State Parks on the Great Lakes

A Complete Outdoor Recreation Guide for Campers, Boaters, Anglers, Hikers and Beach Lovers

Dean F. Miller

Glovebox Guidebooks of America

To our readers: Outdoor travel entails some unavoidable risks. Know your limitations, be prepared, be alert, use good judgement, think safety and enjoy the Great Lakes state parks.

Cover design by Dan Jacalone
Cover photos by Dean Miller
Senior Editor William P. Cornish
Managing Editor Penny Weber

 We have made every reasonable effort to insure accuracy in this publication. Please call ahead to confirm details.

Published by **Glovebox Guidebooks of America**
1112 Washburn Place East
Saginaw, Michigan 48602-2977
(800) 289-4843 or (517) 792-8363

Library of Congress, CIP

Miller, Dean F. 1936-

State Parks on the Great Lakes
(A Glovebox Guidebooks of America publication)
ISBN 1-881139-17-4

Printed in the United States of America

10 9 8 7 6 5 4 3 2 1

Contents

Foreword

This book was written as an outgrowth of my interest in visiting state parks throughout the nation. Every visit, whether summer, winter, fall or spring, presents something new and refreshing.

All 82 state parks on the Great Lakes were visited during the preparation of this book. In some cases the visits were less than a half day. A number of the parks were visited twice, several three or more times. In addition, information was solicited by mail from more than half of the parks.

During the visitations, attempts were made to obtain as much information as possible from park personnel and literature provided to me. Those parks with visitor and information centers were very helpful in providing insights about the park.

My particular interests are hiking and bicycling; so, as much of the park was observed as possible. I'm sure some of this interest will be seen as you use the book.

I have presented what seemed to me the principal feature, or features, of each park. Campgrounds and picnic facilities are described. Also, hiking trails, as well as other types of trails, are explained. Obviously, in some parks it was not possible to hike the complete system of trails. However, from observation and park information some understanding of the trail systems was obtained.

Fishing, wildlife, and some information about the landscape are presented. Many of the parks are open during the winter. Information about winter activities is presented. Where appropriate special events and activities are mentioned.

Other data are presented, such as the amount of acreage of the parks, number of campsites and picnic tables, and other such information. This information was obtained in every case from literature provided to me by the parks.

No book can be written and published without the help of many people. Park personnel and other individuals who answered questions and provided information must be acknowledged. Not every writer has a wife who teaches English and can refine and edit the rough drafts. For this, I thank my wife, Karen. The encouragement of Bill Bailey at Glovebox Guidebooks of America was outstanding from the onset of this project.

Hopefully, this book will excite you about the many outstanding state parks along the Great Lakes. In these parks there is much to see and do for individuals of any age. Almost every type of recreational activity is found in at least one park. Visit them, enjoy them, and be thankful for the wonderful natural resource that is available in the United States—the Great Lakes.

Introduction
The Great Lakes

Nowhere in the world is there as extensive a body of freshwater lakes than that found in the Great Lakes of North America. Nearly one-fifth of all the fresh water on Earth is found in the basins of these five lakes: Lake Superior, Lake Huron, Lake Michigan, Lake Erie and Lake Ontario. The national boundary between Canada and the United States extends through the middle of four of the five Great Lakes. Only one lake, Michigan, is totally within the boundaries of the United States.

From west to east these bodies of water extend more than 800 miles from Duluth, Minnesota, on the western end of Lake Superior to the source of the St. Lawrence River as it flows out of Lake Ontario. There are more than 8,000 miles of shoreline along these lakes; more than 95,000 square miles of water surface make up the Great Lakes.

The Great Lakes

The smallest, as well as the easternmost, is Lake Ontario. This lake extends 193 miles from St. Lawrence River at Wolfe Island, near Kingston, Ontario, Canada, to the western end at Hamilton, Ontario. At its greatest distance Lake Ontario is 53 miles across. The surface area of Lake Ontario is 7,340 square miles. The coastline includes 712 miles. The average depth of the lake is 283 feet, with the greatest measured depth being 802 feet.

The westernmost as well as the most northern lake is also the largest, Lake Superior. This lake extends from Duluth, Minnesota, on the western end to St. Mary's River near Sault Ste. Marie, Michigan, a distance of about 350 miles. At its greatest width the lake is 160 miles across.

The length of the coastline is 2,730 miles—nearly the width of the continental United States!

The waters of Lake Superior are the deepest of the Great Lakes, averaging about 489 feet in depth. At its greatest depth the lake is 1,333 feet. The surface comprises 31,700 square miles. Not only does this make it the largest of the Great Lakes, but it is the largest freshwater lake in the world.

The shoreline of Lake Superior is very rugged and rocky. It is beautiful, but receives heavy pounding by the waves during storms. Waves on Lake Superior, during storms, can reach heights of 30 feet. This makes for treacherous conditions for sailing vessels of all sizes. Even large ships have been lost during storms on the lake.

The southernmost of the Great Lakes is Lake Erie. This lake extends about 241 miles from Buffalo, New York, on the eastern end to Maumee Bay near Toledo, Ohio, on the western end. The lake ranges in width from 38 to 57 miles. The surface of this lake is 9,910 square miles. The coastline is 871 miles. Lake Erie is bordered by four states: Michigan, Ohio, Pennsylvania and New York, in addition to the Canadian province of Ontario.

Lake Erie is the shallowest of the lakes, with an average depth of 62 feet. At the deepest point it is 210 feet. The comparatively shallow nature of the lake can lead to quickly developing, dangerous storms. Storms have caused much damage to the shores of Lake Erie, particularly in the areas east of Cleveland, stretching to Buffalo.

Named for the Huron Indians who lived along its shoreline, Lake Huron is 206 miles long. It stretches north to south from the Straits of Mackinac to Port Huron, Michigan, where the waters enter the St. Clair River. Saginaw Bay and Georgian Bay form part of Lake Huron. At its greatest width this lake is 183 miles across. Including the islands of Georgian Bay, this lake has the greatest amount of coastline, 3,830 miles.

The average depth of Lake Huron is 195 feet, with the deepest part 750 feet. The shores of the lake are relatively low and do not have large sandy beaches.

The only one of the Great Lakes which is entirely within the boundaries of the United States is Lake Michigan. The northernmost point of Lake Michigan is about halfway between St. Ignace and Manistique, in the Upper Peninsula of Michigan. The southernmost point encompasses the industrial complexes of northwestern Indiana: Gary and East Chicago, Indiana. The distance from north to south is 307 miles. At its greatest width Lake Michigan is 118 miles across. The surface of Lake Michigan is 22,300 square miles. The coastline is 1,640 miles.

On the western side of the lake is Door Peninsula of Wisconsin. This peninsula juts out some 80 miles into Lake Michigan from the Wisconsin shoreline, separating Lake Michigan from Green Bay, which is the largest bay in Lake Michigan. The waters in Green Bay are calmer than are those on the Lake Michigan side of the peninsula. Shorelines on the eastern side of the peninsula are more affected by wind, snow, rain and adverse weather conditions than are those within the area of Green Bay. On the eastern side of Lake Michigan are two other bays: Grand Traverse Bay and Little Traverse Bay.

The average depth of Lake Michigan is 279 feet. At its greatest depth, the lake is 923 feet. Along the shoreline of Lake Michigan there are extensive dune formations, providing not only hills for climbing but miles of sand for walking along the shoreline.

Historical Development of the Great Lakes

The origin of these lakes is traced by geologists to the time of the Ice Age some 10,000 years ago. As the glaciers of the Ice Age moved over the landscape, large basins were left. Melting ice filled these basins and comprise the lakes today.

For many years before the arrival of explorers in the 1600s, Native Americans lived along the shores of these lakes. For example, the Ojibwa Indians lived along Lake Superior, the Potawatomi Indians occupied areas along Lake Michigan and Lake Huron, the Erie Indians were at home near Lake Erie, and the Iroquois and Huron Indians lived along Lake Ontario.

By the early 1600s French explorers traveled through the Great Lakes in search of a route to the far east. An early explorer, Jean Nicolet, traveled through the lakes looking for a northwest passage to the Orient. When he came ashore near Green Bay, Wisconsin, he thought he had reached the Orient. Instead he met the Winnebago Indians.

The early explorers established an extensive fur trade. Also, Jesuit missionaries came to the area with the intention of bringing religious faith to the Native Americans. Fathers Marquette and LaSalle were early explorers along these waterways.

During much of the 1700s and 1800s settlement expanded along the shorelines of the lakes. Forts were established at localities where major American cities are now located, such as Fort Dearborn (Chicago), Fort Erie (Buffalo) and Fort Howard (Green Bay).

The waterways of the Great Lakes have served as major "avenues of transportation." Following the travels of the early explorers and settlers during the 1800s, boat cargo transportation became important to the industrial development of cities such as Chicago, Detroit, Cleveland, Buffalo and Milwaukee. Timber, copper and iron became important natural resources available near the lakes. In addition, the waterways were used to transport coal, iron ore and petroleum products. Major grain storage facilities developed in Duluth, Toledo, Buffalo and other cities. From these facilities all kinds of grain, including wheat, corn, and soybeans as well as vegetables, are today transported not only throughout the United States but throughout the world. Since 1959 with the opening of the St. Lawrence Seaway, oceangoing, bulk-carrying vessels have operated on the waters of the Great Lakes. These ships take products to ports throughout the world by way of the lakes and the St. Lawrence River.

From an economic standpoint the waters of the Great Lakes make a major contribution to the lives of millions of Americans.

Not only are the Great Lakes important economically as a major transportation network, but millions of people every year come to the shores of these lakes for recreation. There are national shoreline parks, county, city and other local parks, national wildlife refuges, and numerous private facilities that serve outdoor enthusiasts.

State Parks on the Great Lakes

Along the shores of the five lakes are 82 state parks which provide a variety of activities for millions of people yearly. The state parks on the Great Lakes range in size from Porcupine Mountains Wilderness State Park (Michigan), encompassing more than 58,000 acres stretching some 25 miles along the shoreline of Lake Superior, to the 18-acre Catawba Island State Park (Ohio) on Lake Erie. Some contain miles of hiking trails into wilderness settings, such as Porcupine Mountains, Crosby-Manitou State Park (Minnesota), Tettagouche State Park (Minnesota), Gooseberry Falls State Park (Minnesota), Tahquamenon Falls State Park (Michigan), and Wilderness State Park (Michigan). On the other hand, the skyline of Cleveland can be seen from various locations in Cleveland Lakefront State Park (Ohio). A six-lane highway runs within sight of the beach and fishing pier of this park.

People come to these parks to participate in a variety of activities. In most instances the principal attraction is the water. The beaches provide settings for swimming, sunbathing, playing volleyball, walking and wading along the water's edge. The largest and most spectacular sand beaches tend to be at the parks along the eastern shoreline of Lake Michigan. At parks such as Indiana Dunes State Park, Silver Lake State Park and Warren Dunes State Park, sand dunes as high as 300 feet can be seen. The largest sand beach on Lake Erie in Ohio is at Headlands Beach State Park. Presque Isle State Park, Pennsylvania's only park located on a Great Lake, has nearly seven miles of sand beach on Lake Erie. On the other hand, many parks have small beaches of sand extending just a few feet back from the water's edge.

None of Minnesota's parks on the north shore of Lake Superior has swimming facilities. This is due to the rugged terrain along the shoreline and the temperature of the lake's water. Also, several parks which are historical in nature do not have swimming and sunbathing access.

Boating and fishing attract many visitors to the Great Lakes. Some parks have well-supplied marinas where boaters can purchase any supplies they might need. There are docks and modern marinas at Cleveland Lakefront State Park, Maumee Bay State Park, Geneva State Park and East Harbor State Park in Ohio, at Presque Isle State Park (Pennsylvania) and at Illinois Beach State Park (Illinois).

The waters of the Great Lakes provide excellent sport fishing. Walleye, whitefish, yellow perch and lake herring are native to these waters. Lake sturgeon is another popular native fish, though in recent years it has become seriously depleted. In addition to these fish, rainbow trout, smelt, lake trout, and chinook and cohoo salmon have been introduced into the lakes and are popular among anglers. Fishing in the waters of the Great Lakes is an attraction at many state parks during the spring.

Nearly all of the state parks have camping facilities. Some have more than 400 campsites, including Ludington State Park (Michigan) and Peninsula State Park (Wisconsin) on Lake Michigan and East Harbor State Park (Ohio) on Lake Erie. A few parks are principally camping facilities, such as Baraga State Park (Michigan) on Lake Superior and Straits State Park (Michigan), located next to the Mackinac Bridge at the Straits of Mackinac. Also, Four Mile Creek State Park (New York) and Long Point State Park (New York) on Lake Ontario are mainly camping parks.

Parks without camping facilities usually have several activities for day-use, principally picnicking and water activities. This is the case at Harrington Beach State Park (Wisconsin) on Lake Michigan, Headlands Beach State Park (Ohio) on Lake Erie, and Wilson-Tuscarora State Park (New York) on Lake Ontario. Some campsites are directly on the water's edge, where the views are spectacular. These include the campground at F.J. McLain State Park (Michigan), where from most campsites the sunset over Lake Superior can be seen and Loop B of the campground at Southwick Beach State Park (New York), which is directly on the sand.

Several campsites can only be reached by backpacking in. All of the campsites at Newport State Park (Wisconsin) and at Crosby-Manitou State Park (Minnesota) must be reached on foot. This is also true at Split Rock Lighthouse State Park (Minnesota), where all of the campsites are reached by taking camping gear from the parking lot in carts.

Two state parks have modern resort facilities: Maumee Bay State Park (Ohio) on Lake Erie and Illinois Beach State Park on Lake Michigan. These parks include a range of facilities to accommodate large group meetings, such as retreats and conferences. Golf courses are at Maumee Bay State Park, Peninsula State Park (Wisconsin) and Geneva State Park (Ohio).

Many parks have cabins. Some, such as Maumee Bay State Park, are modern with the best facilities. Others, such as Fair Haven Beach State Park (New York) and Lake Erie State Park (New York), are less modern but comfortable. Rustic cabins are available at J.W. Wells State Park (Michigan), Cheboygan State Park (Michigan) and Wilderness State Park (Michigan). These do not have running water or indoor toilet facilities. They are in rather isolated locations throughout the park and provide beautiful settings nestled in the woods adjacent to the shoreline.

It is necessary at many parks to obtain reservations in advance for cabin facilities or campsites on weekends or holidays during the summer. In some instances, cabin reservations, both modern or rustic, are available only on a lottery system. People have to submit their reservations several months in advance. The park system announces to the public the dates when reservations are due and when the selection process will take place.

Five state parks are on islands from which it is necessary to go by ferry, private boat or small plane. Big Bay State Park (Wisconsin) is on Madeline Island in Lake Superior. Possibly the most popular is Mackinac Island State Park (Michigan) at the Straits, where Lake Michigan and Lake Huron meet. On the far point of Door Peninsula in Wisconsin is Rock Island State Park. At the western end of Lake Erie are two Ohio state parks on islands: South Bass Island and Kelleys Island.

Several parks are historical in nature. These state parks preserve and in most cases tell a history of the particular fort or activity in the area. Most are located in the Upper Peninsula of Michigan. Fort Wilkins State Park on Lake Superior and Fayette State Park on Lake Michigan provide opportunities to visit restored buildings which describe life in the 1800s and early 1900s. At the Straits of Mackinac, Fort Michilimackinac State Park has a restored replica of a fort built in the early part of the 1700s as a military base by the French to protect against the Indians. Fort Niagara (New York) on Lake Ontario was built in 1726. At these historical parks you can reenact the life of the area in the past. At Fort Wilkins State Park (Michigan), it is possible to talk with "soldiers" who lived years ago in this far north outpost. On Mackinac Island, you can spend hours at Fort Mackinac and watch various reenactments of life at this fort. This provides a sense of realism and helps visitors appreciate the history that occurred on the Great Lakes.

Hiking is an important activity in most of the parks. The degree of difficulty and length of the trails vary. Most trails are well marked and provide a challenge for individuals of any age. Opportunities for overnight backpacking experiences are available at Porcupine Mountains Wilderness State Park (Michigan) and at Crosby-Manitou State Park (Minnesota). On the other end of the continuum are several parks which have facilities for easy, quiet walks for anyone, particularly for senior citizens and disabled individuals. At Crane Creek State Park and Maumee Bay State Park (Ohio) on Lake Erie, elevated walkways take you over wetland areas where you can spend hours bird watching or observing the many activities of the marshy wetlands.

Increased interest in bicycling has resulted in the development of bike trails at a few parks. There are bicycle trails at Indiana Dunes State Park, Peninsula State Park (Wisconsin) and Presque Isle State Park (Pennsylvania). In several parks bicyclists are permitted to ride on hiking trails such as those in Albert Sleeper State Park (Michigan) on Lake Huron and at Newport State Park and Potawatomi State Park (Wisconsin) on Lake Michigan. The bicyclist should inquire if it is permissible to ride on the hiking trail system before riding on them. In some parks the bicyclist can see a lot by riding on park roads, fire trails and maintenance roads.

Hundreds of thousands of people visit the parks each year to picnic. Every park has some picnic facilities, if no more than a few tables and grills. The picnic grounds at Evangola State Park (New York) on Lake Erie are well manicured, on a bluff overlooking the lake, with hard-surface walkways throughout the area. On the other hand, the sites at Cascades River State Park and at Gooseberry Falls State Park (Minnesota) are in wooded areas separated from neighboring picnic sites by trees and underbrush. Many parks have picnic shelters which can be reserved in advance for group activities. Some shelters are indoor, protected facilities, such as at Hamlin Beach State Park (New York) where one shelter has a fireplace and four barbecue pits and at Selkirk Shores State Park (New York). The state parks in New York along Lake Ontario, Peninsula State Park (Wisconsin) and Rock Island State Park (Wisconsin) are "carry-in, carry-out" parks. There are no refuse cans at these facilities. People must carry out all of their picnic garbage.

Most visitors come between Memorial Day and Labor Day. It is not unusual on weekends and holidays during the summer for campgrounds and cabin facilities to be filled. Occasionally, people have to be turned away because facilities are filled. This is especially true for parks near large metropolitan areas, such as Warren Dunes State Park and Indiana Dunes State Park, near the Chicago-Hammond-Gary region.

Increasingly, parks are used in other seasons of the year. The fall has become particularly popular for campers, hikers and folks interested in enjoying the crisp autumn and photographing fall foliage in full color. The parks are extremely beautiful from the latter part of September in northern Minnesota, Wisconsin and the Upper Peninsula of Michigan to the end of October along the shores of Lake Erie, Lake Michigan and Lake Ontario. Also in the fall, hunting is permitted at some parks or on public land adjacent to them.

The Great Lakes rest in the part of North America where snow and cold weather are prevalent from mid-November through the early part of March. As Americans become more interested in outdoor winter sport and recreational activities, these parks are receiving increasing activity. Nordic (cross-country) skiing, downhill skiing, snowmobiling and ice fishing are the main attractions. All of the Minnesota state parks along the north shore of Lake Superior are open year-round. In spite of heavy snow and cold temperatures in this area, cross-country skiing, snowmobiling and snowshoeing attract thousands of participants each winter.

Special programs have been established in some parks for winter activity, as at Bay City State Park (Michigan) on Lake Huron. At this park winter camping facilities have been established with heated toilets and shower facilities, plowed campsites and electricity. Ice fishing is popular at this park with individuals being able to walk on the ice or ride their snowmobiles to the fishing hole. Winter camping is available at many other state parks as well. Downhill ski runs are available at Porcupine Mountains Wilderness State Park (Michigan) and at Peninsula State Park (Wisconsin).

A major attraction during the fall and spring at many parks is bird watching. Some parks along Lake Erie are on routes followed by millions of birds flying south in the fall and north in the spring. This is particularly true at Crane Creek State Park (Ohio), Preque Isle State Park (Pennsylvania) and Selkirk Shores State Park (New York). A popular attraction during the spring is seeing Canadian geese with their newborn goslings. Many other waterfowl can be seen this time of year with their little newborn offspring. Hawks can be seen by the thousands along the cliffs of Lake Superior during the migration season at several north shore state parks.

A variety of wildlife is seen at various state parks. Ground animals, such as squirrels, rabbits and chipmunks, are common in nearly every park. Whitetail deer are seen in most parks. In addition, there are coyote and fox sightings. Black bear are seen in the parks of Minnesota and in the Upper Peninsula of Michigan. Moose can be sighted at

Tahquamenon Falls State Park (Michigan) and at most of the state parks along the north shore in Minnesota.

Visitors can learn about the park and surrounding area in visitor and nature centers. The newest visitor center is a modern facility opened in 1996 at Gooseberry Falls State Park (Minnesota). The center at Indiana Dunes State Park provides a number of interesting displays detailing the history of the dunes and the formation of the park. This center also has a library of magazines and other information for the interested visitors. The visitor center at Fayette State Park (Michgian) gives an explanation of the history of the village. There is a very interesting and informative model display of the village. Many visitor centers are used during the school year for field trips for school children. The center at P.J. Hoffmaster State Park (Michigan) is an exceptionally popular place for students to learn about the ecology of the dune environment.

Lighthouses have played an important role in navigation on the Great Lakes. A number of historic lighthouses on the lakes are in the state parks. Though not open daily, most are open at specified times and are popular with visitors. Lighthouses at Lelanau Peninsula State Park (Michigan), Ludington State Park (Michigan), Grand Haven State Park (Michigan), Peninsula State Park (Wisconsin) and Golden Hill State Park (New York) are several of the more interesting ones. One of the most spectacular is Split Rock Lighthouse built on solid rock some 130 feet above the waters of Lake Superior, now within the boundaries of Split Rock Lighthouse State Park (Minnesota). Park authorities say that this is probably the most photographed lighthouse along the Great Lakes shorelines.

There exists great variety in the state parks on the Great Lakes. Everyone can find something of interest to do while visiting these parks. They are all different, some big, some small, some wilderness, some urban; yet each is unique and deserves its place as a park on one of the Great Lakes.

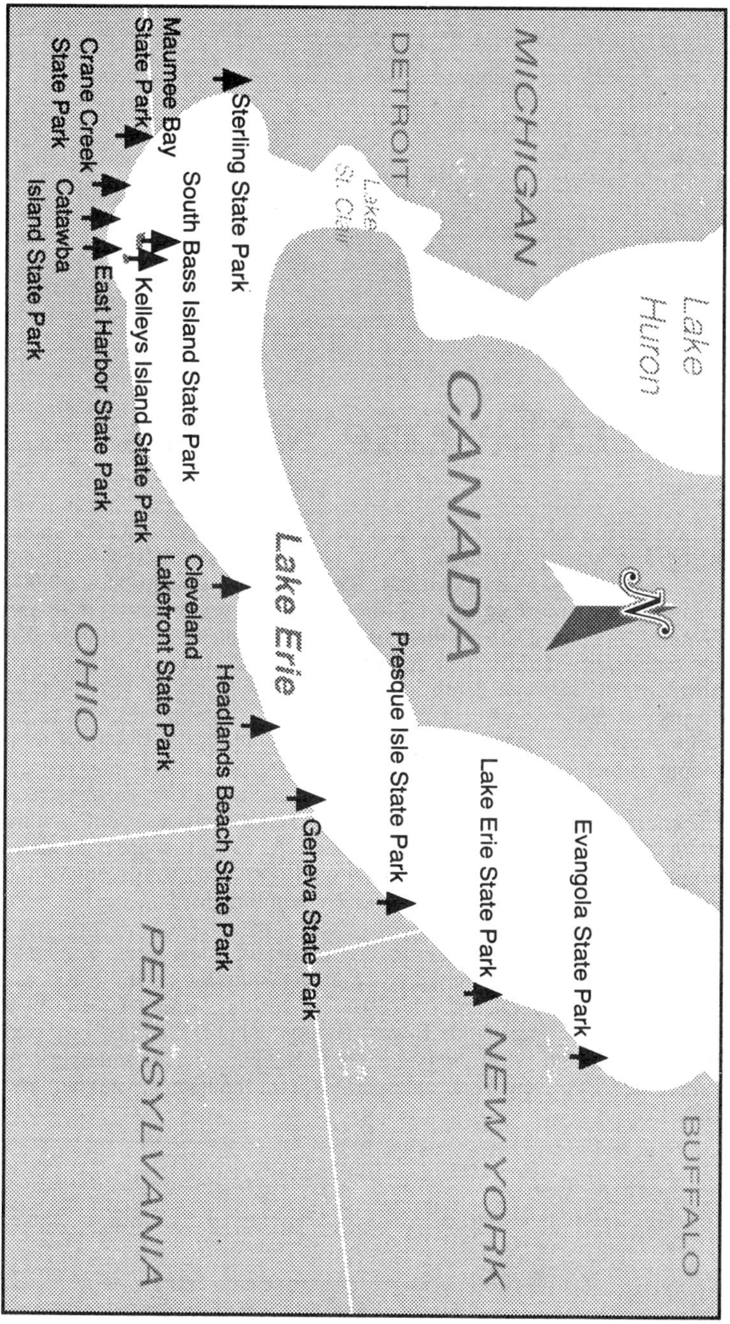

Lake Huron
MICHIGAN
DETROIT
Lake St. Clair
CANADA
Lake Erie
OHIO
PENNSYLVANIA
NEW YORK
BUFFALO
N
Sterling State Park
Maumee Bay State Park
Crane Creek State Park
Catawba Island State Park
South Bass Island State Park
Kelleys Island State Park
East Harbor State Park
Cleveland Lakefront State Park
Headlands Beach State Park
Geneva State Park
Presque Isle State Park
Lake Erie State Park
Evangola State Park

Lake Erie Region

Lake Erie is the southernmost of the five Great Lakes. It is bounded by four states: Michigan, Ohio, Pennsylvania and New York and the Canadian province of Ontario. The lake encompasses about 9,900 square miles, stretching about 240 miles with a width between 38 and 57 miles, making it the smallest of the Great Lakes. Lake Erie is also the shallowest of the Great Lakes, with the deepest point 210 feet. However, the average depth is only about 75 feet. Because of that, storms can cause significant damage along the shoreline. Storms cause serious erosion, washing away sand and reducing the shoreline by a couple of feet a year.

The nutrient level of Lake Erie is higher and the water temperature warmer than any of the other Great Lakes. As a result, there is a greater number of fish in Lake Erie. The annual fish catch nearly equals the fish catches of all the other Great Lakes combined.

There are 13 state parks along the shores of Lake Erie. The only Michigan state park on the lake is Sterling State Park. Nine parks are in Ohio: Catawba Island, Cleveland Lakefront, Crane Creek, East Harbor, Geneva, Headlands Beach, Kelleys Island, Maumee Bay, and South Bass Island. Presque Isle is the only Pennsylvania state park on Lake Erie. Two New York state parks are on the lake: Evangola and Lake Erie.

Catawba Island State Park

The smallest state park on any of the Great Lakes is Catawba Island in Ottawa County, Ohio. Though it is called Catawba Island, it is not actually on an island, but at the north end of the Catawba Peninsula. The park is on land that once belonged to Ottawa and Wyandot Indians. This 18-acre tract is a day-use park with facilities for picnicking, boat launching and fishing.

There are no camping facilities or hiking trails in the park. A couple of miles north of the park, a ferry takes visitors to South Bass Island, a popular summer resort.

Location: Catawba Island State Park is about 10 miles northeast of Port Clinton on Ohio 53.

Features of the Park: Fishing is the primary activity at Catawba Island. Some people come to the park to picnic and enjoy the view.

Fishing: The park has a fishing pier with lights and benches. Anglers

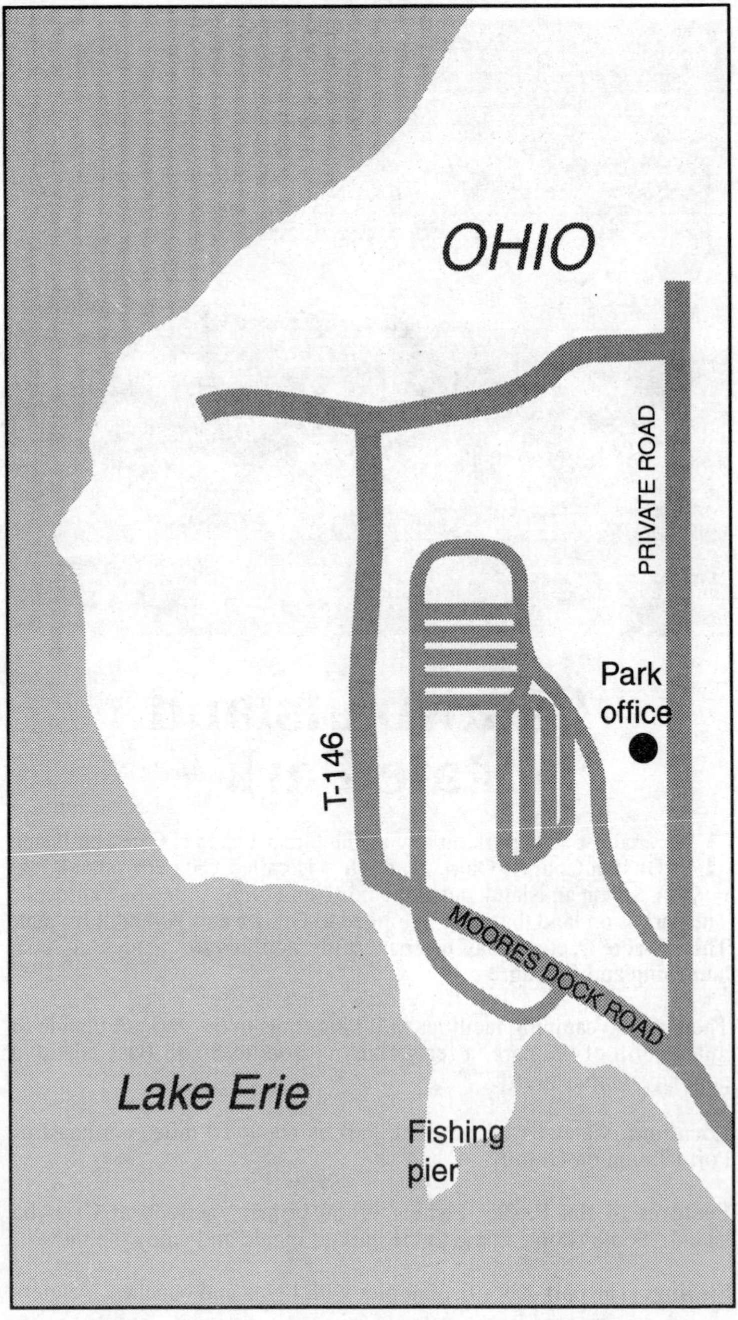
OHIO
PRIVATE ROAD
Park office
T-146
MOORES DOCK ROAD
Lake Erie
Fishing pier

try for bass, catfish and perch. Walleye fishing is very popular in the waters off of Catawba Island, particularly during late spring. Anglers often catch smallmouth bass off the pier.

Many people use the four boat ramps at Catawba Island State Park to launch their boats into the waters of Lake Erie. From here they fish the surrounding waters. On most weekends during the summer, the large parking area is filled to capacity.

Picnic facilities: The picnic area has several tables and grills. The view of the lake from the entire park is quite nice and makes the picnic experience particularly worthwhile. A shelter is available for use during inclement weather.

Winter Activities: In the winter, if the ice on the lake is thick enough, ice fishing is popular off the shore of Catawba Island. However, the ice often is not thick enough for ice activity.

Catawba Island State Park
4049 E. Moores Dock Road
Port Clinton, Ohio 43452
(419) 797-4530

Cleveland Lakefront State Park

The only state park in a major metropolitan area on the Great Lakes is Cleveland Lakefront State Park. This urban state park was established in 1978 and is the busiest in the Ohio park system.

The park is a day-use facility. There are no camping facilities; neither are there hiking trails. The park is composed of six areas.

Settlers first arrived in the area about 1796. As early as 1865, land was set aside along the lake in Cleveland for recreational purposes. The city of Cleveland leased its four lakefront parks to the state in 1977, which became Cleveland Lakefront State Park the next year. Euclid Beach was added in 1982. Today, there are six areas administered through a single park office.

Location: Cleveland Lakefront State Park's six units stretch about 15 miles along the shoreline of Lake Erie. The easternmost units are Wildwood Park and adjacent Villa Angela. Next, moving west, is Euclid Beach Park. Then, closer to downtown Cleveland, is Gordon

Park. The East 55th Marina is just west of Gordon Park. The westernmost unit is Edgewater Park, located in the suburb of Lakewood. Though many consider these separate parks, they are all administered as one state park. Combined, these units that comprise Cleveland Lakefront State Park include about 450 acres of land.

At several locations, the skyline of downtown Cleveland is visible. Also, Ohio 2 and I-90 pass near the park units. You are never out of hearing range of traffic along these busy highways.

Features of the Park: The principal feature of the park is Lake Erie. Nearly all activities at Cleveland Lakefront involve facilities and activities along the shore and in the waters of Lake Erie. Activities include boating, fishing, picnicking, sunbathing, bicycling and swimming.

Beaches: There are three beaches, the largest at Edgewater Park and the others at Euclid Beach and Villa Angela. Edgewater Park's beach is 900 feet long and surrounded by a grassy picnic area. There is a designated swimming area. A bathhouse and concession facility are at the beach, while a 1.6-mile fitness trail passes next to the beach.

The Euclid Beach Park beach was part of a popular amusement park from the turn of the century until the late 1960s. It became a part of the state park system in 1982. As an amusement park, Euclid Beach had a policy of free admission. In addition to the beach at Euclid Beach Park, there are a pavilion and a facility where refreshments can be purchased. There also is a large picnic area between the parking area and the beach. An observation pier provides a place for visitors to look about the shoreline.

Park Units from East to West

The easternmost unit of the Cleveland Lakefront State Park, Wildwood Park, is principally a facility for launching boats and a place where people can fish. There are six ramps and a facility for boat rental. The concession stand provides food, fishing bait and gasoline for boats. The day of my visit, a number of people were fishing from the rocky breakwalls along the shoreline. Fishing is also popular along adjacent Euclid Creek. The Wildwood Park section is connected by bridge to Villa Angela, which has a 900-foot swimming beach and a fishing pier which is handicapped accessible. A bathhouse is located near this beach.

Just west of Villa Angela is Euclid Beach swimming beach, 650 feet long. Also in this area is a large, well-shaded picnic area which groups can reserve.

The two units nearest to downtown Cleveland are Gordon Park and the East 55th Marina. The park headquarters are at the 105-acre Gordon

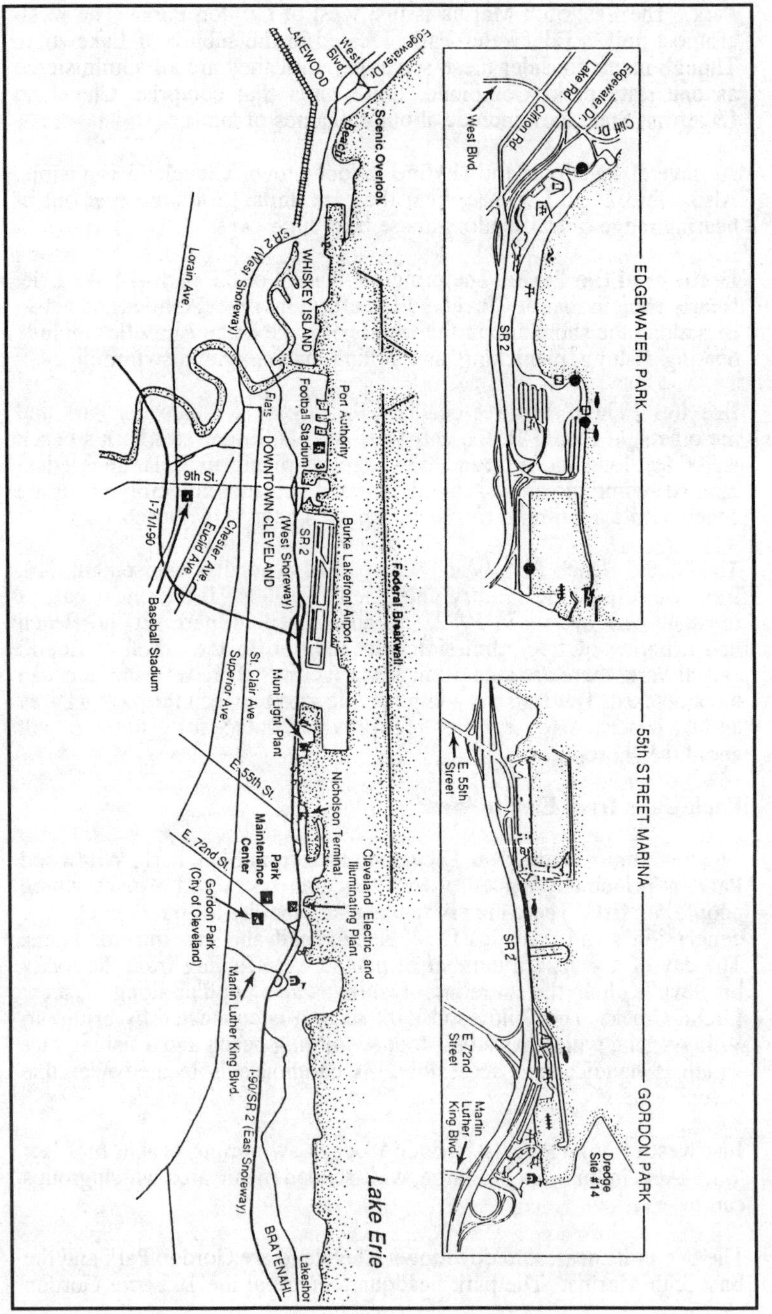
EDGEWATER PARK
Edgewater Dr.
Lake Rd
Cliff Dr.
Clifton Rd
West Blvd.
SR 2
55th STREET MARINA
E. 55th Street
SR 2
GORDON PARK
Dredge Site #14
E 72nd Street
Martin Luther King Blvd.
Edgewater Dr.
West Blvd.
LAKEWOOD
Beach
Scenic Overlook
SR 2 (West Shoreway)
WHISKEY ISLAND
Lorain Ave.
Port Authority
Football Stadium
Flats
DOWNTOWN CLEVELAND
9th St.
I-71/I-90
Chester Ave.
Euclid Ave.
Baseball Stadium
Burke Lakefront Airport
SR 2 (West Shoreway)
Federal Breakwall
Superior Ave.
St. Clair Ave
Muni Light Plant
E. 55th St.
Nicholson Terminal
Cleveland Electric and Illuminating Plant
Park Maintenance Center
E. 72nd St.
Gordon Park (City of Cleveland)
Martin Luther King Blvd.
I-90/SR 2 (East Shoreway)
Lake Erie
BRATENAHL
Lakeshor

Park unit, named after William J. Gordon, a Cleveland businessman in the late 1800s. Mr. Gordon gave much of his estate to the city of Cleveland. He was particularly interested in seeing that the lakefront be developed into a recreational facility for Cleveland residents. The principal facilities are boat launch ramps, a large parking area and picnic grounds.

There are 335 boat slips with water and electrical hook-ups available at the East 55th Marina. Because of the popularity of this marina, slip rentals are available by lottery. Also, there are concessions for food, fishing supplies and marine supplies, as well as gasoline sales for boats.

The breakwall surrounding the marina is extremely popular for fishing. Here, as well as at the other locations along the shoreline, bass, perch, catfish and panfish are caught by anglers. During the early spring and fall, coho salmon are caught in the waters of Euclid Creek at Wildwood Park and in the warmwater discharge of the Cleveland Electric and Illuminating Company at Gordon Park.

The largest unit in the state park is the westernmost section, Edgewater Park. Here you'll find boat docks and 10 launching ramps. As at the other units, there are concessions for purchasing food, fishing supplies and gasoline for boats. A 90-foot "T-shaped" fishing pier is handicapped accessible.

West of the swimming beach, on a bluff overlooking the lake, is a shady picnic area. Here are a number of picnic tables, grills and playground equipment for children. There is a restored pavilion for groups in this section. A paved bicycle trail of less than a mile connects the lower beach and the upper section of the park. Along the bluff are several sites where you can see the Cleveland skyline. In the upper section of Edgewater is the oldest monument in Cleveland, a statue of Conrad Mizar, who was noted for establishing the concept of concerts in the park.

Winter Activities: Winter usually brings cold weather and significant snow to the Cleveland area. Ice fishing is possible at two units, as is ice skating. Opportunities for Nordic skiing exist at the Edgewater Park and Wildwood units. However, there are no ski rental facilities in the park.

Cleveland Lakefront State Park
8701 Lakeshore Blvd., NE
Cleveland, Ohio 44108
(216) 881-8141

Crane Creek State Park

Crane Creek is a day-use park, having no camping facilities. It is relatively small, comprising only 79 acres.

The park gets its name from Crane Creek, which flows into Lake Erie just west of the park. Although no cranes are found in the vicinity, the abundance of egrets and great blue herons in the area led to the naming of this creek, thinking these birds were cranes.

Today the beach and waters of Lake Erie at Crane Creek State Park are clean and provide opportunities for swimming, wading and playing in the water. Not many years ago these waters were polluted and dirty. The first time I visited this park, about 20 years ago, people weren't allowed to swim. However, through the past two decades major initiatives have been undertaken to reduce pollution and environmental destruction throughout the various governmental jurisdictions bordering Lake Erie. Today, on a hot, summer weekend the beach and its waters are filled with people of all ages enjoying the beauty and refreshing nature of Lake Erie's water.

Location: Crane Creek, along the Lake Erie shoreline in Ottawa County on Ohio 2, is about 10 miles east of Toledo.

Features of the Park: Crane Creek State Park is principally a 3,500-foot-beach along Lake Erie. A number of grills and tables for picnicking, toilets and changing shelters are scattered along the beach. The beach-picnic area is shaded by cottonwood trees.

Adjacent Wetlands: Near the entrance of the park, off of Ohio 2, are a park office and maintenance facility. Driving along a two-lane road for a little over a mile, you come to the beach. Along the road you will see marshes and wetlands, although they are not part of Crane Creek State Park. These wetlands comprise the Magee Marsh Wildlife Area and the Ottawa National Wildlife Refuge. The Ottawa refuge is the largest federal wildlife refuge in the state. These two wetland areas adjoin Crane Creek, but are not managed as part of the state park system. The entire area was once part of the Great Black Swamp, which until the mid-1800s extended some 120 miles by 30 to 40 miles in width. With the development of a ditch system to drain the land as well as increased lumbering, the area became a rich farmland.

Birding: Possibly the greatest attraction in this region is the hundreds of different types of waterfowl that reside and/or fly through these reserves. This park rests along two of the four migratory flyways that birds use in the United States. Experienced birdwatchers come to this area from great distances to observe up to 300 species that have been spotted. On a sunny late-April day I spent an hour on the trail along with 50 or more birdwatchers. Most were retired individuals with bird books and binoculars.

We saw numerous small, colorful songbirds, terns, flycatchers, gulls, wrens and swallows. A spectacular view of a great horned owl was being enjoyed by half a dozen photographers with tripods set up in the parking lot. Not being a birder myself, I learned something that day about the joys of watching birds, listening for their song and observing their activities.

On entering the drive into Crane Creek, you can't miss the Canadian geese. The day in early spring that I visited, there were a dozen families of geese with their newborn chicks. The mother and father stayed close to the babies, usually four to six in a family.

Many ducks, geese, gulls and egrets are within easy viewing from the roadway. Several nesting pairs of bald eagles have been reported in this area in recent years. There were 130 sightings of bald eagles already, early in the spring, upon my visit. Six kinds of hawks live in the area, with several thousand sightings.

About a half-mile along the state park entrance drive is the Magee

Marsh viewing tower. From the tower you can see an abundance of birds and other marshland inhabitants. This tower provides an excellent place to photograph birds.

Next to the tower is an informational center which provides displays on the Indians of the Great Lakes. Also, there is an excellent display of birds in the area. Another display provides information about the Bald Eagle Research and Management Program in the park and surrounding wetlands. A stop at the center will familiarize you with what there is to see.

Snakes, turtles, frogs, raccoons and muskrats also reside in the park. The marshes and wetlands provide them with food as well as places of shelter.

Trails/Walking: A one-half mile walking trail is accessible from the parking lot. This trail is a boardwalk which enters the marshlands of the Magee Marsh Wildlife Area. From the trail you can look out on the marshlands and observe numerous birds and other inhabitants, and listen to their calls and songs. This trail is particularly accommodating for elderly persons in that it is short and elevated. It is also wheelchair accessible.

A walk along the roadway also provides opportunity to watch the many birds and other creatures in the marshland. Having walked along this road during the week when traffic was minimal, I can account for the enjoyment of such an activity. However, on weekends when there is a continual flow of traffic, walking might not be as relaxed.

Fishing: Fishing in the waters off the shore in Lake Erie is popular. However, there are no boat ramps in this state park. Anglers must go to nearby private marinas to put their boats into the water. Several types of fish are caught in these waters; walleye, bluegill, white bass, yellow perch and catfish are particularly common.

Hunting: During the fall hunting season, the entrance road leading to the beach is closed, since hunting is permitted in the adjoining Magee Marsh Wildlife Area.

Crane Creek State Park
13531 West State Route 2
Oak Harbor, Ohio 43449
(419) 898-2495

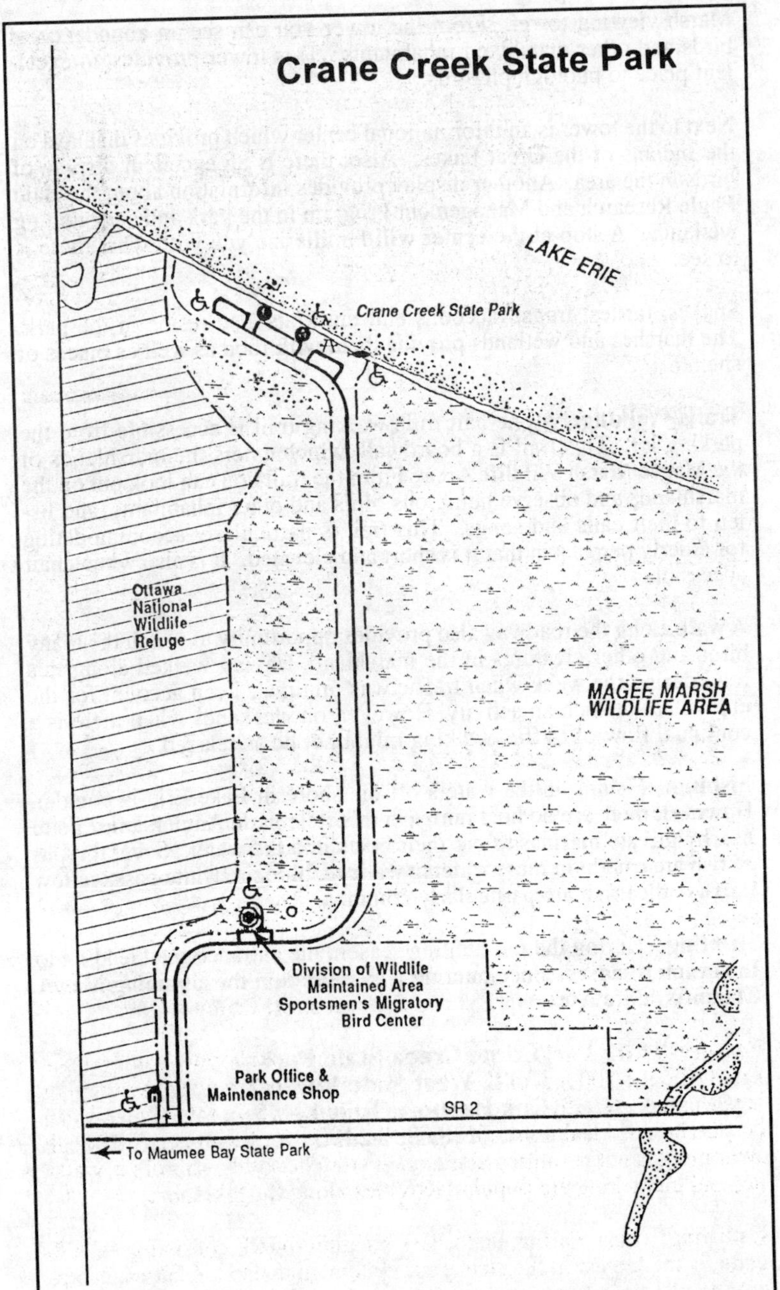

Crane Creek State Park
LAKE ERIE
Crane Creek State Park
Ottawa
National
Wildlife
Refuge
MAGEE MARSH
WILDLIFE AREA
Division of Wildlife
Maintained Area
Sportsmen's Migratory
Bird Center
Park Office &
Maintenance Shop
SR 2
To Maumee Bay State Park

East Harbor State Park

East Harbor State Park, on a peninsula stretching into Lake Erie, opened as the first state park in Ohio on Lake Erie in 1947. The park contains three harbors: East Harbor, Middle Harbor, and West Harbor. Middle Harbor is a game sanctuary. The park consists of 1,152 acres.

Location: East Harbor State Park is about seven miles east of Port Clinton, Ohio, on the Marblehead Peninsula, off Ohio SR 269.

Features of the Park: There is nearly a mile of shoreline along Lake Erie. About 1,500 feet of this shoreline is sand beach where swimming is permitted. Nearby is a concession building where refreshments can be purchased. There are changing facilities for swimmers. Though swimming is not permitted along other stretches of the shoreline, walking and picnicking are popular activities along the lakeshore.

Camping: East Harbor State Park's campground, consisting of 570 units, is the largest in the state park system, and also the largest campground of any state park on the Great Lakes. It is almost always filled on week-ends and holidays during the summer. There are hot shower facilities, flush toilets, a dump station and a commissary for campers to purchase supplies. Several playgrounds and playfields are scattered throughout the camping area.

All campsites at East Harbor State Park are available on a non-reservation first-come, first-served basis, with a 14-day maximum for occupancy. Each campsite has a picnic table and fire ring; none has electricity. However, passage of a recent bond issue to install electricity will make available electrical outlets in the near future. The campground is open year-round.

The campground is not within sight of the Lake Erie shoreline. It is about a half-mile from the campground to the lake. Five days a week, a park naturalist presents informational and entertaining programs of interest to people of all ages.

Two group camping units are available by reservation. One of these units, designated for youth groups, has a capacity of 50. The adult camp unit can accommodate up to 100 individuals.

Picnic facilities: Picnic tables and grills are at several locations around the park, including some on the water's edge, providing excellent views of Lake Erie. Another picnic area is situated at Middle Harbor. There are two picnic shelters available on a rental basis, one in a grassy area near the park entrance road and the other on the edge of East Harbor.

Marina: Less than a mile north of the main entrance are the marina, store, restaurant and boat launch. Boats launch into West Harbor, from where they cruise down a channel into Lake Erie.

Fuel, boat supplies, fishing equipment and fishing licenses can be purchased at the marina. Also, there are full-time mechanics available at the marina. More than 120 boat docks are available for rental at the marina. During the winter, the marina provides storage for boats and camping vehicles.

A restaurant providing breakfast and lunch from early May through mid-September is located at the marina.

Fishing and Hunting: As at other state parks along Lake Erie in this part of Ohio, fishing is popular. Walleye, yellow perch, channel catfish, and smallmouth and white bass are caught in Lake Erie. Also bluegill, carp and crappie are found in the waters of East Harbor and West Harbor.

During the duck hunting season, hunting is permitted on several offshore islands near the park. There are five duck blinds in the park.

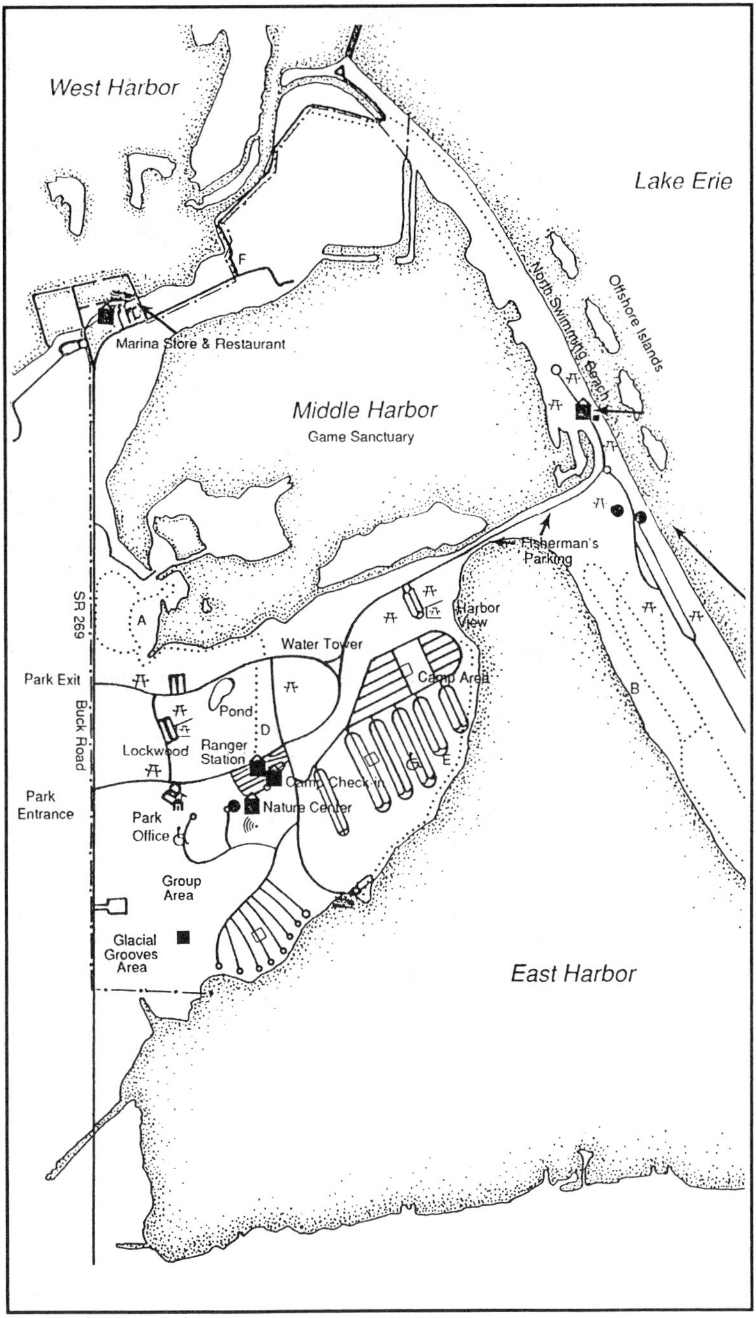
West Harbor
Lake Erie
North Swimming Beach
Offshore Islands
Marina Store & Restaurant
F
Middle Harbor
Game Sanctuary
Fisherman's Parking
SR 269
A
Harbor View
Water Tower
Camp Area
Park Exit
Buck Road
Pond
D
B
Lockwood
Ranger Station
Camp Check-in
E
Park Entrance
Nature Center
Park Office
Group Area
Glacial Grooves Area
East Harbor

Permits to use these blinds are made available by lottery.

Trails: East Harbor State Park has about seven miles of hiking trails. One, South Beach Trail, stretches for 2.5 miles along East Harbor. At places you can get good views of the shoreline.

The West Harbor Trail travels between West Harbor and Middle Harbor. This was a much more scenic trail than the others. On the West Harbor side of the trail, a boat channel entered Lake Erie. On summer weekends boats are lined along the channel almost like a major urban interstate highway at rush hour.

Middle Harbor, on the opposite side of the trail, is a game sanctuary. Several species of ducks, other waterfowl, herons, egrets and shorebirds are seen on hikes. The trail is about three-fourths of a mile long. It ends at the shore of Lake Erie, north of the swimming beach.

There are no bicycle paths in the park. However, you can ride several miles along the park roads from the campground to the parking lot by the lake, and then to the marina. These roads are busy on holidays and weekends in the summer, however, I bicycled these roads early in May when there was little motor-vehicle traffic and thoroughly enjoyed the park.

Nature: A wide variety of waterfowl can be seen at East Harbor State Park. The great blue heron is part of the park's logo. This bird with a six-foot wingspan is often seen in the surrounding waterways and marshlands. Egrets, other species of herons, Canada geese and numerous ducks are frequent visitors during the spring and summer.

Winter Activities: East Harbor State Park provides trails for cross-country skiing during the winter. Also, ice fishing and ice skating in the harbor sections of the park are popular.

East Harbor State Park
1169 N. Buck Road
Lakeside-Marblehead, Ohio 43440
(419) 734-4424

Evangola State Park

New York's Evangola State Park, is a 745-acre park, that is popular, particularly on weekends from the end of June through Labor Day.

The road entering the park is a double-lane highway with a broad, grassy parkway between the lanes. The grass between the lanes, and throughout the park, is trimmed and well-manicured.

From Memorial Day to the end of June the park is open only on weekends. Other days during this time no services are available and swimming is prohibited because of the absence of lifeguards on duty. From the last weekend in June until Labor Day, park services and the beach are open daily.

Location: Evangola State Park is in Erie County, New York. Take I-90 to exit 58 and immediately get on N.Y. 5. The park entrance is four miles from exit 58 on N.Y. 5. The park is 27 miles southwest of Buffalo.

Features of the Park: The two principal features of this park are the sandy beach and the extensive picnic area.

Beach: The intimate sandy beach extends about a half-mile along the Lake Erie shoreline. The sand extends back several hundred yards from the water's edge. At each end of the beach, the shoreline continues with bluffs of about 20 feet. The picnic areas rest on these bluffs overlooking the lake.

A large bathhouse with concession is at the entrance to the beach, separating the two picnic sections. A hard-surface walkway overlooks the beach near the bathhouse. Two hard-surface walkways lead to the beach. In addition, there are several dirt pathways from the picnic area to the shoreline.

Swimming is permitted only when lifeguards are on duty.

The shoreline away from the beach contains driftwood, stones and shale.

Picnic Facilities: A key feature of the park is the large picnic area with hundreds of tables. There are several open shelters with a half-dozen picnic tables in each, which are available by reservation. Restroom facilities are found in these large shelters.

The picnic area is shaded by many large trees. Throughout the park are many hard-surface walkways, which along with the well-manicured grass give the appearance of an urban park setting.

Scattered throughout the picnic grounds are grills. There are no refuse barrels in the park - "carry-in, carry-out."

At several places throughout the picnic grounds are tables on cement pads which are reserved for handicapped use. A hard-surface connector to the walkway accommodates wheelchairs.

Bluffs extend along the shoreline the length of the park. Several picnic tables and grills sit on the edge of the bluffs, providing an excellent view of the lake.

Several softball diamonds and children's swingsets are scattered throughout the picnic grounds.

There is a large parking lot adjacent to the picnic and beach area.

Camping: The 82-site campground is nearly a half-mile from the park entrance.

The first loop (campsites #58-#80) is in a wooded and grassy area atop a bluff. A fence along the edge of the bluff provides some protection. Electricity is not available at these campsites. Each site has a picnic table. Campsite #75 sits back a little from the others, directly on the

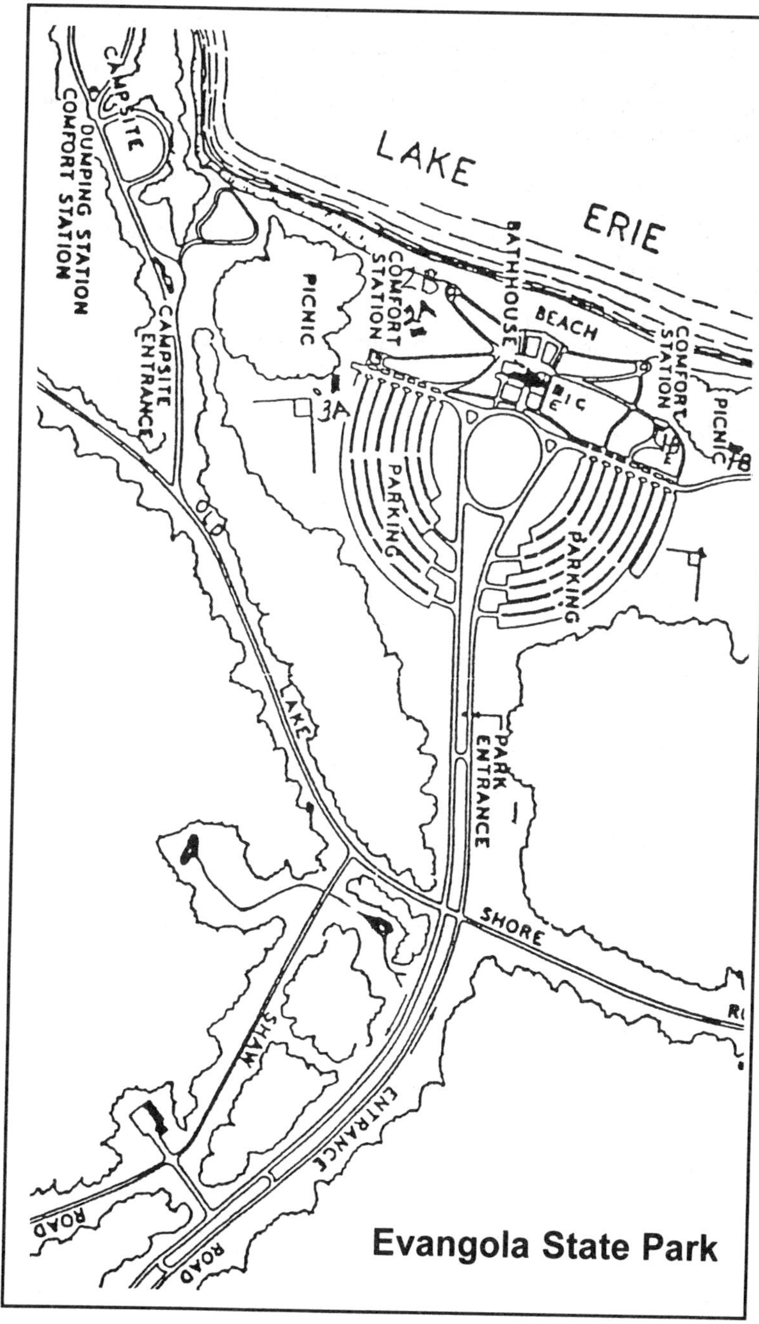

Evangola State Park

edge of the bluff.

The second circle (campsites #1 - #18) is open with little shade. These campsites do not have electricity. The odd numbered campsites are on the edge of the bluff, with a fence providing protection.

Campsites #19 - #57, a third loop, are shadier than the other loops and the spacing is slightly greater between campsites. Electricity is available at campsites #19-#53. Campsite #22 is handicapped accessible, having a cement hard-surface pad.

A recreation area includes tennis courts, basketball courts and a recreation hall for camper use. Also, laundry facilities are available for campers.

Trails: No hiking trails exist in Evangola State Park. A short nature trail which departs from the campground is only for camper use.

Scattered over the land are stones brought in from Canada by glaciers during the last Ice Age. These stones are often black and white speckled or striped. Anglola shale is exposed in the low cliffs at the edge of the beach. It contains calcareous concretions and nodules which weather in interesting rounded shapes.

Evangola State Park
Rte. 5
Irving, NY
(716) 549-1760

Geneva State Park

Geneva State Park receives significant damage from storms and waves, especially in the Chestnut Grove Picnic Area on the east border of the park. Until the mid-1980s the park's principal beach along the shoreline was in this area. This beach was closed in 1991. Surf caused by heavy pounding of storms over time destroyed much of the beach. Today, the beach is washed away and the waters of the lake wash upon the debris and rocks of the picnic area.

The land that is now Geneva State Park was acquired between 1964 and 1972. The Chestnut Grove section was first purchased by the state as a park. Today, the park contains 698 acres and encompasses more than a mile of Lake Erie shoreline.

Three creeks, Cowles Creek, Wheeler Creek and No Name Creek flow into Lake Erie at Geneva State Park. Freshwater marshes at the mouths of these creeks contain a variety of plants and submerged aquatic vegetation.

Location: Geneva State Park is about three miles north of Ohio 2 in

Ashtubula County in northeast Ohio. Leave I-90 at exit 218 and turn north onto Ohio 534 to the town of Geneva. The distance from the interstate to the park entrance is six miles.

Features of the Park: On the eastern edge of the park is Chestnut Grove Picnic Area, a well-shaded picnic area with many large white oak trees. Many picnic tables and grills are spread throughout the picnic grounds, located on the edge of the water. Next to them is the modern Geneva State Park Marina. A swimming beach, called Breakwater Beach, is west of the marina; on the western end of the park are eight cabins.

Marina: The modern marina, completed in 1989, has docks for 383 boats. The boat entrance to the lake is between breakwaters and a fishing pier. The boat ramp has provision for launching six boats. A large parking area for motor vehicles and boat trailers sits adjacent to the boat launch ramp. Bicycles and various types of watercraft are available for rental at the marina.

There is a full-service store at the marina where fishing and picnic supplies as well as gasoline are available. Also, refreshments including ice cream, soft drinks and sandwiches can be purchased. Mechanical boat service is available.

Beach: To replace the destroyed beach, a new beach was built, called the Breakwater Swimming Beach. It is about 300 feet long and extends 30 to 40 yards from the waterline. This swimming beach is just west of the marina, about a half-mile from the campground and the cabins.

Picnic Facilities: There are a number of picnic facilities in the park. The most scenic, and most popular, is Chestnut Grove. This area has many old white oak trees which provide shade for picnicking and make for a scenic view.

At the Crabapple Picnic Area, there are two shelterhouses available on a first-come, first-served basis.

Camping: The campground has 91 campsites, all equipped with electrical outlets. There are hot shower and flush toilet facilities. The campground is not within sight of Lake Erie; it is more than a half-mile to the beach along a road. It is more than a mile to the marina and Chestnut Grove Picnic Area. The campground is popular during the summer. It is usually filled on holidays and on most weekends from Memorial Day until Labor Day.

Three rent-a-tent campsites are available in the campground. In the 10-by-12-foot tent are a dining canopy, two cots, a cooler, propane cooking stove, lantern, broom and dustpan.

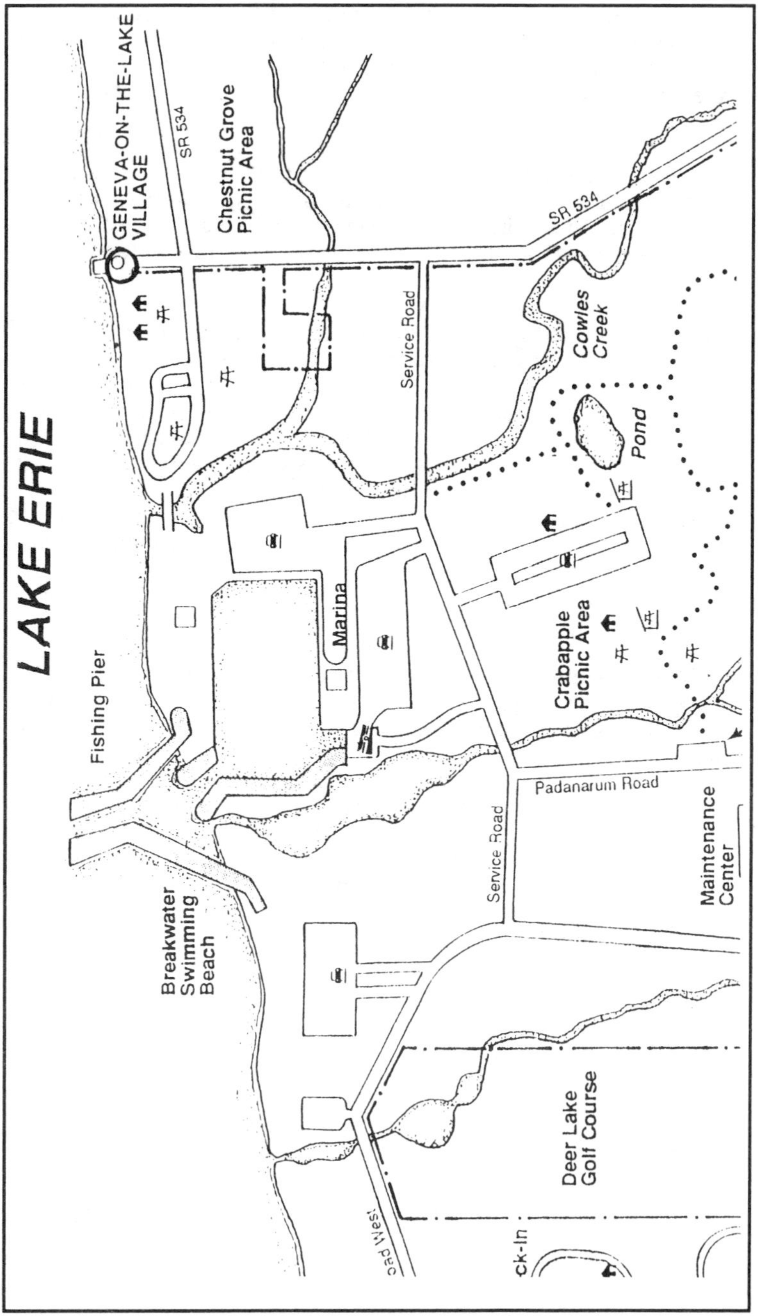
LAKE ERIE
GENEVA-ON-THE-LAKE VILLAGE
SR 534
Chestnut Grove Picnic Area
SR 534
Service Road
Cowles Creek
Pond
Marina
Fishing Pier
Crabapple Picnic Area
Padanarum Road
Service Road
Maintenance Center
Breakwater Swimming Beach
Deer Lake Golf Course
oad West
ck-In

Cabins: Eight cabins on the western edge of the park overlook Lake Erie. These cabins have facilities for six people. They are situated in a semi-circular formation providing excellent views of the lake. There are eating and cooking utensils in each cabin, as well as cable television.

It is about a half-mile walk along a path to the beach. To get to the marina, you must drive. Reservations for the cabins must be made months in advance. They can be made starting in January on a first-come, first-served basis for the coming year. They are allotted on a lottery basis.

Within park boundaries, but privately operated, is an 18-hole golf course adjacent to the campground.

Trails: There are three miles of hiking trails in the park. The trails travel from the Crabapple Picnic Area and the Rod and Gun Club Picnic Area bounded on the east to Cowles Creek and on the south by the south boundary road, Lake Road West.

There are no bicycle paths in Geneva State Park, yet bicycles are available for rental at the marina. Bikes are fun to traverse the roads of the park. However, these roads can get crowded in the summer, particularly on weekends and during holidays.

Winter Activities: Geneva State Park is in an area of Ohio that receives large amounts of snow. As a result, cross-country skiing and snowmobiling are popular. Also, it is possible to ice fish during many winter days.

Geneva State Park
P.O. Box 429
Padanarum Road
Geneva, Ohio 44041
(216) 466-8400

Headlands Beach State Park

Headlands Beach State Park is a relatively small, 126-acre day-use park. When the park opened in 1953, it was known as Painesville Beach State Park. In 1955, the name was changed to the current one.

Location: Headlands Beach is in Lake County, Ohio, east of Cleveland, on Ohio 44 (Heisley Road), about seven miles north of exit 200 and head north on SR44, which ends at the park entrance.

Features of the Park: The primary feature of Headlands Beach State Park is the mile-long beach, which extends the length of the park. The beach is the largest natural sand beach among Ohio state parks on Lake Erie. In places, the beach extends 150 yards from the water's edge. It is extremely popular for swimming and sunbathing during the summer.

In the huge parking lot, there are 38 rows of parking spaces between the entrance of the park and the beach. These parking spaces run the width of the park from east to west. There are places available for close to 4,000 vehicles. During hot summer weekends, this parking facility often is filled.

Two concession stands are located on the beach. Here food and soft drinks are available to visitors during the summer. There are changing facilities and several restrooms along the beach.

Picnic Facilities: A small picnic area can be found about mid-point along the beach. It includes one shelter near the beach, which can be reserved in advance.

Trails: Within the park is less than one mile of hiking trails. The northern terminus of the 1,200-mile Buckeye Trail is on the eastern edge of Headlands Beach State Park. A sign marks this point.

Fishing: Within the park is a small pond, Shipman Pond, surrounded by trees. There is a small fishing dock; however, it did not appear as though many people came to this park to fish. Most people the day of my visit were on the beach.

Nature Preserves: As is the case with many state parks in Ohio, Headlands Beach is surrounded by several hundred acres of state nature preserves. To the east is Headlands Dunes State Nature Preserve and to the south is Mentor Marsh State Nature Preserve. Both possess a variety of plant life.

The Headlands Dunes Nature Preserve has been preserved by Ohio legislation. It encompasses one of the finest remaining examples of Lake Erie beach. Here you can find a variety of coastal plants which are typically located along the Atlantic coast, such as beach pea, seaside spurge, beach grass and purple sand grass.

There is a five-mile hiking trail, the Zimmerman Trail, which leaves from the state park, across from the office, and provides access to the Mentor Marsh preserve.

Also, a federal breakwater wall where anglers enjoy fishing is located here. They walk a short access trail from the east end of the park service road onto the breakwall. Fishing for bluegill, coho salmon, catfish, bass, perch, bullhead and several other types of fish attract anglers throughout the year.

Winter Activities : Snowfall is often heavier in this section of Ohio, east of Cleveland, than along the western section of Lake Erie. Sledding and cross-country skiing bring people to the park in the winter. There are no ski rentals nor groomed trails in the park.

Headlands Beach State Park

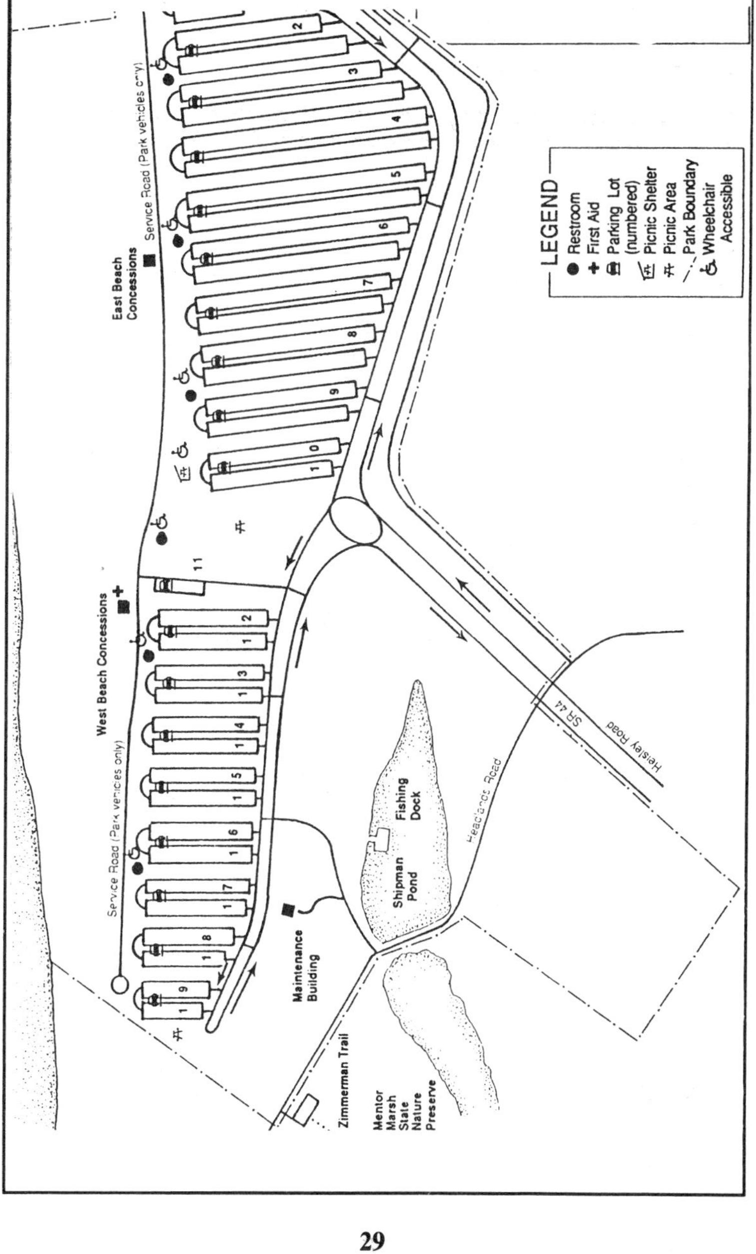

Observation: One of the more humorous observations of my visits to state parks took place along the road going past Shipman Pond. A squirrel was "walking" down the road. There was a backup of half a dozen motor vehicles behind the squirrel. This was a most amusing scene. Usually we see squirrels running to cross the roadway when there is traffic present. Not this time.

Headlands Beach State Park
9601 Headlands Road
Mentor, Ohio 44060
(216) 257-1330

Kelleys Island State Park

Kelleys Island State Park is a 661-acre park on the north side of an island by the same name in Lake Erie. Travel to the island is by ferry from either Sandusky or Marblehead, Ohio. The ferry from Marblehead is the shortest, taking about a half hour. This island has a number of interesting tourist attractions. It's not as crowded in the summer as its near neighbor, South Bass Island.

Location: It is about two miles from the ferry docks on the island to the entrance of Kelleys Island State Park. Most people come to the park in motor vehicles that they have brought over on the ferry. It is possible to rent bicycles or golf carts to get about the island, however. I visited this park by bicycling along the various roads of the island. The traffic on the island is not particularly heavy and some of the roads follow the shoreline, providing a beautiful bicycle ride.

Features of the Park: There are three basic features of Kelleys Island State Park: the glacial grooves, campground and Horseshoe Lake.

The most unique natural feature in Kelleys Island is the glacial grooves. These grooves into bedrock were made more than 10,000 years ago when the last glacier retreated from this part of North America. A fenced walkway keeps people from walking on the grooves, taking them along the area where the glacial grooves are located. Along this walk are several plaques which provide information about how these grooves were formed and other factors of interest.

Most of the state park acreage is south of the campground in the middle of the island. This area in the 1930s was an important quarry where the Kelleys Island Lime and Transport Company removed a significant amount of limestone. The quarry ended at the head of Horseshoe Lake. This lake is today a popular place to fish, picnic and hike. Smallmouth bass and sunfish are the most commonly caught fish in the lake. Swimming is not permitted in Horseshoe Lake.

Camping: There are 129 campsites in the park. Several campsites are directly on the Lake Erie shoreline. A beautiful view of the lake can be seen from a trailer, tent or picnic table at those campsites. There are showers and restrooms available for use by campers. Several campsites have been set aside for people with pets. Across the road from the campground is a small store where basic camping supplies and food can be purchased.

Within walking distance of the campground is a small, 100-yard-long beach. It is a nice place to enjoy the sunshine in the summer.

A short distance from the beach are a boat launching ramp and a fishing pier. A walk out onto the pier provides a very good view of both the campground and the lake.

Trails: There are about five miles of hiking trails in the state park, most in the East Quarry area. Hiking, particularly along the shore of Horseshoe Lake, is popular. Many people were walking along this area the day I visited. Though not designated as bicycle trails, bicycling is permitted. It is an interesting area.

There is a 1.5-mile trail along the north shore that begins near the North Quarry. This quarry, opened in 1830, was the second quarry on Kelleys Island. The stone from this quarry was used to construct buildings in Cleveland and other cities throughout the eastern United States. The stone for the first American lock at Sault St. Marie, Michigan, was dug from this quarry.

Many individuals who worked in this quarry were immigrants from Europe and Slavic communities. The North Shore Trail takes you past a structure where stone was loaded into rail cars to be taken to lime kilns. Today old roads associated with the quarry are used as fire lanes and hiking trails.

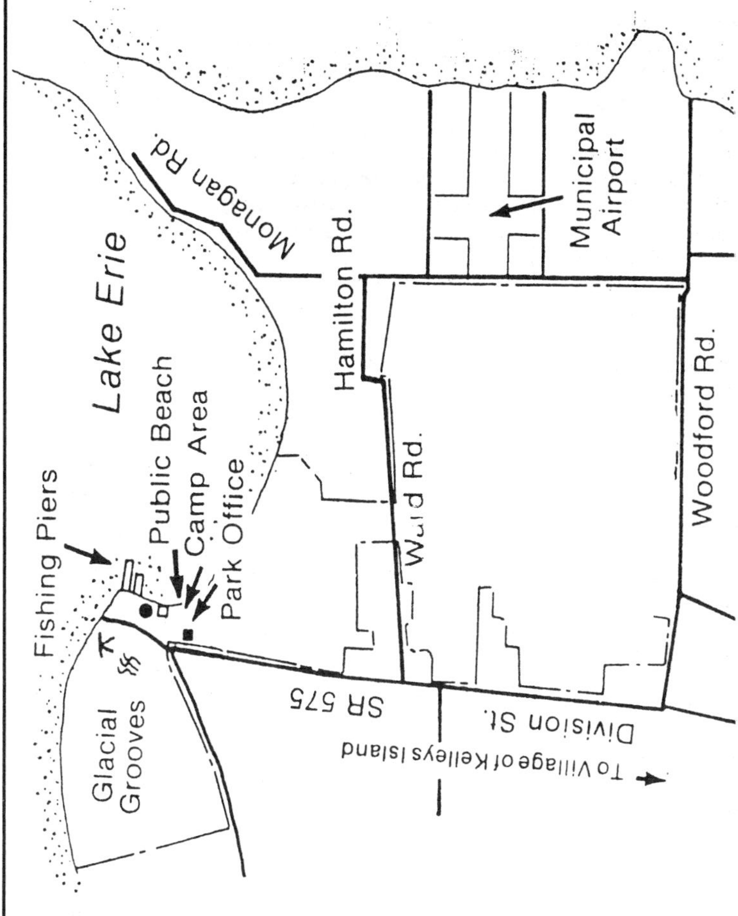

Kelleys Island State Park

Fishing/Boating: Boating and fishing are popular activities for individuals who come to camp at Kelleys Island State Park. As is the case in other state parks in the western basin of Lake Erie, fishing for walleye, perch and bass is popular.

Winter Activities: Even though most visitors to Kelleys Island come in the summer, a variety of activities exist in the winter. Ice fishing, cross-country skiing and snowmobiling are favorite pastimes.

Kelleys Island State Park
Kelleys Island, Ohio 43438
(419) 746-2546

Lake Erie State Park

Lake Erie State Park is one of the oldest state parks in New York, established in 1928. The park, comprised of 355 acres, is one of two New York state parks on Lake Erie.

The park is well manicured, with cut grass along all the roads, the picnic area and campground.

Location: Lake Erie State Park is in Chautauqua County, one of the leading grape-growing counties in New York. It is situated along New York 5, between Barcelona and Dunkirk. The park is about five miles south of Dunkirk.

After entering the park at the toll booth, the road divides. The road to the left leads to the camping and cabin area while the road to the right goes to the picnic area.

Features of the Park: The principal feature of the park is the Lake Erie shoreline with high bluffs about 40 feet above the beach. On top of the bluffs are small trees and thick shrubs. The major tree species is the black locust.

Camping: There are 125 campsites in the campground. Most campsites are close to each other, in the open with little shade, and on mostly grass-covered ground. Each campsite has a picnic table, but not every campsite has a grill. Several campsites (#10, #11, #13, #14, #17, #18, #20 and #21) are on the edge of the bluff. There is one semicircle with 11 campsites (#87 -#97) without electricity.

Campsites #82 and #83 have hard-surface pads and are reserved for the disabled. There are two modern hot shower and flush toilet facilities in the camping area.

The campground is not heavily used during the week. On summer weekends and holidays, the campsites and cabins are filled.

Cabins: Situated on the bluffs overlooking the lake and adjacent to the campground are 10 semi-primitive cabins. They provide a good view of the lake from the top of the bluff. The views from cabins #1, #3 and #6 provide one of the best views looking out on Lake Erie. Cabin #6 is handicapped accessible.

Picnic Facilities: There is a large grass-covered picnic area extending from the parking lot to the shoreline. Several picnic tables are scattered throughout the area. Many maple trees surround the picnic area. There is a small open pavilion with four inside barbecue pits for use by picnickers.

A recreational area with a basketball rim and a softball diamond is located in the picnic area along with children's playground equipment.

Boats/Fishing: Fishing is available along sections of the beach. There are no boat ramps in the park, but there are several in nearby Westfield and Dunkirk.

Trails: Within the park are two hiking trails, each about 1.5 miles long. They are level and easy walking. However, during my visit, I found no signs indicating trailheads nor were there any signs giving directions or distances of the trails. At one place near the parking lot there were a bridge over a stream and some steps which led to the top of the bluff.

A short woodland handicapped-accessible nature trail was completed in 1995.

Beach: The shoreline extends about .75-mile. There is a lot of driftwood, rocks and stones along the shoreline with very little sand. Only a couple hundred feet of sand beach is available for swimming.

Birding: As at other state parks on Lake Erie, birding is popular in this

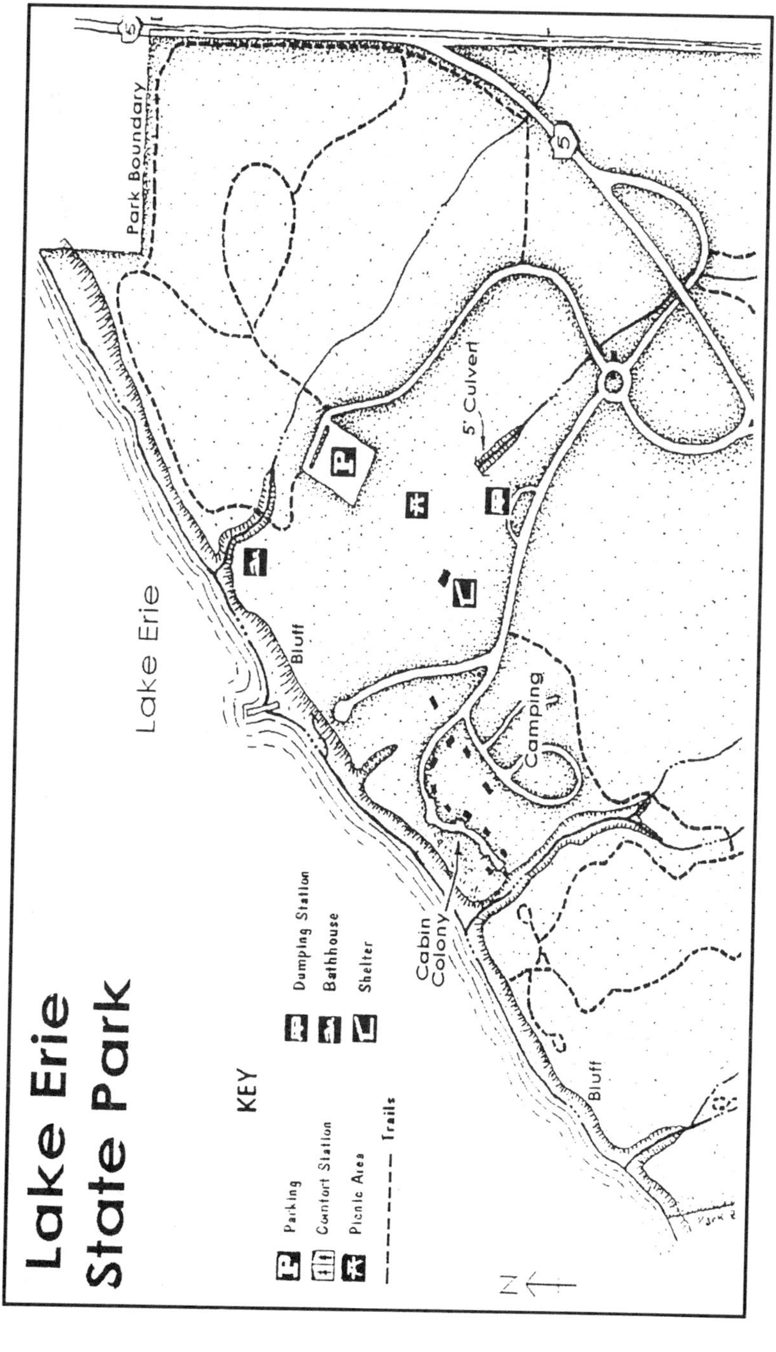
Lake Erie
State Park
KEY
Parking
Comfort Station
Picnic Area
Trails
Dumping Station
Bathhouse
Shelter
Lake Erie
Park Boundary
5
Bluff
5' Culvert
Camping
Cabin Colony
Bluff
N

area. The park is a natural stopping place for birds flying across the lake during the spring and fall migrations.

During the winter, nearby Dunkirk harbor is an excellent place to observe wintering waterfowl. Because a local power plant discharges warm water, ice does not form between the shore and breakwall, providing open water for many types of waterfowl year-round.

Winter Activities: Lake Erie State Park is not open during the winter. However, many people use the trails for cross-country skiing.

Lake Erie State Park
R.D. #1
Brocton, NY 14716
(716) 792-9214

Maumee Bay State Park

Anyone visiting Maumee Bay State Park a decade ago would have been unimpressed. This park, which became a state park in 1975, was little more than a camping area with little development around the water. On my first visit to this park, in the late 1970s, about all that I noticed was the camping area in the midst of a flat farming area.

Today this park is the most comprehensively developed state park recreational and resort facility on any of the Great Lakes. It consists of about 1,450 acres of land.

Adjacent to the east boundary of the park is a 2,000-acre state wildlife area and the Cedar Point National Wildlife Refuge. The general public is not permitted to enter the wildlife refuge; special permits are required.

Location: Maumee Bay State Park is on the east side of Toledo, about 10 miles from the center of the city. The park entrance is at the end of North Curtice Road, which is reached by turning north off of Ohio 2.

Lodging facilities: Today, as you enter the park, you will first see the lodge, which opened in 1991. The lodge, sitting on the shore of Maumee Bay, is the newest state park lodge in Ohio and one of only two such facilities on the Great Lake's state parks. The lodge is officially known as Quilter Lodge, named after a local state government representative who was instrumental in moving legislation that created the state park.

There are 120 guest rooms in the resort lodge, each with a private balcony that overlooks Lake Erie. Numerous services and activities are available in the lodge: saunas, whirlpools, game rooms, racquetball courts, a weight room, and both an indoor and outdoor swimming pool. The lodge restaurant provides a full-meal menu for both guests at the park and for visitors who come just to enjoy the beauty and scenery of the lakefront.

Throughout the year many professional, educational and religious organizations hold conferences, retreats and meetings at the lodge. Eleven meeting rooms can accommodate up to 600 individuals. There are audio-visual, fax and copy services for use by conference participants.

In addition to the lodge, there are 20 modern cottages in Maumee Bay State Park. Both two-and four-bedroom cottages are available on a daily or weekly rental basis. Some of these cottages are adjacent to the golf course; others are alongside the wetlands to the north. Each cottage has a gas fireplace, a kitchen, living area and two or four bedrooms. They also are air-conditioned and heated. Television sets and telephones are available in each cottage. Guests using the cottages have access to all of the facilities throughout the park, including the lodge. Facilities at the lodge and the cottages are open year-round.

Features/activities of the park: Next to the lodge is a marina, which opened in 1994. This marina has 32 boat slips where you can dock your boat. Twenty-two of the slips have accommodations for electricity for overnight stays for a maximum of seven days. The 10 docks without electrical power are available for docking up to four hours. They can be reserved overnight, but cannot be reserved in advance. Potable water is available at each boat slip. A lighted concrete walkway makes up each dock. Boats up to 40 feet long can be accommodated. Every boat slip is accessible for people with disabilities.

There are several recreational facilities in the park, including tennis courts and an 18-hole Scottish Link golf course. The par 71 course was constructed in the style of Scottish courses. Sand bunkers, ponds and the fairways are as rough as the courses of Scotland. Lessons are provided by a resident golf professional. During the summer, it is usually necessary to reserve tee times since the course has become very popular, both by guests to the park and citizens in the area.

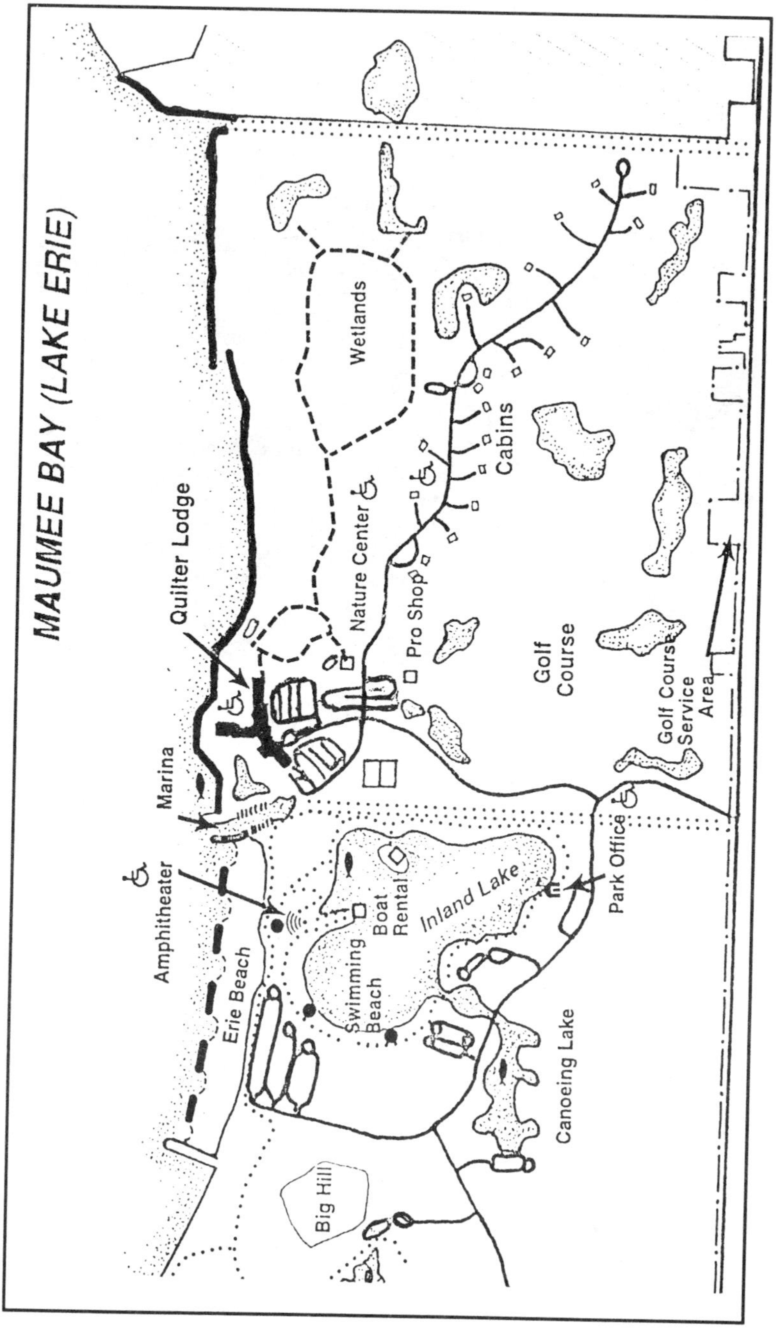
MAUMEE BAY (LAKE ERIE)
Quilter Lodge
Marina
Amphitheater
Erie Beach
Wetlands
Nature Center
Pro Shop
Cabins
Golf Course
Golf Course Service Area
Park Office
Boat Rental
Inland Lake
Swimming Beach
Canoeing Lake
Big Hill

There are two swimming beaches in the park. Along the shore of the bay is a 1,500-foot sandy beach. This beach tends to be most popular for sunbathing and walking rather than for swimming. Most swimming occurs on the beach of Inland Lake, about 2,000 feet in length. This manmade lake, consisting of 57 acres, is several hundred feet from the Lake Erie shoreline. There are changing facilities and a concession area near the beaches.

Connected to Inland Lake is Canoeing Lake, another manmade lake of about 12 acres. Here canoes can be rented and canoeing can be enjoyed. There is no place for canoeists to go other than about the waters of this small lake. However, it provides opportunity for individuals who have little experience with canoes. Sailboats, paddleboats, and rowboats can be rented on these two small inland lakes. Motorized boats are prohibited. There are no launching ramps into Lake Erie at the state park. Visitors to the park with boats must put their boats in at private marinas in the area.

Camping: There is a large modern campground at Maumee Bay State Park. This facility, including 256 campsites, is equipped with modern toilet facilities, showers, electricity and a playground. Each campsite includes a picnic table and fire ring. The campground is well-planned with adequate space between the sites.

Most of the campground was developed in recent years. As a result, there are few trees and not much shrubbery. You can look out over the entire campground. It is somewhat like camping in a nicely developed farm field. Throughout the camping area are ponds where fishing is encouraged, but swimming is prohibited. The campground is about a mile from the lodge, the beach and the golf course. These facilities are connected to the campground by a hiking and bicycling trail. Camping is provided on a first-come, first-served basis, with no advance reservations taken.

There is a Rent-a-Camp program available by reservation. A tent, cooler, cook stove and other facilities can be rented during the summer.

Trails: Ten miles of trails exist in Maumee Bay State Park. Some of them are combination bicycle, hiking and jogging trails. The trail system goes through a natural meadow between the campground and Inland Lake. It also follows the edge of Lake Erie on the west side of the park.

A nature trail of about two miles begins behind the nature center. This is a boardwalk trail that is elevated above marsh wetlands and swamplands. The hiker is provided with an excellent opportunity to see more closely what a marshy wetland is like. This is an easy trail to walk, particularly for older individuals. It is also handicapped accessible. At the far eastern end of the circular trail is a lookout from which you can see Lake Erie. From this tower you can obtain a good understanding of what this region must have been like years ago when the entire area for miles around was swamp and marshland. During the spring and fall, many songbirds can be seen along the nature trail.

Nature Center: The nature center, known as the Milton B. Trautman Nature Center, provides information about the surrounding wetlands region. There are a number of educational interactive displays for children and adults. A couple of these displays are situated in front of large picture windows looking over the wetlands. The day I visited the center a senior citizen group was enjoying the displays.

A theater in the nature center offers audio-visual presentations about the surrounding wetland environment. Anyone spending a little time at the center will have a better understanding of the importance of wetlands in this part of Ohio.

During the summer, numerous nature programs are provided at, or originate from, the nature center. These include bird hikes and walks in which the characteristics and importance of marshes and swamps are explained. Nature walks with instruction about butterflies, plants, reptiles and amphibians in the area are conducted. One evening each week there is a night hike when visitors learn about owls, bats and other creatures.

Fishing/Hunting: As with all state parks on Lake Erie, fishing is a common activity. All of the ponds in Maumee Bay State Park are stocked and fishing is permitted. Also, two miles of Lake Erie shoreline can be fished.

Walleye is particularly good in this part of Lake Erie. So is fishing for bass, yellow perch and channel catfish. Fishing is permitted on the manmade inland lake of the park. An Ohio fishing license is required by anyone fishing in the waters of the state park.

Fishing in Lake Erie is very popular. However, there are no boat ramps in the park. Within a 20-minute drive from the park are several marinas and boat ramps where anglers can launch a boat.

Hunting is not permitted in the state park; however, you can hunt in the adjacent Mallard Club Marsh Wildlife Area.

Winter Activities: This park has become increasingly popular during the winter. The campground, lodge and cottages are open year round, with many organizations meeting during this time. When there is adequate snow, cross-country skiing is popular on the many trails. A hill about 50 feet tall serves as a place for sledding.

Special Activities: Throughout the year many special activities are scheduled at the park. A unique activity provided at Maumee Bay is kite flying. Two triathlon races and a duathlon race are held in addition to a bike rodeo. There is a two-day stunt kite-flying competition, a two-day windsurfing championship race, and an arts and crafts festival. In the fall, a Halloween campout with related activities attracts hundreds of people.

Maumee Bay State Park
1400 Park Road #1
Oregon, Ohio 43618
(419) 836-7758

Presque Isle State Park

The only Pennsylvania state park on a Great Lake is Presque Isle which is on a peninsula which juts seven miles into Lake Erie, across Presque Isle Bay from Erie, Pennsylvania. The park is comprised of 3,200 acres and is open year-round. Today, the manager lives in Presque Isle Lighthouse, built in 1872.

Energy for the park's buildings is provided by a natural gas well on the peninsula. A downwind windmill at Beach No. 6 produces electrical power for the park office.

Information about the park can be obtained by turning to 1480 AM on the radio dial.

Location: To reach the park, leave I-90 at Exit 5 or U.S. 20 at Pennsylvania 832. The park entrance is about eight miles north of I-90, about two miles north of U.S. 20, and one mile north of Pennsylvania 5.

It is also possible to take a ferry from Erie to the park. The ferry leaves the Erie Public Dock at the end of State Street and arrives at the dock in the park near the Waterworks Picnic Shelter and Beach Area.

Features of the park: The location of the park provides much variety for recreational opportunities. Despite the size and location of the park and its wide popularity, this is a day-use only facility. There are no overnight camping facilities nor cabins within the park. Near the park in the city of Erie are many privately owned campgrounds, cottages and motels. A listing of these facilities is provided by the park office upon request.

Presque Isle Bay is protected by the Presque Isle peninsula. This provides for calmer waters than is found on Lake Erie. It also provides the state of Pennsylvania with its only port on the Great Lakes. All kinds of water activities are possible on the bay: water skiing, motor boating, personal watercrafts, windsurfing, canoeing and fishing.

A part of the park is designated as an ecological reservation. In this area, you will find a combination of wetlands, woods and sand ridges. This area is a haven for wildlife.

Because of the location of the park, thousands of birds migrate through the area during the middle of May and again in September. More than 300 species of birds have been identified on the peninsula. Many visitors come to the park to birdwatch. More than 600 species of plants have been found here.

Geological, biological and historical interest: Presque Isle State Park is of geological interest because here you can see the effects of winds, currents and waves on glacial sand. On this peninsula it is possible to observe a complete ecological succession from newly forming sand beaches to climax forests. Nowhere else in the world is this possible to see in such a short distance.

The park is of interest biologically because of extensive plant life. Here one can go from a sand and water lakeshore to a forest within two miles. In the ponds of the park is extensive aquatic life.

This area has an interesting history. Four states have claimed ownership.

This area was important in the early 19th century history on the Great Lakes. In 1812 the British were in command of the waters of Lake Erie. Late that year navy lieutenant Oliver H. Perry arrived at Presque Isle Bay to build ships to engage the British. Here in Misery Bay, there were adequate resources and protection to build six ships for battle.

The shores and waters of this area provided protection for Perry's fleet while it was being constructed until he went out into Lake Erie to engage the British in the War of 1812. Perry engaged the British at Put-n-Bay, in the western end of Lake Erie. On Sept. 10, 1813, the American naval fleet under Perry defeated the British. After the victory, the ships returned to Misery Bay. Perry's Monument at Presque Isle State Park commemorates this event in American history.

Nature/Interpretative Center: About a mile from the park entrance near Barricks Beach is the Stull Interpretive Center. Displays explain the geological and ecological development of the peninsula. One display explains how various weather forces have impacted the development of Presque Isle. Also, information is provided about the wildlife in the area, the birds and the flowers. An audio-visual presentation telling of the history of the park and surrounding area is available.

Marina: Situated on West Fisher Drive is a large full-service marina. The marina, which has 473 slips, many of which are rented for the season, is on the south shore of Marina Lake. Boats leaving the marina go into Presque Isle Bay, passing between East Pier and West Pier.

Picnic Facilities: More than 800 picnic tables are scattered throughout the park for use year-round.

At the East Pier picnic area are dozens picnic tables, grills and an open shelter. This site includes facilities for wheelchair accessible fishing.

Another picnic area is on a little peninsula on the edge of Misery Bay at the point on which Perry's Monument stands. There is water on both sides of the peninsula: Misery Bay and Presque Isle Bay, providing a delightful picnic setting.

Trails: About 10 miles of hiking trails are found in the park; most are in the wetlands section and pass along the various ponds. Most originate across from the parking lot near the Presque Isle Lighthouse. Bicycles are prohibited on the hiking trails.

Most of the trails are relatively short. The longest is the Fox Trail (2.25 miles), which winds through wooded swamps and oak-maple forests. The Dead Pond Trail (2 miles) traverses several former dunes where you can observe sand plains, pines and an oak-maple forest. The Gull Point Trail (1.5 miles) loops through the Gull Point Natural Area. The trail goes to an observation platform where you can see shorebirds in the Special Management Area. An interesting trail is the Sidewalk Trail (1.25 miles), which was constructed by the lighthouse keeper to provide a path connecting the lighthouse to Misery Bay, where the keeper docked his boat. The trail originally was a wooden boardwalk. However, concrete was poured in 1925.

Other trails, which are less than a mile in length, include the Self-Guided Interpretive Trail (.2 miles), near the Stull Interpretive Center,

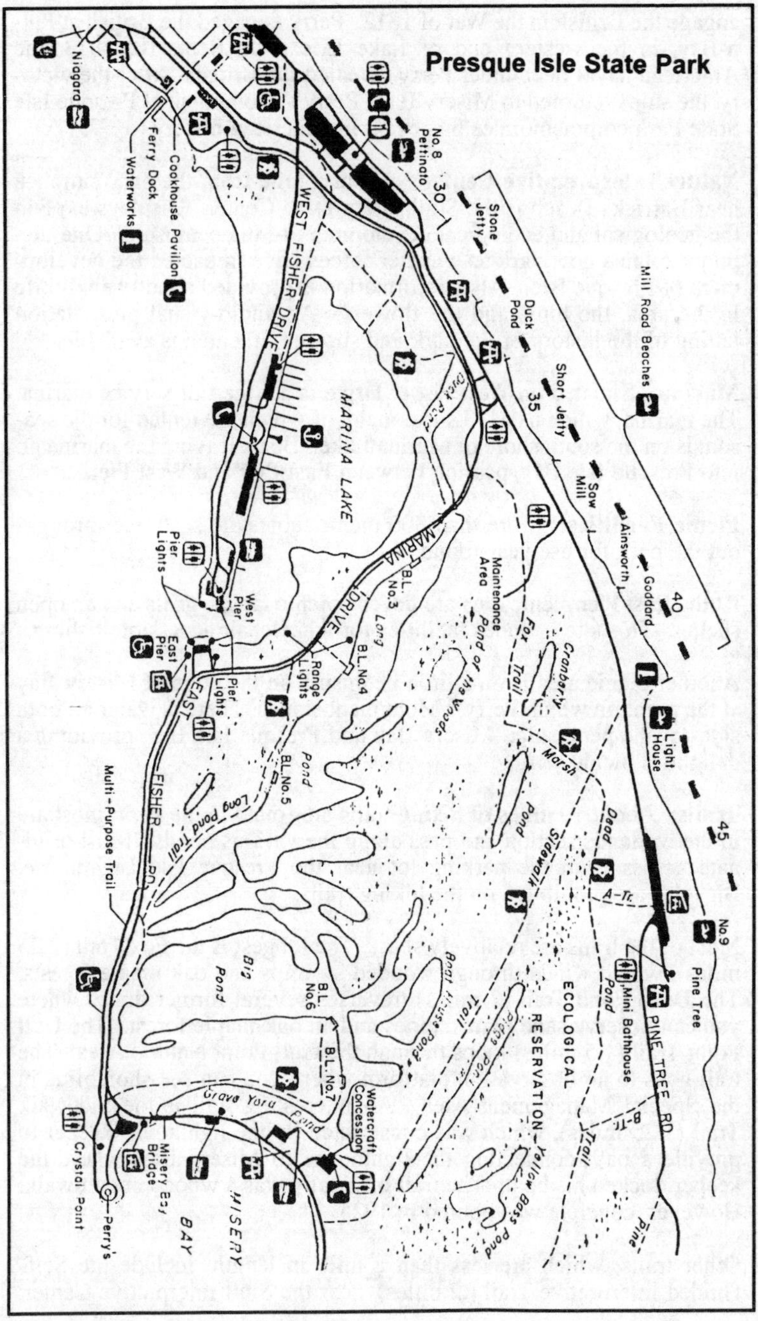
Presque Isle State Park
No. 8 Pettinato
Stone Jetty
Duck Pond
Mill Road Beaches
Short Jetty
Saw Mill
Ainsworth
Goddard
Light House
No. 9
Pine Tree
Mini Bathhouse
PINE TREE RD
Niagara
Ferry Dock
Cookhouse Pavilion
Waterworks
WEST FISHER DRIVE
MARINA LAKE
MARINA DRIVE
Pier Lights
West Pier
East Pier
Range Lights
B.L. No.3
B.L. No.4
B.L. No.5
B.L. No.6
B.L. No.7
Maintenance Area
Fox Trail
Cranberry
Marsh
Pond of the Woods
Long Pond
Long Pond Trail
Dead Pond
Sidewalk Trail
A-Tr.
B-Tr.
Big Pond
ECOLOGICAL RESERVATION
Boat House Pond
Boat House Trail
Yellow Bass Pond
Grave Yard Pond
Watercraft Concession
EAST FISHER RD
Multi-Purpose Trail
Misery Bay Bridge
MISERY BAY
Crystal Point
Perry's
30
35
40
45

Old-Gas Well Trail (.5 mile), Canoe Portage Trail (.25 mile), Ridge Trail (.5 mile), Marsh Trail (.25 mile), Pine-Tree Trail (.7 mile), North Pier Trail (.7 mile), and Graveyard Pond Trail (.75 mile). The trailheads for most are well marked, with a small dirt parking area at the trailheads.

An excellent feature of Presque Isle State Park is the 5.8 mile, multipurpose, hard-surface trail which begins at the park entrance and leads to Perry's Monument. This popular trail is used by thousands of people every year for bicycling, jogging, walking, roller blading and cross-country skiing. It is also wheelchair accessible.

This multipurpose trail winds through the park, generally paralleling the road. Sometimes it goes directly along the water's edge of Presque Isle Harbor, other times in the woods, and occasionally adjacent to the roadway. Distances in tenths of a mile are marked along the trail. For example, at the 2.9-mile mark is the Waterworks Ferry Dock. The last mile, the trail follows Presque Isle Bay. From here you can see downtown Erie. The trail ends at Perry Monument.

Boating/Fishing: There are six boat launch ramps in five areas of the park. In addition, several other places permit hand carried watercraft to be taken into the water.

You can rent canoes, rowboats, motorboats and electric-powered boats. Canoes and boats can be rented at the East Boat Livery near the Misery Bay Bridge from 8 a.m. to 8 p.m. Visitors navigate in three ponds and interior lagoons in the ecological reservation area where power boats are prohibited.

During the summer, a free interpretive pontoon boat tour leaves from this location and provides an opportunity for visitors to learn and see more of this environment.

Fishing is good in the various ponds and lagoons of the park. Bass, panfish, walleye, rainbow trout and perch are caught in these waters. Perch, walleye, bass, muskie, northern pike, smelt and coho are caught in Presque Isle Bay. Yellow perch, walleye, coho and chinook salmon, smelt, bass and rainbow trout are caught in Lake Erie. Salmon are plentiful during the fall as they move from deeper parts of the lake to streams for spawning.

Beaches: There are several miles of beaches along the Lake Erie shoreline. Generally, the sand extends back several hundred feet from the edge of the water to low-lying dunes with wild grass and shrubs. Along the edge of the beach among the trees are picnic tables.

Swimming is permitted only at beaches where lifeguards are present. Guards are available from 10 a.m. to 8 p.m. from Memorial Day to

Labor Day. Concession buildings where refreshments are available are located at several beaches. These are available at Budny Beach No. 10, Pettinato No. 8, Waterworks No. 7, and No. 6.

Beach No. 7 has a handicap accessible ramp. Also, near this beach are three small cabins surrounding a pond. These cabins provide shelter for group picnics. Each of these buildings has a fireplace and a dozen or more picnic tables.

Extending the length of the park is a road running parallel to the lake. In places you can't see the lake from the road because of dunes separating the road and the beach. However, in places the beaches and water are in sight of the road, such as at Ainsworth Beach.

Winter Activities: The park is open during the winter. Often this section of the country has significant snowfall from December through February.

Ice fishing is particularly popular. Fishing on Misery Bay, in the marina area, and on Presque Isle Bay is very good. Also, five miles of cross-country ski trails are maintained in winter.

Snowmobiles are not permitted in the park. There is a winter sports concession at the all-purpose building from November through the end of March.

Lodging: This is a day-use only park. There are no camping facilities. A listing of nearby restaurants, motels, campgrounds and cottages are provided by the park office.

Presque Isle State Park
P.O. Box 8510
Erie, PA 16505-0510
(814) 871-4251

South Bass Island State Park

South Bass Island State Park is a small 36-acre park on the southwest shore of South Bass Island, in Lake Erie just north of Catawba Island. Not only is the island a popular resort, but it has an important history. Here, during the War of 1812 the Americans, under the command of Oliver Perry, defeated the British. The entire British fleet was captured during this battle. This was the first time in British history that such a defeat had occurred. This victory is commemorated by a national monument, the Perry Victory International Peace Memorial, near Put-in-Bay on the island.

In the campground are the ruins of the former magnificent Victory Hotel. In the late 1800s and early 1900s this area was a popular tourist site. People came from Detroit, Cleveland and Toledo on steamships. The Victory Hotel, which opened in 1892, was a popular facility for those who made these trips. This hotel, which once was advertised as the largest hotel in the world, had a main dining room with 60 foot ceilings and seating for 1,200 people. Three United States Presidents stayed at the hotel in the early 1900s.

The hotel was destroyed by fire in August 1919. The blaze was visible 22 miles across the water in the city of Sandusky. Today visitors can see the concrete shell of the hotel's swimming pool. This nearly Olympic-size heated pool was one of the first to allow men and women to share the pool at the same time.

Today, most tourists come to the island during the summer by ferry from either Port Clinton or Catawba. The ferry run from Catawba is the shorter trip, about three miles long. Many boaters, both sailors and power boaters, come to the town of Put-in-Bay on South Bass Island for a weekend or a couple of days' visit. During the summer the boat docks at Put-in-Bay are full. There are numerous places in and around Put-in-Bay for activity and entertainment.

Camping: The principal activity that attracts people to the park is camping. There are 134 sites; those near the water provide a beautiful view of Lake Erie. Most campers come to enjoy the activities on the island or to boat and fish in Lake Erie. There is a boat launching ramp at the park. However, there is no marina for mooring boats in the park. One has to go to the town of Put-in-Bay to find a marina.

There are four small cabins for weekly rental in the park. These cabins are hexagonal-shaped, containing an efficiency kitchen, a shower, a picnic table and bunks for sleeping up to six people. They are referred to as "cabents." They must be rented on a weekly basis from Memorial Day to the end of September. Renters are selected by lottery, with applications due by the end of January. The cabins are usually occupied throughout the entire summer.

Picnic facilities: There is a shelter house and picnic area with tables and grills for those who come to the park for a picnic.

Fishing: As is the case in nearly all of the parks at the western end of Lake Erie, fishing is very popular. The most commonly caught fish are perch, crappies, smallmouth bass and walleyes. At South Bass Island State Park there is a pier from which individuals can fish. There is a facility near the camping area where fish can be cleaned.

Trails: There are no hiking or bicycle trails in the park. However, the roads of the island serve as an excellent place to bicycle. There are several miles of roadways that cyclists can take where the views of the waters of Lake Erie are spectacular. Fields of grapes growing in the interior sections of the island provide interesting backdrops for individuals sightseeing on bicycle or by motor vehicle along the roadways.

Winter Activities: This area is popular in the winter for various outdoor activities. Ice fishing brings many fishermen to the park. Walleye

South Bass Island State Park

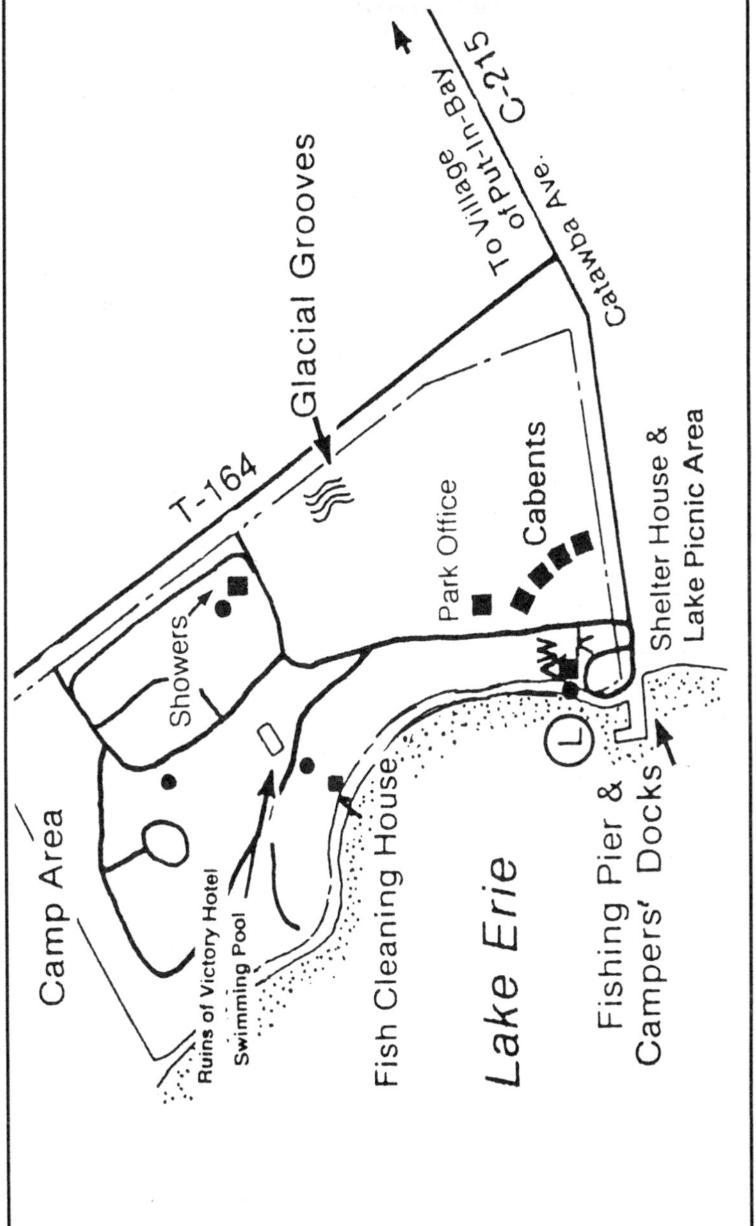

fishing is particularly good at this time of the year as well as in the early spring. When the waters are frozen between the mainland and the island, snowmobiling and the operation of all-terrain vehicles on the ice become popular.

Care must be taken to assure that the ice is thick enough for these activities. Special attention must be given to anyone on the ice when the temperatures start to rise. Regardless of the depth of the ice, an unusually warm day, even in the middle of winter, can cause openings in the ice and result in individuals being trapped.

Transportation to the island during the winter is by airplane. This service is provided not just in the winter when the passageway between the mainland and island is ice covered, but throughout the entire year.

South Bass Island State Park
Put-in-Bay, Ohio 43456
(419) 285-2112

Sterling State Park

Four of the five Great Lakes form part of the boundaries of Michigan. A small section of Lake Erie constitutes part of the boundary in the southeast portion of the state. Here, on the north edge of the city of Monroe, in Monroe County, is Sterling State Park. This park, which was established in 1935, is comprised of 1,000 acres and is the only Michigan state park on Lake Erie.

Location: Sterling State Park is about a half-mile east of I-75 exit 15 on Dixie Highway. The park entrance is .75-mile east of the interstate exit.

Features of the park: Two natural features are the primary focus of this park: the beach and wetlands. A rather narrow beach extends about a mile along Lake Erie. In places the sandy portion of the beach extends only 10 or so yards back from the edge of the water. Nowhere does the beach extend more than 25 yards from the shoreline.

Preservation of several lagoons constitutes a major part of Sterling State Park.

Picnic facilities: Behind the sand beach is a large grassy area for picnics, games and lying in the sunshine during the summer. On most holidays and weekends during the summer, this area is packed with families and other groups having picnics. The lake water is warm enough during the summer to enjoy swimming, wind surfing or just wading and playing in the water. A beachhouse with toilets is in the designated swimming area. A concession building with picnic supplies and refreshments is near the beach.

At the south end of the park are picnic tables and grills in a grassy area on the lagoon. This is a nice shaded picnic facility.

Trail: The only hiking trail in the park circles the largest lagoon. This 2.6-mile loop, the Marshview Nature Trail, is best to travel in a clockwise direction. The reason for this is that three-tenths of a mile from the trailhead, which is located at a parking lot between two lagoons, is an interpretive shelter. The shelter offers information about the wetlands and things to look for along the trail. The interpretive shelter is open during the summer.

The trail is hard-surfaced asphalt, and very easy to walk. It is convenient for disabled individuals and for the elderly. Several young mothers were walking with small children in strollers on the day that I visited the park.

About a mile from the trailhead, traveling clockwise, is an observation tower. From this tower you can get a good view of the entire wetlands area. It is an excellent location from which to view the many species of birds in the park. The only negative feature is that the tower is located directly below two sets of electrical high tension wires. These make it rather difficult to get good pictures without having the towers and wires of the electrical company in your photograph.

Along the southern edge of the park, between the lagoon and a stream, an eight-foot fence with barbed wire top has been installed. This fence separates the stream from the trail.

While visiting Sterling State Park, you're not far from a heavily populated urbanized area. At several locations along the nature and hiking trail, you can look about a mile in the distance and see, and hear, the traffic on I-75, the major interstate highway connecting Detroit and Toledo. Across the stream at the south edge of the park is a nuclear power plant. To the north, you can see two towers of another power plant. On a clear day you can look across the lake toward Ohio and see the tower of yet another power plant, the Davis-Bessey Nuclear Power Plant.

Although this is not a wilderness setting, numerous sounds may interest nature lovers, particularly bird watchers. Many kinds of waterfowl

Sterling State Park

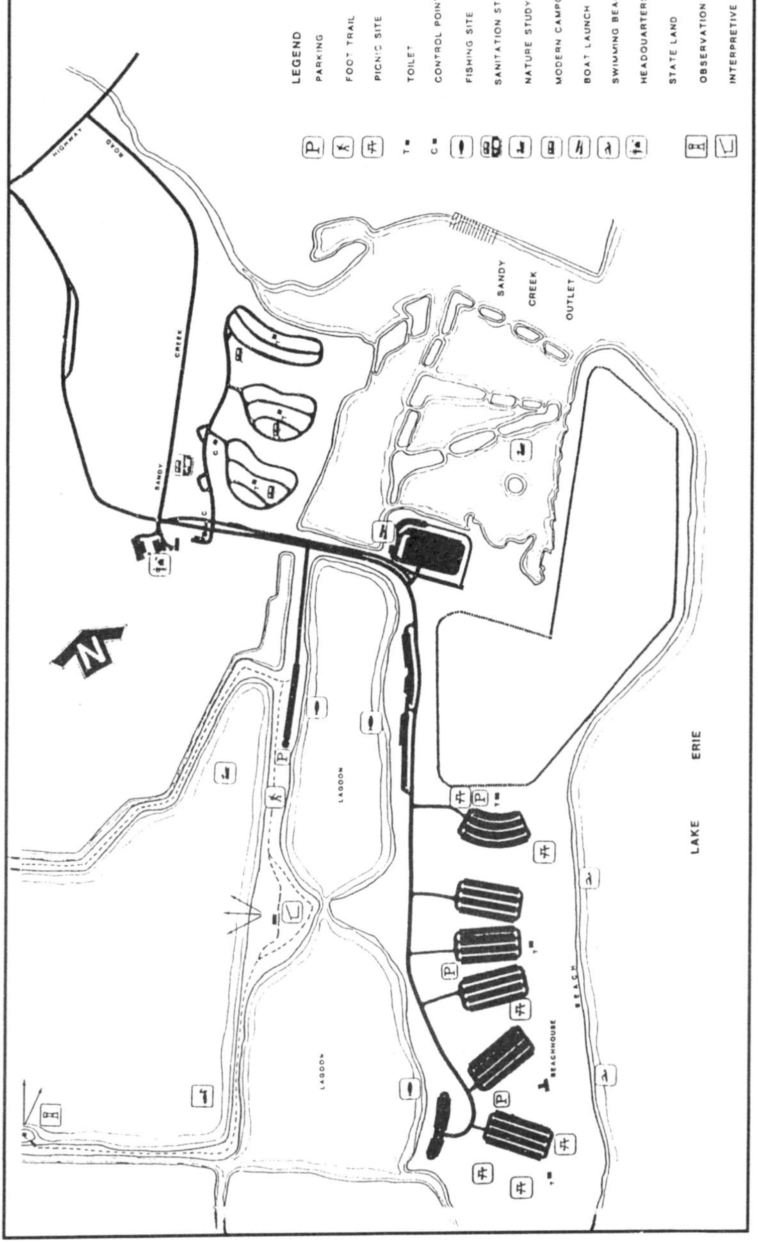

are seen along the trail. The swooshing sounds of a large blue heron and egret can be heard at times. The singing of songbirds takes your mind off of the urban sounds outside the park.

Many types of waterfowl can be seen while hiking in the area. Egrets, blue herons, Canadian geese and ducks are commonly seen. The day of my visit, I saw turtles sunning themselves on logs in and along the water. Twice we saw a dozen turtles enjoying the spring sunshine.

Camping: The park campground is near the park entrance booth. There are 288 campsites, each with a picnic table and in-ground fire pit. The campground is grass-covered in an open area with little shade; most of the sites are exposed to the sun, wind and rain. The sites are rather close to each other and are not within sight of Lake Erie.

The sites are arranged around three circles. Circle A provides a little shade. There is a modern shower and toilet facility in the middle of the loop.

Circle B resembles camping in a field. There are no shrubs, bushes or mature trees. A few relatively new trees are scattered throughout these sites. A children's swing set and other play equipment are between Circle A and B.

Campsites along circle C are grass-covered. The even numbered campsites from #44 - #64 back up on Sandy Creek Outlet. A group camping area with picnic tables and in-ground fire rings is provided. Reservations are required to use this facility.

Fishing/boat ramp: Sandy Creek, which serves as the northeast boundary to the park, flows into Lake Erie at Sterling State Park. The park has a large boat ramp with five cement ramps and a large parking area. There is no fee to use this boat launch.

Lake Erie has become an excellent body of water for fishing, particularly walleye. On weekends and holidays there are many boats in the lake with fishermen trying to catch their limit.

Fishing is also popular along the lagoons of the wetland marshes. There are small piers in the lagoon from where you can fish. I saw anglers seeking bluegills and catfish.

During the summer, rowboat, canoe and paddleboat rentals are available at the park for use in the lagoons.

Sterling State Park
2800 State Park Road
Monroe, MI 48193
(313) 289-2715

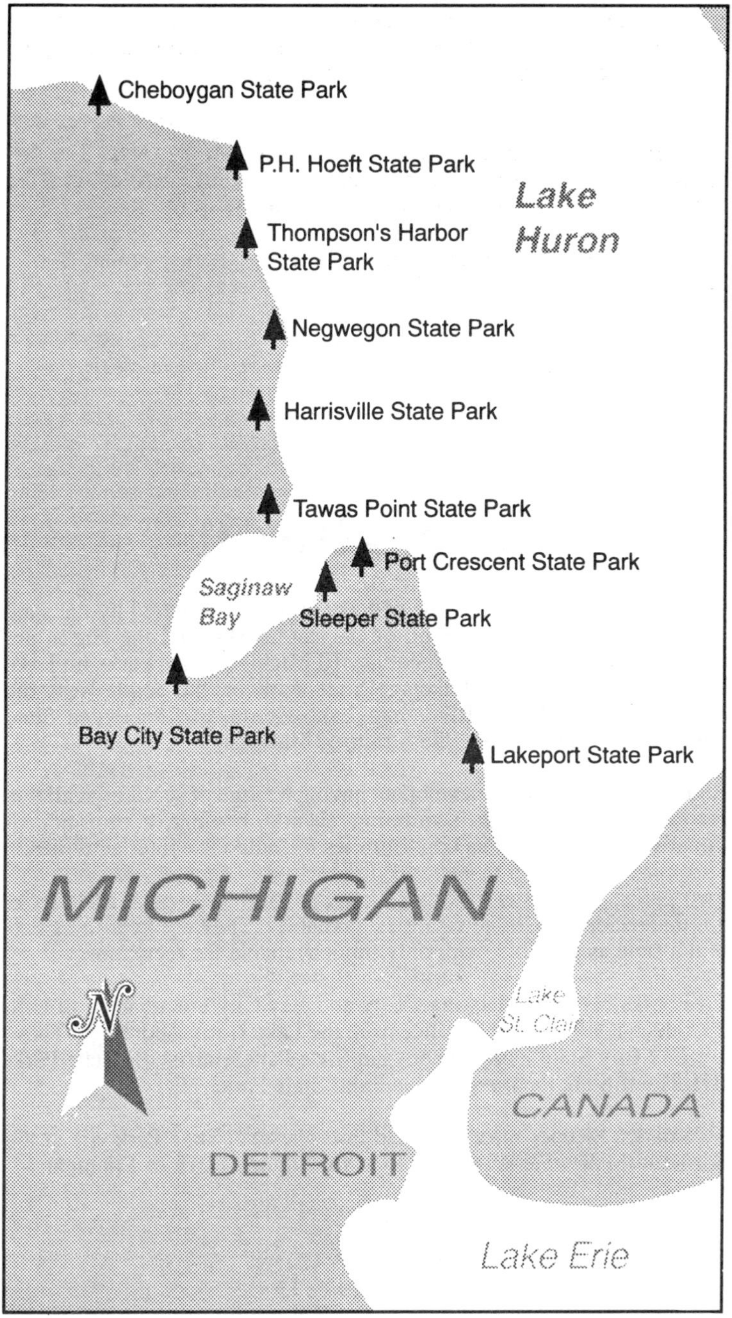
Cheboygan State Park
P.H. Hoeft State Park
Lake Huron
Thompson's Harbor State Park
Negwegon State Park
Harrisville State Park
Tawas Point State Park
Port Crescent State Park
Saginaw Bay
Sleeper State Park
Bay City State Park
Lakeport State Park
MICHIGAN
N
Lake St. Clair
CANADA
DETROIT
Lake Erie

Lake Huron

The entire western shoreline of Lake Huron is bordered by the state of Michigan. Therefore, all of the state parks on Lake Huron are administered by that state. There are 10 Michigan state parks on Lake Huron, stretching from Lakeport State Park on the south, near the entrance of the Detroit River into Lake Huron, to Cheboygan State Park at the northern point, the Straits of Mackinac.

Eight of these parks are developed, having a range of services available for the visitor: camping, swimming, fishing, boating, hiking, educational services, as well as opportunities for outdoor winter activities.

Two parks, Thompson's Harbor State Park and Negwegon State Park, are undeveloped with no facilities available. They are kept in as natural a state as possible, with only trails available for recreation.

Five parks between Mackinaw City and Bay City are adjacent to U.S. 23, which is just a short distance from the Lake Huron shoreline. These are Bay City State Park, Cheboygan State Park, Harrisville State Park, P.H. Hoeft State Park and Tawas Point State Park.

Two parks, Sleeper State Park and Port Crescent State Park, are at the northern tip of what is referred to as the "thumb" area of Michigan.

Bay City State Park

Bay City State Park is a relatively small park, comprising about 196 acres. Despite its small size, it is popular, close to the heavily populated region between Detroit and Flint. Even closer are Saginaw and Bay City.

Located next to Bay City State Park is the Tobico Marsh State Game Area, encompassing 2,000 acres of marsh and wetlands. Many visitors to Bay City State Park don't realize that this area is not part of the state park. Within the refuge are a variety of trees, plant life, waterfowl, birds and animals. There are several miles of hiking trails. Two 30-foot lookout towers provide excellent views over the surrounding marshlands.

Location: The park is about five miles north of Bay City in Bay County, Michigan, on Saginaw Bay. This park can be reached by leaving I-75 at exit 168 (Beaver Road). Seven miles east of the interstate on Beaver Road you will arrive at the park entrance.

Features of the Park: The sandy beach along Saginaw Bay is the primary feature of Bay City State Park. Along the beach are continuous wide-angle views of Lake Huron. In several places are shaded areas for those who desire to sit in the shade on a hot, sunny day. Here, during the summer, thousands of people come to enjoy the waters of Lake Huron, to sunbath, to picnic and to relax. On summer holidays and weekends the beach is often heavily populated.

Picnic Facilities: Behind the beach, between the sandy shoreline and the parking area, is a grass-covered day-use picnic area with numerous tables and grills. There are two picnic shelters in this area which are available for group picnics, reunions and other group activities. Many families and small groups enjoy the facilities of the day-use area throughout the summer and fall. In this area are a bathhouse for changing into swimsuits and a small concession building which is open during the summer.

Trails: Bay City State Park is not known as a hiking park. There is only one short trail, a little over a half-mile which circles the Tobico Lagoon. The lagoon provides a place where individuals can fish from a small pier. Along the trail are several places where you can get a good picture of this small body of water and the surrounding vegetation. There are several miles of trails in the adjacent Tobico Marsh State Game Area. This wildlife refuge is accessed from the state park by a three-quarter mile trail called the Frank Andersen Trail.

Camping: The park campground is across Beaver Road from the day-use picnic area, beach and parking lot. There are 264 campsites, each having a picnic table, fire ring and electricity. It's not possible to see Saginaw Bay from the campground. The camping area is well-shaded, and walking distance from the campsite to the beach ranges from a quarter-to a half-mile.

Also within the park is a group camping area. Picnic tables, a fire circle and rustic facilities stand beside a large field which can be used for a variety of group activities.

At Bay City State Park, you will find Rent-a-Tent (Tipi) facilities, tents which already are set up for rental. Included are two cots. Sleeping bags are also available for rental, as are lanterns and propane stoves. There also are two mini-cabins in the campground, each having two night minimum rentals.

Fishing: Fishing in Saginaw Bay is not permitted from the beach. There is no ramp for launching boats within the state park boundaries. Fishing is allowed only in Tobico Lagoon. Here, from a small pier, panfish may be caught. The day of my visit four boys were on the pier, fishing as boys have done through the centuries, but they were having little success.

Bay City State Park

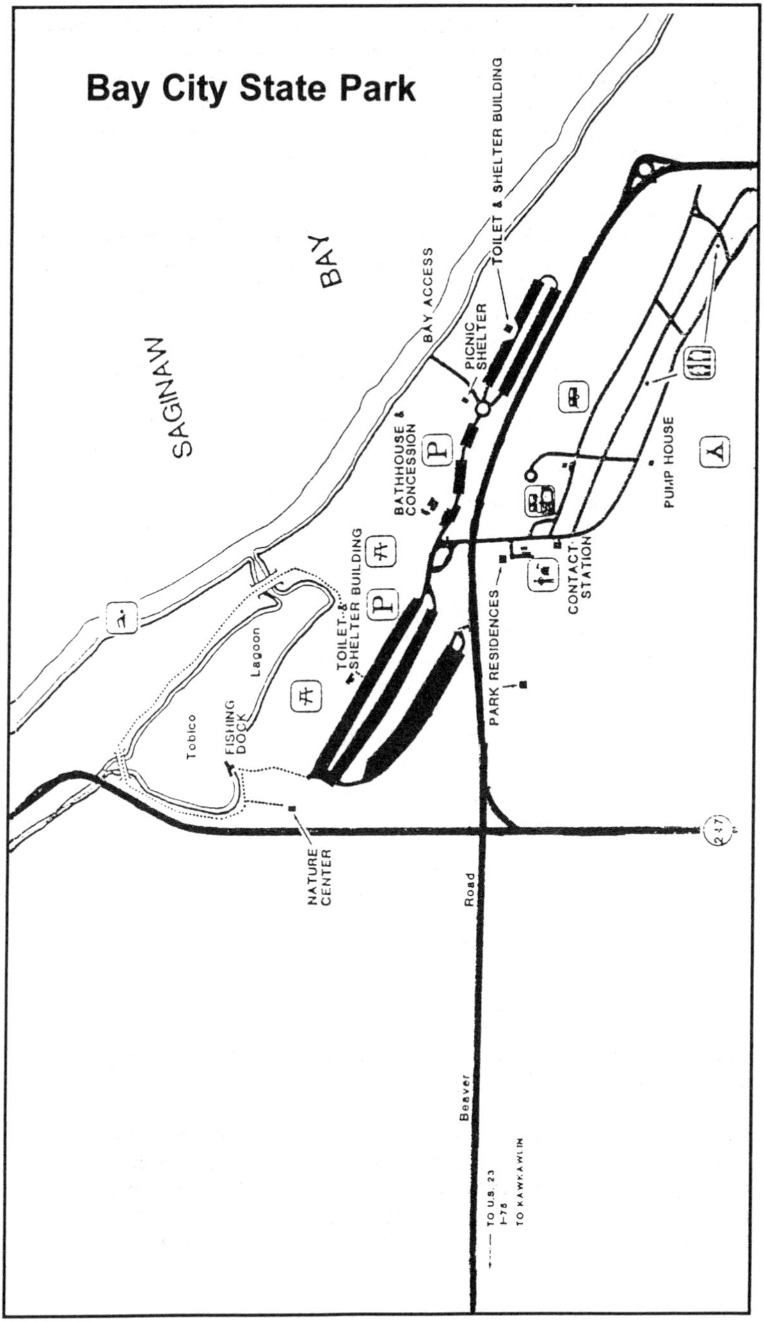

SAGINAW BAY
BAY ACCESS
TOILET & SHELTER BUILDING
PICNIC SHELTER
BATHHOUSE & CONCESSION
TOILET & SHELTER BUILDING
Lagoon
Tobico
FISHING DOCK
PARK RESIDENCES
CONTACT STATION
PUMP HOUSE
NATURE CENTER
Beaver Road
TO U.S. 23
I-75
TO KAWKAWLIN
247

Nature Center: The Saginaw Bay Visitors Center opened in early 1996. During the previous year the old Jennison Nature Center was closed and renovated. It was enlarged to triple its previous size. This center has a collection of exhibits which depict the surrounding environment. Included are hands-on educational displays, information about the history of the region, and an historical display of duck hunting in the marsh in earlier times.

In the newly remodeled center there is an auditorium for group presentations, a classroom, both temporary and permanent exhibit halls, and a nature gift shop. Tours of Tobico Marsh are provided by nature center personnel to various groups and organizations as well as to school classes.

A visit to the center offers you a greater understanding and appreciation of the unique features that encompass the surrounding marshlands.

Winter Activities: The campground at Bay City State Park is open for winter camping. There are heated toilet-shower facilities available in one of the three available restroom buildings. The campsites are plowed and electricity and picnic tables are available on each site.

The two most popular wintertime activities are Nordic skiing and ice fishing on the waters of Lake Huron. There are five miles of cross-country ski trails available for winter enjoyment in the adjacent Tobico Marsh Wildlife Refuge.

The ice is usually thick enough to walk or drive a snowmobile out to your fishing spot.

A winter festival is held in the park. Among the various activities is a popular snow sculpting contest for high school students. Local schools are invited to enter teams in this competition.

Bay City State Park
3582 State Park Drive
Bay City, MI 48706
(517) 684-3020

Cheboygan State Park

Cheboygan State Park, comprised of 1,200 acres, sits on Lake Huron with the western part of the park on Duncan Bay, a part of Lake Huron. Little Billy Elliots Creek flows through the park into Duncan Bay. Along this creek are many marshes and bogs.

The park entrance road divides, with the left fork going to the beach and picnic area on Duncan Bay and the right taking you to the campground. All roads in this state park are gravel or dirt.

Location: Cheboygan State Park is about three miles east of Cheboygan, Michigan, in Cheboygan County on U.S. 23.

History of the Park: In 1851 the Cheboygan Point Lighthouse was built on the shore of Lake Huron where Cheboygan State Park now stands. The lighthouse originally was built on a pier in Lake Huron. Because of winter ice and rough water of the lake, the lighthouse was rebuilt on the shore in 1859. It remained in operation until 1930, when the lighthouse and surrounding land were given to the state of Michigan as a park.

From 1958 until 1960 there was a state forest campground covering about 13 acres. In 1960 the administration of this forest campground was turned over to the Parks Division of the Department of Natural Resources and given the name Poe Reef State Park. In 1962 the park's name was changed to Cheboygan State Park at the request of Cheboygan business leaders.

Features of the Park: The principal feature of the park is the beach, on Duncan Bay about a mile from the park entrance. Looking out from the beach, you can see the Mackinac Bridge some 15 miles in the distance. The sandy beach, excellent for swimming, extends several hundred feet from the water's edge. The beach continues into the water with a gradual slope. The beachhouse has modern toilets and changing facilities. No lifeguard services are available.

Camping: The campground is on Duncan Bay, about four miles by park road from the beach. There are 78 well-shaded campsites. Electricity, a picnic table and an in-ground fire ring are provided at each site. Foliage, including shrubs and bushes, provides privacy between campsites.

A number of the campsites (odd numbered sites from #19 - #29 and even numbered sites from #30 - #46) rest along the water's edge. These campsites are wide, yet provide privacy. However, from the campsites it is not possible to see the water because of the heavy woods and foliage.

A bath and shower building with hot water and modern restroom facilities is located in the middle of the campground.

Campsites #1 and #78, near the entrance building to the campground are reserved for people with disabilities.

At Duncan Bay Campground, there is a small boat ramp designed only for hand-carried watercraft.

Near the beach is Lakeshore Campground, with eight campsites (Campsites #79 - #86). Each campsite has a ground fire pit and a picnic table. These campsites are on sand at the rear of the beach, next to the beach parking lot. This campground actually appears to be a continuation of the parking lot, with no trees, brush or shade and only barriers separating the lot.

Duncan Bay is within sight of the campsites. The park naturalist indicated that some people prefer this campsite despite the fact that it is on the sand with no vegetation, because it is near the water and beach. It is used at times for overflow when the Duncan Bay Campground is full.

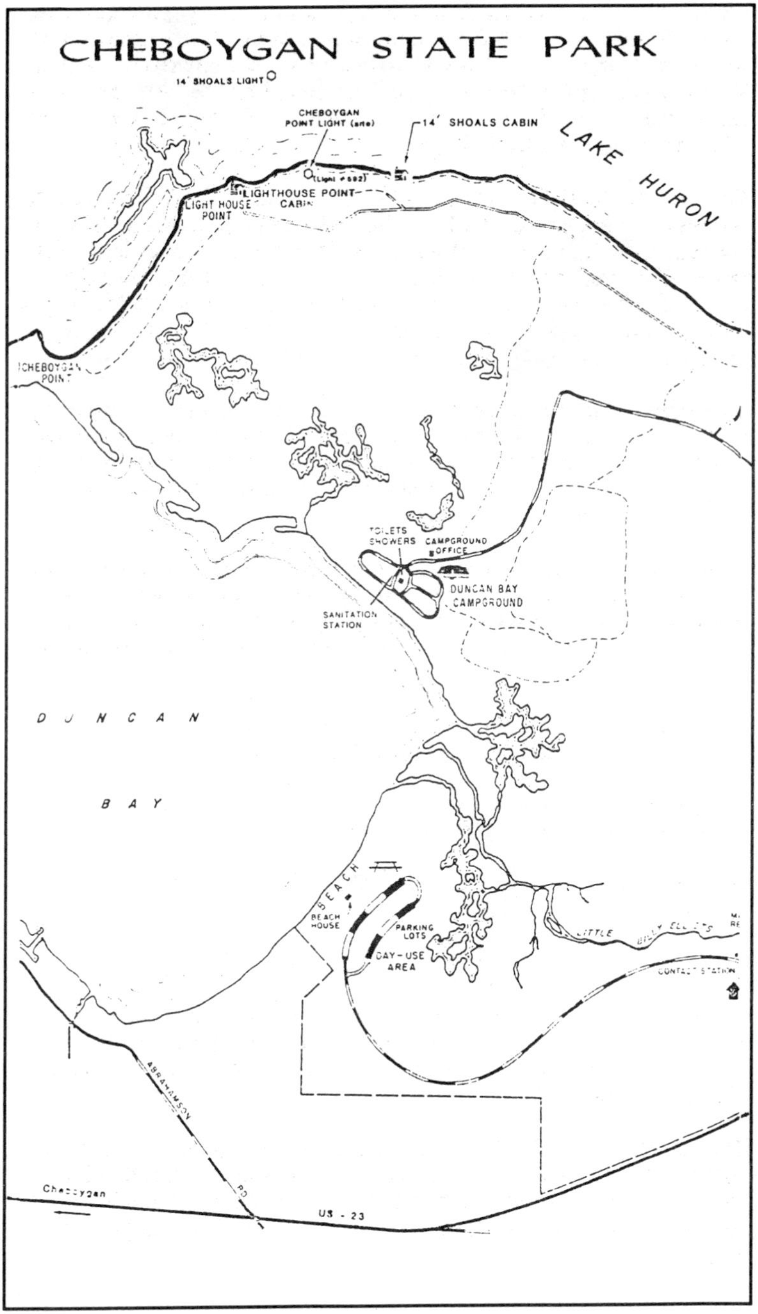
CHEBOYGAN STATE PARK
14' SHOALS LIGHT
CHEBOYGAN
POINT LIGHT (site)
14' SHOALS CABIN
LAKE HURON
(Light #692)
LIGHTHOUSE POINT
CABIN
LIGHT HOUSE
POINT
CHEBOYGAN
POINT
TOILETS
SHOWERS
CAMPGROUND
OFFICE
DUNCAN BAY
CAMPGROUND
SANITATION
STATION
D U N C A N
B A Y
BEACH
BEACH
HOUSE
PARKING
LOTS
DAY-USE
AREA
LITTLE
CONTACT STATION
ABRAHAMSON
RD
US - 23

A group camping facility looks out over a flat area with little shade. Evergreen trees surround the campsite. No modern facilities are available, just a vault toilet.

Cabins: Along the shore of Lake Huron are three isolated rustic cabins in the woods near the shoreline. These cabins are named Poe's Reef Cabin, Fourteen Foot Shoals Cabin, and Lighthouse Point Cabin. Fourteen Foot Shoals Cabin gets its name from a lighthouse which can be seen just off the shore.

Lighthouse Point cabin is at Lighthouse Point, near the site of the old Cheboygan Point Lighthouse. The actual site of the lighthouse was about halfway between Fourteen Foot Shoals Cabin and Lighthouse Point Cabin. They are isolated, but set in a very beautiful location within sight of the lake.

Outside each cabin are a picnic table, an in-ground fire ring, water pump, firewood and vault toilet. Within each cabin are bunk beds, a wooden table and a wooden fire stove. No running water is available. The cabins are available on a daily or weekly rental basis.

The cabins sit among trees on the edge of the sand along the shoreline of Lake Huron, making it excellent for swimming, fishing and walking.

walking. From the sandy beaches near the cabins you can see the Mackinac Bridge.

The cabins are about a quarter-mile from a narrow one-lane dirt forest road that extends for 1.25 miles and ends at the Lighthouse Point Cabin. It is possible to drive to the cabins; however, the road is not easy to drive. There is a locked gate at the entrance to the road, but provisions can be made to unlock it.

The cabins are good for people seeking a wilderness experience. You won't drive into town to the store several times each day from these cabins. If you like a beach to yourself, you will enjoy the rustic cabins. There are no interpretive programs or other recreational activities near these cabins.

Trails: There are a number of hiking trails in Cheboygan State Park. Trailhead signs with a series of colored markings are on wooden map boards.

Picnic Facilities: There is a day-use picnic area near the parking lot at the beach, with playground equipment for children along with tables and grills.

Fishing: Fishing is popular in the surrounding area. Little Billy Elliot Creek flows through the park into Duncan Bay. Speckled brook trout fishing is excellent in this creek.

Also, fishing for bass, perch and northern pike is good in Duncan Bay.

Winter Activities: The principal winter activity at Cheboygan State Park is cross-country skiing. There are about four miles of groomed cross-country ski trails.

Though not groomed, the access road to the cabins is often used for skiing. There is no ski rental in the park.

Cheboygan State Park
4490 Beach Road
Cheboygan, MI 49721
(616) 627-2811

Harrisville State Park

The smallest state park on Lake Huron is Harrisville State Park. This 94-acre park is comprised of a half-mile beach, picnic area, campground and nature area.

Location: Harrisville State Park is in Alcona County, one-half mile south of Harrisville, Michigan on U.S. 23, which forms the western boundary of the park.

Features of the Park: The sandy beach is bordered by cedar and pine trees a couple of hundred feet from the water. The bottom of Lake Huron is a combination of sand and small pebbles. Playing in the water and sunbathing on warm summer days are popular activities for many visitors to the park. There is no lifeguard at the beach.

At the far south end of the park, at the edge of the picnic area, is an access site for individuals with hand-carried boats. You can drive your vehicle to the edge of the sand to put the boat in the water. However, you cannot drive onto the beach or into the water.

Harrisville State Park

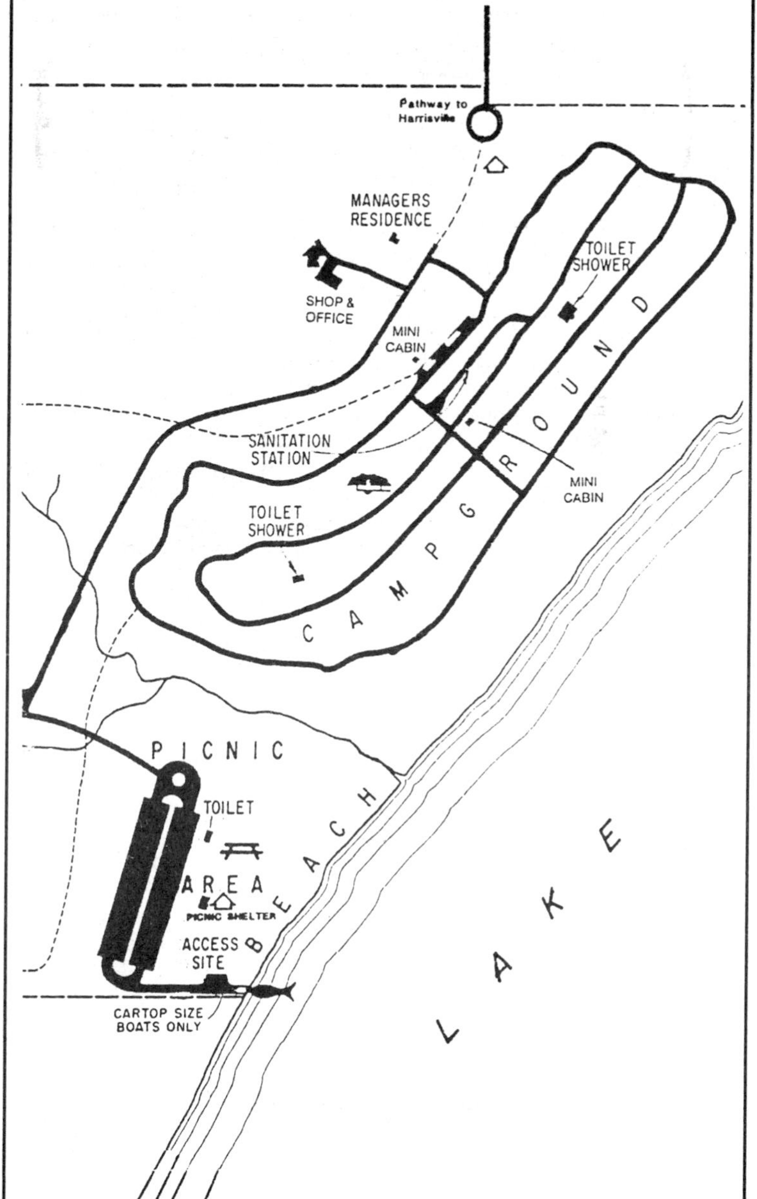
Pathway to Harrisville
MANAGERS RESIDENCE
SHOP & OFFICE
MINI CABIN
TOILET SHOWER
CAMPGROUND
SANITATION STATION
MINI CABIN
TOILET SHOWER
PICNIC
TOILET
AREA
PICNIC SHELTER
ACCESS SITE
BEACH
CARTOP SIZE BOATS ONLY
LAKE

Camping: The campground is in the north section of the park. It has 229 well-spaced campsites. Modern facilities including electricity are available throughout the campground. About 30 campsites, all with electrical outlets, are as close to the beach as you can get in a Great Lakes state park campground. The view of the rising sun is particularly rewarding for campers along these sites.

The rest of the campground is well shaded with a variety of large trees. The ground is covered with grass. This campground is not a highly congested facility.

The day of my visit, on a beautiful day in mid-week in early June, there were about a dozen campers scattered throughout the park.

Also in the campground are two rustic mini-cabins. Electricity is provided in these cabins; however, there is no running water. Water is available in the campground during the summer and at the headquarters building during the fall, winter and spring. In both cabins there is provision for four people with two bunk beds. In one cabin, the A-frame, there is an eating area and a wood stove used for heat. Outside is a grill. Inside the mini-cabin is an electric wall heater, but there are no cooking facilities.

Trails: There is only one walking trail in Harrisville State Park, the Cedar Run Nature Trail. The trail is about one mile long. It leaves the campground from near the mini-cabin and campsite No. 1. The trail is flat and very easy to walk. About half of the trail's distance is covered by wood chips. There are 14 marked signs along the trail, pointing out items of interest for the walker. A brochure is available telling what to look for at each sign.

Near the manager's residence is a hiking/bicycling pathway which goes about a mile to the nearby town of Harrisville. Within the park, bicycles can be operated only on the roadways.

Picnic Facilities: There is a nicely shaded and grassy covered picnic area south of the campground. Here you will find a picnic shelter and a bathhouse, as well as tables and grills for those enjoying a day at the beach. There are slides, swings and climbing equipment scattered throughout the picnic area.

Harrisville State Park
248 State Park Road
P.O. Box 326
Harrisville, MI 48740
(517) 724-5126

P.H. Hoeft State Park

The land of P.H. Hoeft State Park was deeded to the state of Michigan in 1922 by Paul H. Hoeft, a logging baron who also owned a department store in nearby Rogers City. Today the park consists of 301 acres.

Location: P.H. Hoeft State Park is in Presque Isle County, about four miles northwest of Rogers City, Michigan, off of U.S. 23.

Features of the Park: The principal feature of P.H. Hoeft State Park is the one-mile scenic beach along the Lake Huron shore. Along the beach are rolling hills of sand. These hills extend up to 300 yards from the water's edge to the tree line. The actual sand beach extends 20 to 50 yards from the edge of the water. The beach is excellent for walking, reading or sunbathing. The lake has a tough bottom with many small stones. As the water warms in the summer, increasing numbers of visitors enter the water to play and swim.

During the summer a number of activities are conducted on a daily basis. There are nature walks, craft presentations, sand sculpture contests and campfire presentations. P.H. Hoeft State Park is usually filled on summer holidays. Also, the first two weeks of August are very popular because of two festivals in nearby Rogers City. The first weekend in August is a "Nautical City Festival," and the second is the annual salmon fishing tournament. Both events result in much activity and many visitors to the area.

Camping: There is a 144-site campground at P.H. Hoeft State Park. This campground has complete modern facilities among pine trees. None of the campsites is within sight of the beach, and the rolling dunes prohibit campers from seeing the lake. However, it is only a short walk from the campsites to the beach.

There are four rent-a-tents in the campground. These are 10-by 12-foot tents on wooden platforms. Inside are two cots and pads. A stove, light and cooler also can be rented. Adjacent to each tent is a picnic table, fire pit and an electrical outlet. There is also one rustic mini-cabin at campsite #48. Reservations for these facilities, plus any camping reservations, may be made through the state park central reservation system.

There also is a group campsite.

Trails: There are 4.5 miles of hiking trails in the park. The Nagel Creek Trail, about three-quarters of a mile, loops around the south section of the park to Nagel Creek. The creek flows into Lake Huron near the south boundary of the park. Two other trails, the Beach Trail and Hardwoods Trail, are each about a 1.5 miles long. The Hardwoods Trail crosses U.S. 23 and forms a loop away from the Lake Huron shoreline. This trail passes through a typical northwoods forest of oak, maple and beech trees. The Beach Trail exits the campground between campsites #21 and #23, traverses along the dunes and loops back through the wooded section of the park.

The Pavilion Trail, about a quarter-mile in length, leaves from the pavilion and is connected to the other trails.

The hiking trails are well marked, flat and easy walking for all ages. Bicycles are prohibited on the trails.

The highway passes alongside the trails and picnic area, less than a quarter-mile away. When hiking the Nagel Creek Trail, you can hear the passing traffic.

Picnic Facilities: The day-use picnic area is just inside the park entrance. The focal point of the picnic area is the stone and log shelter which groups can rent in advance. This pavilion was built in 1938-1939 by the Civilian Conservation Corps. The CCC also was instrumental in the development of the day-use area in the 1930s. There are a number of picnic tables and grills throughout the wooded area near

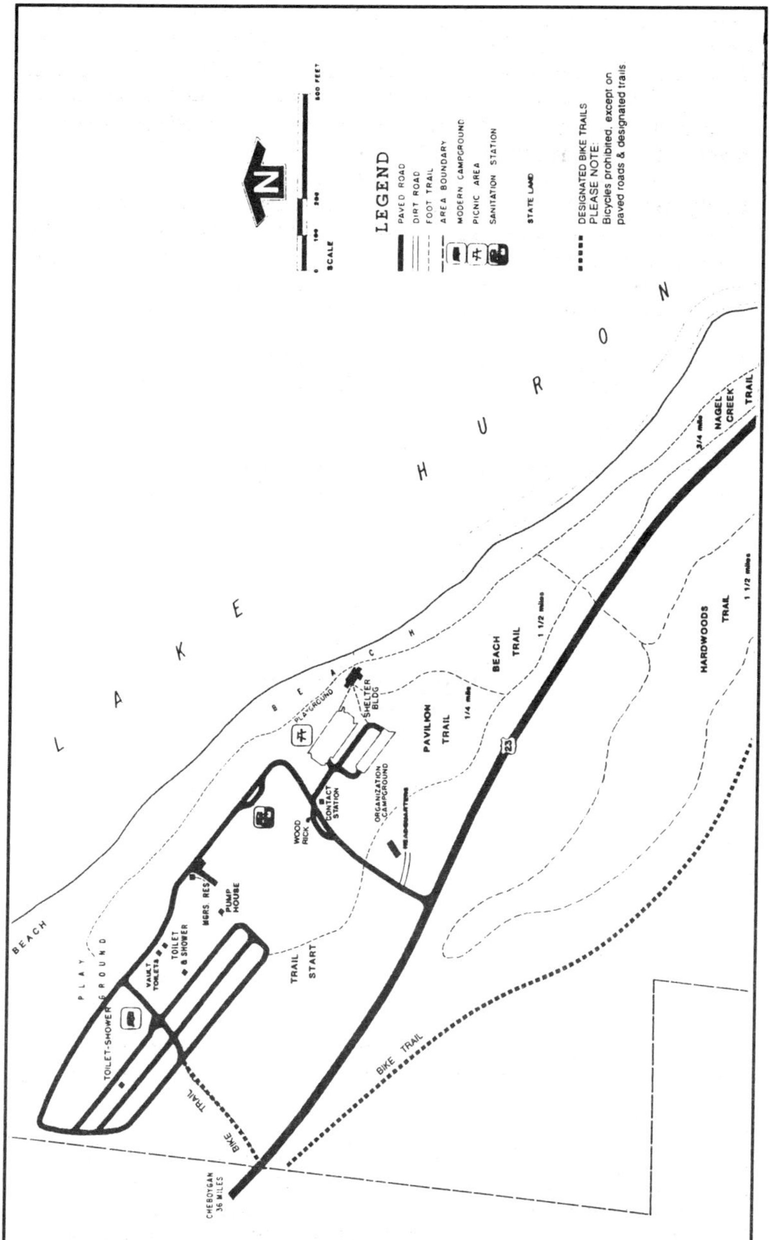

P.F. Hoeft State Park

the pavilion.

Fishing: Fishing is popular in the surrounding waters of Lake Huron. Salmon, lake trout and brown trout are favorite among anglers.

However, there are no boat ramps at the park. Anglers wishing to launch their fishing boats must go to Rogers City to find the nearest ramps. Charter boats are available in Rogers City and other nearby localities. The only fishing that occurs within the boundaries of the park takes place in Nagel Creek.

Winter Activities: P.H. Hoeft State Park is open during the winter. This includes the campground, having electricity and pump water available. Vault toilets are used instead of the restrooms. The trails are groomed during the winter for Nordic skiing, and campers can ski directly from their campsites to the trails.

The terrain, being relatively flat, makes skiing enjoyable for the novice cross-country skier.

There is no snowmobiling in the park. However, many snowmobile trails are on nearby public lands.

P.H. Hoeft State Park
U.S. 23
Rogers City, MI 49779
(517) 734-2543

Lakeport State Park

Lakeport State Park is a 565-acre park divided into two units. The campground and a small beach comprise the northern unit. About 1.5 miles to the south is the Franklin Delano Roosevelt day-use unit. The village of Lakeport is between the two units. To go from one unit to another, you must travel on M-25.

Lakeport State Park, the southernmost state park on Lake Huron, is within an hour's drive of the Detroit metropolitan area.

Location: Lakeport State Park is 10 miles north of Port Huron, Michigan, on M-25 at Lakeport.

Features of the Park: Lakeport State Park is a camping and picnicking facility with a beach where people can swim, sunbath and enjoy the Lake Huron waterfront.

Camping: A campground with 315 sites is in the north unit. The shady campground is about a quarter-mile from Lake Huron. There are three modern toilet and shower facilities in the campground. One section of the campground, consisting of 56 campsites (#301 - #356), has black-top pads with surrounding grass.

The day of my visit in early October, there were a number of people camping under the colorful trees. Most campers were sitting in the warm fall sun outside their trailers and RVs reading or playing cards.

Two group campgrounds can be reserved in the northern section of the park.

From the campground, a short walk along any of several paths will lead you to the beach, stretching about a mile along the Lake Huron shoreline. The beach is a combination sand and pebble strip.

Picnic Facilities: The day-use unit, the Franklin Delano Roosevelt unit, includes a large parking lot accommodating up to 2,000 vehicles. Next to the parking lot is a picnic area. Two shelters can be reserved for group activities. On the east side of the highway are additional picnic tables and grills, as well as a bathhouse and concession building.

The beach in this day-use unit is about a half-mile long. It is wider and nicer than the shoreline beach to the north at the campground unit. It's not very wide, so during the summer the beach is often crowded on weekends and on holidays.

Connecting the parking lot on the west of the highway and the beach and picnic area on the east is a pedestrian overpass, protected by a high fence.

Trails: There are no hiking or bicycle trails in the park. At the northern unit, between the campground and the Lake Huron shoreline, are a series of short paths for walking; however, none is identified as a hiking trail.

Boating: Many people who come to Lakeport State Park go boating and fishing in Lake Huron. However, there is no boat ramp in the park facilities. Boats can be chartered from commercial establishments about 10 miles north of the park in Lexington. There also is a boat launch facility in Lexington.

Lakeport State Park
7605 Lakeshore Road
Lakeport, MI 48059
(810) 327-6224

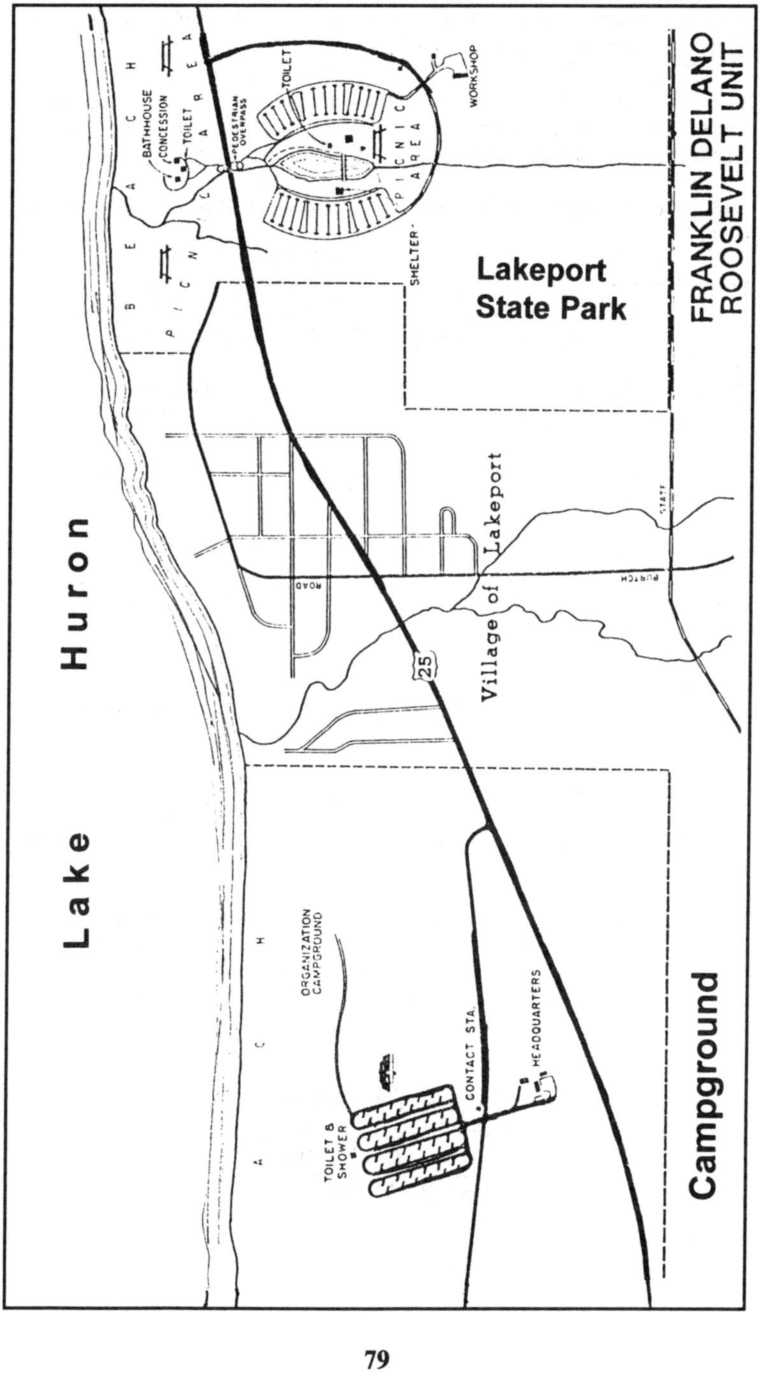

Lake Huron
Lakeport State Park
FRANKLIN DELANO ROOSEVELT UNIT
Campground
Village of Lakeport
25
BEACH
PICNIC AREA
BATHHOUSE
CONCESSION
TOILET
PEDESTRIAN OVERPASS
TOILET
WORKSHOP
SHELTER
ROAD
BURTCH
STATE
BEACH
ORGANIZATION CAMPGROUND
CONTACT STA.
HEADQUARTERS
TOILET & SHOWER

Port Crescent State Park

Port Crescent State Park consists of 569 acres and is located at the old town of Port Crescent. This community thrived from the latter 1800s to the early 1900s with up to 500 people residing here. At its peak the town had two hotels, a grist mill, a carriage, wagon, and sleigh factory, and a brewery. There also were two large docks built into the lake where ships came to be loaded with lumber from the surrounding forests. Lumbering, fishing and salt manufacturing were the principle sources of income for people residing in this town.

By the end of the 1930s, however, there were no residents in Port Crescent and today nothing remains of the town except a chimney from the sawmill.

The park is comprised of two sections: the day use area and the campground. By way of M-25 these two sections are about two miles apart. However, they are connected along the shoreline, forming a continuous park. The Pinnebog River separates the two sections.

Location: Port Crescent State Park is in Huron County about five miles west of Port Arthur, Michigan.

Features of the Park: The principal feature of Port Crescent State Park is the nearly three miles of sandy beach. Not only is the beach very clean, the waters of Lake Huron along the state park shoreline are extremely clear. The beach is popular for the typical recreational activities of walking, sunbathing, playing in the water and swimming.

The western section of the park, acquired in 1975, is the day-use area known as "The Dunes." There are facilities for picnicking, walking and hiking, sunbathing and swimming, though there are no lifeguards on duty. Here the beach extends along the shoreline about three miles and is at its widest. There are a picnic shelter and beach house with changing facilities, as well as restrooms close to the lake. The shelter can be reserved for special occasions.

The section of the park east of Pinnebog River comprises the campground and a series of hiking trails.

Trails: In the day-use section about 1,000 feet of boardwalk permits visitors to walk along the crest of the dunes. This boardwalk connects five picnic decks that overlook Lake Huron, where you can find excellent views.

There is a 10 station, three-quarter-mile fitness trail in this area. At each station are the instructions for various stretching and calisthenics exercises.

Also, there are about 3.5 miles of hiking trails in the day-use area bordered by the beach and sand dunes. Park literature suggests that the trails are well marked.

About 2.5 miles of hiking trails are located on an island in the Pinnebog River. Access to these trails is from the campground or the iron bridge over the Old River Channel of the Pinnebog River.

Camping: There are 181-sites, each with an electrical outlet, fire circle and picnic table. Several sites on the beach shoreline are blacktopped. Also, several campsites rest along the old river channel and provide access to handicapped accessible fishing piers. There are two bath and toilet facilities in the campground. Access to the beach and the hiking trails is near the playground between campsites #119 and #122. The campground is well shaded. During the summer the campground is usually filled each weekend and holiday. There is one rustic mini-cabin in the campground, but more are in the planning stages.

An area set aside for group camping is on an island bounded by the Old River Channel, the Pinnebog River and Lake Huron. Access to this area is off of M-25 over an iron bridge. Because vehicles are not permitted on the island, campers must enter on foot. This rustic camping area is available by reservation.

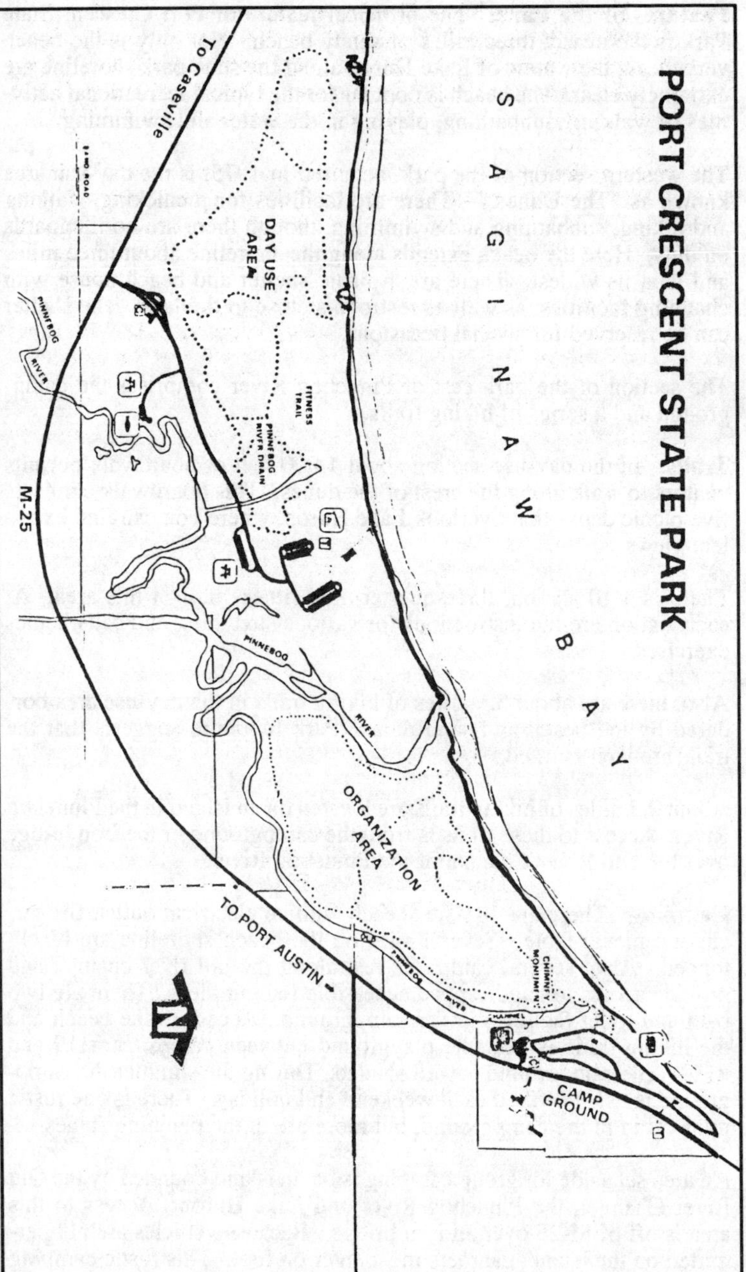
PORT CRESCENT STATE PARK
S A G I N A W B A Y
To Caseville
SAND ROAD
DAY USE AREA
FITNESS TRAIL
PINNEBOG RIVER DRAIN
PINNEBOG RIVER
M-25
PINNEBOG RIVER
ORGANIZATION AREA
TO PORT AUSTIN
PINNEBOG RIVER
CHIMNEY MONUMENT
CHANNEL
CAMP GROUND
N

Fishing: The Pinnebog River, flowing into Lake Huron, runs for about two miles through the park. Fishing along this river is popular. Bass, panfish, salmon, northern pike and perch are caught. Canoeing along the river also is popular during the summer. Canoes are available at a commercial rental facility on M-25, just outside of the park.

In addition to fishing along the river, walleye fishing is popular in the lake. There is an access site for canoes and small, hand-carried boats in the day-use area. However, there are no boat ramps within the park. The nearest ramps are in Port Austin, about five miles from the park.

Winter Activities: Port Crescent State Park is open year round, providing a range of winter activities including camping. As with other parks in this area of Michigan, there is adequate snow in the winter for outdoor activities.

Four miles of the trail system are groomed for Nordic (cross-country) skiing, with the trails being relatively flat with some slight rolling terrain. During the winter candlelight ski events are scheduled.

Ice fishing in the surrounding waters is another activity that visitors to Port Crescent State Park participate in during the winter. There is no snowmobiling in the park; however, snowmobiles can be operated in several places near the park.

Special Activities: On the Saturday following Memorial Day weekend, a Kite Fly and Trunk Flea Market are held at Port Crescent State Park. Also, the springtime finds flocks of birds migrating through this area. The Huron Audubon Club holds an annual hawk watch, when it is often possible to see several thousand hawks a day.

Port Crescent State Park
1775 Port Austin Road
Port Austin, MI 48467
(517) 738-8663

Sleeper State Park

Sleeper State Park includes 723 acres on the Saginaw Bay. It began as a small county park in the 1920s. By 1927 it became part of the state park system, called Huron State Park. The name was changed in the 1940s to honor Albert E. Sleeper, who was the governor of Michigan when the state park system was signed into law by the state legislature. Mr. Sleeper was from Bad Axe, the Huron County seat.

Location: Sleeper State Park, on the northern shore of the Michigan "Thumb," is bisected by M-25 about five miles from Caseville.

Features of the Park: There is a half-mile of sandy beach, with clear waters. A beach house, toilet/shelter facility, rentable picnic shelter and tables and grills are near the beach.

Though most summer visitors come to enjoy the water and beach, the largest section—300 acres—is across M-25. In this area deer and small game hunting is permitted in season, as are trapping and snow-mobiling. The highway bisects the beach and picnic area from the campground, hiking trails and undeveloped section of the park.

The weekend before Memorial Day weekend, there is a dulcimer concert and Art Expo at Sleeper State Park.

Camping: The campground contains 280 wooded campsites. Each site has an electrical outlet, picnic table and a fire pit. Within the campground are three toilet/shower buildings with flush toilets and hot-water showers. The entire campground is tree-covered. You can't see the lake from the campground. There is one rustic mini-cabin available.

A group outdoor camping center was constructed following World War II. Wilderness cabins can sleep up to 120 individuals and have a kitchen and dining hall, along with an outdoor council ring where instruction can be conducted and campfire programs held. This facility can be rented by organizations desiring to provide an outdoor educational experience for young people for one night to a week. School, church groups and other youth organizations use the facility at various times throughout the year. The camp buildings are remodeled Civilian Conservation Corps buildings built in the 1940s. The facility is operated by the National Wildlife Education Foundation of Warren, Michigan.

Because of the popularity of this region and its proximity to Detroit and Flint, the campground usually fills up on weekends and holidays during the summer. Reservations should be made particularly during the summer. There is a two-night minimum. The toilet/shower buildings are not open during the late fall and winter months. Usually they are opened about the first of May.

Picnic Facilities: The picnic area along the beach includes several picnic tables and grills along with playground equipment. There is a modern changing building with restrooms. A shelter can be rented for picnics and other events. Overlooking the beach and the water is a handicap accessible deck.

It is necessary to cross the highway to get from the campground to the beach and picnic sections of the park. A pedestrian overpass, constructed in 1980, connects the beach and campground.

Trails: There are 4.5 miles of excellent and well-marked hiking trails in the park. The trailheads begin from the campground. The Mile Circle Trail is a half-mile trail that connects the two campground sections. The Ridges Nature Trail is a 1.5 mile circular trail that begins and ends on the Mile Circle Trail. There are 14 marked points of interest along this trail. The various points identify trees along the trail, including red pine, often referred to as Norway pine, red oak, red maple, white oak, jack pine, aspen, birch and white pine. Some white and red pines are more than 100 years old.

This trail traverses land where at one time the shoreline of Saginaw

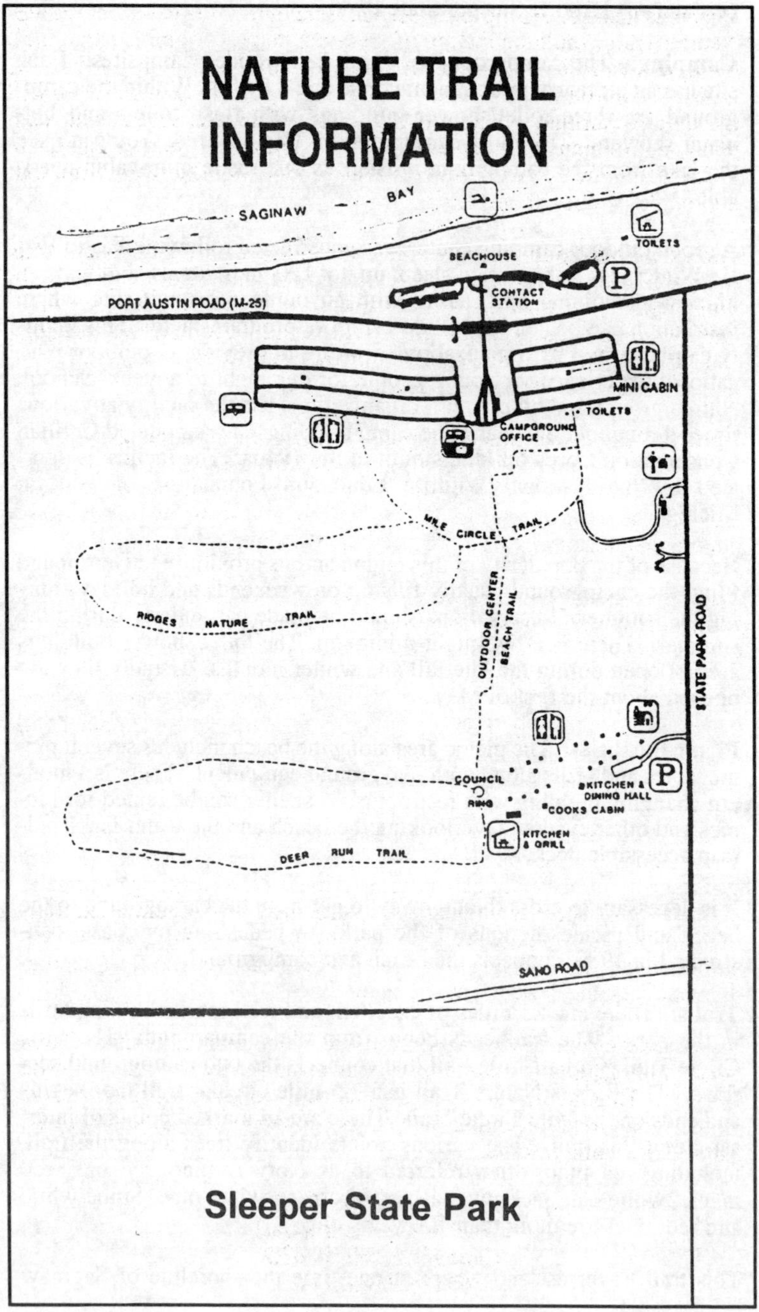
NATURE TRAIL
INFORMATION
SAGINAW BAY
BEACHOUSE
CONTACT STATION
TOILETS
PORT AUSTIN ROAD (M-25)
MINI CABIN
TOILETS
CAMPGROUND OFFICE
MILE CIRCLE TRAIL
RIDGES NATURE TRAIL
OUTDOOR CENTER BEACH TRAIL
STATE PARK ROAD
COUNCIL RING
KITCHEN & DINING HALL
COOKS CABIN
KITCHEN & GRILL
DEER RUN TRAIL
SAND ROAD
Sleeper State Park

Bay was located. As the lake receded, sand dunes formed. The Ridges Nature Trail is built on the top of these old dunes. An informative trail guide is available to educate the hiker of points of interest along the trail. The third trail, Deer Run Trail, is a 2.5 mile circular trail. I hiked these trails during the height of fall color, which was spectacular with many reds of maples, bronze of oaks, and yellow of birches. There are no bicycling trails here. Bicyclists can ride on the Deer Run Trail, but not on the Ridges Nature Trail.

Traversing the south edge of the park is a dirt road, Sand Road. This road was once the original stagecoach trail running from Bay City to Port Austin. The road is excellent for bicycling. The day of my visit there were no cars or people on the road and the foliage in the forest was spectacular. To the east of the park, Sand Road extends through the Rush Lake State Game Area.

Nature: The usual ground animals can be seen throughout the park. Deer are common, best seen along the Deer Run Trail since it is away from the campground and picnic areas. Hunting is permitted in some areas of the park during the fall. The hiker must be aware of where hunting can occur and take precautions when hiking the trails.

Fishing: Fishing is popular on this part of Lake Huron. Perch and walleye fishing is good in Saginaw Bay, while lake trout and salmon are particularly good in Lake Huron. There are no boat ramps in the park; however, the town of Caseville is five miles away and has several ramps. Charter boat fishing reservations are available at several locations near the park. Fishing festivals and contests are conducted in Caseville at various times during the year. In the spring there is a perch festival and in the summer a walleye tournament.

Winter Activities: This part of Michigan, the "Thumb," usually has heavy snow during the winter. The park is open year-round, with opportunity for a variety of winter activities. Nordic skiing is popular in the region. There are four miles of groomed cross-country ski trails in the park. These trails are excellent for the novice skier in that they are relatively flat. During the winter on several occasions, a candlelight ski is held. These events begin at dusk.

Nearby Reserve: To the east of the park is the Rush Lake State Game Area. This 2,000-acre game reserve is managed by the state wildlife division. This facility offers additional acres to hike, bicycle or drive on the forest roads. Hunting as well as snowmobiling is permitted on parts of the game reserve.

Sleeper State Park
6573 State Park Road
Caseville, MI 48725
(517) 856-4411

Tawas Point State Park

Tawas Point State Park, a 183-acre site, is at the end of a sand spit which separates Tawas Bay from Lake Huron. This area has been called the "*Cape Cod of the Midwest*" because of the beautiful sand shoreline and lighthouse.

Location: The entrance to Tawas Point is on Tawas Beach Road in Iosco County, Michigan, three miles southeast of East Tawas.

Features of the Park: The principal features are the Tawas Point Lighthouse and beach. The lighthouse, built in 1876, was operated by the U.S. Coast Guard until 1991, when a different Coast Guard facility was constructed just outside the park entrance. The old lighthouse station was decommissioned at that time. The lighthouse was equipped with a lens built in Paris in 1880. The lighthouse is 70 feet tall and the walls at the base are six feet thick. Today the lighthouse can only be visited by making advance arrangements.

Tawas Point State Park has a beautiful sandy beach on both the Lake

Huron side as well as near the campground on the Tawas Bay side of the peninsula. The beach near the campground, on Tawas Bay, is shallow, sandy and well suited for swimming by young children during the summer.

The beach on Lake Huron, stretching from the picnic area to Tawas Point, a distance of nearly three-fourths of a mile, is very fine sand. The beach extends back from the water's edge as far as 300 feet, the largest expanse of sand beach on any state park beach on Lake Huron. It provides an excellent location for all water activities such as walking, sunbathing, playing in the water and fishing.

Camping: The modern campground, having 210 campsites, is on the Tawas Bay side of the park. At each campsite is an electrical hookup, fire pit and picnic table. A few campsites are near, or on, the bay. The campground is grassy, having very little shade because there are few mature trees. The campsites are fairly wide, but not deep. In the center of the campground are two play areas for children and two modern toilet-shower buildings. There is a quarter-mile trail that leads from the campground across the park to the picnic area.

Also in the campground are two mini-cabins equipped with four bunks, electricity, a table and an electric heater. They can be rented for a minimum of two nights throughout the year.

Trails: Only one nature trail exists for hiking in Tawas Point State Park. This is the Sandy Hook Nature Trail which leaves the parking lot at the picnic area near the lighthouse and goes along Tawas Bay. A series of numbered signs provides information about trees, berries, geological formations and other items of interest along the trail. The trail takes you out to Tawas Point, where you can see the "sandy hook" for which the nature trail was named. A century ago this sandy section of land did not exist. The point was formed by Lake Huron currents which through the years have dropped sand at the point as they round the ever-changing point and enter Tawas Bay.

The trail then crosses to the Lake Huron side and follows the U.S. Coast Guard road for a short distance. To your right along this road is a sand hill which keeps you from seeing the sandy beach and Lake Huron. About halfway back to the picnic area, the trail comes to a point where Lake Huron can be seen. The hiker then passes a couple of inland ponds before returning to the starting point. Many waterfowl are seen among these ponds. It is interesting to note that the level of water in the ponds fluctuates with the water level of Lake Huron.

Bicycling is not permitted on the Sandy Hook Nature Trail. However, there is a one-mile bike trail from the entrance to the picnic area with a short spur going to the campground. This trail connects to a bicycle trail at the park entrance, which goes for several miles toward East

Tawas Point State Park

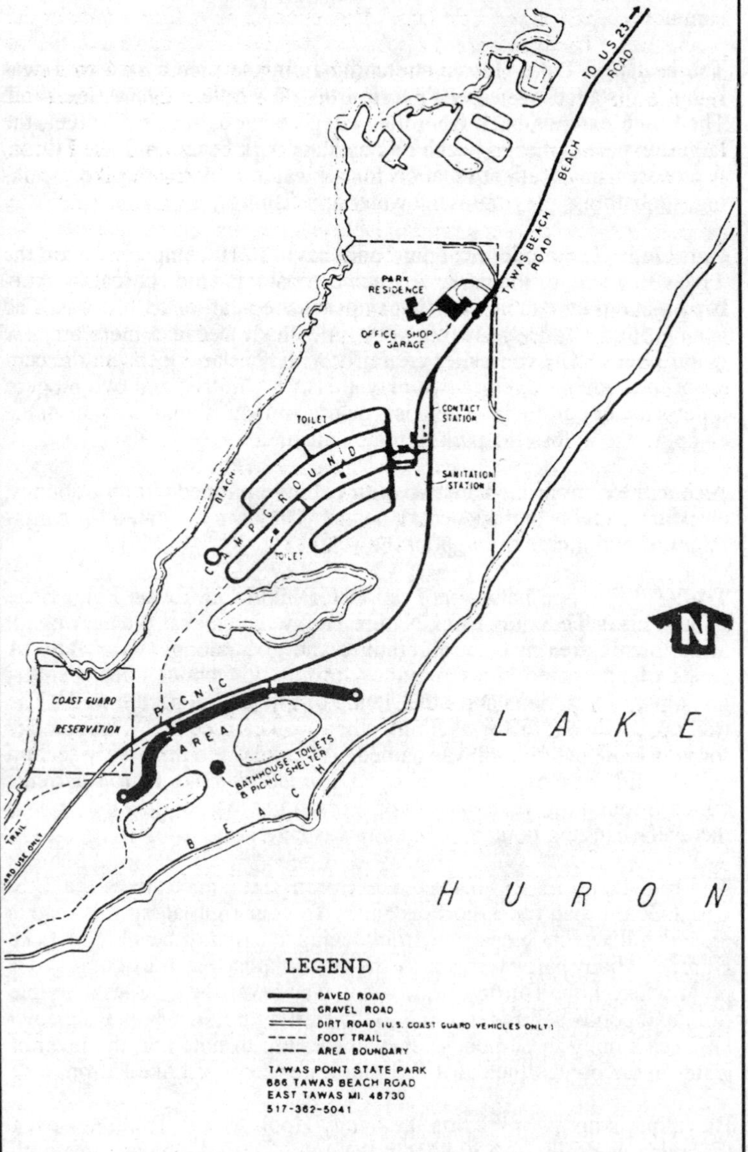
TO U.S. 23
BEACH ROAD
TAWAS BEACH ROAD
PARK RESIDENCE
OFFICE SHOP & GARAGE
CONTACT STATION
TOILET
CAMPGROUND
SANITATION STATION
BEACH
TOILET
COAST GUARD RESERVATION
PICNIC AREA
BATHHOUSE TOILETS & PICNIC SHELTER
BEACH
TRAIL
N
LAKE
HURON
LEGEND
PAVED ROAD
GRAVEL ROAD
DIRT ROAD (U.S. COAST GUARD VEHICLES ONLY)
FOOT TRAIL
AREA BOUNDARY
TAWAS POINT STATE PARK
686 TAWAS BEACH ROAD
EAST TAWAS MI. 48730
517-362-5041

Tawas.

Picnic Facilities: There are picnic tables and grills in a grassy area between the parking lot and lake. However, there is little shade in the picnic area. The views from a wooden walkway out onto Lake Huron are excellent. There are a shelter and beach house with modern toilets and changing facilities in the picnic area. The shelter can be reserved.

Fishing: Fishing is popular in Tawas Bay as well as on Lake Huron, especially for walleye, coho and chinook salmon, northern pike, perch, smallmouth bass and lake trout. There are no boat launching ramps in the park. However, ramps are available at a marina just outside the park and in the nearby towns of East Tawas and Tawas.

Winter Activities: Tawas Point is open during the winter. Vault toilets are available. There are miles of cross-country and snowmobile trails available within a few miles of the park. Ice fishing in Tawas Bay is popular by winter fishing enthusiasts.

Tawas Point State Park
686 Tawas Beach Road
East Tawas, MI 48730
(517) 362-5041

TWO UNDEVELOPED STATE PARKS NEGWEGON AND THOMPSON'S HARBOR

Along the shoreline of Lake Huron are two undeveloped state parks in Michigan: Negwegon State Park and Thompson's Harbor State Park. Neither has camping, picnic grounds, boat ramps or nature centers. It is nearly impossible to find the parks unless you have specific information about their location.

Negwegon State Park consists of 1,775 acres on Lake Huron in Alcona County, about halfway between Alpena and Harrisville. There are no signs on U.S. 23 indicating the turnoff to the park, which is named after a Chippewa Indian chief. Part of the road leading to the parking lot at the entrance to the park is gravel and sand. It can be difficult to drive this section of the road, particularly if sand has blown on the road. At the parking lot there are vault toilets and a water spigot. A sign provides information about trails for hikers.

There are more than six miles of shoreline along Lake Huron. Those who have seen them suggest that they are some of the best beaches on Lake Huron. If you want an isolated, non-developed beach experience, visit Negwegon State Park.

The only other activity in the park is several miles of hiking trails. These trails begin at the parking area and go through forests of white birch, maple, cedar and other hardwood trees. Part of the trails are along old two-track roads. One trail goes south from the parking lot along the shore of the lake.

A much larger park, Thompson's Harbor, is off of U.S. 23 about 10 miles southeast of Rogers City in Presque Isle County. This park is comprised of 5,029 acres.

There is no extensive trail system, but the park is composed of heavy woods with a seven-mile shoreline along Lake Huron.

Generally, activity at both of these undeveloped parks is limited primarily to people who live in the surrounding communities. With no information about them available, no facilities and little indications of their location with signs on the highway, most people are unaware of them.

Information about Thompson's Harbor State Park can be obtained at P.H. Hoeft State Park; about Negwegon State Park, contact Harrisville State Park.

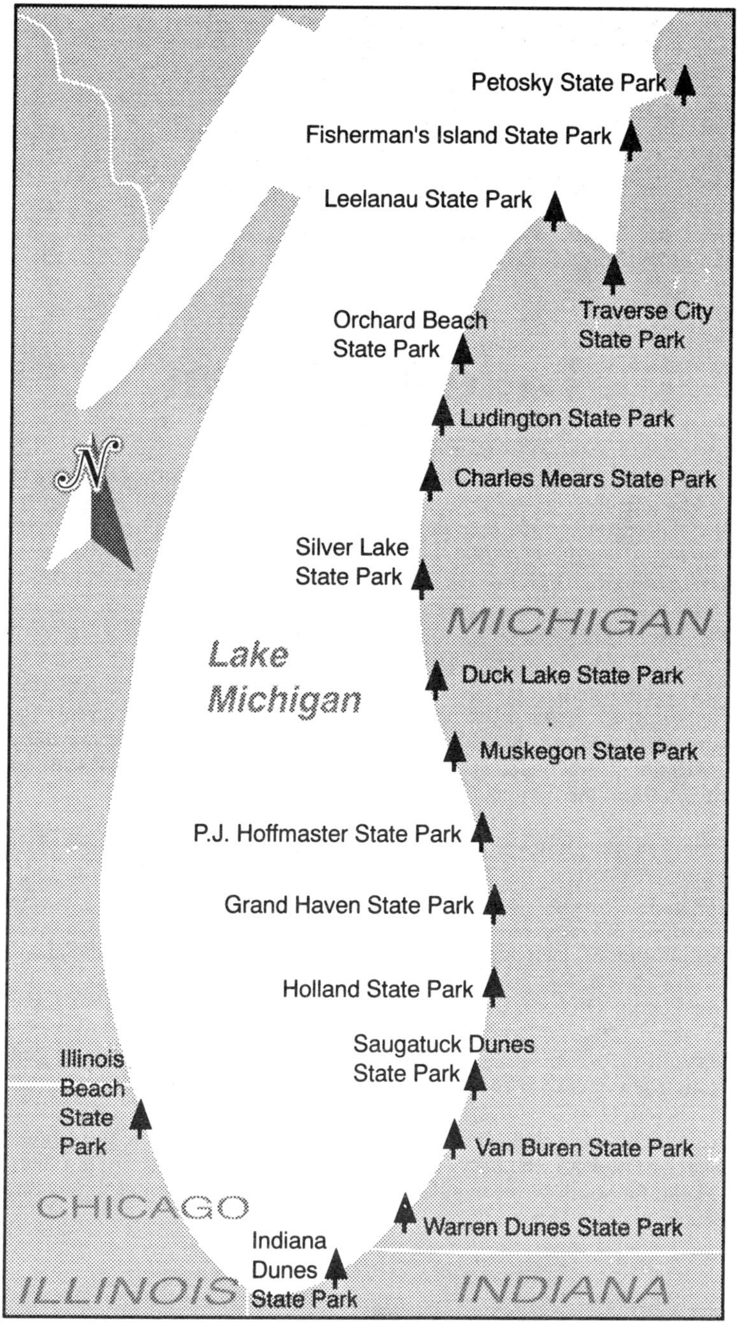
Petosky State Park
Fisherman's Island State Park
Leelanau State Park
Traverse City
State Park
Orchard Beach
State Park
Ludington State Park
Charles Mears State Park
Silver Lake
State Park
MICHIGAN
Lake
Michigan
Duck Lake State Park
Muskegon State Park
P.J. Hoffmaster State Park
Grand Haven State Park
Holland State Park
Saugatuck Dunes
State Park
Illinois
Beach
State
Park
Van Buren State Park
CHICAGO
Warren Dunes State Park
Indiana
Dunes
State Park
ILLINOIS
INDIANA

Lake Michigan

Along the eastern shoreline of Lake Michigan are some of the most beautiful beaches in the world. These beaches resulted from several thousand years of geological development since the Great Ice Age. The oldest sand dunes that we see today are 10,000 years old. Some are as recent as 3,500 years.

The largest sand dunes along the Great Lakes are found on the eastern shore of Lake Michigan. This is due principally because of the westerly winds which blow across the lake. The sand comes primarily from glacial drift left when the Ice Age glaciers melted. Over the years the dunes formed as winds blew grains of sand onto shore. Today these dunes and sandy beaches provide some of the best recreational settings anywhere in the nation.

From Indiana Dunes State Park on the south to Petoskey State Park in Emmet County in the northern section of the Lower Peninsula, there are 17 state parks.

All but one of these are in Michigan: Duck Lake, Fisherman's Island, Grand Haven, P.J. Hoffmaster, Holland, Leelanau, Ludington, Mears, Muskegon, Orchard Beach, Petoskey, Saugatuck Dunes, Silver Lake, Traverse City, VanBuren, and Warren Dunes. All of these parks have very clean, white sandy beaches. The parks have sand dunes ranging from a few feet to several hundred feet in height.

Also included in this section are Indiana Dunes State Park and Illinois Beach State Park, the only Illinois state park on one of the Great Lakes. On the far south western side of the lake, it has a long and interesting beach.

Duck Lake State Park

Duck Lake State Park consists of 704 acres in Muskegon County, about eight miles north of Muskegon, Michigan. This day-use park has no hiking trails or camping facilities. It became a state park in 1988.

Most of Duck Lake State Park is on the north shore of Duck Lake and is a heavily wooded undeveloped area. It is colorful during the fall because of its many different kinds of hardwoods. Duck Lake is quite large, forming most of the southern boundary of the park stretching eastward from Lake Michigan.

Location: Duck Lake State Park is on Michillinda Road in northern Muskegon County. To arrive at the park, take Scenic Drive, which runs parallel with Lake Michigan, to Michillinda Road. Turn right (east) onto Michillinda and travel a short distance to the entrance of the park.

Features of the Park: Features include a picnic area on Duck Lake, a one-ramp boat launch, and a sandy beach with one dune separating the Lake Michigan shoreline from Scenic Drive. The sand dune compris-

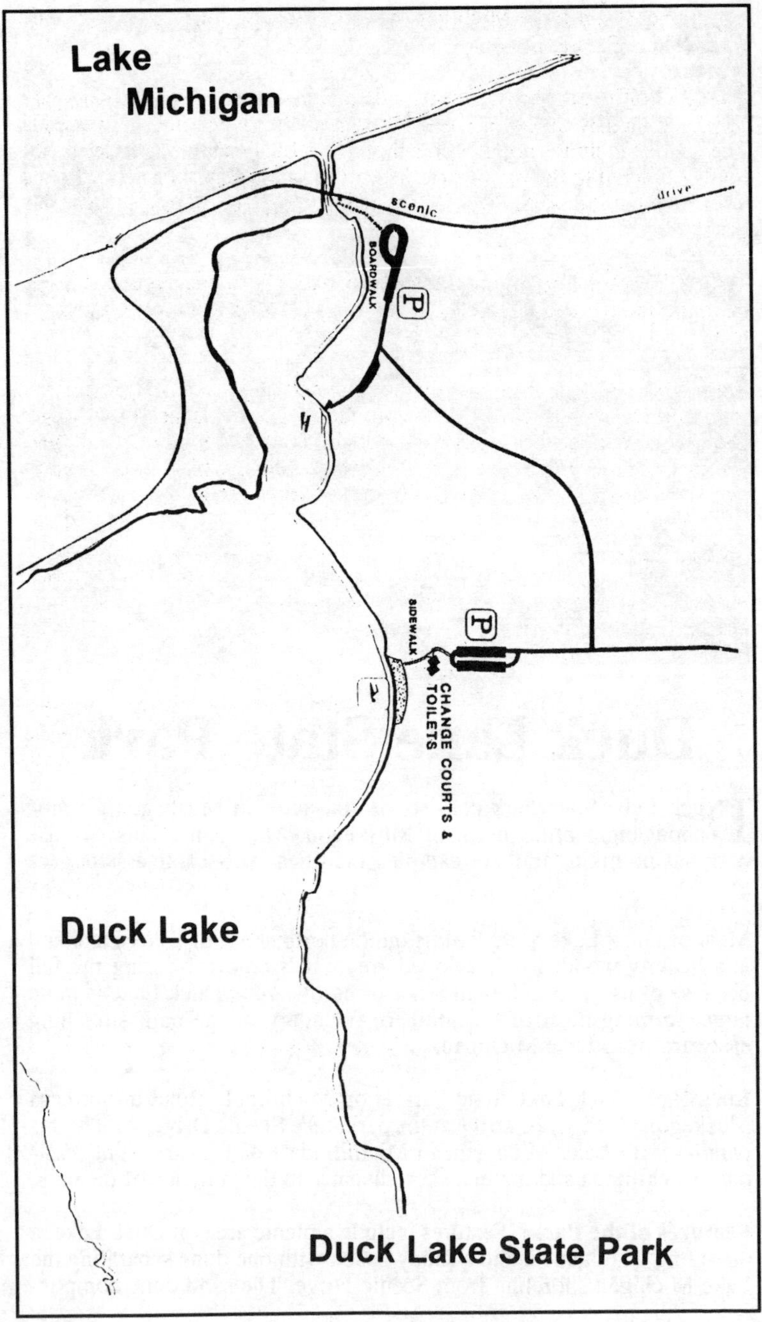

Duck Lake State Park

ing the beach on Lake Michigan is separated from the rest of the park by two-lane Scenic Drive.

Picnic Facilities: The entrance road ends in a parking lot at the wooded picnic facility on Duck Lake. A brick shelter is available for rental. The shelter includes about a dozen picnic tables as well as toilet facilities. Adjacent to the picnic area is a small sandy beach on Duck Lake. There is a bathhouse facility for changing into swimming gear near the beach.

Trails: There are no hiking trails in this park. A short paved trail leads from the picnic area to Duck Lake, a distance of only several hundred feet.

From a parking area between the boat launch and Lake Michigan, you can walk to Lake Michigan. The wooden walkway near the outlet of Duck Lake connects the parking lot to the Lake Michigan beach. The walkway brings visitors to Scenic Drive, the road which separates the two sections of the park. Here it is necessary to cross the road to the Lake Michigan beach.

The walkway is only about a quarter of a mile long. At this point also is a stream flowing into Lake Michigan from Duck Lake. A small dam under the road bridge makes it impossible for any type of boat traffic from Duck Lake to enter Lake Michigan.

Boat Ramp: A single-lane boat launch is available for small boats wishing to enter Duck Lake. Boats can't reach Lake Michigan from here because the channel connecting Duck Lake and Lake Michigan has a small dam under the bridge. At the ramp is a small parking area.

Beach: The Lake Michigan shoreline is a sand beach, including a large dune that extends 50 to 75 yards from the water's edge. On the side of the dune is the typical development of sand, grass and trees. There is no parking along the road for beach users. Neither are there any bathhouse or toilet facilities or concession stand on the beach.

Duck Lake State Park
3560 Memorial Drive
North Muskegon, MI 49445
(616) 894-8769

Fisherman's Island State Park

Fisherman's Island State Park consists of 2,678 acres stretching about five miles along the Lake Michigan shoreline. There is only minimal development at this park, mostly at the northern part of the park. Development includes camping facilities and a sandy beach. There are no picnic facilities for day use in the park.

South of Inwood Creek, the park is undeveloped with no trail system or facilities. You may enter this area by driving six miles south to Norwood Road. Traveling west on this road, you come to a small parking spot where the road ends. From here, you can walk along a two-lane sandy road as far as Whiskey Creek. There are some private lands in this area and also some state park lands.

Location: Fisherman's Island is about two miles south of Charlevoix, Michigan, in Charlevoix County. Exit U.S. 31 about two miles from Charlevoix at Bell's Bay Road. Turn on Bell's Bay Road and go west to the entrance of the park.

Features of the Park: The principal features of this park are the five miles of Lake Michigan shoreline and the rustic campground in heavy woods.

Beach and Shoreline: The 3.2-mile park road parallels the lake from the park entrance to a small parking area, where Inwood Creek flows into Lake Michigan. It is here where most people come to enter the sandy Lake Michigan beach.

The beach is scenic, stretching both north and south from the path which leads to the beach from the parking lot. There are a few picnic tables in the sand, but no organized picnic facility.

The first mile of the park road is asphalt, while the remainder is gravel. Though gravel, it is an excellent road to bicycle. It is adjacent to Lake Michigan with no brush or trees between the road and the water. Looking out on the water, it is possible to see miles in all directions. A couple of large lake freighters were seen in the distance the day of my visit. The beach along this northern shoreline is stony.

Fisherman's Island: The park namesake, Fisherman's Island, is several hundred feet offshore. There is no development or organized activity on the island, only woods. During the summer some visitors swim across to the island.

Camping: Ninety rustic campsites are spread out across two camping areas in the park. No modern facilities, showers or flush toilets are available. Neither is there electricity. A picnic table and in-ground firepit and grill are found at each campsite.

The north campground is near the entrance booth. Sites #1 - #26 are around two circular gravel drives in heavily shaded woods. Campsites #27 - #40 are just a few feet from the water's edge. These well-spaced sites are encircled by trees, shrubs and brush. It is not possible to see the next campsite. The ground is mainly sand, with little grass cover.

At the south campground (sites #41 - #90), the campsites are well-spaced and isolated from the next by heavily wooded trees, shrubs and brush. Some sites are separated from the adjacent site with small ridges of sand dunes. Very few of the campsites are within sight of neighbors. Some are quite large and back up into the woods.

The south campground is some distance from the lake. It is necessary to walk up to a half-mile across the park road to the beach. However, for isolation and quiet from neighboring campsites, this campground is one of the best in a state park on the Great Lakes.

The campground generally is full during summer holidays and weekends. However, during weekdays, campsites often are available.

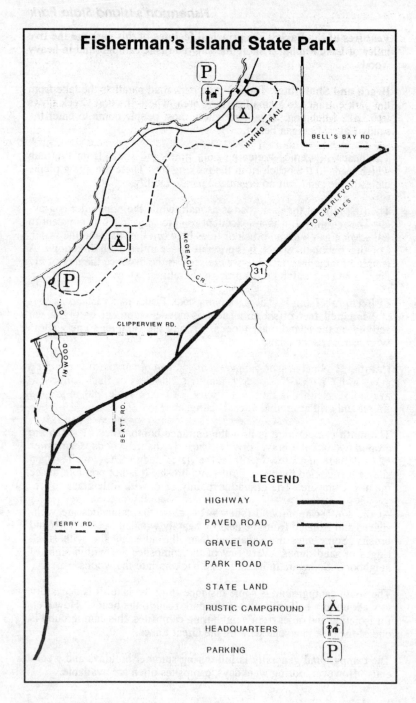

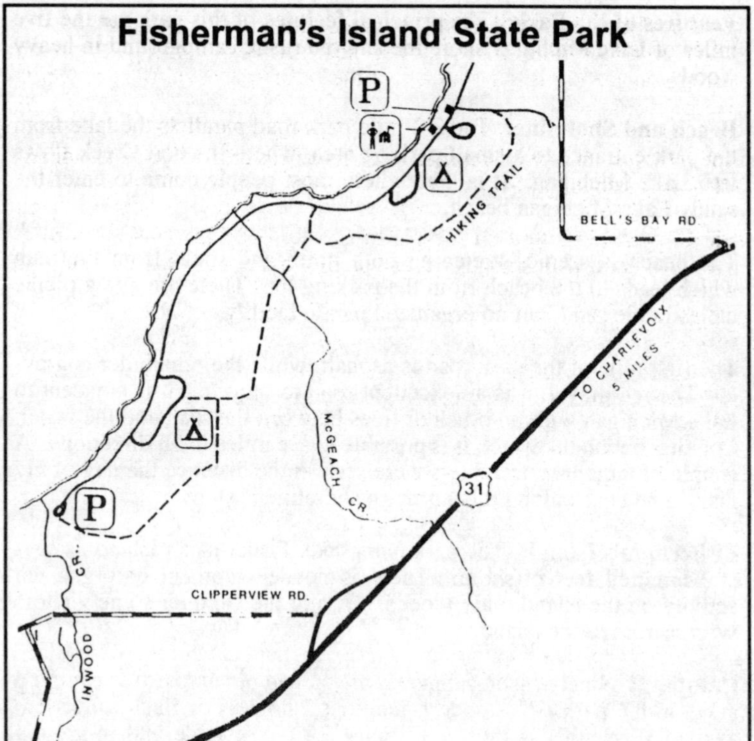
Fisherman's Island State Park
HIKING TRAIL
BELL'S BAY RD.
TO CHARLEVOIX
5 MILES
McGEACH
CR.
31
CR.
CLIPPERVIEW RD.
INWOOD
BEATT RD.
FERRY RD.
LEGEND
HIGHWAY
PAVED ROAD
GRAVEL ROAD
PARK ROAD
STATE LAND
RUSTIC CAMPGROUND
HEADQUARTERS
PARKING

Trails: There are three loops in the park. The North Campground Loop is a one-mile trail starting near the park gate. The South Campground loop is 2.1 miles, and the beach and picnic area loop is 3.2 miles.

The trail system is well-marked with distances and objectives indicated at the various trailheads.

Bicycling is permitted on the North Campground Loop. It is a relatively flat trail, with some roots and stones, but not terribly difficult for bicycling.

Winter Activities: During the winter, cross-country skiing is possible. However, the trails are not groomed and there is no winter camping or ski rental available.

Fisherman's Island State Park
P.O. Box 456
Charlevoix, MI 49720
(616) 547-6641

Grand Haven State Park

Grand Haven State Park is the smallest state park on Lake Michigan, 48 acres. When you arrive at the park, you see a beautiful beach with hundreds of camping trailers.

The park in the heart of Grand Haven, Michigan, is surrounded by houses and condominiums. The town is an extremely popular summer resort with many shops, restaurants and galleries. Without the indications that this is a state park, you would think this was just a city park. During the summer, a trolley takes people along the waterfront to various locations in the city.

Though small, Grand Haven is an extremely popular park due to the beach and the town's amenities. More than a million people visit this park each year. In the summer, the state park parking lot is often filled before mid-morning. Many people park in the town and take the trolley or walk the mile or so from town to the beach.

Location: To arrive at Grand Haven State Park, turn west off of U.S. 31 in Grand Haven, and follow the signs to the waterfront.

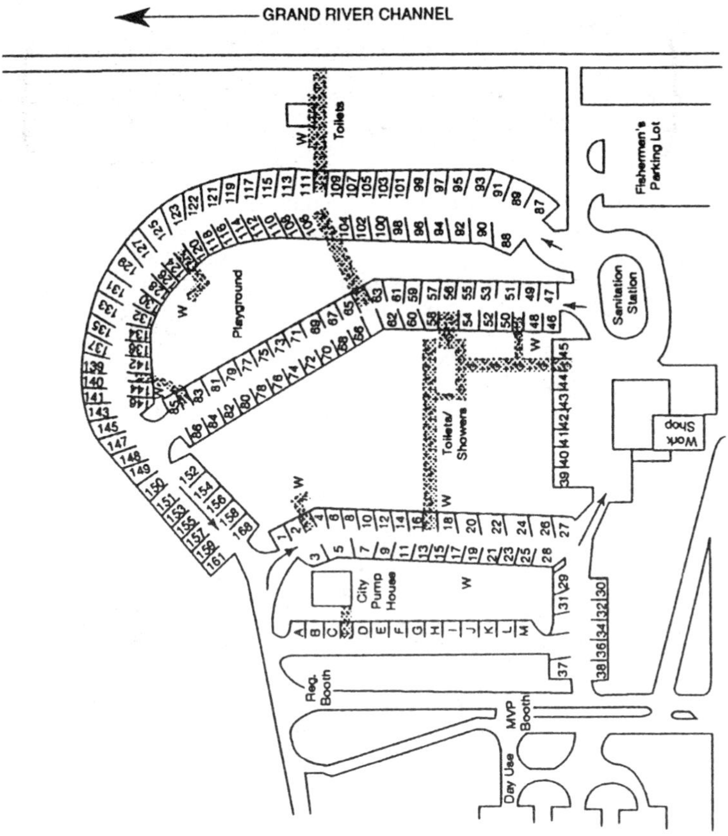

Grand Haven State Park

Campground: The campground has 182 sites on asphalt, with sand between the campsite rows. There is no shade and the sites are close to each other. Most people camping at Grand Haven State Park are in recreational vehicles (RVs) and motorhomes. Some people pitch tents in the sand; however, it is often windy along the lake and therefore necessary to drive pegs deep into the sand to anchor a tent.

About a dozen campsites (odd numbers from #127 - #147) are situated directly on the edge of the Lake Michigan beach. A modern flush toilet and hot shower building is in the center of the campground.

Up to 80 percent of the sites are reserved in advance. Reservations can be made beginning in the fall for the following season. Even though 20 percent of the total occupancy is not reserved, this does not mean that it is easy to obtain a site. With people extending their stays, it is unlikely that campsites can be obtained without a reservation.

Beach: The sandy beach extends from the pier along the entire length of the park. It is a wide and beautiful beach. There is a concession facility, bathhouse and several picnic tables at the beach.

Fishing: Many people fish on the pier connecting the Grand Haven Lighthouse, adjacent to the park, to the mainland. Anglers fish for salmon or trout.

No boat ramps exist in the park. However, public boat launches are nearby in the city. Also, there are charter fishing boats in the vicinity for individuals wishing to go out by charter into Lake Michigan.

Grand Haven State Park
1001 Harbor Avenue
Grand Haven, MI 49417
(616) 842-6020

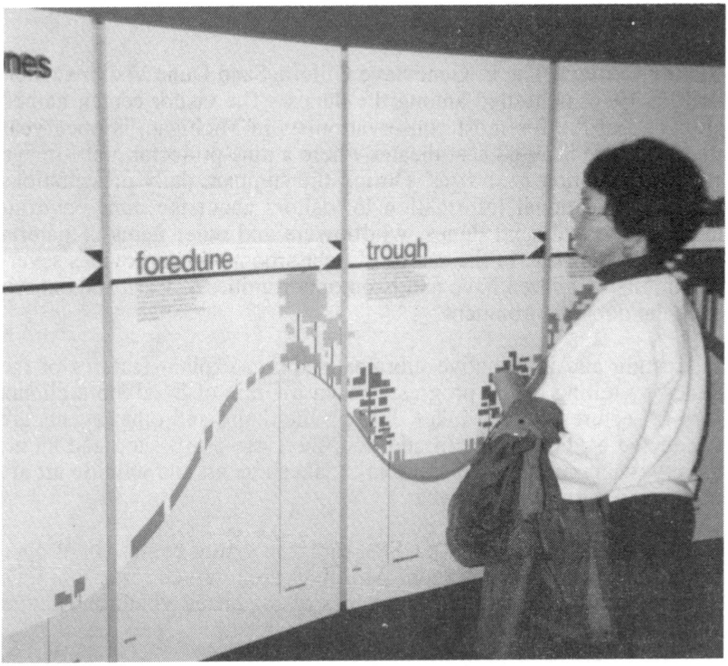

P.J. Hoffmaster State Park

P.J. Hoffmaster State Park, comprised of 1,043 acres, is named after Percy J. Hoffmaster, who was director of Michigan state parks in the 1920 and 1930s.

Location: P.J. Hoffmaster State Park is in Muskegon County, Michigan, three miles west of U.S. 31. After exiting U.S. 31, take Pontaluna Road to the park entrance. The drive into the park is a scenic wooded road. In the fall, this entrance has spectacular color.

Features of the Park: The principal features of this park are the dunes and beach along the Lake Michigan shoreline. Also, one of the most informative visitor centers in any state park on the Great Lakes is located here.

Most of the dunes at Hoffmaster State Park are stabilized by a hardwood forest. The windward side, facing Lake Michigan, is less stable due to the winds from the lake.

Visitor Center: The E. Genevieve Gillette Sand Dune Visitor Center, built in 1976, is nestled among the dunes. The visitor center, named after one of the foremost conservationists in Michigan, is open year round. There is an 82 seat theater where a nine-projector multi-image slide presentation is shown. During the summer, daily presentations provide educational information to visitors about the dune environment, individual sand dunes, wildflowers and other items of natural interest in the area. In the center is a classroom which provides several exhibits. Children have hands-on opportunities to learn and experience the dune environment.

Interesting and informative diorama graphics explain features of the dunes by telling of the progress "From a Grain of Sand" to a climax forest. Lectures, guided hikes through the dunes and other events are conducted at the center. In addition, there are a gift shop and an art gallery where a variety of exhibits of lakeshore art and wildlife art are on display throughout the year.

During the fall, winter and early spring, the visitor center is not open for public visits until afternoon. Mornings are reserved for school field trips, scouting groups and other types of organized youth and senior citizen activities.

Trails: There are more than 10 miles of hiking trails in P.J. Hoffmaster State Park. Several trails depart from the visitor center. The best known is the Dune Climb Stairway. This trail is about a five-minute walk from the visitor center to the stairway. The 168-step stairs proceed to the top of a sand dune, where a walkway leads to an observation deck. Along the stairway are several benches where you may rest.

The observation deck provides a spectacular panorama of the surrounding area. Lake Michigan is in view; however, because of dunes in the foreground, the beach cannot be seen. The observation deck is 190 feet above Lake Michigan, 770 feet above sea level. Nearby is Mount Baldy, a 756-foot sand dune.

Along the walkway are signs explaining the grasses growing in the sand. They offer you a good understanding of how sand dunes can eventually stabilize, grasses take over and eventually forests develop. Today in this park, there is a variety of hardwoods.

Marram grass, also known as beach grass, is extremely important in stabilizing sand. It grows fast and has an underground stem and eventually develops into a network that binds the sand together. By late summer, the grass goes to seed. Another grass in the area is wormwood, a plant found on the stabilized dunes.

P.J. Hoffmaster State Park

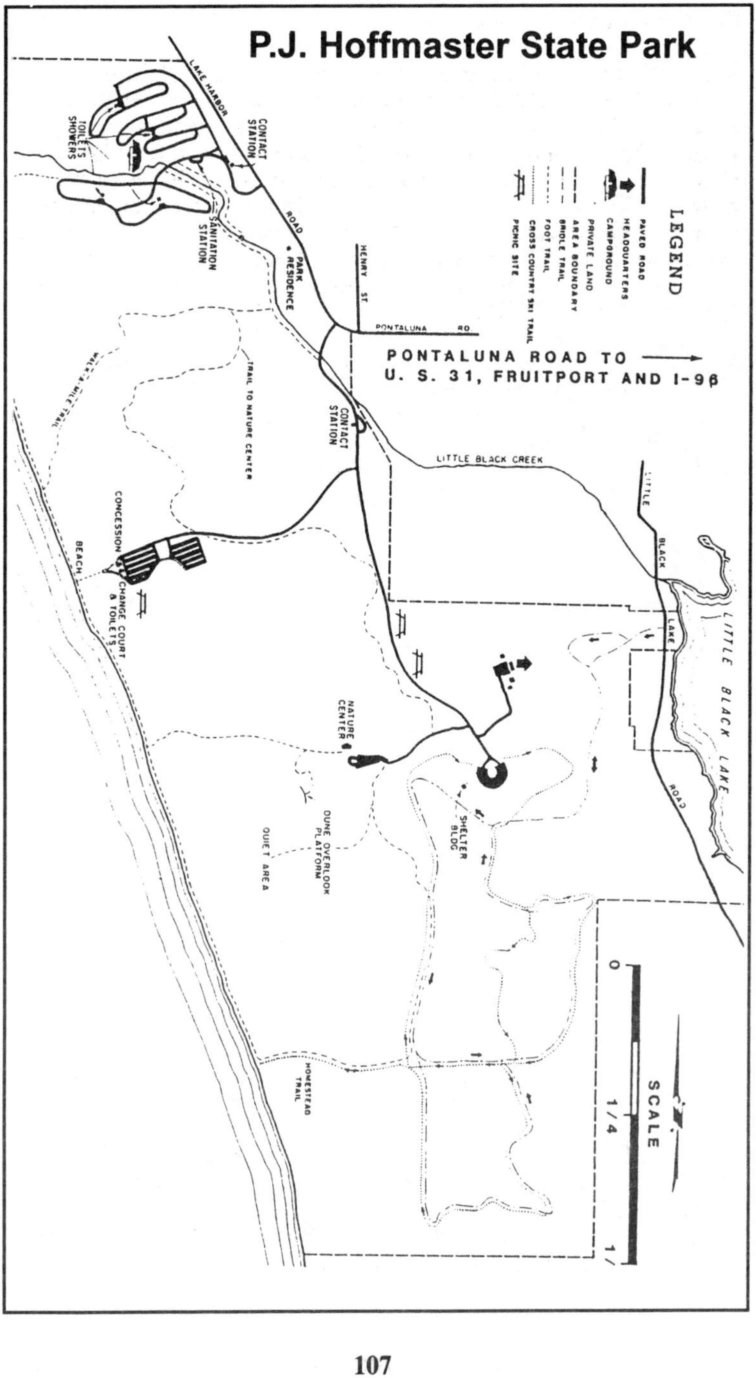

LAKE HARBOR
ROAD
CONTACT STATION
TOILETS SHOWERS
SANITATION STATION
PARK RESIDENCE
HENRY ST
PONTALUNA RD
PONTALUNA ROAD TO
U. S. 31, FRUITPORT AND I-96
LEGEND
PAVED ROAD
HEADQUARTERS
CAMPGROUND
PRIVATE LAND
AREA BOUNDARY
BRIDLE TRAIL
FOOT TRAIL
CROSS COUNTRY SKI TRAIL
PICNIC SITE
TRAIL TO NATURE CENTER
CONTACT STATION
LITTLE BLACK CREEK
LITTLE BLACK LAKE ROAD
LITTLE BLACK LAKE
CONCESSION
BEACH
CHANGE COURT & TOILETS
NATURE CENTER
SHELTER BLDG
DUNE OVERLOOK PLATFORM
QUIET AREA
HOMESTEAD TRAIL
SCALE
0
1/4

Another trail from the visitor center to the beach goes part of the distance along an elevated, wooden walkway. This trail heads through the woods with sandy dunes on one side and on the other side trees and grass growing in more stabilized dunes. The walk to the dunes takes about 10 minutes, about a half-mile in length.

There are no bicycle trails in the park. Bicycling is permitted on the roadways in the park, but may not be taken on the hiking trails.

Beach: There are nearly three miles of beach extending the length of the park. This provides plenty of beach for walking, sunbathing, jogging and all of the other activities associated with beautiful clean sandy beaches. The beach is long enough that visitors can find, even on busy days, an isolated location to enjoy the sun, sand and water.

The beach, like other state parks along Lake Michigan, has clean, soft, fine sand. There are no rocks or stones in the beach. The beach extends back from the water's edge 50 to 100 yards. At that point, the dunes with grass and small trees begin.

Camping: To reach the campground, exit the main park and go about a quarter-mile along Lake Harbor Road to the entrance. The campground has 333 sites. It is well shaded and quite scenic, with adequate spacing between most campsites. At each campsite are a picnic table, a circular fire pit and electricity. There are modern hot shower and flush toilet facilities.

The campground is not within sight of Lake Michigan. A trail of about a half-mile leads from the campground to the campers' beach. From here, you can walk along the beach the entire length of the park. Reservations should be made for camping during the summer, as this campground is often filled, especially on holidays and weekends.

Picnic Facilities: There are three picnic areas in the park. Two are in scenic wooded settings with picnic tables, grills and a water pump, as well as vault toilets. The third site is next to the large parking area and concession building near the beach.

Just inside the entrance to the park, a road leads to this picnic area. There are beach bathhouse changing facilities and modern flush toilets here. It is just a short walk from the parking lot to the beach.

Winter Activities: Hoffmaster State Park is open year-round. One section of the campground, 60 to 70 sites, is kept open during the winter. Some of these sites are along Little Black Creek, which flows through the campground.

Cross-country skiing is particularly popular during the winter months. There are three miles of groomed cross-country trails. The shelter where the ski trails begin is at a parking area at the end of the road running through the park.

A map describes where the ski trails go, their intersections and distances.

From the campground, you could ski through the woods to the beach and along the lakeshore.

The nature center is open during the winter in the afternoon only. No snowmobiles are permitted in the park.

P.J. Hoffmaster State Park
6585 Lake Harbor Road
Muskegon, MI 49441
(616) 798-3711
(616) 789-4470 (fax)

Holland State Park

Holland State Park is a relatively small 142 acres, yet is one of the most heavily used state parks on the Great Lakes during the summer. Surrounding the park are condominiums, beach houses, restaurants, marinas and other buildings. Across the road from the Lake Macatawa Campground are a condominium and a motel.

The park is divided into two sections: the beach and campground on Lake Michigan, and the Lake Macatawa Campground about three-fourths of a mile from Lake Michigan.

Given the surrounding populations of Holland, Grand Rapids, northern Indiana and Chicago, coupled with the spectacular beach, this park is crowded during summer weekends and holidays. It is not unusual for the large parking facility to be filled by midday.

Location: Holland State Park is in Ottawa County on the edge of Holland, Michigan, between Lake Macatawa and Lake Michigan. This park can be reached by taking U.S. 31 to the north side of Holland and exiting onto Lakewood Blvd. West about three miles, the road becomes Ottawa Beach Road. This road comes to the entrance of the park, about seven miles from U.S. 31. The area along these seven miles is built up with homes, restaurants, inns, condominiums, motels and marinas.

Features of the Park: The principal feature of the park is the beach along the Lake Michigan shoreline. Also, there are two popular campgrounds.

Beach: The Lake Michigan beach at Holland State Park stretches nearly half a mile. It is a beautiful beach extending back up to 150 feet from the water. In the summer, every kind of water and beach activity can be experienced here: sunbathing, walking along the beach, playing in the water, using personal watercraft, windsurfing and sailing. There are a shelter and large parking lot near the beach.

At the south end of the beach is the breakwater leading into Lake Michigan from the channel connecting Lake Michigan and Lake Macatawa. Several grills and many picnic tables rest in this area between the channel and the parking lot. Fishing is very popular along the channel. Boats from marinas along Lake Macatawa can enter Lake Michigan through this channel.

On the breakwater is the Holland Harbor Lighthouse, which was first built in 1872. The present structure was erected in 1907 and was automated in 1932. This red lighthouse often is affectionately called "Big Red."

Camping: Two campgrounds in the park have a total of 368 sites. The Lake Michigan Campground is next to the parking lot near the Lake Michigan beach. This campground is on blacktop with sites designated by paint markings. There is no shade. This campground is principally designed for recreational vehicles.

Connecting the two campgrounds is a walking and bicycle path along Ottawa Beach Road. The distance between the two campgrounds is about three-fourths of a mile.

Two hundred and twenty campsites are at the Lake Macatawa Campground. Sites to the left of the entrance road sit in the open, with little shade and foliage. Each site has a picnic table. A few on the outer edge are among some trees, but overall it is much like a field with picnic tables. When filled during the summer, little privacy exists between campsites.

The east part of the campground is more wooded with pine trees and

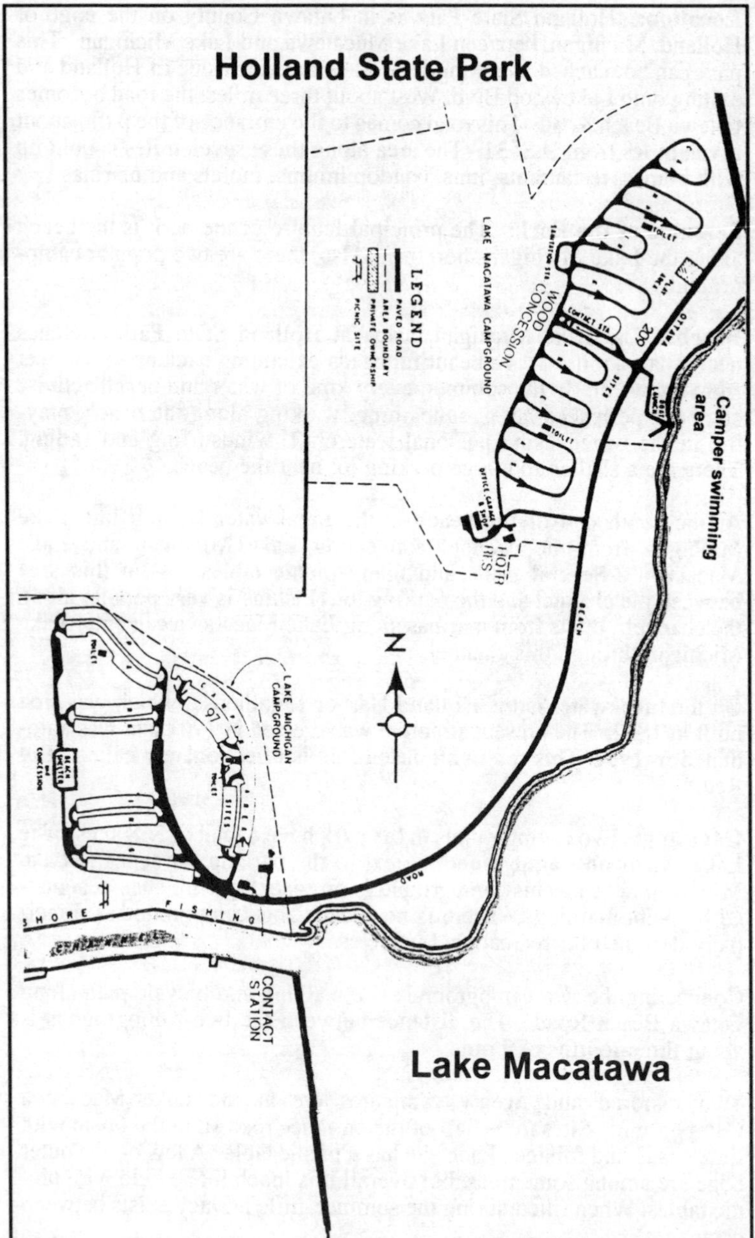

Holland State Park
LEGEND
PAVED ROAD
AREA BOUNDARY
PRIVATE OWNERSHIP
PICNIC SITE
LAKE MACATAWA CAMPGROUND
WOOD CONCESSION
TOILET
CONTACT STA
209
SITES
OTTAWA
Camper swimming area
BEACH
ROAD
N
LAKE MICHIGAN CAMPGROUND
SITES
BEACH SHELTER and CONCESSION
SHORE FISHING
CONTACT STATION
Lake Macatawa

several kinds of hardwoods. The campsites are close to each other in this section; however, there is more shade. Along the northern edge of the campground the sites are a little bit more spread out and shaded. On the south side of the circle, sites back directly on the road leading into the park. Several sites back up to a popular commercial inn on the outside of the park.

At the entrance to the campground is Papa Don's Rentals. Bicycles, paddle boats, funcycles, and adult trikes are available for rent.

Across from the campground on Lake Macatawa is a small beach about 300 yards in length. This beach accommodates campers. At this location is a single boat launching ramp into Lake Macatawa. However, there is no parking for the vehicle and trailer. There are several marinas and boat docks near the park. Across the lake from the park are many private homes.

Both campgrounds are full most of the summer. It is almost always necessary to have reservations. The campgrounds are closed from Nov. 1 to April 1.

Fishing: Lake Macatawa is popular as a fishing lake for bass, walleye and perch. Fishing in Lake Michigan for coho salmon and lake trout is good from the pier stretching out from the channel into the lake.

Trails: There are no hiking trails in this park. The bicycle trail connecting the two campgrounds is part of a trail system in the surrounding area. It is possible to ride for several miles on trails maintained by local agencies.

Winter Activities: Winter brings heavy snow to this section of the Midwest. However, the park is not open during the winter. Local residents come to the area to ice fish, but there are no cross-country ski trails or winter camping.

Holland State Park
2215 Ottawa Beach Road
Holland, MI 49424
(616) 399-9390
(616) 399-5830 (fax)

Illinois Beach State Park

Illinois Beach State Park was established in 1954. The park consists of two sections, the northern and southern units. The two sections are separated by the Zion Nuclear Power Plant, which was built in the early 1970s. Then, it was located on the northern edge of the park. Later, the park was extended all the way to the Wisconsin state line.

The northern unit, Camp Logan day-use section, is comprised of 1,925 acres and has 2.5 miles of shoreline. The unit was a prisoner-of-war camp during the Civil War and an Army basic training center for World Wars I and II. Some of the structures are still standing from the time when this area served as a military camp.

There are four day-use areas: facilities for picnicking, swimming, a boat marina, and a trail system for hiking, bicycling and cross-country skiing.

The southern unit comprises 2,235 acres with 3.5 miles of shoreline. This section houses the Illinois Beach Resort and Conference Center, swimming beach, the park camping facilities and a series of hiking trails. In the southern part of the park are a nature preserve and wildlife refuge. Entrance to the preserve is limited to individuals with permits, which are available at the park office.

Combining the two units, the park includes 4,160 acres. Much of this land originally was part of the Algonquin Indian nation. Through the years many Indian artifacts, such as arrowheads and axeheads, have been found. Today it is the only section of lakeshore dunes from Wisconsin to Gary, Indiana, that have been preserved in their natural state.

In the southern section of the park is Dead River. This stream drains the southern part of the dunes along with runoff waters from the surrounding terrain. Most of the time, the mouth of the river is blocked by an elongated sandbar. When this happens, the water forms a pond. When the pond reaches a high level, the water breaks through the sandbar and the pond drains.

Location: Illinois Beach State Park is in Lake County, Illinois, stretching 6.5 miles along the Lake Michigan shoreline, from the Wisconsin-Illinois state line to the city of Waukegan, Illinois. This park is reached by turning east on one of four roads off of Illinois 137 (Sheridan Road), just north of Waukegon at Zion. To enter the south unit, take Wadsworth Road east to the park entrance.

Features of the Park: Looking out on the beach, you can imagine what this area looked like more than 100 years ago, before heavy urbanization of the Chicago metropolitan area.

The park shoreline attracts hundreds of thousands of people every year. Also, the Resort and Convention Center is an attraction for groups scheduling a meeting or a stay in a resort facility overlooking the lake. This park also is popular among individuals wishing a camping experience within close proximity to their homes in the surrounding heavily populated Chicago area.

Resort and Conference Center: The Illinois Beach Resort and Conference Center has modern accommodations that include 96 guest rooms, an indoor heated swimming pool, a cocktail lounge and a full-service health club. A restaurant is open seven days a week. There are 12 meeting rooms, which can accommodate up to 500 people. These facilities are popular for educational, business, religious and other group meetings.

The Resort and Conference Center has been closed for five years for renovations. According to information provided by park personnel, plans are for the facility to be reopened sometime in 1997.

Interpretive Center: An excellent interpretive center in the nature preserve area offers information about the history of the area and an explanation of the natural development of dunes.

Camping: A large modern campground with 244 sites is located in the southern section of the park. Facilities for both tent and trailer camping are available. The campground is spread out and nicely shaded. Each campsite has a grill and picnic table. Lake Michigan cannot be seen from the campground because of small dunes with trees, shrubs and grass. However, it is just a short walk over these dunes to the lakefront.

Modern hot shower and flush toilet facilities are available at several places in the park. Near the campground is a camper store where refreshments, gifts and souvenirs, in addition to camping supplies, are available.

Campsites #150 - #219 are in an area with little shade and are close to each other. The campsites on the east side of the camp road back up to the dunes stretching to the lake. These campsites are within a few hundred yards of the lake.

Campsites #104 - #149 on the east side of a road overlook a marsh. These campsites are well-shaded. Twenty-two campsites (#500 - #521) are on blacktop pads.

The campground is open year-round. Forty campsites in the northern part of the campground are available by reservation at least two weeks in advance during the late spring and summer. A group camp area is available.

Beach: The extensive beach offers swimming, fishing, walking and sunbathing. There are about 1,000 feet of shoreline where swimming is permitted. This is an unsupervised beach with no lifeguards present. Nearby are two bathhouses with hot showers, flush toilets and changing rooms. At one end of the beach is a concessions facility with refreshments. Here, you can purchase a Chicago hot dog - the only state park on a Great Lake where it's available. Also, souvenirs and some groceries can be purchased here.

Another beautiful sandy beach is located adjacent to the North Point Marina at the northern edge of the park. This is the Winthrope Harbor Unit. Along this beach are picnic tables and grills. All along the beach, the view of Lake Michigan is spectacular, made so by numerous boats coming and going from the marina.

Trails: There are a nearly 20 miles of trails in the park. Five marked nature trails ranging from two tenths of a mile to 2.25 miles are available for the walker and nature observer. These trails begin at the interpretive center. These nature trails provide access to sand dunes, plants growing on the beaches, the Dead River and trees in the area.

The Dead River Trail is 1.8 miles, proceeding along the banks of the river for most of its length. This well-defined hiking trail provides a continuous view of the river. The day of my hike, I saw a variety of waterfowl, including many ducks. The trail ends near the mouth of the Dead River, where it flows into Lake Michigan.

From here, you can return to the interpretive center along the Sand Trail. This nine tenths of a mile trail parallels the lakeshore behind a ridge of sand. The lake is not in view along this trail; however, you can hear the water and observe the sea gulls and other features of this grass sand dune. Along both of these trails, Dead River and Sand Trail, there are lookouts where hikers can see the surrounding terrain and Lake Michigan. It provides a particularly good place from which to photograph the park. The trails in the interpretive trail system are for hiking only.

The Loop Trail (2.25 miles) is a gravel trail that winds through an oak forest. Two short trails in the same section are the Oak Ridge Trail (.6 mile) and Beach Trail (.2 mile).

Cross-country skiing and bicycling are prohibited in this area.

The trails in Illinois Beach State Park are the best marked of any state park on the Great Lakes. At each trailhead is a sign providing information about the name of the trail, its length, a clear map showing where the trail goes and any connectors, along with a brief description of what to expect along the trail.

In the northern unit, the Marsh Trail (6.7 miles) is the longest trail in the park.

In addition to the hiking nature trails, there are about 10 miles of trails which serve both bicyclers and hikers. These trails principally run between the northern and southern units. Nordic skiing is permitted on these trails during the winter. It is forbidden on the nature trails.

The bicycle trail starts at the Interpretive Center, then proceeds along the beach and Lake Michigan shoreline past the campground. It then goes onto city streets to pass the nuclear power plant and enters the roadway system of the northern section of the park. In the southern section of the park, it is hard-surfaced; however, in the northern section the surface varies.

Picnic Facilities: In the Camp Logan area (northern section) are several picnic areas with pit toilets, picnic tables and grills. These include Dunes Day-Use Area, Beach Ridge Day-Use Area, Logan Day-Use Area and Sailing Beach. Lessons and rentals are available at Sailing

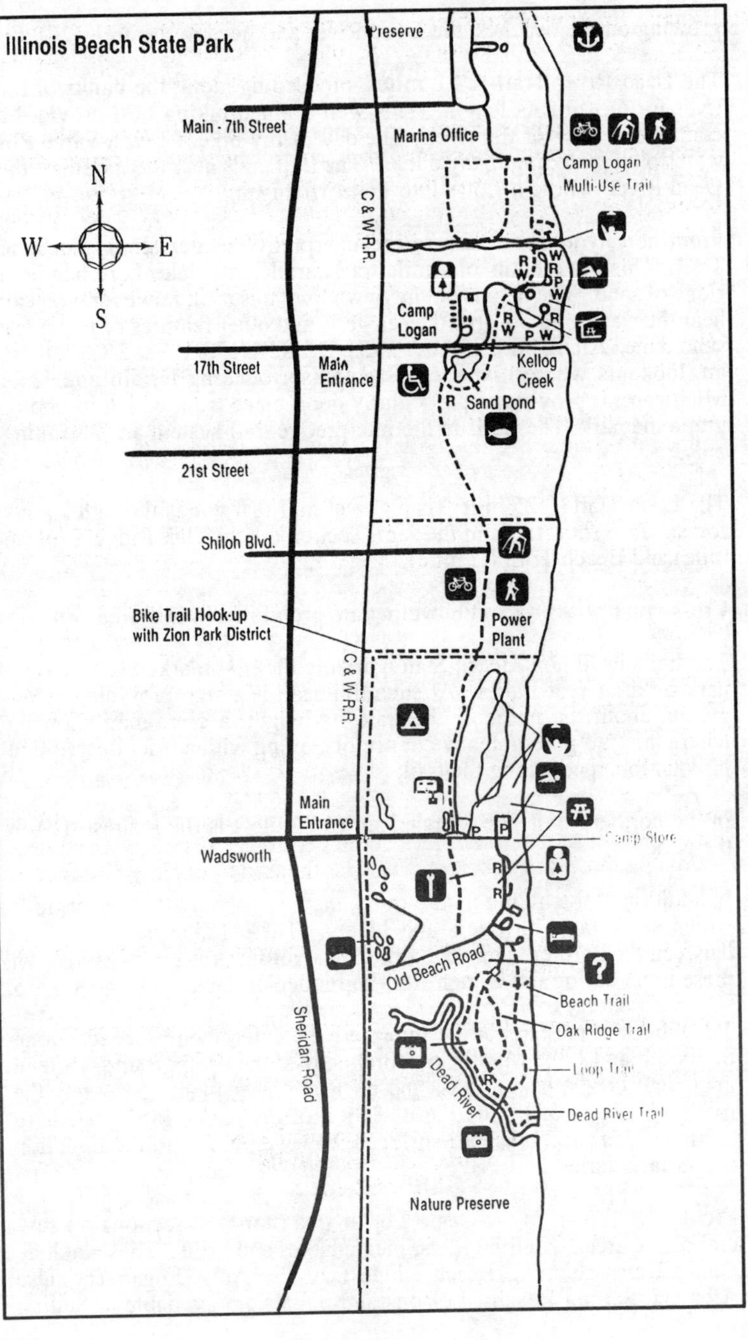
Illinois Beach State Park
Preserve
Main - 7th Street
Marina Office
Camp Logan
Multi-Use Trail
N
W
E
S
C & W R.R.
Camp Logan
17th Street
Main Entrance
Kellog Creek
Sand Pond
21st Street
Shiloh Blvd.
Power Plant
Bike Trail Hook-up with Zion Park District
C & W R.R.
Main Entrance
Camp Store
Wadsworth
Old Beach Road
Beach Trail
Oak Ridge Trail
Loop Trail
Dead River Trail
Dead River
Sheridan Road
Nature Preserve

Beach. Two picnic shelters, not available by reservation, are in this area. A concession facility can be found in the Camp Logan section, where picnic and camping supplies can be purchased.

Fishing: Fishing is permitted along the Lake Michigan shoreline except in the designated swimming section. Fishing is permitted also in small inland ponds within the park. Sand Lake, a small, popular fishing lake, is stocked with rainbow trout. There is a small fishing dock on the pond which is often used by children.

North Point Marina: At the northernmost part of the Camp Logan unit is North Point Marina, a full-service facility with a large 10-lane boat launch. There are 1,550 slips at this marina, which is reached by driving to Seventh Street in Zion, Illinois, and proceeding to the lake.

At the marina you can rent a variety of boats, catamarans, sailboards and windsurfing units. In addition, there is a food-service facility.

Nature: Illinois Beach State Park is an excellent place to observe birds and a large variety of plants. This area is a popular migration route for a variety of birds. More than 250 species of birds have been identified at the park. Many ducks and geese are seen at Illinois Beach State Park. Bird watching is popular throughout the year, including the winter.

More than 600 species of plants have been documented in the dunes. The park provides an excellent place to study plants ranging from those which grow in stabilized dunes and ridges, to the prairie grasses and forests further from the shoreline of Lake Michigan.

Special Events: During May, a two-day camper show is held at Illinois Beach State Park. A number of exhibitors display their various camping units and equipment. Several thousand people are drawn to this annual event.

In July, the two-day National Jet Ski Championships are held at the park. This often draws 50,000 people.

Winter Activities: Illinois Beach State Park is open year-round. Particularly popular is cross-country skiing on the many trails of the northern section. Ice fishing also is a winter activity.

Illinois Beach State Park
Zion, Illinois 60099
(708) 662-4811

Indiana Dunes State Park

The only Indiana state park on one of the Great Lakes is Indiana Dunes State Park. This park was established in 1926 and today comprises 2,182 acres.

Location: Indiana Dunes State Park, in Porter County along the south shore of Lake Michigan, is two miles north of I-94 on Indiana 49, about halfway between Gary and Michigan City, Indiana. This park is less than an hour's drive from Chicago.

Features of the Park: By far the most spectacular, and popular, feature of this state park is the more than three miles of Lake Michigan beach with its sand dunes. The beach is wide with very clean, beautiful sand.

Swimming is restricted to parts of the beach where and when lifeguards are on duty. Swimming is permitted from the weekend before

Memorial Day through Labor Day.

All along the lakefront behind the beaches are sand hills rising nearly 200 feet high. In addition, within the park are 1,800 wooded acres, which contain flora unique to the sand hills in the dunes region.

The entrance road, which ends in a large parking lot near the pavilion and beach house on the shore of Lake Michigan, is on the western end of the park. The picturesque pavilion, on the edge of the lake, has snack bar facilities, a souvenir shop and bathhouses, as well as shelter from inclement weather.

Trails: There are about 17 miles of hiking trails throughout the park. The trails are numbered (#1 - #10) and range from less than a quarter mile (Trail #1) to 5.5 miles (Trail #10). The trails traverse the various dune formations and each has different features.

Regardless of which trail you hike, it is likely that a portion of the hike will be in sand. Several trails are almost completely in sand.

Anyone planning to hike at Indiana Dunes Beach State Park should realize that it will not be easy walking. There are times when it seems as though you are sliding two steps backward while walking one step forward through the sand. You cannot hike at the same pace on the sandy trails as you can on firm, hard-packed dirt or blacktop trails.

One trail (Trail #8) that is particularly challenging travels over the tops of the three highest dunes in the park: Mt. Tom at 192 feet, Mt. Holden at 184 feet, and Mt. Jackson at 176 feet. This 1.5-mile trail begins at the Wilson Shelter at Wilson Picnic Grounds and ends at the beach about a half-mile east of the pavilion and beach house. There are excellent views of the lake and the surrounding area from many points along the trail.

The view from Mt. Tom looks westward along the lake. It is a very scenic view. However, like other views along the shoreline of Lake Michigan near urban areas, you see a huge steel manufacturing plant at nearby Burns Harbor, Indiana, just a few miles to the west.

The shortest trail in the park, Trail #1, leaves a parking lot on the western section of the park and takes the hiker to a lookout tower where he/she can get an excellent view of the beach and the lake.

The longest hiking trail (Trail #10), about five and a half miles, extends along the edge of the lake. This trail begins at the pavilion and ends along the eastern section of the park in an area of white pines. Trail #2 is a three-mile walk which departs from the Wilson Picnic Grounds and extends through a wooded climax forest and marshlands.

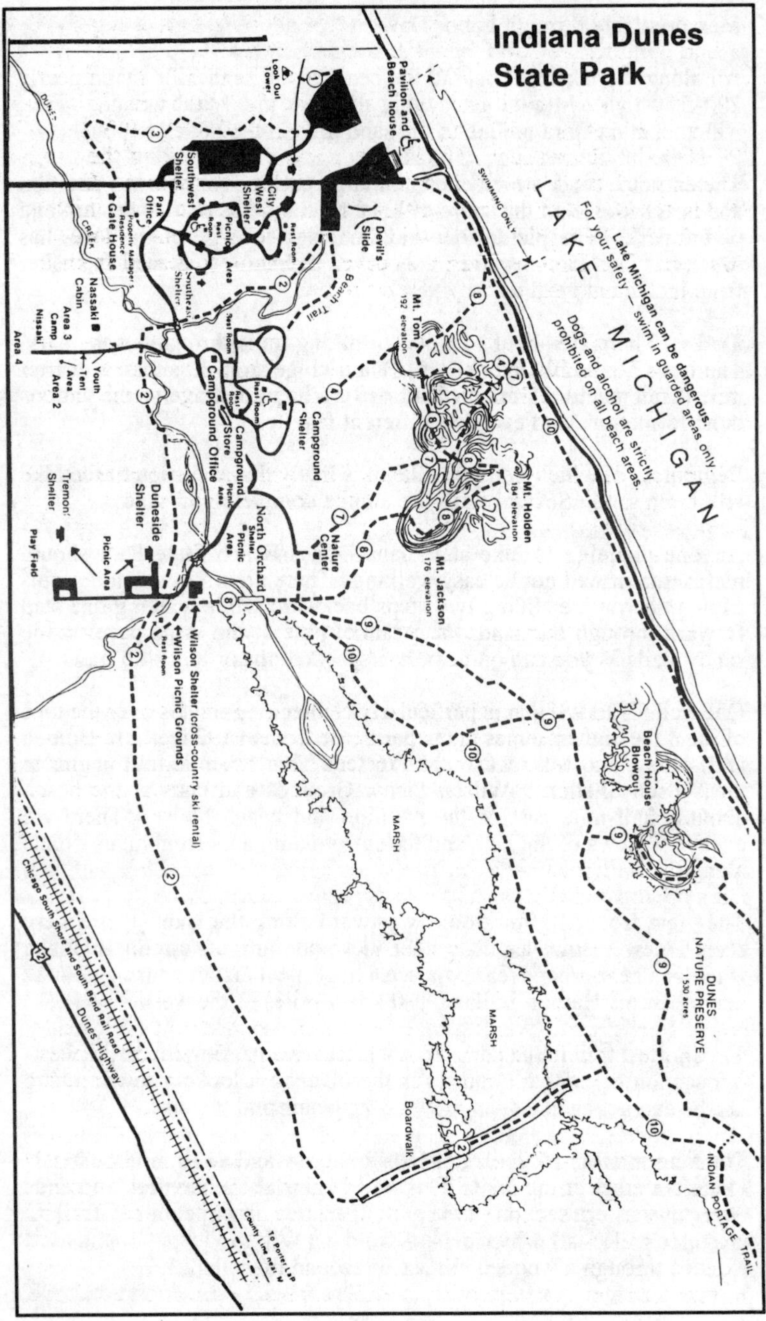

Indiana Dunes
State Park
LAKE MICHIGAN
Lake Michigan can be dangerous.
For your safety — swim in guarded areas only
Dogs and alcohol are strictly
prohibited on all beach areas.
SWIMMING ONLY
Pavilion and
Beach house
Look Out
Tower
DUNES
CREEK
Southwest
Shelter
City
West
Shelter
Park
Office
Gate House
Property Manager's
Residence
Picnic
Area
Rest
Room
Rest Room
Southeast
Shelter
Devil's
Slide
Beach Trail
Nassaki
Cabin
Area 3
Camp
Nissaki
Area 4
Youth
Tent
Area
Area 2
Campground Office
Campground
Store
Campground
Shelter
Rest Room
Picnic
Area
North Orchard
Shelter
Picnic
Area
Nature
Center
Duneside
Shelter
Tremont
Shelter
Play Field
Picnic Area
Wilson Shelter (cross-country ski rental)
Wilson Picnic Grounds
Rest Room
Mt. Tom
192 elevation
Mt. Holden
184 elevation
Mt. Jackson
176 elevation
Beach House
Blowout
MARSH
MARSH
Boardwalk
DUNES
NATURE PRESERVE
1,530 acres
INDIAN PORTAGE TRAIL
Chicago South Shore and South Bend Rail Road
Dunes Highway
12
To Porter
County Line near

Information about all 10 hiking trails can be obtained from a map available at the entrance booth or at the nature center.

A trail which runs next to the state park is the Calumet Trail. This 9.2-mile trail is designated for bicycling, jogging and hiking. It is part of the National Recreational Trail System and extends along the south boundary of the state park, continuing to the neighboring Indiana Dunes National Lakeshore. In this national lakeshore is the highest sand dune in the region, Mt. Baldy, at an elevation of slightly more than 700 feet. The Calumet Trail was developed on land leased from the Northern Indiana Public Service Company.

Though this trail is not in the state park, many individuals who come to Indiana Dunes State Park to camp or visit bring their bicycles. There is a solid, firm base along the Calumet Trail, providing a good surface for cycling.

Camping: The campground is just a short walking distance from the waterfront. Many campsites are at the foot of sand dunes. Each includes electricity and picnic facilities. The lake is not seen from the campsites because of the dunes. However, a short walk over the dunes brings you to the beach.

The campground is in a shaded, yet sandy area, with the dunes providing protection from the winds blowing off of the lake.

During weekends and on holidays during the summer, the campground is filled. Written reservations are needed for the busiest summer periods. There is a two-week maximum camping limitation. To camp at Indiana Dunes State Park, one person in the party must be at least 21 years of age.

A small campground store where wood, groceries and other supplies can be purchased is close to the campground office.

There is also a group camping area. Advance reservations are required to use it.

Picnic Facilities: Several designated picnic areas have tables, grills, shelters and playfields. At these picnic areas are several shelters (Wilson Shelter, North Orchard Shelter, Duneside Shelter and Tremont Shelter) which can be reserved for group outings.

Nature: In the park are numerous wildflowers and ground animals. Raccoons and deer are the most commonly observed animals. Waterfowl also are seen in the park. There are no facilities for fishing, such as a pier or a boat launching ramp at this park.

Nature Center: A nature center provides much information about the dunes, the historical development of the park, the wildlife and flowers in the region, and where you can learn about the relationship between the wetlands, the woods and the beach.

The geological history and development of the dunes is explained using a variety of displays. Film and naturalist presentations are conducted in the auditorium throughout the summer.

There is also a library for those wishing to find information and/or do extensive research relevant to the natural character of the region.

The park sponsors a program for children who can earn a patch. The youngster must complete several activities, such as reading and observation, to qualify for the state park patch. This program motivates children who come to the park.

Winter Activities: This part of northern Indiana receives large amounts of snow. As a result, cross-country skiing is popular. Several miles of trails are groomed within the park. The hills along the dunes provide an excellent challenge to the more experienced Nordic skier. Skis are available for rental at Wilson Shelter.

Sledding is another popular activity on the hills during the winter.

Indiana Dunes State Park
1600 North 25 East
Chesterton, IN 46304
(219) 926-4520

Leelanau State Park

Leelanau State Park, on the northern tip of the Leelanau Peninsula about 40 miles north of Traverse City, Michigan, consists of 1,300 acres and is divided into two sections. The northern section includes the beach, campground and the Grand Traverse Lighthouse. The southern section includes the trail system of the park. The two sections are about four miles apart. The word Leelanau is an Indian word which means "a land of delight."

Location: Leelanau State Park is reached by taking M-22 north from Traverse City to Northport. From Northport, it is an eight-mile drive to the park entrance. Follow the state park signs to the park.

The drive from Traverse City through the Leelanau Peninsula to the park is beautiful, particularly during May. The entire peninsula, including the hillsides overlooking Grand Traverse Bay, is covered with flowering cherry trees at this time of the spring.

Features of the Park: Leelanau State Park is in a forest at the far point of the Leelanau Peninsula. The park features the Grand Traverse

Lighthouse and a rustic campground on the shoreline where Lake Michigan and Grand Traverse Bay meet. Also, there are several miles of hiking trails in the park.

Shoreline: The shoreline at the tip of the park is rocky and stone-covered along with a lot of reeds which grow in the water. There is no sand along the shoreline. However, the view is beautiful. You can see water in nearly every direction.

The shoreline is not conducive for swimming at the northern section.

The Lake Michigan shoreline at the southern section of the park is wide and sandy with coastal dunes. Entrance to this beach is from the trail system. It is necessary to walk nearly a mile along the hiking trails to reach the beach.

Grand Traverse Lighthouse: The Grand Traverse Lighthouse, on the tip of the peninsula in Leelanau State Park, is one of the oldest lighthouses on the Great Lakes. The lighthouse, which is on the Manitou Shipping Passage, marks the entrance to Grand Traverse Bay. Today it is on the National Register of Historic Places.

The lighthouse was erected in 1858 by the United States Lighthouse Service. In 1899 a fog signal, which could be heard by vessels for many miles, was added to the lighthouse. In 1900 the facility was converted to a two-family dwelling and continued operating until 1972 when an automatic light tower system was erected. The lighthouse was then closed and in 1986 it was opened to the public as a museum. The lighthouse museum and grounds are operated by the Grand Traverse Lighthouse Foundation.

The lighthouse is open daily from mid-June until Labor Day. From Memorial Day through mid-June and after Labor Day through mid-October, it is open only on weekends. A gift shop is located in the old fog-signal building. It is open weekends from noon until 5 p.m. Also in this building is a display explaining how foghorns work with compressed air.

Camping: Fifty rustic campsites are in a beautiful site at the tip of the Leelanau Peninsula, on the water's edge in a heavily wooded area. Each campsite has a picnic table and a pit fireplace. There are no modern shower or toilet facilities, only pit toilets. Also, no water faucets are in the campground. You must get water from a pump in the picnic area. The campsites are not large, but provide excellent views of the water.

Most campsites are near the water. A number of the campsites (#31 - #39, #41 - #47) face the rocky, reed-covered shoreline, which is about 100 yards away. Most of the campsites in the 20s are on the water's

Leelanau State Park

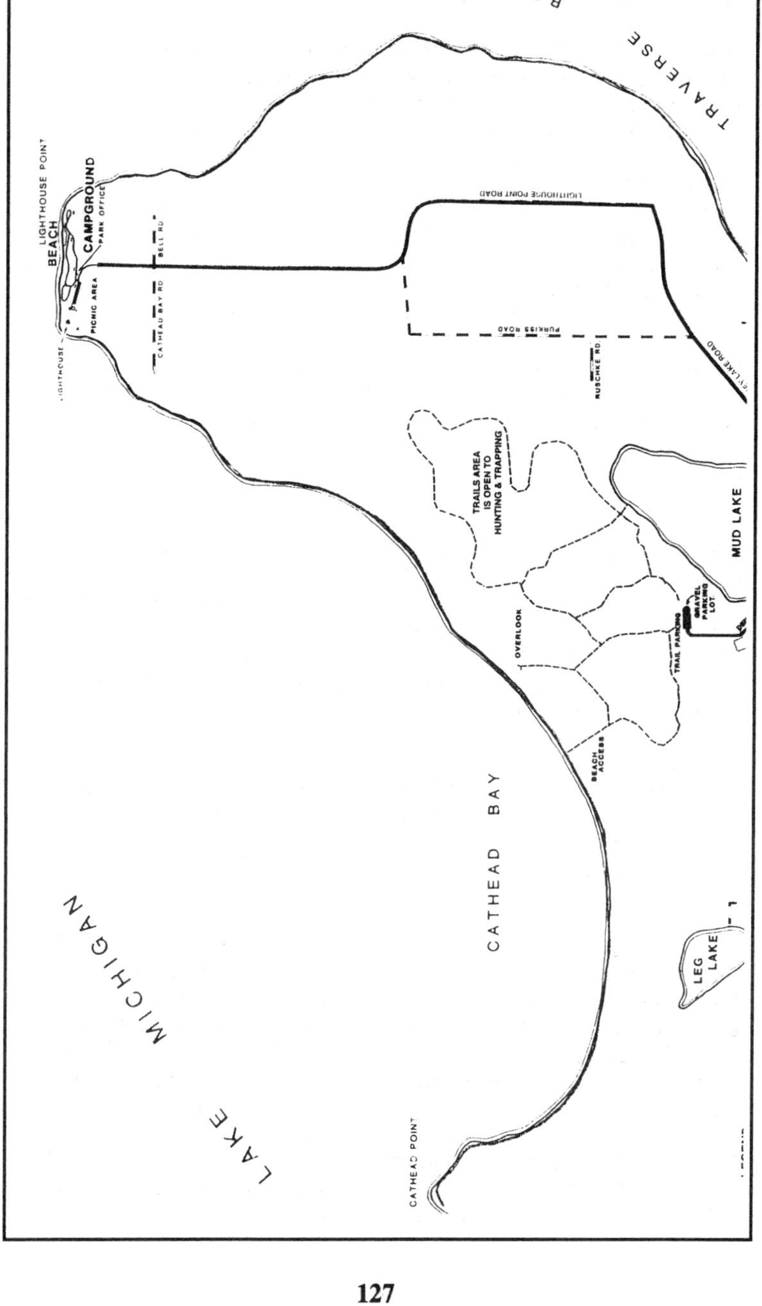

edge, on sand. The campsites are shaded by evergreen trees.

Also included in the campground are two rustic mini-cabins, each having room for four individuals. These mini-cabins have bunks and mattresses. There is also a small table inside and a picnic table and fire circle outside. Bedding, cooking and other necessities must be provided by people using the cabins. During much of the season, it is necessary to make advance reservations. There is a two-night minimum. The campground fills up on weekends from late June until Labor Day.

Picnic Facilities: A nice grass-covered picnic area, including a shelter and children's playground with slides, swings and climbing equipment, is located across the road from the park entrance. In this area are a number of picnic tables and grills. Several picnic tables are also near the lighthouse.

Trails: The hiking trails are in the southern section of the park. All of the trailheads originate at a gravel parking lot at the end of Densmore Road. This section of the park is between the Cathead Bay section of Lake Michigan and Mud Lake, a small lake along the southern boundary of the park.

There are seven miles of trails, all in a heavily wooded section of the park. The trails are relatively level, with a few small sand dune hills. They are very well marked. These trails are used for hiking as well as skiing in the winter. Bicycles are prohibited on the trails.

The two main trails are Mud Lake Trail (orange markers), which is 3.2 miles, and the Lake Michigan Trail (light blue markers), a 1.2-mile trail. Branching off of, and connecting, these two trails are several small (.1 to .2 mile) spurs. A section of Mud Lake Trail passes Mud Lake, where there is an observation dock. Leelanau State Park is on a migratory pathway for songbirds and hawks. Therefore, the area around Mud Lake is popular for observing birds of various species.

An overlook gives the hiker an excellent view of the Lake Michigan shoreline with its coastal sand dunes. This area of the park is open for hunting after Sept. 10.

Winter Activities: The southern trails are excellent for cross-country skiing. Densmore Road and the parking lot are plowed during the winter; however, there is no ski rental at the park.

Leelanau State Park
15310 N. Lighthouse Point Road
Northport, MI 49670
(616) 922-5270
(616) 386-5422 (summer)

Ludington State Park

Ludington State Park is a 5,202-acre park between Hamlin Lake on the east and Lake Michigan on the west. There are about 5.5 miles of Lake Michigan shoreline on its west boundary and four miles of Hamlin Lake shoreline on the east. The park stretches along Lake Michigan from the park entrance to its northern boundary at the Manistee National Forest at the Point Sable Lighthouse. The northern part of the park is an undeveloped section of wilderness dunes.

The park is one of the most popular in Michigan. There is something to do for people with any interest: hiking, fishing, bicycling, canoeing, camping, sunbathing, swimming, picnicking and just relaxing.

The park entrance is about four miles from the center of Ludington.

The roadway passes through the park for three miles, adjacent to the shoreline of the water. This is a most interesting drive. The water's edge is less than 300 feet from the road during much of this section. However, because of sand dunes and hills separating the road from the water, it is not possible to see the lake along much of the drive. In places the sand was blown across the road and you get the feeling of being in a desert.

There is a little grass coverage on the dunes.

Location: Ludington State Park is in Mason County, Michigan, seven miles north of Ludington on M-116, which ends at the park.

Features of the Park: The Lake Michigan shoreline and adjacent sand dunes and hills are principal features of this park. In addition, Hamlin Lake with its many possibilities for recreational activities provides another major feature.

Visitor Center: A visitor center is open from about Memorial Day to the middle of October. The Great Lakes Visitor Center is south of the Big Sable River among the dunes in a very picturesque setting. The walkways leading to the center are covered by large hardwood trees. In the center, there is a small auditorium where presentations are given during the summer. The center is open Saturdays and Sundays from 10 a.m. to 5 p.m. weekdays from 2 p.m. to 5 p.m.

Beach: The beach on Lake Michigan extends several miles along the shoreline. Visitors can enjoy the beach anywhere along the five plus miles of shoreline. The shoreline is comprised of beautiful soft sand as far as you can see and extends back several hundred yards from the water's edge. No lifeguards are provided along the beach.

There is a beachhouse with a concession facility (Ludington Park Cafe) near the parking lot near the Big Sable River at the park entrance. A commercial fast-food chain has the concessions at the cafe.

There is a small swimming beach on Hamlin Lake. At the beach is a bathhouse and concession building. Also, boats can be rented in this area.

Hamlin Lake: Hamlin Lake is the largest manmade lake in Michigan, comprising 4,490 acres and extending nearly 10 miles. The lake was created when a dam was built on the Sable River more than 100 years ago. This dam was built to create a lake on which logs could be floated to the mill for sawing. The lumber was then hauled by mule carts on a tramway to long piers on Lake Michigan, where it was loaded onto boats. The lumbering town of Hamlin was located here on the Big Sable River. In 1888, because of pressure from logs that filled Hamlin Lake, the dam broke and the waters washed the village into Lake

Michigan. Later, the dam was replaced and today regulates the water level of Hamlin Lake. Remains of the old mill can be seen at the dam site.

The Big Sable River flows from Hamlin Lake into Lake Michigan. A road from the toll booth extends along the river to the parking lot and beach on Hamlin Lake. Along this section of the park is a hard-surface bicycle path between the road and the river. Picnic tables are scattered along the road.

Point Sable Lighthouse: A picturesque feature in the park is the Point Sable Lighthouse, built in 1867. This facility can be reached only by hiking trail or a hard-packed sand road, which is not open to motorized vehicles. The road departs from the Pines Campground (between campsites #67 and #69) and goes 1.5 miles to the lighthouse. On the lake side of the road are sand dunes, and on the opposite are grass and forested dunes.

The lighthouse is listed in the National Register of Historical Places. It sits on the edge of the lakeshore. The Big Sable Point Lighthouse has been active since it was constructed and the light first illuminated in 1867. In 1968 the station became automated and is no longer manned. The lighthouse is not open to visitors except for three Saturdays during the season, one each in May, July and August from 10 a.m. to 4 p.m. Tours originate in downtown Ludington.

Camping: There are 398 campsites in three campgrounds. Reservations are necessary during the summer, since Ludington State Park is the most popular camping park in Michigan. You can make reservations for the following season starting Oct. 1.

The Beechwood Campground (campsites #250 - #405) is a wooded area near Lost Lake and Hamlin Lake. Picnic tables, circular fire pits and electrical outlets are available at each site, which are well spaced. However, there is no underbrush or ground foliage, so it is possible to see from one campsite to another. There is a modern shower and toilet facility in the park. Several campsites are on the edge of Lost Lake, a small body of water which is an extension of Hamlin Lake.

Stretching along Lost Lake the length of the campground is a wooden walkway. A short spur of the walkway goes to a small island. This provides an excellent place to walk, particularly for the disabled and senior citizens. There is a rustic cabin (campsite #400) in this campground.

Cedar Campground (campsites #130 - #240) is about halfway between Hamlin Lake and Lake Michigan, along two oblong roads. Sites on the interior of the circles are smaller and have less shade. Campsite 161 is a mini-cabin.

Ludington State Park

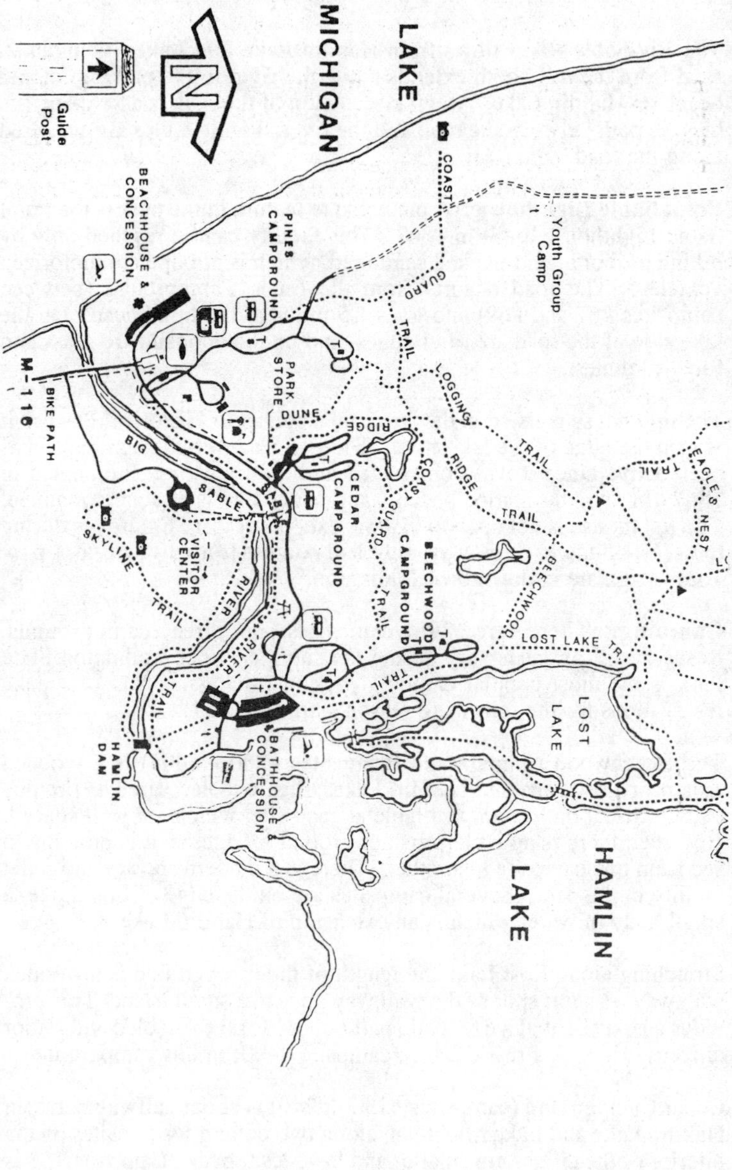

A children's playground with swing sets, slides and other apparatus can be found in the campground. A well-stocked park store at the entrance to the Cedar Campground is open during the summer from 9 a.m. to 9 p.m.

Pines Campground is separated from the Lake Michigan by sand dunes. One hundred and eleven campsites extend along two roads, with sites on each side. Every campsite has electricity, picnic table and circular fire pit. Generally, the campsites are open with grass and sand groundcover. Flush toilets and shower facilities are available. A rustic mini-cabin (campsite #1) is at the entrance to the park.

A group camping area along the sand road to the lighthouse is an open space in the middle of the dunes. Water and picnic tables are available in this camping area.

Trails: The park includes 18 miles of hiking trails. Eleven trails traverse the woods and dunes between Hamlin Lake and Lake Michigan. Along the various trails are four shelters which can be used for resting or having lunch or a snack. They are not available for overnight camping.

The longest trails are the Ridge Trail and the Logging Trail, each 2.7 miles. The Island Trail (1.6 miles) follows the shoreline of Hamlin Lake. The Sable River Trail (1.6 miles) runs along the Big Sable River. The Coast Guard Trail (1 mile) end at a scenic lookout on Lake Michigan and the beach. Lighthouse Trail (1 mile) takes the hiker across dunes to the Point Sable Lighthouse. Other trails include the Dune Trail (.7 mile), Lost Lake Trail (1.3 miles) and Eagle's Nest Trail (.6 mile).

A short but scenic trail is the half-mile Skyline Trail. Three stairways, one at each end of the walk and the other at the visitors center, bring hikers to the boardwalk trail. This trail goes along the ridge above the visitor center south of the Big Sable River. There are 13 marked points of interest along the trail. Several of these are spectacular vistas looking out across the dunes. Lake Michigan can be seen from various points along the trail, as can the Big Sable River.

A one-mile hard-surface bicycle path runs along the Big Sable River from Hamlin Lake to Lake Michigan, then extends south along the highway, coming into the park from the south. The bicycle trail connects the three campgrounds with the park headquarters. Along the pathway, you can see a variety of waterfowl in the river, numerous picnic tables and sitting benches. A spur of the bicycle trail crosses the river to the visitors center.

Bicyclists are not permitted on any hiking trails, but may travel on the dirt road leading from the Pines Campground to the Point Sable

Lighthouse. Also, bicycles can be ridden along the entrance road along the Lake Michigan shoreline into the park.

A unique trail in the park is the Ludington State Park Canoe Pathway. Canoes can be rented at the Hamlin Lake concession facility near the swimming beach. The trail is a loop that extends along the shore of Hamlin Lake and goes through several ponds. There are canoe trail markers along the way to tell canoeists where to go. There are a couple of places where it is necessary to portage a short distance.

An informative brochure provides detailed information on where the trail goes and what you are likely to see along the way. The brochure recommends that the time required to make the entire loop trail is one to three hours, depending upon the skill level of the canoers and the interest they have in taking in the surrounding scenery.

Fishing: Fishing is popular at several places in Ludington State Park. Along the shoreline of Lake Michigan, many people fish for salmon and trout. Fishing in Hamlin Lake is particularly good for muskellunge, northern pike and bass. Also, fishing is excellent along the Big Sable River. A fishing pier is about a quarter-mile from Beechwood Campground.

A one-ramp boat launch with adjoining parking lot for motor vehicles and trailers is located on Hamlin Lake. Next to the boat ramp is a handicapped accessible fishing site.

Picnic Facilities: Throughout the park are picnic tables for day use. Along the road by the Big Sable River are many tables in a beautiful wooded area. A large picnic area with tables and grills also is at the beach on Hamlin Lake.

Winter Activities: Ludington State Park is open year-round. During the winter, cross-country skiing and ice fishing are particularly popular. There are four cross-country ski trails constituting a total of 16 miles, with loops ranging from the shortest, River Loop of 1.5 miles, to the longest, the Jack Pine Loop, a four-mile trail. All of the ski trails are south of the Big Sable River.

The trails originate from the visitors center. Snowmobiles are not permitted in the park. Camping, including electricity, is available in the winter. Pit toilets and water are available at the park office for winter campers.

Ludington State Park
P.O. Box 709
Ludington, MI 49431
(616) 843-8671

Charles Mears State Park

One of the smallest state parks on the eastern shore of Lake Michigan, only 50 acres, is Charles Mears State Park. The park is named after Charles Mears, the father of Carrie Mears, who donated the land in 1920 that is today the state park.

Location: Charles Mears State Park is on Business Route U.S. 31 north of Pentwater, Michigan, in Oceana County. From U.S. 31, exit at mile marker 159 and proceed to Pentwater.

Features of the Park: This is a camping park with 179 sites on asphalt, having the appearance of a large parking lot. The campsites are about 10 feet wide and are very close to each other. They are just large enough for a recreational vehicle.

Each campsite has a picnic table, a circular fire pit and an electrical outlet. A few trees are planted throughout the campground; otherwise, there is no vegetation. It is possible to see throughout the entire park from about any place in the campground. None of the campsites are within sight of the lake because there is a ridge of sand dunes between the campground and the lake. There are modern flush toilet and hot shower facilities. The campground is extremely popular and is usually filled during much of the summer, from late June to Labor Day.

Beach: The beach extends for less than a half-mile. It is a very wide beach, extending back from the shoreline up to 500 yards, providing plenty of space for beach and water activities. The sand is very beautiful and soft. Along the beach are a number of permanent benches. On the beach is a bathhouse with a concessions store which is open during the summer. It is just a short walk of a few hundred yards from the beach to the camping sites.

Next to the beach is a large parking area, which is full by late morning on many summer weekends and holidays. Often at these times, visitors must park in town and walk to the park.

Looking beyond the park boundary, the shoreline appears somewhat like a wilderness. There are no developments, houses or other buildings as you look up the shore. You can do a great amount of walking along the water's edge beyond the park.

Picnic Facilities: Several picnic tables are scattered throughout the park.

Trails: A half-mile trail starting at the east of the campground goes to the top of a sand dune called Old Baldy. From the top of this dune, you can get a good view of the lake and of the town of Pentwater.

This is not a park for bicyclists. Even on the cement sidewalk leading to the campground from the beach is a "no bicycling" symbol.

Fishing: On the south edge of the park, is a channel with a pier from which visitors can fish. Perch and bass fishing is often good during the summer. In late fall, surf fishing from the beach for salmon and steelhead trout attracts many anglers.

Winter Activities: There is little winter activity at Charles Mears State Park. The campground is open; however, there is no electricity nor bathroom facilities available. Ice fishing brings a few visitors. There are no groomed cross-country ski trails in the park.

Charles Mears State Park
P.O. Box 370
W. Lowell St.
Pentwater, MI 49449
(616) 869-2051

Muskegon State Park

Muskegon State Park, comprised of 1,165 acres, is on a peninsula between Lake Michigan and Muskegon Lake. It was established as a Michigan state park in 1923. Connecting the two lakes is a ship channel, which is the south boundary of the park. This park has a variety of activities to offer the visitor.

Location: Muskegon State Park is in Muskegon County, just north of Muskegon, Michigan. The park is reached by taking U.S. 31 to Holton Road (M-120). Take Holton Road west about eight miles to the park entrance.

Features of the Park: Muskegon State Park features the beach along Lake Michigan, the day-use area on Muskegon Lake, and winter sports, particularly cross-country ski trails and the luge run.

Beach: The beach extends along the Lake Michigan shoreline for 2.9 miles. From the middle through the northern part of the park, the beach is not particularly wide, extending from the water's edge only 10 to 20 feet in places and averages 25 feet from the shoreline. Behind the beach, the dunes with grass and trees extend as far as 500 feet.

In the southern part of the park, the beach is wider and better for sunbathing, swimming and beach activities. There is a large concession stand open during the summer on the beach. A lot with 564 parking spaces is near the beach. In places small trees grow on the dunes.

In addition to the beach along the Lake Michigan shoreline, there are 2.1 miles of shoreline on inland lakes in the park.

Picnic Facilities: A day-use area with picnic facilities is just inside the park entrance on Snug Harbor, a body of water that is part of Muskegon Lake. This area is well-shaded and grass covered. Two picnic shelters can be reserved; numerous tables, grills and a playground are at this location.

Boat Launch: At one end of the day-use picnic area is a boat launch with two ramps. Here visitors can launch boats into Muskegon Lake. There are 29 parking spaces at the Snug Harbor boat launch for vehicles with boat trailers.

A second boat launch is near the Channel Campground on Muskegon Lake.

Ship Channel: Connecting Muskegon Lake and Lake Michigan, forming the southern boundary of the park, is a ship channel. Along this channel is a 4,000-foot sidewalk. Many people enjoy sightseeing along the walkway as boats pass through the channel during the summer. Fishing is popular from the walkway. The day of my visit, there were people fishing for trout.

Camping: There are three campgrounds in Muskegon State Park. The Channel Campground, with 147 campsites, is along the navigation channel and on Muskegon Lake. There is a blacktop pad, picnic table, grill and electricity at each campsite. The campground is quite sandy with some shade scattered throughout. Also, a fish cleaning building is in the campground.

The Lake Michigan campground, having 178 campsites, is in the north section of the park. This is a shaded campground with each site having an electrical outlet, table and grill. Because the sites are sandy it is difficult to anchor a tent. One section backs up to a large grass-covered, tree-shaded dune. People are asked not to walk on the dune, as part of erosion control. Just over the dune is Lake Michigan. It is not possible to see Lake Michigan from this campground.

The campground is between the large sand dune and Scenic Drive running into the park from the north entrance. Many campsites are small and close together. At one section, several sites back up directly to the

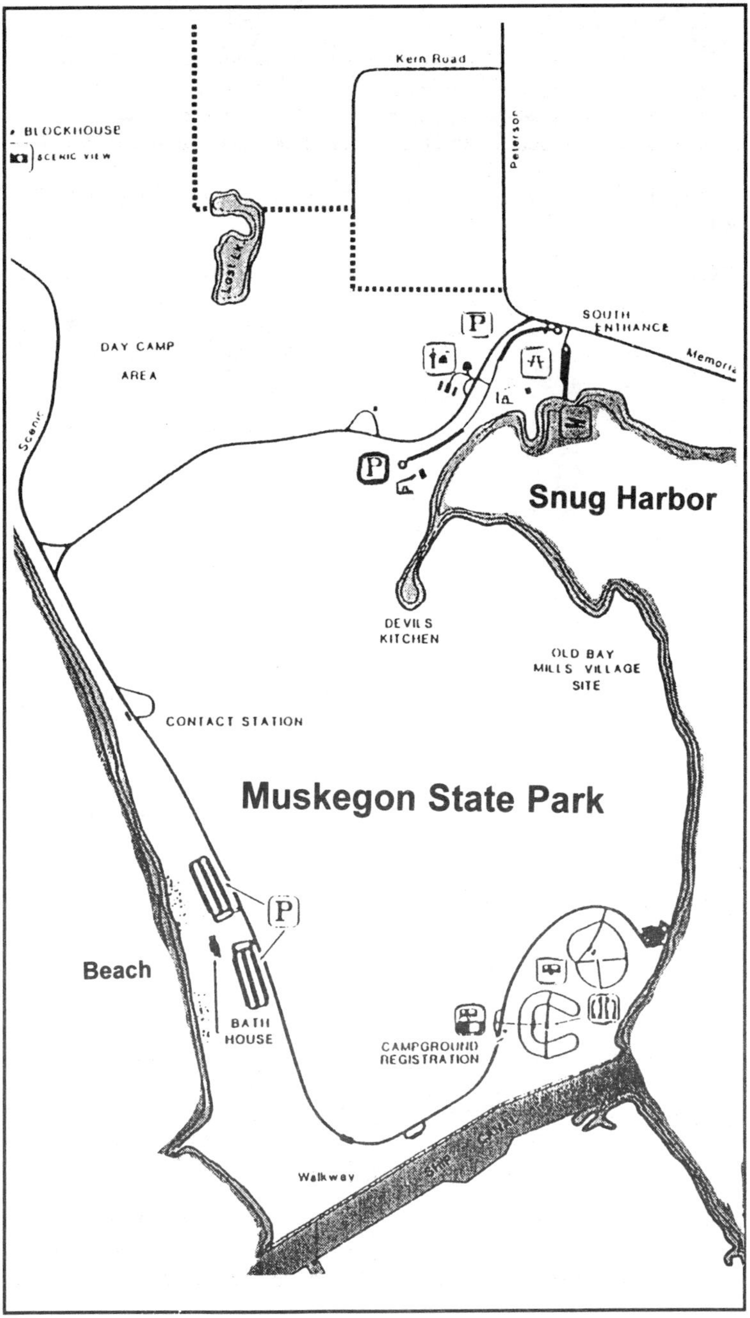

BLOCKHOUSE
SCENIC VIEW
Kern Road
Peterson
Lost Lk.
SOUTH ENTRANCE
Memorial
DAY CAMP AREA
Scenic
Snug Harbor
DEVILS KITCHEN
OLD BAY MILLS VILLAGE SITE
CONTACT STATION
Muskegon State Park
Beach
BATH HOUSE
CAMPGROUND REGISTRATION
Walkway

park boundary. On the edge of the campground just outside the park, is a commercial ice cream stand.

There are modern bath and shower facilities in the campground, along with two rustic cabins that can accommodate four persons each.

There is a 52-site campground across from the Lake Michigan Campground. This campground is open year-round. During the summer it has flush toilets and central water supply, but no electricity. This campground is used in the winter by people coming to the park for cross-country skiing and luging. Access to the lighted ski trails originate from this campground.

Also, a youth campground can accommodate up to 100 individuals. This facility is available by reservation only. It is used by school groups, church groups, scouts and other youth organizations.

Blockhouse: A scenic blockhouse is situated along Scenic Drive which runs from the north park entrance along the Lake Michigan shoreline. The building was completed in 1935 by the Civilian Conservation Corps. It was destroyed in 1962 by fire and rebuilt in 1964. The blockhouse has the appearance of old colony forts located throughout the Great Lakes built 200 to 300 years ago. This building has been built to serve as a scenic overlook. From the blockhouse you can look out through small windows in all four directions and see the surrounding terrain, which is spectacular in the fall when trees are in fall colors.

Trails: Six hiking trails with a total of 12 miles traverse the dunes and go through woods. All of the trails except one, the Loop to Loop Trail, are one to two miles in length. They all have color-coded markings. Motorized vehicles and bicycles are prohibited on the hiking trails. The Devil's Kitchen Trail is a one-mile trail which goes from the boat launching ramp on Muskegon Lake in the Channel Campground to the parking facility on Snug Harbor. This trail traverses along dunes and marshlands, providing a nice view of Muskegon Lake.

The longest trail is the Loop to Loop Trail, a distance of five miles. This trail begins at the blockhouse parking lot and passes the luge run. Portions of the trail are lighted in the winter for cross-country skiing.

The Dune Ridge Trail is a 1.75-mile trail which passes through both wooded and open dunes. It is possible to see Lake Michigan, Muskegon Lake, the Channel and several ponds along this interesting trail. Several locations along this hike are designated as scenic spots where it is possible to get excellent views of the surrounding territory. There is also a short hiking trail from the Snug Harbor parking lot that goes to Lost Lake, less than a mile. This is a small lake near the park boundary east of the youth camping area.

Winter Activities: A unique feature of Muskegon State Park is the availability of winter sports facilities. Directly across from the Lake Michigan Campground next to the East Campground is the Sports Lodge.

This facility was built by the volunteer non-profit corporation, the Muskegon Sports Council. During the summer the facility is managed by the state park and rented for business meetings, receptions and reunions. In the winter the lodge is operated by the Sports Council as a place where visitors coming to cross-country ski and luge can relax. There are five miles of lighted cross-country ski trails. These ski trails were established as a project of the Sports Council. Cross-country ski rental facilities are provided at the lodge.

A luge run was built with community support in the 1980s. This luge run is one of only four in the United States. The luge is operational starting in early January for as long as winter weather permits. Throughout January and February, a variety of luge competitions are held at the park.

Muskegon State Park
3560 Memorial Drive
North Muskegon, MI 49445
(616) 744-3480

Orchard Beach State Park

Orchard Beach State Park is a 201-acre park that was a farm during the late 1800s. At one time an apple orchard dominated this area. During the first part of the 20th century, the property was sold and the land became a popular park until about the time of World War I. In 1921 the property was given to the state for use as a park.

Location: Orchard Beach State Park is about two miles north of Manistee, Michigan, on M-110. The park campground, beach and day-use area are between M-110 and Lake Michigan. East of the highway is the wooded trail section.

Features of the Park: This park features a picnic area and a campground with a beach backed up by high bluffs overlooking Lake Michigan. The bluffs rise about 100 feet or more from a small sand beach.

Camping: The campground has 176 sites on three parallel drives. The campground is grass-covered with hardwood trees providing adequate shade. However, there are no shrubs or foliage separating the campsites. It is possible to stand at the entrance booth and see throughout the campground.

Each campsite has a hard-surface pad, picnic table, circular fire pit grill and provision for electrical hook-up. Overlooking the bluff on the lakeside of the campground is a large stone shelterhouse. This facility can accommodate up to 200 people and can be reserved at the park office.

It is not possible to see the lake from most of the campsites. On the far end of the campground are a half-dozen sites overlooking the bluffs, having a view of the lake. Five of these campsites (#49, #50, #51, #53 and #54) sit between the campground road and the bluff and back up directly to the bluff. These sites provide a spectacular view of the lake. Also, directly on the bluff at the south end of the campground is a mini rustic cabin.

Between the edge of the bluffs and the road running through the campground is a large grassy area for walking, playing and enjoying various activities.

A playground for children and a fish cleaning house are in the campground.

Though there are no boat ramps into Lake Michigan in the park, many people go to the nearby town of Manistee to put their boats in or to charter fishing boats.

The last row of campsites on the east side of the park backs up directly to M-110, separated only by a chain fence. There is no foliage separating the campsite from the traffic along the highway. The campground has modern toilet and shower facilities.

Beach: The only walkway to the beach is down steep stairs south of the shelterhouse. Otherwise, along the edge of the bluffs are signs and a wooden fence warning visitors to stay away from the steep bluff dropoffs.

The beach runs the length of the park, about a half-mile.

Picnic Facilities: At the north end of the park is a picnicking area with tables, grills a four-posted open shelter and, play equipment for children. At the north end of the day-use area is a softball field.

As the name of the park implies, this area was once an orchard. Today, scattered through the day-use area, as well as in places in the campground, apple trees still stand.

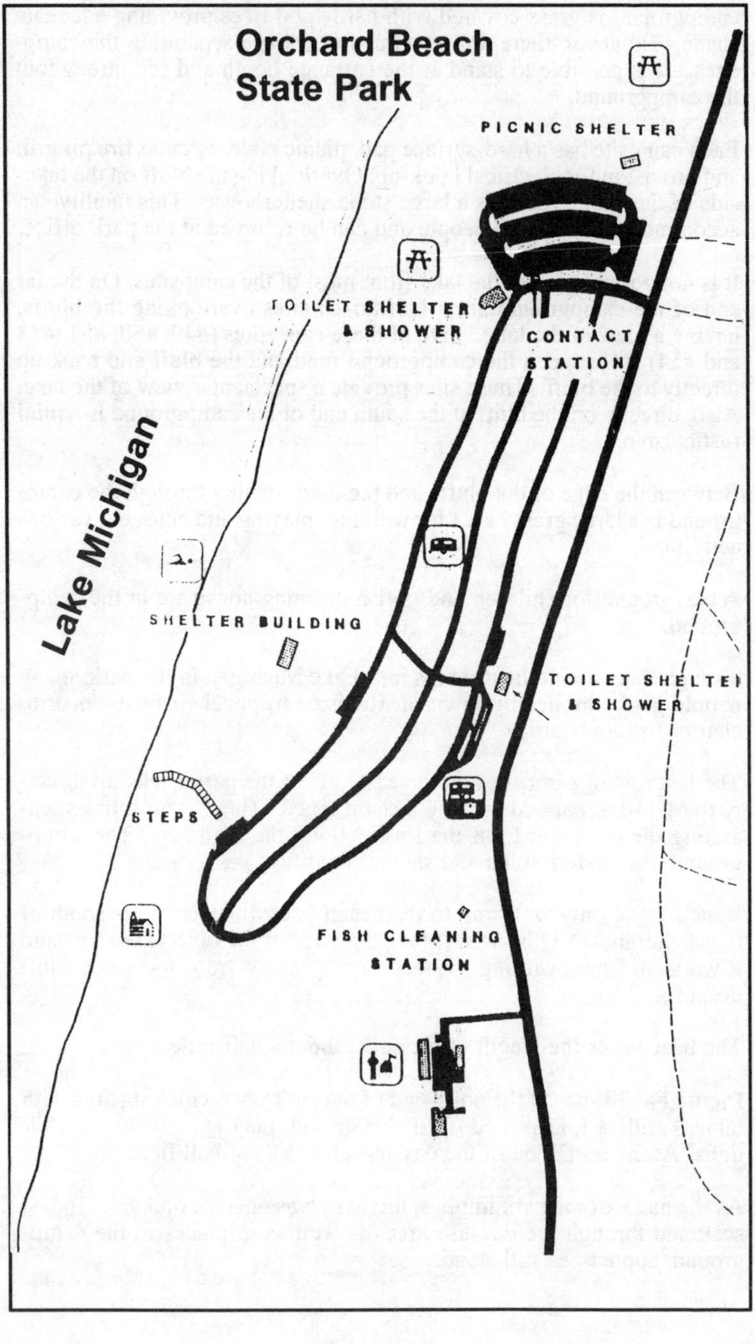
Orchard Beach State Park
PICNIC SHELTER
TOILET SHELTER & SHOWER
CONTACT STATION
Lake Michigan
SHELTER BUILDING
TOILET SHELTER & SHOWER
STEPS
FISH CLEANING STATION

Trails: Directly across M-110 from the park entrance is a trailhead for the only hiking trail in the park. This trail is a half-mile self-guided nature trail. The loop has numbered stations through the woods that connect with two miles of hiking trails.

These trails are not identified by name or color marking, except that at intersections a map indicates the direction of the trail.

Winter Activities: During the winter there are about three miles of cross-country ski trails that extend from the nature trail. The trails are relatively level. There is no facility for ski rental nor warming shelter at this park. Snowmobiling is prohibited in the park.

The campground is closed during the winter and there are no winterized facilities in the park. The park is not plowed.

Orchard Beach State Park
2064 Lakeshore Road
Manistee, MI 49660
(616) 723-7422

Petoskey State Park

Petoskey State Park, on the north end of Little Traverse Bay, consists of 304 acres along 1.25 miles of bay shoreline.

The park was established as a state park in 1970 after serving as a Petoskey city beach for at least 30 years.

Location: Petoskey State Park is on M-119 in Emmett County, Michigan, half-way between Harbor Springs and Petoskey.

Features of the Park: The park includes the sandy beach and shoreline, dunes and Little Traverse Bay.

Camping: In Petoskey State Park are 170 campsites at two campgrounds. The largest is the Tannery Creek Campground in the southern section of the park, where there are 100 modern sites with electric hook-ups and a modern shower and toilet facility. Each campsite has a paved, hard-surfaced pad, convenient for trailers and recreational vehicles. There are a picnic table and in-ground grill at each site. The campsites are on four semi-circular roads, with little distance between them. At the end of each semi-circle is a wooden walkway through the sand dunes, connecting the beach and campground.

The beach has fine pebbles and stones in places, and a ridgeline of sand with fine grass and small trees on top. The ridgeline is about 25 feet tall. Then there is a valley of sand and grass, then another ridgeline of sand dune covered with larger trees and the beginning of the woods.

Two rustic cabins (campsites #164 and #168) are available for rental. Also, several campsites are reserved for people with disabilities.

There are 70 campsites at the Dunes Campground, which is close to the park entrance and beach house. There are two circles, each with 35 campsites.

This is a well-shaded campground. The distance between most campsites is good, with ground brush and trees separating them. Each campsite has a picnic table and in-ground fire pit grill. A hot shower and bath facility is in the middle of the campground. There are electric hook-ups at this campground. The sites are not paved. Several of the campsites back up to a large sand dune. Sites #58, #60, #62 and #64 are rather small.

Facilities for group camping are just inside the park entrance. The area includes a cement block shelter with a tin roof and two vault toilets. Also, several picnic tables and grills are in the surrounding area.

Petoskey State Park is popular, so reservations for camping are necessary from mid-June until the end of the summer.

Trails: There are two trails in the park: Old Baldy Trail and Portage Trail. The trail up Old Baldy is steep.

The old Blady trailhead is across the road from the Dunes Campground registration booth. The start of the trail up Old Baldy is a series of steps. Then the trail proceeds along a ridge line with a drop-off on either side. Further along the trail is another set of 102 steps to the top of Old Baldy. The top of Old Baldy is a flat sandy area surrounded by trees. There are no resting benches or lookouts.

It took me about 10 minutes to climb to the top. The return trail follows a different ridgeline. It is steeper and a little more difficult to walk than the trail coming up.

The Portage Trail crosses the road from the Dunes Campground and winds through woods to restroom facilities at the Tannery Creek Campground. This trail is about 1.5 miles round trip. The trail is relatively flat and quite sandy. It is not a difficult trail to walk. Bicycles are not permitted on the trails of Petoskey State Park.

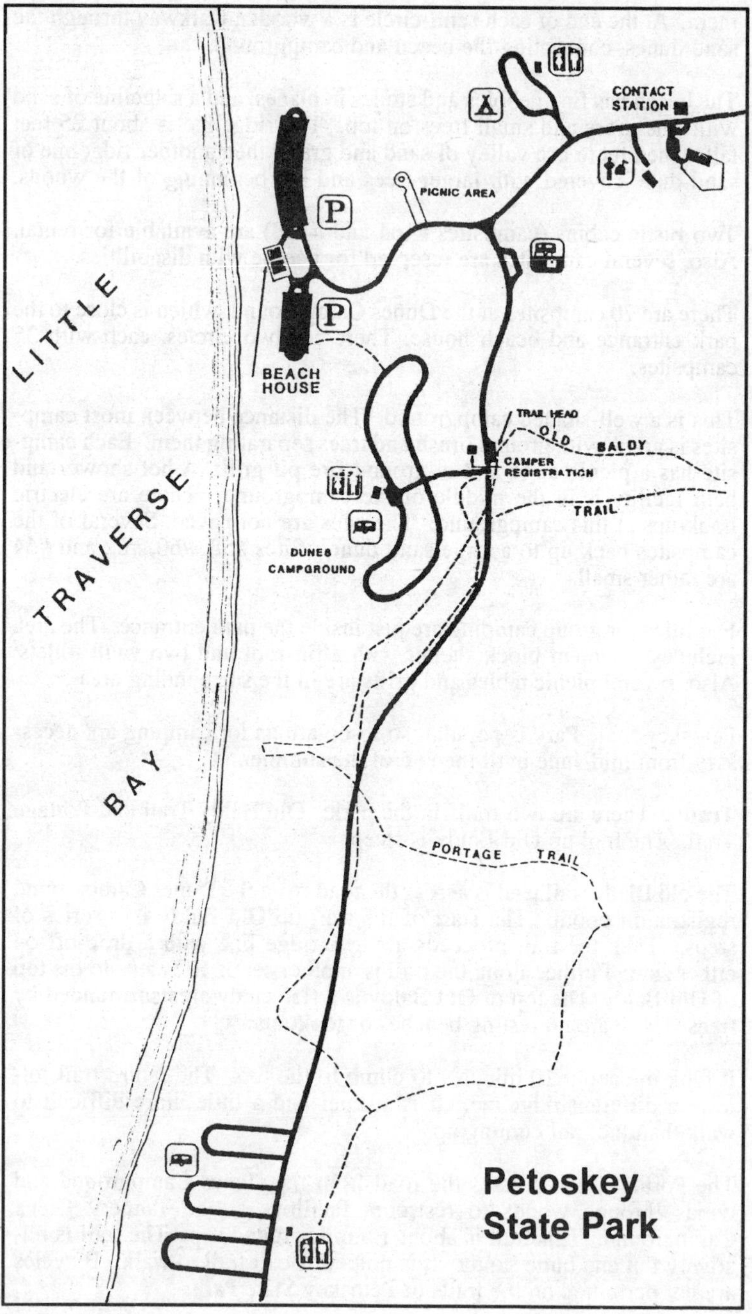

CONTACT STATION
PICNIC AREA
P
P
BEACH HOUSE
LITTLE
TRAVERSE
BAY
TRAIL HEAD
OLD
BALDY
TRAIL
CAMPER REGISTRATION
DUNES CAMPGROUND
PORTAGE TRAIL
Petoskey
State Park

Beach: The road extending from the park entrance to the beach has tall sand dunes on either side. There is a large parking lot near a beach house with changing facilities. No concessions are available.

The beach is typical of those along the eastern shoreline of Lake Michigan—nice, scenic, with clean sand stretching in both directions from the beach house. Behind the beach are high sand dunes, rising 50 to 70 feet. The sand dunes are covered with grass, small trees and brush. These provide opportunity for walking and climbing along the dunes. There are no lifeguards at this beach.

There is a volleyball net on the beach.

Boating: There are no boat launches at the park, although several launch facilities on Little Traverse Bay are available in both Harbor Springs and Petoskey. A short distance from the park are many inland lakes, also with boat launch facilities.

Picnic Facilities: About a quarter-mile from the beach is a small picnic area with about a dozen tables and several grills. Most of the tables are spread out among trees. The picnic area is separated from the beach by tall sand dunes.

Winter Activities: There is no winter activity at Petoskey State Park, since there is too much competition from surrounding commercial ski centers. Throughout this area are hundreds of miles of groomed cross-country ski trails and some of the best downhill skiing in the Midwest.

The park closes in the fall and reopens in May.

Petoskey State Park
2475 M-119
Petoskey, MI 49770
(616) 347-2311

Saugatuck Dunes State Park

Saugatuck Dunes State Park is an 866-acre day-use only facility. There are no camping nor concession facilities in the park. It is located between Holland and the resort town of Saugatuck, Michigan.

A series of trails lead to the lake.

Location: Saugatuck Dunes State Park is reached by leaving I-96 at exit 41 south of Holland, and traveling west on Blue Star Highway to 64th Street. Take 64th Street about two miles to 138th Avenue, turn west and proceed to the park entrance.

Features of the Park: The park features the two-mile-long beach which can be reached only by walking in at least one mile along an extensive hiking trail system. This isolation of the beach makes for a less congested beach during the busy summer season. Once you get there, this park provides a spectacular place to enjoy all of the activities associated with a Lake Michigan beach.

At the park entrance are an open picnic shelter, several picnic tables, grills, and pit toilets.

Trails: There are four hiking trails with a combined distance of about 13 miles. The trailheads all begin at the parking lot. The longest is the South Trail (blue markers), a loop of 5.5 miles. In the center of the park are two trails, the Livingston Trail (red markers) and Beach Trail (yellow markers). Each of these is 2.5 miles and served by connecting trails. The North Trail (white markers) is another 2.5-mile trail, which ends at the lakefront.

We hiked the North Trail. This trail winds in among the dunes. A climax forest with a variety of evergreens and hardwoods is situated on these dunes. At places the trail is hard-packed and easy to walk; other places, the trail is sandy and footing is more difficult. The closer to the lake and beach, the more the trail becomes sand. Part of this trail passes through a pine forest. The trail ground is covered by needles from these trees. This is a scenic and enjoyable walk.

At several points the trail was not well-marked.

Beach: Behind the beach, the dunes rise 100 feet or more in a series of hills. The sandy beach extends 25 to 50 yards from the water back to grass. The beach is very sandy with clear water and soft, fine sand.

As you look to the south along the beach, there is no sign of development: buildings, factories and so forth. It makes you believe you are in a wilderness. All you see are tree-covered and grass-covered dunes, making for a very scenic view.

There are no changing facilities or lifeguards at the beach.

Winter Activities: Saugatuck Dunes is an excellent park for cross-country skiing. The trails are rolling enough to challenge the Nordic skier. The South Trail is the flattest and best for the novice skier. The trails are groomed; however, there are no ski rentals or warming shelter. Snowmobiling is not permitted in the park.

Saugatuck Dunes State Park
Ottawa Beach Road
Holland, MI 49424
(616) 399-9390

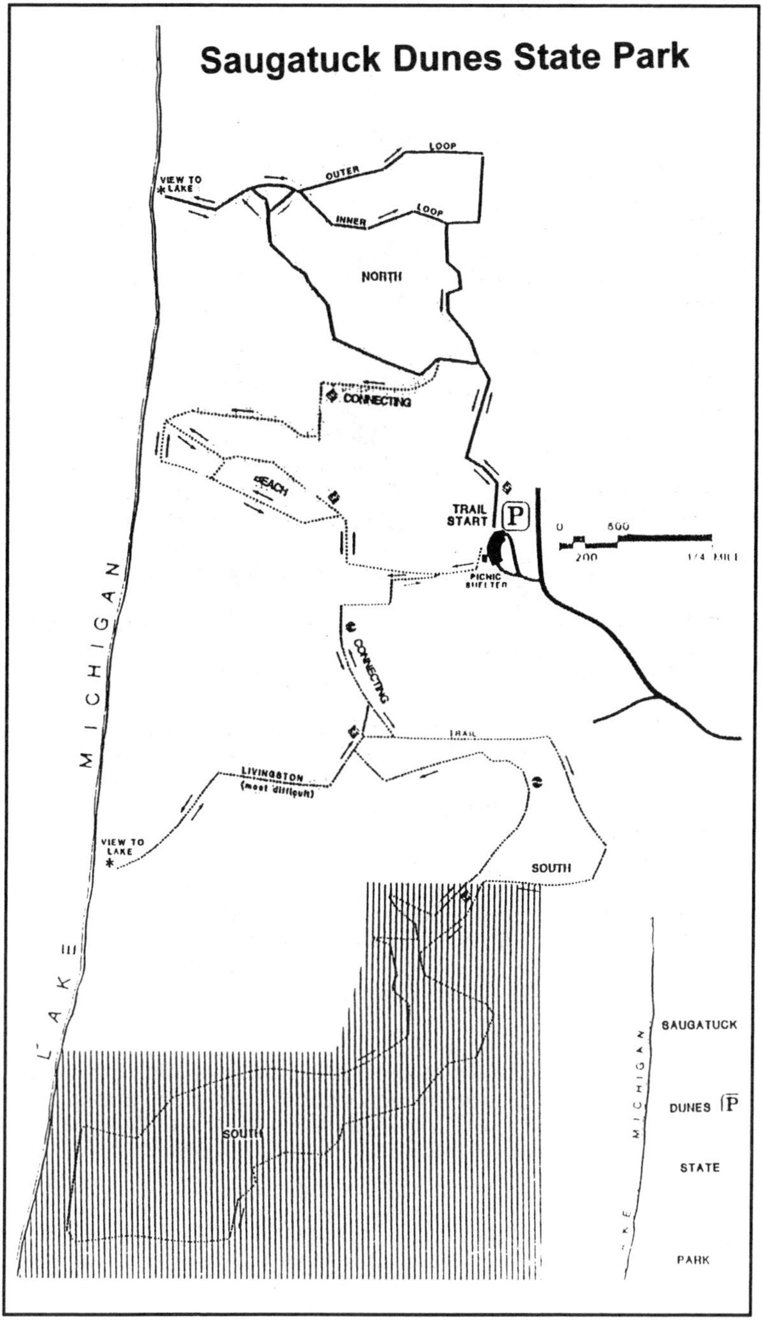
Saugatuck Dunes State Park
VIEW TO LAKE
OUTER
LOOP
INNER
LOOP
NORTH
CONNECTING
BEACH
TRAIL START
P
0
600
200
1/4 MILE
PICNIC SHELTER
CONNECTING
TRAIL
LIVINGSTON (most difficult)
VIEW TO LAKE
SOUTH
SOUTH
LAKE MICHIGAN
SAUGATUCK
DUNES
STATE
PARK

Silver Lake State Park

Silver Lake State Park encompasses 2,860 acre in Oceana County, Michigan, between Lake Michigan and Silver Lake.

Location: To visit Silver Lake, leave U.S. 31 at the Shelby Road exit and go west for 6.5 miles to Scenic Drive (County Road B-15). Turn north on Scenic Drive for about two miles, where the huge barren sand dunes of Silver Lake State Park become visible. The campground entrance is another 2.5 miles on Scenic Drive.

Features of the Park: Silver Lake features high dunes with no vegetation of any kind for about 3.5 miles along the Lake Michigan shoreline. The park includes a beach near the Little Point Sable Lighthouse, spectacular, desert-like, barren sand dunes between Lake Michigan and Silver Lake, and a unique area designated for off-road vehicles on the sand dunes.

Little Point Sable Lighthouse: To reach the beach near the Little Point Sable Lighthouse, drive a narrow, winding road leading past a number of private cottages in a heavily wooded area. The road ends

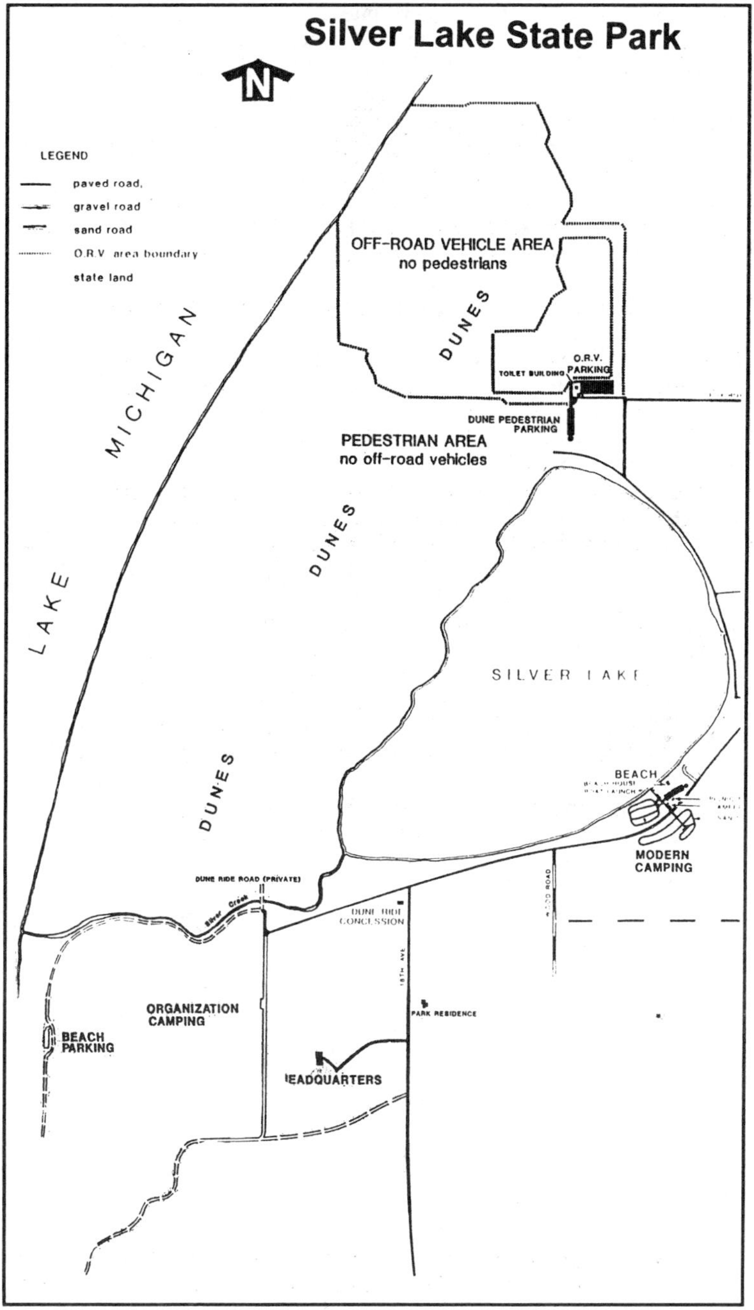
Silver Lake State Park
N
LEGEND
paved road,
gravel road
sand road
O.R.V. area boundary
state land
LAKE MICHIGAN
OFF-ROAD VEHICLE AREA
no pedestrians
DUNES
TOILET BUILDING
O.R.V. PARKING
DUNE PEDESTRIAN PARKING
PEDESTRIAN AREA
no off-road vehicles
DUNES
SILVER LAKE
BEACH
MODERN CAMPING
DUNES
DUNE RIDE ROAD (PRIVATE)
Silver Creek
DUNE RIDE CONCESSION
18TH AVE
ORGANIZATION CAMPING
BEACH PARKING
PARK RESIDENCE
HEADQUARTERS

near the lighthouse. The picturesque 107-foot-high lighthouse, was built in 1878, on the edge of the sand dunes. The beach at this spot is quite wide, stretching back to the parking lot. The sand is fine, clean and soft. Behind the beach are several small grass-covered dunes rising 40 to 50 feet. When we visited this beach, it was quite desolate and had only a half-dozen visitors. There are no lifeguards at this beach.

The Dunes: In the central part of the park are several miles of tall, barren sand dunes. Walking these dunes feels like walking across a desert. There is no vegetation - trees, shrubs, brush or grass. Eventually you come to the Lake Michigan shoreline, with almost endless sandy beach. The beach can be reached only by walking over and along the sand dunes. From the Dunes Pedestrian Parking Area off of Fox Road, walk over the sand dunes, at least one mile, before reaching the Lake Michigan shoreline.

Off-Road Vehicle Area: In the north section of Silver Lake State Park is an area that is open from April 1 through the end of October, set aside for the use of off-road-vehicles. There is a large parking area for vehicles pulling the ORVs. You must have a valid off-road vehicle permit before entering the area. A page of rules is provided to assure safety for riders and protection of dunes. Helmets and safety harness straps are mandatory. Also, one-way traffic on the dunes is required. The ORV area is open from 8 a.m. to 10 p.m., unless otherwise posted. Pedestrians are not permitted to enter this area.

Camping: The park campground, with 249 sites, is on the east side of Silver Lake. The campground is somewhat shaded, with each site having a picnic table and fire pit. The campground also has a picnic shelter and boat launch. A small beach is on Silver Lake near the campground. Surrounding the campground is a commercial area with stores, houses, cabins and private campgrounds. A group campground is available in the south section of the park.

Commercial Dune Buggy: Located near the boundary of the park is a commercial dune buggy company, which operates in certain areas of Silver Lake State Park. Visitors can take a seven-mile ride on the dunes in an open buggy that seats up to 20 individuals. The driver explains the history, environment and other features of the dunes as you travel over the dunes. The trip passes Silver Lake, provides many spectacular views from the top of the dunes, and also stops to permit visitors to wade in the waters of Lake Michigan.

Silver Lake State Park
9679 W. State Park Road
Mears, MI 49436
(616) 873-3083

Traverse City State Park

Traverse City State Park is situated on Grand Traverse Bay, two miles from the center of Traverse City, Michigan. The small park consists of 45 acres that is mainly the park campground. The park is surrounded by all kinds of development: upscale restaurants and resorts, inns, beach condominiums and motels. Within a mile of the campground are many commercial fast-food restaurants. The result is a very urbanized state park.

U.S. 31 bisects the park. On the north side of the highway are the beach and day-use picnic area. On the opposite side is the 342-site campground.

A walkway bridge over U.S. 31 connects the beach with the campground. The highway is so heavily traveled that during the summer, turning left out of the campground or the beach area is almost impossible.

Features of the Park: The park features the campground. Because Traverse City is the main community of a widespread resort region, people come to camp and then visit the many surrounding areas of interest.

The Shoreline: Along the shoreline are parking facilities and a small beach of about .3-mile. The sand extends 25 to 30 yards from the water's edge. A few picnic tables are along the beach in this area; however, there are no extended picnic facilities in the park.

The view from the beach looking out onto Grand Traverse Bay is very enjoyable and relaxing.

The Campground: The campground is not within sight of the lake. It is across the busy highway.

The campground includes modern hot shower and flush toilet facilities. It is well shaded. The campsites are small and close to each other. Each site has a picnic table and in-ground fire pit.

Sites #35 to #45 along the backside of the campground are adjacent to a railroad line. Several sites (odd numbers in the 70s and 80s) back-up to U.S. 31.

Two rustic cabins are near the campground entrance. A children's playground features swings, slides and climbing apparatus. A camp store is across the street from the campground.

The walkway bridge is at campsite #100.

There is an organizational campground area within the park.

Winter Activities: The campground is open year-round. This area of Michigan receives heavy snowfall; as a result, cross-country skiing and downhill skiing at several popular commercial resorts attract many people to this region.

Traverse City State Park
1132 U.S. 31 North
Traverse City, MI 49686
(616) 922-5270

Van Buren State Park

Location: Van Buren State Park, in Van Buren County about four miles south of South Haven, Michigan, is reached by taking the Blue Star Memorial Highway south from South Haven to Ruggles Road. Turn west on Ruggles to the park entrance.

Features of the Park: Van Buren State Park, comprised of 326 acres, the sandy beach along Lake Michigan, which extends about a half-mile, a campground, and a day-use area for picnicking.

Camping: A campground, which has 220 sites with modern toilet and shower facilities, is widely used during the summer. Each campsite has a picnic table, a metal fire ring for campfires and electricity. Some campsites are shaded with trees; however, most are open with little foliage around them. The campsites are close to each other, providing little privacy in the summer when the park is often filled. The campground is not on Lake Michigan, but is about a quarter-mile, a five-to 10-minute walk, from the beach.

The campsites along the south end of the campground are along a fence, beyond which is the Palisades Nuclear Plant. There are no trees or shrubs to hide this facility.

The campground is closed from the first of December through the end of March.

In addition to the general campground, there is a group campground.

Picnic Facilities: A day-use picnic area has numerous picnic tables and grills. Also in this area are toilet, shower and changing facilities, as well as a concession stand adjacent to the beach.

Three large parking lots at the end of the road into the park lead to a broad cement walkway leading past the dunes to the beach.

Beach: The beach extends for about one mile along the shore of Lake Michigan. The beach is composed of very fine sand, extending between 25 and 50 yards from the shoreline. Behind the sandy beach are small dunes with grass, shrubbery and a variety of trees.

Trails: There are no identified hiking trails in the park. However, you can walk along the dunes and the surrounding woods between the beach and parking lots.

Boating: Although no boat launching facilities exist at the park, in nearby South Haven there are public launching ramps. Also, marinas and charter fishing boats are available in this resort town.

Palisades Nuclear Plant: Adjacent to the park on the south end is the Palisades Nuclear Plant. In the pamphlet welcoming visitors to the park is an announcement for tours of the plant. Also included is information about the early warning sirens in case of an emergency involving a nuclear accident or other disaster requiring evacuation.

Van Buren State Park
23960 Ruggles Road
P.O. Box 122-B
South Haven, MI 49090
(616) 637-2788

Warren Dunes State Park

Warren Dunes State Park is comprised of 1,950 acres, most of it sand dunes.

Visitors can participate in a variety of activities at Warren Dunes. The water is comfortable during the summer. As a result, the beaches are packed most every weekend in the summer with people swimming, sunbathing and playing. In addition, windsurfing has become increasingly popular.

Fishing is very good in the waters adjacent to the park. However, there are no boating facilities, fishing piers or ramps in the park. These can be found outside of the park.

The park is named for the Warren family of nearby Three Oaks, who gave the land to the state for recreational purposes. In the mid-1800s Edward K. Warren, a partner in a local general store, bought sandy

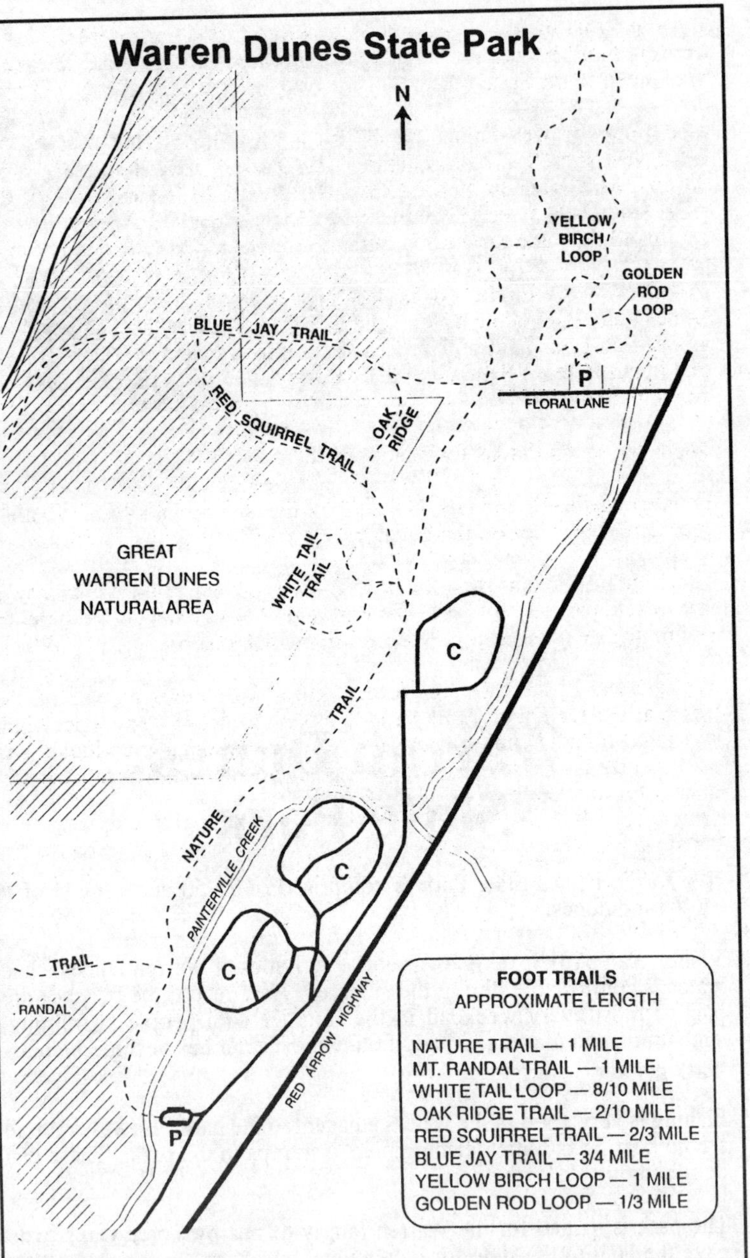
Warren Dunes State Park
N
YELLOW BIRCH LOOP
GOLDEN ROD LOOP
BLUE JAY TRAIL
RED SQUIRREL TRAIL
OAK RIDGE
P
FLORAL LANE
GREAT WARREN DUNES NATURAL AREA
WHITE TAIL TRAIL
C
TRAIL
NATURE
PAINTERVILLE CREEK
C
C
TRAIL
RANDAL
RED ARROW HIGHWAY
P
FOOT TRAILS
APPROXIMATE LENGTH
NATURE TRAIL — 1 MILE
MT. RANDAL TRAIL — 1 MILE
WHITE TAIL LOOP — 8/10 MILE
OAK RIDGE TRAIL — 2/10 MILE
RED SQUIRREL TRAIL — 2/3 MILE
BLUE JAY TRAIL — 3/4 MILE
YELLOW BIRCH LOOP — 1 MILE
GOLDEN ROD LOOP — 1/3 MILE

duneland that many considered of no value. As a person interested in conservation, he had the foresight to purchase this land and in time it was given to the state.

Location: Warren Dunes State Park is on Lake Michigan along the southwest shoreline of Michigan. This park is 15 miles south of St. Joseph, Michigan, in Berrien County. To get to the entrance of the park, leave I-94 at exit 12 in Sawyer. Go west a quarter of a mile, turn north and the park entrance is two miles away.

Features of the Park: By far the most impressive feature of Warren Dunes State Park is the beach, which stretches nearly three miles along Lake Michigan. The sand dunes extend inland from the shoreline several hundred feet. Sand dune hills along the beach rise up to 240 feet above the lake.

There are several areas for picnicking in the park.

Beach: The beach extends the length of the park and is one of the most spectacular beaches on the Great Lakes.

There are no lifeguards on the beach. A large concession building is at the beach parking lot and campground. Souvenirs, refreshments, swimming gear and sun protection are available here.

We saw one of the most interesting and unique items for use on the beach at Warren Dunes State Park - a dune wheelchair. The wheelchair has large inflated rubber tires, available for disabled individuals and senior citizens. These dune wheelchairs can be obtained from park personnel for no charge.

Most people who come to Warren Dunes State Park for a weekday visit in the summer will find adequate parking. However, on weekends and holidays it is not unusual for the beach parking facility to be filled by late morning.

The Dunes: The sand dunes formed over thousands of years as a result of receding ice glaciers reducing bedrock to the sand we see today. Over centuries, wind and water have helped form the dunes.

At Warren Dunes there are five sand dunes, as high as 200 feet or more, along the shoreline. These are Mt. Edward on the northern portion of the park, Great Warren Dune, Mt. Randall, Tower Hill and Mt. Fuller. Mt. Randall is on the edge of the campground. Tower Hill, the tallest at 240 feet, is the dune you see upon entering the beach area. Mt. Edwards is mostly covered with trees.

Hang Gliding: Warren Dunes is the only state park along the Great Lakes where hang gliding is permitted. The environment is particularly conducive to this activity. Winds coming off the lake are excellent for hang gliding. The soft sand along the shoreline provides a perfect landing surface. Gliders from throughout the country come to this park. Individuals desiring to hang glide must have a U.S. Hang Gliding Association proficiency rating card and a Warren Dunes State Park hang gliding permit from the headquarters office. Safety helmets must be worn while flying. On two of my visits to Warren Dunes State Park, there were gliders on Tower Hill. One of the gliders was particularly skilled, providing a beautiful scene to photograph with the colorful glider and the blue sky and sandy background.

Camping: A campground of 180 modern sites is on the east side of the park. Tower Hill and Mt. Randall separate the campground from the beach and shoreline. The campground is sandy with some groundcover, but shady. Each campsite has electrical outlets, an in-ground fire pit and picnic table. The campsites are relatively small and are close to each other. The campsites are on two circles. A modern hot shower and flush toilet facility is available for camper use. In the campground are three mini-cabins. Each can accommodate four individuals and have electricity.

A short hiking trail goes from the campground to the beach, circling Mt. Randall. During the summer this campground is usually filled on weekends and holidays. Reservations can be made at least seven days in advance, and are suggested through Labor Day. There may be opportunities to camp in an overflow section of the park on these busy days. From Memorial Day through Labor Day, Beach Campground is open. This campground, with 122 sites, is on the edge of the beach at the foot of Tower Hill. It is located on asphalt. There are modern flush toilets, but no showers or electricity in this campground.

A group campground with seven campsites is available. Each campsite has fire circles and picnic tables for youth groups. Pit toilets and hand pumps are available. There are no shower facilities or electricity. To use these facilities, the group must consist of young people 18 years and under and there must be qualified supervision.

Picnic Facilities: Thousands of people come to Warren Dunes State Park to enjoy a picnic. Just to the right after passing the park entrance booth is a large, heavily shaded picnic area. Many picnic tables and grills are adjacent to the sand dunes; however, they are in the shade. Three additional picnic areas are along Painterville Creek as it flows along the road to the beach. Another picnic area is about a quarter-mile from the campground. It is here that the Nature Trail trailhead is located.

Trails: About five miles of hiking trails are in the park. These trails traverse the open dunes, proceed over the hills, and go through wooded terrain. Most people do not come to Warren Dunes State Park to hike, however, the most enjoyable hiking activity is just climbing around on the several large dunes.

There is a one-mile Nature Trail which has 10 items of interest for the hiker/walker. Walking this trail will give you a better understanding of the geological and historical development of the area. For example, trees noted on the trail are various hardwoods, such as oak, maple, ash and tulip. The cottonwood is one of the first trees to grow in an area of shifting sands. The white pine and paw paw tree are unique to this region of Michigan and are seen along this trail.

The paw paw tree is particularly interesting since it grows only in southern Michigan. It is a member of the tropical custard apple family. It is small, rarely growing over 10 feet in height. It produces a three-to five-inch-long green fruit resembling a banana, which ripens in the fall. The fruit is hard to find in Warren Dunes State Park because it is usually eaten by squirrels, raccoons and opossums. The raccoon is the most common animal in the park. This animal is most active at night. Raccoons eat wildberries, eggs, crayfish and frogs. Turtles, crayfish, clams and frogs are found in Painterville Creek, which forms the south boundary of the park. It is shallow, usually less than a foot deep.

The Mt. Randall Trail connects the Nature Trail and beach campground. It passes over Mt. Randall and is one mile long. In the north part of the park are two loop trails: Yellow Birch Loop (1 mile) and Golden Rod Loop (1/3 mile). Other trails which are less than a mile long are Oak Ridge Trail (.2 mile), Red Squirrel Trail (2/3 mile), and Blue Jay Trail (3/4 mile).

Winter Activities: This park provides a variety of opportunities for winter activity. Six miles of trails are available for cross-country skiing in the park. However, there is no ski rental nor are the trails groomed. The hills provide an opportunity for sliding, sledding and tobogganing. One of my most enjoyable times spent at Warren Dunes was a winter day with a significant amount of snow on the ground and the trees covered with snow. Walking with snowshoes over the hills was a special treat, seeing the white of the ground, the blue of the sky and the ice on the water. Winter camping is available. Electricity is provided; however, water must be carried to the campsite and there are box toilets.

Other Information: All alcoholic beverages are prohibited in Warren Dunes State Park.

Warren Dunes State Park
Red Arrow Highway
Sawyer, MI 49125
(616) 426-4013

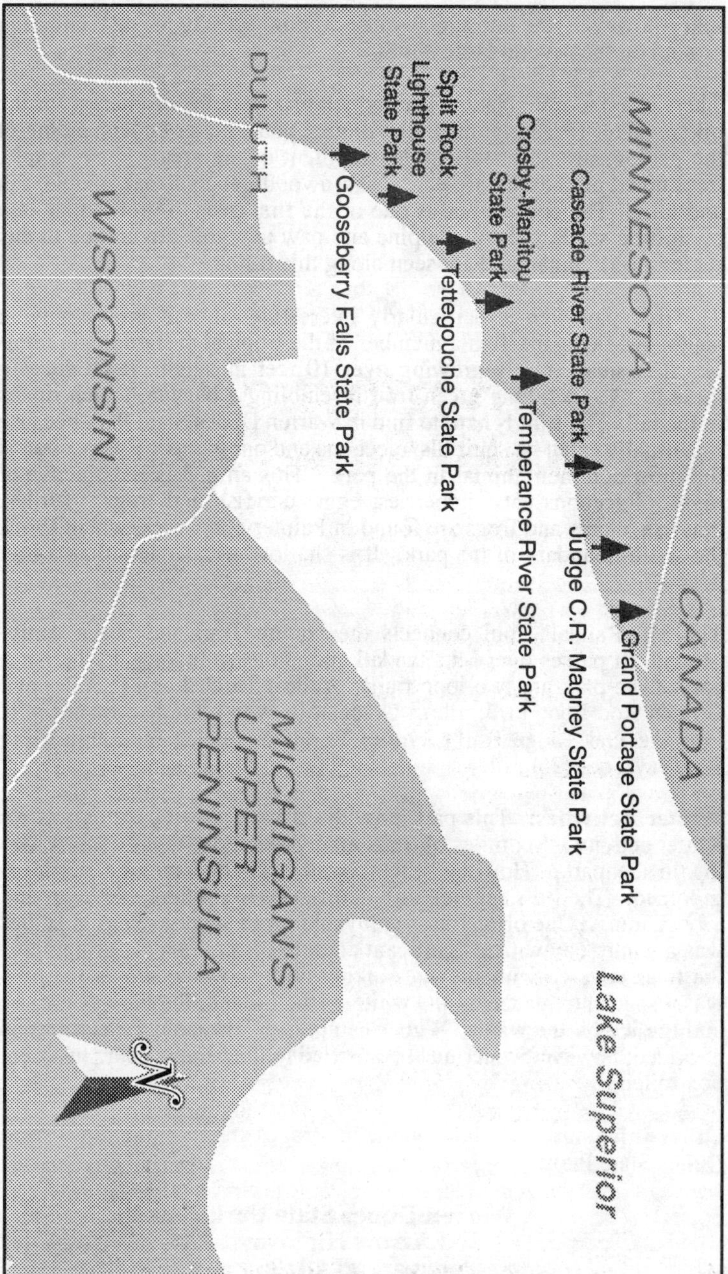
MINNESOTA
CANADA
Lake Superior
Grand Portage State Park
Judge C.R. Magney State Park
Cascade River State Park
Temperance River State Park
Crosby-Manitou State Park
Tettegouche State Park
Split Rock Lighthouse State Park
Gooseberry Falls State Park
DULUTH
WISCONSIN
MICHIGAN'S UPPER PENINSULA
N

The Northshore of Lake Superior

Stretching 150 miles between Duluth, Minnesota, and the Canadian border is the North Shore of Lake Superior. Along the shoreline is some of the most beautiful scenery in the United States. There are no sandy beaches, sand dunes or hills to walk along, nor comfortably warm water to swim and wade in. The waters of Lake Superior seldom rise above 55 degrees, even in summer, and the shoreline is more a reminder of the rugged, rocky ocean coast.

Along most of the North Shore, forests come down to the rocky, cliff-dominated shoreline. These are boreal forests, consisting primarily of coniferous trees such as balsam fir, spruce, birch and poplar.

These forests provide an environment conducive to a variety of wildlife. Small ground animals are common. However, it is the larger wildlife found in the wilderness and forests of this area that interests many visitors. Deer, black bear, timber wolves and moose live in the woods and forests of the North Shore. They often are seen along the trails, streams, rivers, lakes and campgrounds of the North Shore.

Many streams and rivers flow from Canada to the north, cutting through stone, rock and gorges, finally tumbling into Lake Superior. Along most of these rivers are scenic rapids and waterfalls. These serve as the principal attraction for several Minnesota state parks.

Along the shoreline you can find a variety of beautiful rocks and stones. Agates are a favorite of any rock collector. Other gems include jasper, thomsonite, greenstone and quartz crystals.

Minnesota 61 runs parallel to the Lake Superior shoreline from Duluth to the Canadian border. Seldom is a person traveling this highway more than a half-mile from the lake. At times the highway is adjacent to the water's edge. As a result, the lake is within sight of the highway nearly the entire 150 miles.

The state of Minnesota has established eight state parks along the North Shore. The entrance to all but one is from Minnesota 61. They include: Gooseberry Falls, Split Rock Lighthouse, Tettegouche, Temperance River, Cascade River, Judge C.R. Magney and Grand Portage. Crosby-Manitou is reached off of a county road.

One of the finest long-distance hiking trails in the United States is the Superior Hiking Trail. Construction of the trail began in 1987. It eventually will extend the length of the North Shore from Duluth to the Canadian border, a distance of nearly 300 miles. Currently, about 200 miles of the trail are complete. The trail connects all eight state parks along the North Shore. It ranges in elevation from 602 feet to more than 1,800 feet.

The trail appeals to both the backpacker who plans an extensive long-range hike and the day hiker wishing to walk just a couple of miles with family. It is operated as a cooperative venture of the Superior Hiking Trail Association, the U.S. Forest Service, the Minnesota Department of Natural Resources, and county and private landowners.The Superior Hiking Trail Association, a non-profit organization of volunteers, manages and maintains the trail.

The Superior Hiking Trail provides many spectacular views of Lake Superior as it passes through the northern boreal forest and along the many rivers and streams along the North Shore of Lake Superior.

Camping reservations at Minnesota state parks can be made 90 days in advance by calling (800) 246-CAMP.

Information about the Superior Hiking Trail:

Superior Hiking Trail
P.O. Box 4
Two Harbors, MN 55616
(218) 834-2700

Cascade River State Park

Cascade River State Park is comprised of 2,813 acres along the rugged, scenic shoreline of Lake Superior. Different sections of the park stretch along the shoreline for nearly 12 miles. The main area of the park is at the mouth of the Cascade River north along Lake Superior for about 1.5 miles. The park extends inland from the shoreline about a half-mile.

Location: Cascade River is in Cook County, Minnesota, about 10 miles southwest of Grand Marais. The park entrance is near mile marker 101 on Minnesota 61.

Features of the Park: The park highlights the Cascade River, which flows through the park to Lake Superior. Two waterfalls, Cascade Falls and The Cascades, are in the park. Hiking during the summer and fall and cross-country skiing in the winter are the major activities here. Two excellent overviews provide fantastic views: Lookout Mountain (600 feet above the lake) and Moose Mountain (500 feet above the lake).

The Lake Superior shoreline is very scenic and rugged in the park. The forest comes directly to the rocky shoreline. All along the shoreline are large boulders, lava and cliffs. You can walk from rock to rock along the shoreline.

Camping: The campground with 40 campsites is in the forest. The sites are well-spaced and sit in the brush and trees off of the campground road. Most sites are not within visual distance of the adjacent site. Included in the campground are shower facilities, flush toilets and a year-round screened picnic shelter.

A backpacking campsite is on the Lake Superior shoreline. This site can be reached by hiking a little over a mile on the trail that parallels the shoreline. Also, four additional backpacking camping sites are located in the park interior. These sites provide a shelter, pit toilet, picnic table and fire ring.

Two group camping facilities are found in the park on a short road just after passing the park entrance building. Each has space for several tents. Also, there are several picnic tables and two in-ground fire pits at each site. No modern facilities are available, only a pit toilet and water. Each group site can accommodate up to 25 people. They must be reserved in advance.

Hiking: Eighteen miles of hiking trails provide access throughout the park's birch and spruce forests. The Superior Hiking Trail passes through the park and is accessible from the park trails.

If you are traveling along Minnesota 61 and stop at the mouth of the river, it is well worth your time to walk a .3-mile trail to the bridge at The Cascades, walk over the bridge and return to the highway on the opposite side. This short walk gives you an opportunity to see The Cascades and the Cascade Falls as well as to gain an understanding of what the hiking trails deeper in the park are like.

Another short trail, also about .3-mile, leads from the bridge at The Cascades to a ridge which runs parallel to the shoreline and Minnesota 61, ending at a commercial lodge and restaurant. Along this walk are several excellent views of Lake Superior. Though the highway is down the hill from the trail, it cannot be seen because of the woods.

A 7.7-mile Cascade River Loop Trail takes the hiker along the river from the highway bridge at highway 61 to Cook County Road 45, where you will cross the river and return on the opposite side. The trail on the east side of the river is the Superior Hiking Trail. Along this trail are a number of falls and an old mine.

The Superior Hiking Trail passes through Cascade River State Park. It can be taken to reach Lookout Mountain, which is 600 feet above Lake

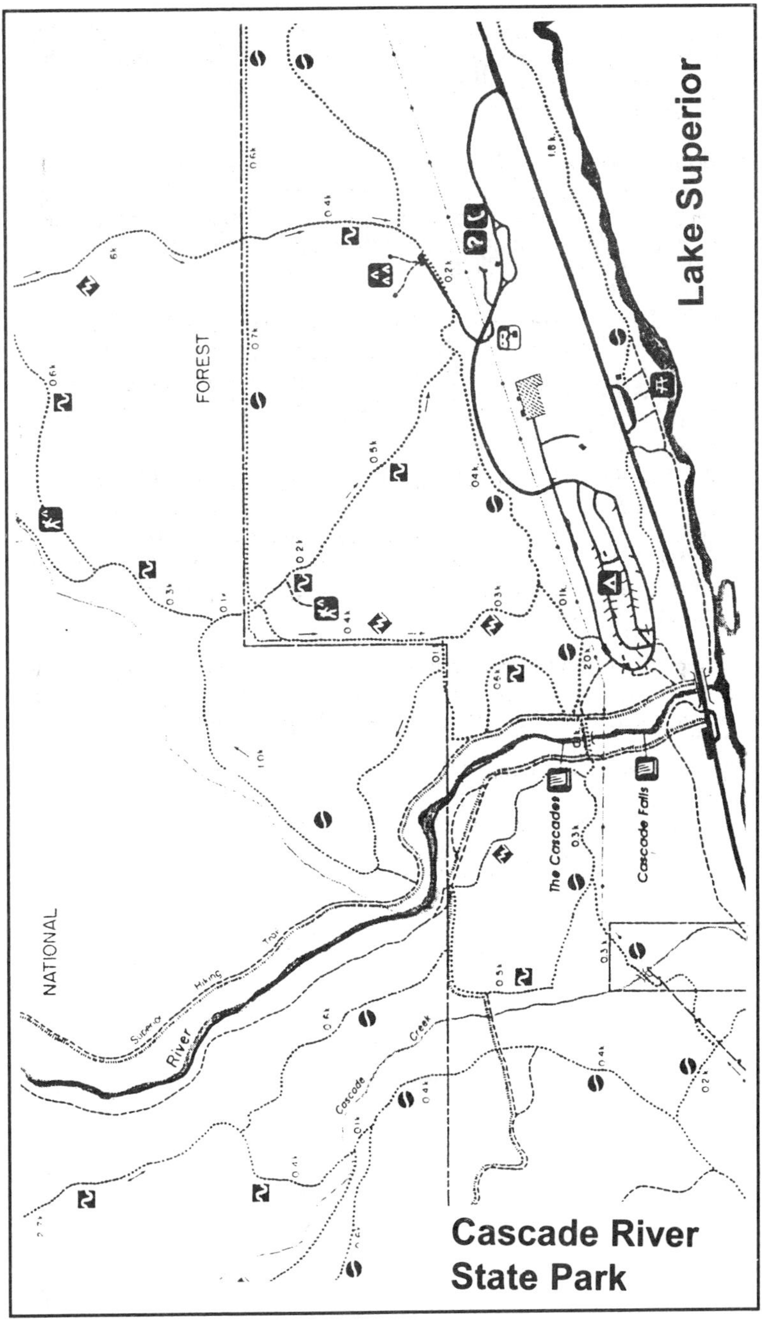
Cascade River State Park
Lake Superior
NATIONAL
FOREST
Superior Hiking Trail
River
Cascade Creek
The Cascades
Cascade Falls

Superior. Though not an easy climb, the view from this lookout is outstanding, providing views of Lake Superior, the Sawtooth Mountain Range and the Cascade River valley. The Superior Hiking Trail proceeds along the west side of the river through the park to the bridge on the highway, then traverses the east side of the river and leaves the park, continuing along the river into the Superior National Forest.

Picnic Facilities: A picnic area with seven picnic sites is located on Lake Superior. It is necessary to walk about 75 yards from the parking lot to the picnic sites which are separated by woods, brush and undergrowth. The picnic tables and fire ring are on the edge of the lake, characterized by large boulders. People can walk along the shore, stepping from one boulder to another.

Fishing/Wildlife: Fishing for lake trout is good, both in Lake Superior and at the mouth of the river. Rainbow trout and brook trout fishing occurs in the upper portions of the river. Also, in the fall many anglers fish for chinook salmon along the riverbanks. These fish return to spawn in the fall.

The largest winter deer yarding area in Minnesota is located adjacent to the park. Here, in an open area, deer seek protection from the cold wind and temperatures during the winter. Moose, black bear, wolves, fishers, pine martens and many other common smaller wild animals are seen in the park and surrounding area.

Winter Activities: Seventeen miles of cross-country ski trails are groomed in Cascade River State Park. In addition, the park trails connect to trails in the surrounding Superior National Forest and the North Shore mountains ski trail system. Groomed cross-country ski trails lead to the top of both Lookout Mountain and Moose Mountain.

Also, two miles of snowmobile trails in the park provide access to hundreds of miles of snowmobile trails in the surrounding area.

During the winter, the waterfalls freeze; ice climbers climb the frozen waterfalls.

Cascade River State Park
HCR 3, P.O. Box 450
Lutsen, MN 55612
(218) 387-1543

George H. Crosby-Manitou State Park

George H. Crosby-Manitou State Park is a hiking and camping park, comprised of 5,259 acres. It is a wilderness park with nearly the entire acreage being non-developed park land.

The park was named after George H. Crosby, who donated the land to the state for a park, and after the Ojibwa name for the river, Manitou, which runs through the park. Manitou in the Ojibwa language means "spirit."

The Manitou River, which runs the length of the park, empties into Lake Superior. At the mouth of the river, near Minnesota 61, is a small parcel of state park land. However, most of the land surrounding the mouth of the river is private property, not accessible to the public.

Location: Crosby-Manitou is in Lake County, Minnesota. The only entrance is off of Lake County Road 7 about 12 miles from Finland, Minnesota. To reach the entrance, leave Minnesota 61 about one mile beyond Tettagouche State Park at Ilgen City on Minnesota 1. Drive six miles to Finland. At Finland turn east on County Road 7 and proceed 7.5 miles to the park. This road becomes a dirt road about 1.5 miles outside of Finland.

Crosby-Manitou has the most remote entrance to any state park on the Great Lakes. It is a single-lane dirt road through the forest. The parking lot is the trailhead for all of the marked hiking trails in the park.

Features of the Park: Crosby-Manitou State Park features the Manitou River and wilderness, which includes isolated backpacking campsites and miles of hiking trails. The Manitou River drops 600 feet as it passes through the park.

Camping: Twenty-two campsites are spread throughout the park. Hikers must register for a campsite at the office or on a sign-in board next to the office if the office is closed. Five sites (#18-#22) are near Bensen Lake. These sites are within a 15-minute walk from the parking lot.

The other campsites are at various points along the Manitou River. The farthest ones are 2.5 to 3 miles from the parking lot. Campsite #1 is reached by taking the Humpback Trail, about an hours walk. Campsite #2 is near the Manitou River Cascades. The farthest campsite from the parking lot is #16.

Each site has one or two dirt pads for tents and an in-ground fire pit. There is no picnic table; however, a bench or two made of large logs provides a table and bench for campers.

Drinking water must be boiled, treated or obtained from a pump behind the information building at the park entrance. All garbage must be taken to refuse containers near the parking lot.

Campers must take caution in storing food since there are black bears in the park.

Trails: There are 24 miles of rugged hiking trails in Crosby-Manitou State Park. Hikers must wear strong footgear and insect repellent during the summer.

The Bensen Lake Trail circles the lake. This relatively flat trail proceeds along the edge of the lake, providing good views.

At the south end of Bensen Lake is the beginning of the Matt Willis Trail (1.5 miles). This trail goes to a shelter at the far end of the park,

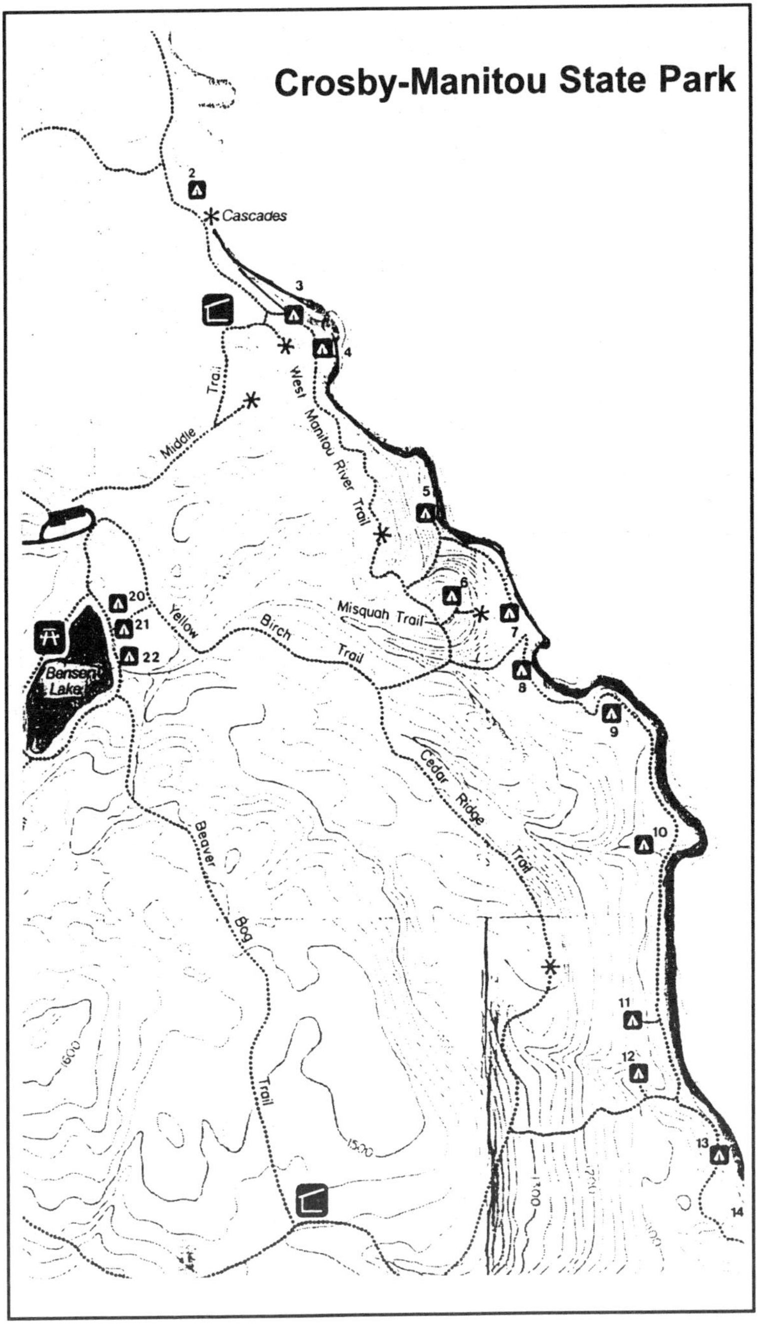
Crosby-Manitou State Park
2
Cascades
3
4
Middle
Trail
West Manitou River Trail
5
6
7
8
9
10
11
12
13
14
Misquah Trail
20
21
22
Yellow
Birch
Trail
Bensen Lake
Cedar Ridge Trail
Beaver Bog Trail
1600
1500
1300

at the junction of the Matt Willis Trail and the Beaver Bog Trail. Beaver Bog Trail returns to Bensen Lake (1 mile) near campsite #22.

The Humpback Trail and Middle Trail form a circle to the Manitou River Cascades. The Humpback Trail is a strenuous trail. Along the river is the West Manitou River Trail. The Yellow Birch Trail takes hikers toward the river. As the name implies, there are many yellow birch trees along this trail. Along this trail the Cedar Ridge Trail circles around and meets the Beaver Bog Trail.

Picnic Facilities: The only picnic facility in the park is on Bensen Lake, about a five-minute walk from the parking lot. A half-dozen tables and an in-ground fire pit and grill are at this site.

Fishing: Rainbow and brook trout are excellent catches along the Manitou River.

Wildlife: Because of the park's isolation the likelihood of seeing wildlife is very good. Deer, black bear, timber wolf and moose are in these woods along with many smaller species. Ruffed and spruce grouse are in the park as are many other species of birds.

Winter Activities: Crosby-Manitou State Park is open year-round. Cross-country skiing and winter camping are the primary activities during the winter. Several miles of hiking trails are groomed for skiing.

Snowshoeing on the trails attracts some winter activists. Trails can be rugged and the most isolated campsites can be difficult to reach should a major snowstorm develop.

George H. Crosby-Manitou State Park
P.O. Box 482
Finland, MN 55603
(218) 226-4492

Gooseberry Falls State Park

Gooseberry Falls is the most popular state park in Minnesota, attracting more than 800,000 visitors a year.

This area originally was covered with gigantic white pines. In the 1890s, loggers cut down the trees and took them to Lake Superior for rafting to sawmills. The pines disappeared by the early 1920s. Today the park is covered with conifer, aspen and birch forests.

Gooseberry Falls State Park was developed by the Civilian Conservation Corps (CCC). Beginning in 1934, two CCC companies began their work on the park. Several stone buildings and trails were built and the campground was laid out. Some of the quarried stones they used weighed several tons. The CCC camp closed in 1941 at the start of World War II.

The park received its name from the river which flows through it. The river was named for French explorer Sieur des Groseilliers, whose name translates into English as "gooseberry."

The area was established as a state park in 1937 and today it is comprised of 1,662 acres.

Location: Gooseberry Falls State Park is in Lake County on Minnesota 61 at mile marker 39. It is about 15 miles north of Two Harbors.

Features of the Park: The park features five falls on the Gooseberry River. Also, the newly constructed modern Gooseberry Falls State Park Visitor Center provides information for people about the park and surrounding points of interest.

Of the five falls on the Gooseberry River, three are most commonly visited. The Lower Falls, which is 60 feet high, is just below the highway bridge crossing the river near the park visitor center. Upstream a few hundred feet is the 30-foot Upper Falls. Many people traveling Minnesota 61 stop and see these two falls without having to hike into the woods. A third falls, Fifth Falls, is about 1.5 miles upstream from the bridge.

A visitor center with a variety of exhibits and audio-visual presentations recently was built.

The Gooseberry River enters the park at a height of 240 feet and drops over a series of waterfalls to Lake Superior.

Visitor Center: The newest visitor center in any of the state parks on the Great Lakes is at Gooseberry Falls State Park. The modern stone and wood constructed facility was dedicated and opened in September 1996. Historical and informational displays are available at the center. A park naturalist offers educational activities about the park and surrounding area.

An audio-visual presentation depicts information about the history of the various state parks on the North Shore. Information about animals, plants, recreation and natural resources are provided. Interactive displays inform about the history of the park, about wildlife in the surrounding area, and other items.

A section of the facility is a gift shop and nature store selling books, educational materials and gifts.

Camping: A campground with 70 sites includes hot showers, flush toilets and a dumping station. At each campsite are a picnic table and an in-ground fire pit. The campsites are spread out and large, most having grass ground cover. These sites are as large as any in the state parks on the Great Lakes. Several large rocks at nearly every campsite keep motor vehicles and trailers off of the grass.

The campsites are around four circular roads. Campsites #1 - #27 are on circle 1; circle 2 has campsites #28-#44; circle 3 has campsites #45-#57 and circle 4 has campsites #58-#70. Circle 4 is the nearest to Lake Superior. A modern toilet and shower building is in each circle. The campground is set in an aspen and birch woods. The underbrush is not as thick as at other parks along the North Shore.

An indoor shelter with toilet facilities and picnic tables is located at the campground. No refuge disposals are available, making it necessary to carry out any trash and refuge.

An outdoor amphitheater and lodge are next to the campground. Naturalist programs are conducted at the Lady Slipper Lodge several nights a week during the summer and on weekends during the fall. Films, slide shows and talks about wildlife in the area, voyageurs, the Great Lakes, birds and other interesting topics are presented.

In addition to the main campground, a rustic group campsite is located in the park. This facility can accommodate up to 150 individuals. Reservations are required.

Trails: Hiking is one of the most popular activities of visitors to the park. Eighteen miles of trails are spread throughout the park. Five trails lead to the river and falls.

As part of renovations taking place in 1996-97, a hard-surface, handicapped accessible trail now departs from the visitor center and provides access to both the Lower and Upper Falls. This trail brings people to a newly constructed overlook near the Lower Falls. With a five-minute walk upstream, passing under the highway bridge, you come to the Upper Falls. Excellent views of the Lower Falls are obtained by hiking along the Lower Rim Trail to a newly constructed bridge. This circular walk provides several places where a person can observe the Lower Falls.

The Lower Rim Trail follows the river from the Lower Falls, passing through the river picnic area and ending at the mouth of the river on the Lake Superior shoreline.

The Gitchi Gummi Trail begins on the east side of the Minnesota 61 bridge and passes through aspen and white pine forests. Along this trail is a scenic overlook of Lake Superior. The trail loops back along Nelson's Creek.

The Fifth Falls Trail extends about 1.5 miles along the Gooseberry River to Fifth Falls. Crossing a bridge at the falls permits hikers to return on the opposite side of the river, making for a circular hike of

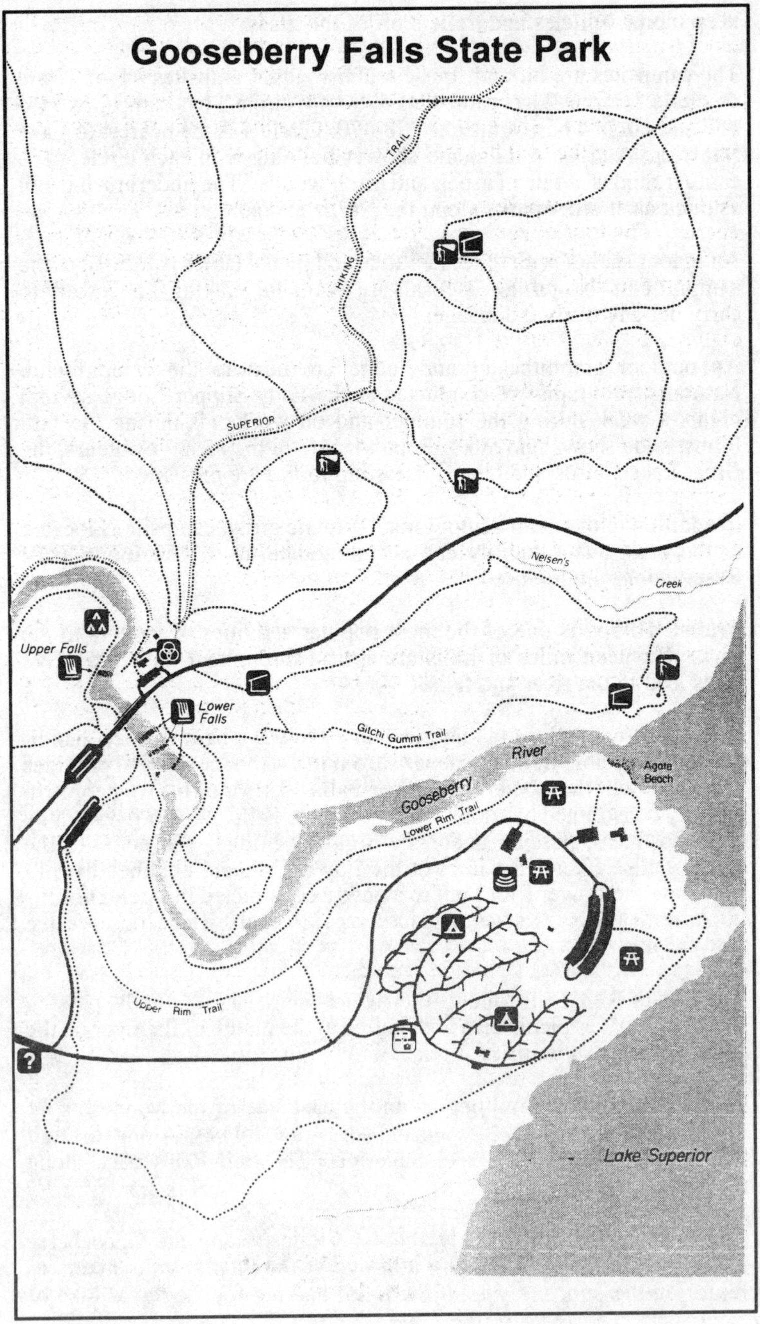
Gooseberry Falls State Park
HIKING TRAIL
SUPERIOR
Nelsen's
Creek
Upper Falls
Lower Falls
Gitchi Gummi Trail
River
Agate Beach
Gooseberry
Lower Rim Trail
Upper Rim Trail
Lake Superior

about three miles. Along the eastern side of the river, the Fifth Falls Trail is part of the Superior Hiking Trail. As you walk along this trail at the edge of the river, the water flows through rapids. Several places along the trail are overlooks where log benches are available to rest and enjoy the scenery. The best view to photograph the falls is two to three minutes along the trail before the bridge on the west side of the river.

About three minutes down river from the bridge along the trail is a shelter. The trail on the west side of the river is not as easy to walk as is the east side. It is steeper in places and the footing includes tree roots and some rocks. Along the way, the trail ascends to a ridge line above the falls. There are 10 miles of mountain bike trails in the park. Bikers should call ahead before riding the trails.

Lake Superior Water Trail: The Lake Superior Water Trail for canoers and kayakers extends between Gooseberry Falls State Park and Tettegouche State Park, a distance of 20 miles. The water trail passes Split Rock Lighthouse State Park. Along this section are many spectacular cliffs and sea caves. The first phase of the trail opened in 1994. There are several campsites along the trail. Anyone venturing into Lake Superior to kayak and canoe must be skilled. Plans are underway to expand the trail further along Lake Superior.

Picnic Facilities: The Lakeview Picnic Area is at the mouth of the Gooseberry River. The lakeshore at this point is hardened lava rock from volcanic eruptions millions of years ago. Picnic tables are spread along the lakeshore in a very scenic area, which includes the Lakeview Picnic Shelter on a bluff. The shelter, with a fireplace and several picnic tables, is available by reservation. Agate Beach is located down a short trail from the shelter at the mouth of the river. This beach is a little stretch of stones where people can walk along the shoreline, looking for agates and other gems. At the mouth of the river is a large stone and rock bar. The river flowing into the lake is a small, quiet channel.

Fishing/Wildlife: A variety of birds and animals live in the park. Some 142 species of birds nest or visit the park including herring gulls, woodpeckers and the common loon. Deer and black bear are found in the park. Deer feed in a park deer yard during the winter.

Winter Activities: Fifteen miles of groomed cross-country ski trails are maintained throughout the park, most north of Minnesota 61 and east of the Gooseberry River. There also are three miles of snowmobile trails in the park, providing access to the North Shore State Trail. Park naturalists offer snowshoe instructions to winter visitors.

Gooseberry Falls State Park
1300 Minnesota 61 East
Two Harbors, MN 55616
(218) 834-3855

Grand Portage State Park

Grand Portage State Park is the newest state park on the Great Lakes, officially opening to the public in October 1994. The park was established by the state of Minnesota in cooperation with the Grand Portage Band of Chippewa Indians in 1989, and has been in various stages of use and development since then. The park helps preserve High Falls on the Pigeon River.

The park, on the Grand Portage Indian Reservation, is the only state park in Minnesota not owned by the state. The land is leased to the state by the Federal Bureau of Indian Affairs.

The 300-acre park is a day-use park. A visitor center and nature store offer information about the park and items for sale on Minnesota state parks. The park is open year round.

The park boundaries are not on the lake; Lake Superior is about a mile beyond the park boundary, where the Pigeon River flows into the lake.

Location: Grand Portage State Park is in Cook County, Minnesota, at the United States and Canadian border. The park is six miles north of Grand Portage, Minnesota, on Minnesota 61. The park entrance is next to the United States Port of Entry from Canada. The Pigeon River, which is the boundary between Canada and the United States, is the northern boundary of the park. The Pigeon River, the largest river on Minnesota's North Shore, flows through a series of rapids and falls for some 20 miles before arriving at the park. Park frontage on the Pigeon River is about 2.5 miles.

Features of the Park: The park highlights High Falls, the highest falls in Minnesota. Here the water flows over High Falls, a drop of nearly 120 feet. The water then flows through a steep walled gorge and exits about a half-mile later as a gentle, slow-moving river. Upstream from High Falls is another falls, the Middle Falls, 90 feet in height.

Trails: Five miles of trails are in the planning stages. Only one trail is open to the public. The Falls Trail, about one-half mile long, begins at the park office and extends through the woods toward the Pigeon River. The last part of the trail (700 feet) is a boardwalk, which provides easy access for disabled individuals and senior citizens to three overlooks. These overlooks provide spectacular views of High Falls.

Falls Trail is a level dirt and stone roadway. It is accessible to wheelchairs.

The longest trail in the park, about 3.5 miles, will be the Middle Falls Trail. It will start at the office and extend to Middle Falls in the northwest section of the park. A hike to Middle Falls can be extended about one mile by taking the Middle Falls Loop Trail. This trail follows the river bank and winds through a heavily wooded forest of birch, aspen and spruce trees.

Picnic Facilities: The picnic area is on the Pigeon River near the visitor center and nature store. A half-dozen picnic tables and grills are spread across this area. Each picnic site has two tables and a grill and is separated from others by about 20 yards with bushes, trees and undergrowth. The picnic sites are within sight of the river.

Camping: This is a day-use only park. There is no camping.

Nature: The park is covered by a hardwood forest of mostly white birch and aspen trees. Also, there are balsam fir, white cedar, poplar and black ashes. Numerous waterfowl, blue herons, geese and ducks can be found in the park area.
Also, eagles and hawks are common. Moose, black bear and red fox are occasionally seen in the park.

Grand Portage State Park

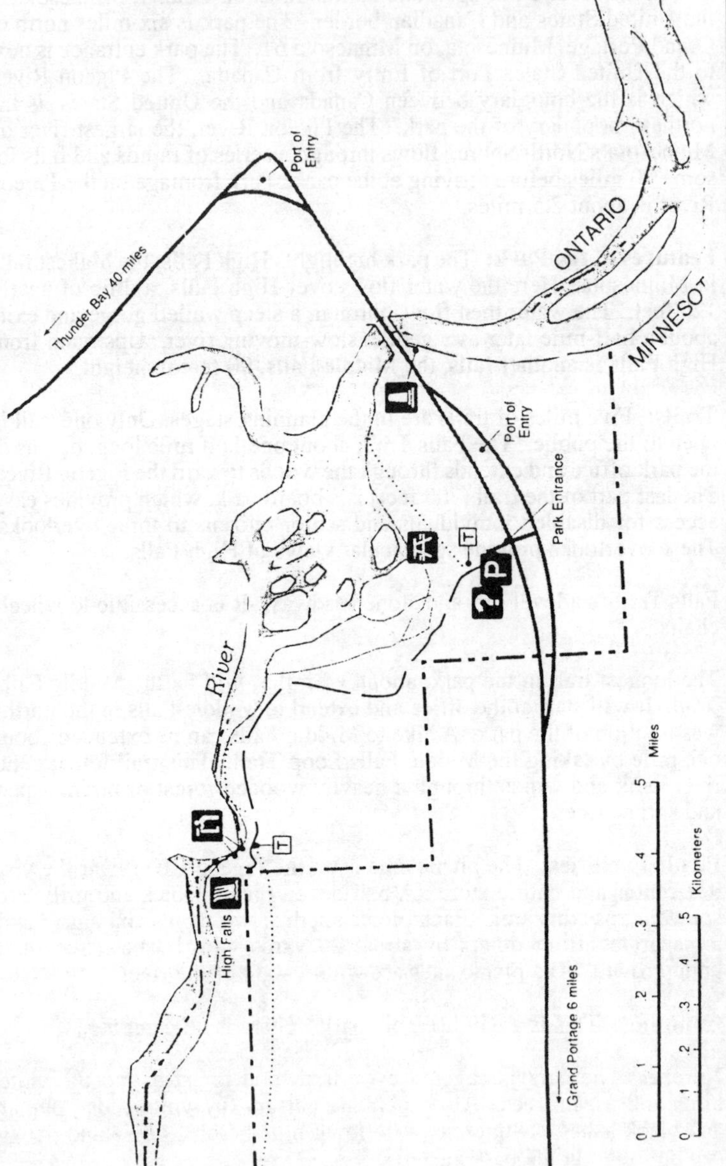

Year-round naturalist programs are given at the park. One interesting program explains storytelling among the Ojibwa Indians. Traditions, history and beliefs were passed from one generation to another by storytelling. A traditional Ojibwa story is told as part of this program.

Grand Portage State Park
HCR 1, P.O. Box 7
Grand Portage, MN 55605
(218) 475-2360

Judge C.R. Magney State Park

Judge C.R. Magney State Park is comprised of 4,514 acres, the major portion non-developed wilderness. The park is bounded on all sides by the Grand Portage State Forest.

In 1957 a section of land along the Brule River was set aside as the Bois Brule River State Park. In 1963, the park was renamed as a memorial for Judge Clarence R. Magney, a lawyer who was once the mayor of Duluth. He also served on the Minnesota Supreme Court and was a strong advocate of the state park system. The area along the Brule River was one of Magney's favorite locations.

During the 1930s the state of Minnesota built a camp, known as the Grover Condzet Camp, on the west side of the Brule River to serve as a work camp for transient, homeless and unemployed men. The camp, designed to accommodate 400 men, included 27 buildings. The men did forestry work, built trails, fought forest fires, and performed other public service and construction work. The camp was phased out at the end of the Great Depression. Today, the foundations of some of these buildings can be seen partially buried in the park, especially in the park campground and picnic areas.

Most people come to this park to hike and fish. The only road in the park extends for less than a half-mile from the entrance to the campground and the dirt parking lot, from where the trail system begins.

Location: Judge C.R. Magney State Park is on Minnesota 61 near mile marker 124 in Cook County, Minnesota, 15 miles northeast of Grand Marais and five miles south of Hovland.

Features of the Park: The Brule River traverses the park and empties into Lake Superior. As this scenic river passes through the park, it forms many whitewater rapids and waterfalls. The lower part of the park is the most popular and accessible to visitors. Along the river in this section are three falls that attract hikers: the Upper Falls, the Lower Falls and the Devil's Kettle Falls.

The other major feature of the park is the extensive non-developed wilderness area.

Trails: Nine miles of hiking trails exist in Judge C.R. Magney State Park, most of which is the Superior Hiking Trail. All of the trails start at the parking lot at the end of the park road. Here is a pit toilet and a spigot for drinking water.

The Superior Hiking Trail is a relatively easy trail to hike, having a slight upgrade but firm and hard-surface footing. The trail is elevated from the flowing river, which can be heard but not seen through the woods of predominantly aspen and birch. Along this section of the trail, you pass Lower Falls. A short spur takes the hiker to the falls.

Further upstream is Upper Falls, a powerful, impressive and picturesque falls. Just before reaching Upper Falls is a stairway with 182 steps, constructed to bring the hiker from the top of the ridge line to the river. From the foot of the stairway, it is about 200 feet to the Upper Falls. Another 700 feet from Upper Falls is Devil's Kettle Falls.

The Devil's Kettle Falls is scenic and interesting. Here, the Brule River is divided by a huge rock formation, causing the water to drop in two falls. The eastern section drops 50 feet into a gorge and pool. The western part plunges into a huge pothole.

Beyond the Devil's Kettle Falls, the Superior Hiking Trail continues along the edge of the Brule River. Along this stretch of the river are numerous small rapids and falls. It is an excellent trail to walk. There are numerous places to observe the river, to fish, and to take photographs. More than two miles beyond Devil's Kettle Falls, the trail

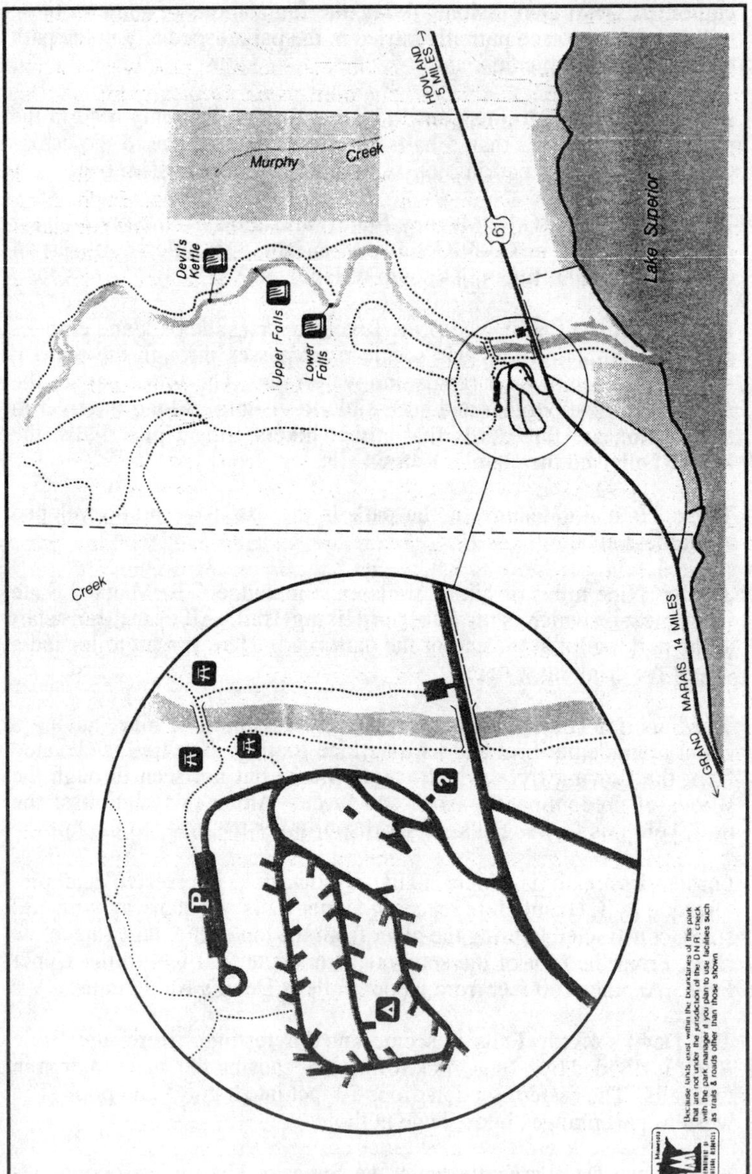
HOVLAND 5 MILES →
Murphy Creek
Lake Superior
61
Devil's Kettle
Upper Falls
Lower Falls
Creek
← GRAND MARAIS 14 MILES
P
?
Because lands exist within the boundaries of this park that are not under the jurisdiction of the D.N.R. check with the park manager if you plan to use facilities such as trails & roads other than those shown

Magney State Park

turns away from the river and enters the Grand Portage State Forest.

Backpackers can hike several miles to a shelter along the western side of the Brule River. The trail at this point is the farthest point into the park where there are maintained trails.

Camping: A semi-modern campground with 33 sites is near the park entrance in a heavily wooded white spruce and pine forest. Each campsite has a picnic table, an in-ground fire pit and a grill. The campsites are not as isolated from neighboring sites as are those in the other state parks along the North Shore. Shower facilities and flush toilets are provided.

Picnic Facilities: Along the banks of the Brule River just a few yards from the parking lot are several picnic sites with tables and an in-ground fire pit. This picnic area is next to the bridge that crosses the Brule River.

Fishing/Wildlife: Fishing is excellent along the Brule River. The river is a designated trout stream. The Department of Natural Resources stocks the river each year with brook and rainbow trout. Steelhead trout spawns in the spring. Salmon run in the fall.

Moose, timber wolves, black bear and deer are found throughout the park, principally in the non-developed sections. Also, fisher, red fox, otter and coyote are in the undeveloped areas.

Many species of birds can be seen in the park. Grouse, woodpeckers and jays are in the area year round. During the fall, hawks migrate along this section of Lake Superior.

Winter Facilities: As is true of all the state parks on the North Shore, C.R. Magney is open during the winter. There is plenty of snow in this area. Five miles of cross-country ski trails are groomed.

Judge C.R. Magney State Park
Grand Marais, MN 55604
(218) 387-2929

Split Rock Lighthouse State Park

Split Rock Lighthouse State Park stretches for three miles along the Lake Superior shoreline. It encompasses 1,872 acres, most of it northwest of the highway. The major trail into this section of the park is the Superior Hiking Trail. Most of the park development is between Minnesota 61 and the lakeshore, where visitors enjoy the lighthouse, campground and hiking trails. Twenty-five acres include the History Center and restored Split Rock Lighthouse. Some say that Split Rock Lighthouse is the most photographed lighthouse in the United States.

The first white people living in this area were commercial fishermen. They lived in a small village, called Little Two Harbors, in the cove near the island, about a half-mile west of the lighthouse. These fishermen fished for herring during the first two decades of the 1900s.

The Split Rock River passes through a narrow, steep-walled canyon and enters Lake Superior at the south end of the park. During the early years of the 1900s logging operations were conducted at the mouth of the river. At that time the forest was predominantly Norway and white pine. Logging and fires took most of these stately trees. Today, birch, spruce, fir and ash constitute the bulk of the forest along the Lake Superior shoreline.

Location: Split Rock Lighthouse State Park is in Lake County, four miles from Beaver Bay and 22 miles north of Two Harbors, Minnesota. It is four miles north of Gooseberry Falls State Park at mile marker 46 on Minnesota 61.

Features of the Park: The park features the lighthouse built in 1910, the History Center operated by the Minnesota Historical Society, nearly three miles of Lake Superior shoreline, and the campground.

Split Rock Lighthouse: On a cliff 130 feet above Lake Superior is one of the most picturesque sights on the Great Lakes. Split Rock Lighthouse stands on a cliff along the shoreline which appears at water level to be split in two parts. The lighthouse stands 50 feet high with stairs leading to its tower. The lighthouse became operational on Aug. 1, 1910, and served as a warning to mariners on Lake Superior until 1969. The beacon, flashing at 10-second intervals, could be seen a distance of 20 to 22 miles. The accompanying fog horn siren could be heard for up to five miles.

The lighthouse was operated by the United States Lighthouse Service until 1939, when the U.S. Coast Guard took over its operation. The station closed in 1969 when modern navigational equipment and techniques made this lighthouse obsolete. In 1971 the Minnesota Historical Society obtained the lighthouse and has developed a historic site and restored the lighthouse as it was in the 1920s. A History Center provides information to visitors.

Since 1971 the lighthouse, surrounding buildings and 25 acres of land in the state park have been administered and operated by the state of Minnesota as a public historic site. Included on the grounds in addition to the lighthouse and fog signal building are three houses which served as residences for the lighthouse keeper and his assistants. Today, one house is restored to the pre-1924 appearance and is open to visitors. The other two serve as private residences. There is a separate fee for entry to the History Center and light station buildings and grounds.

The History Center and buildings are open daily from May 15 to October 15 from 9 a.m. to 5 p.m. From Oct. 16 to May 14, just the History Center is open on weekends from noon to 4 p.m. During this time, the other buildings are not open but visitors can walk the grounds.

The History Center includes a theater which has a seating capacity of 90. A 22-minute film, Split Rock Light: Tribute to the Age of Steel, depicts life of commercial fishing and the development, building and operation of the lighthouse. In the museum portion of the center are

interesting displays that depict the history of the North Shore, navigation on Lake Superior and aids to navigation on the Great Lakes.

Books and other novelties can be purchased at the center's gift shop. A one-hour guided tour takes the visitor to the restored keeper's home, the fog signal building and the lighthouse. At each point of interest is a guide in the role of the keeper's wife, the lighthouse keeper and the operator of the fog signal system. The keeper's wife takes you on a tour of the home, and the keeper explains in detail his activities at the lighthouse.

Camping: Split Rock Lighthouse State Park has one of the most unique campgrounds on the Great Lakes: a "cart-in" campground. The park provides small carts that tent campers can load with their equipment and haul back to their secluded and quiet sites.

Campers must walk in to their site from a parking lot. Twenty widely spread sites are along the rocky shoreline of the park which can be reached only by walking. Distances from the parking lot to the sites range from 350 feet (campsite #3) to the farthest site 1,950 feet from the parking lot (campsite #20). Some sites are on the edge of the cliffs overlooking the lake; most of them are away from the walkway in the woods, providing even greater isolation.

Lightweight, garden-type carts are provided with campsite rentals. The

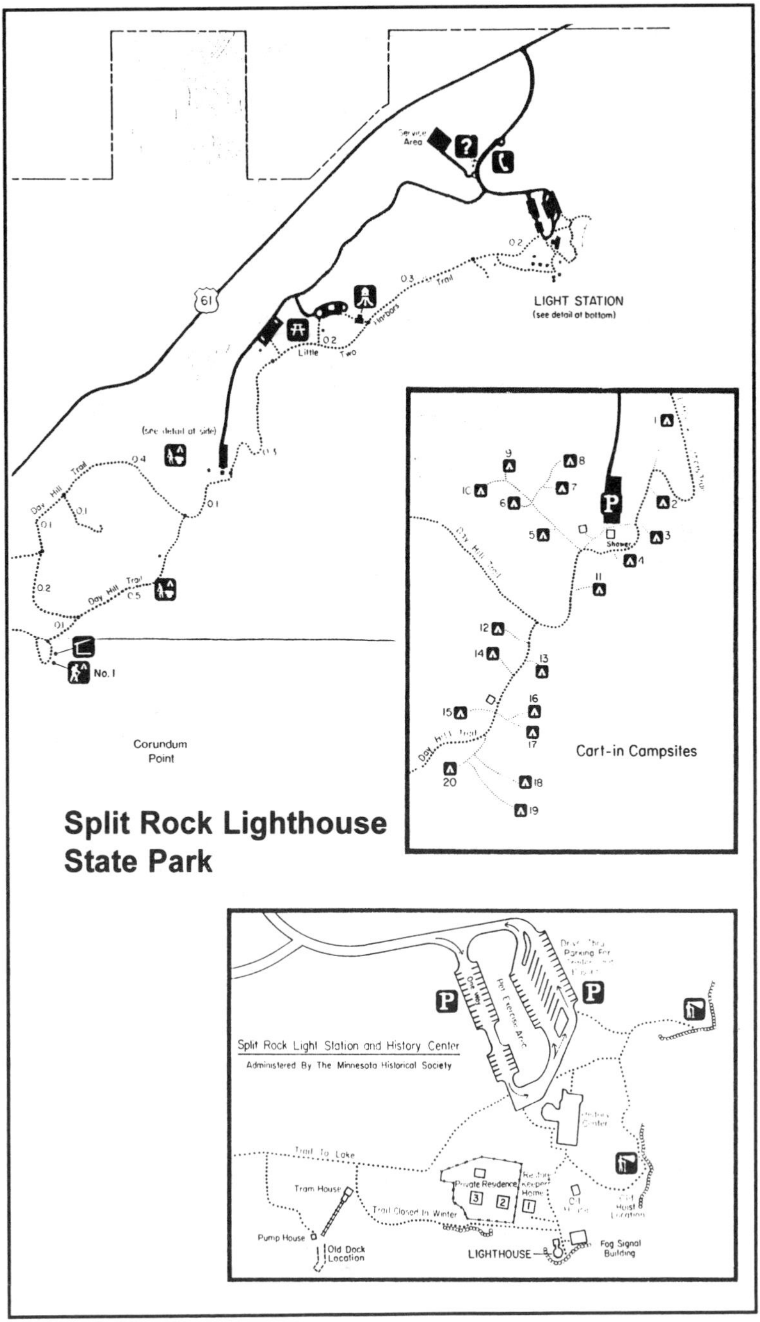
Service Area
61
LIGHT STATION
(see detail at bottom)
0.2
0.3
Trail
Little Two Harbors
(see detail at side)
0.4
Day Hill Trail
0.1
0.2
0.5
No. 1
Corundum Point
Split Rock Lighthouse State Park
Cart-in Campsites
Shower
P
Split Rock Light Station and History Center
Administered By The Minnesota Historical Society
One Way
Pet Exercise Area
Trail To Lake
Tram House
Private Residence
Trail Closed In Winter
Pump House
Old Dock Location
LIGHTHOUSE
Fog Signal Building

carts can be wheeled along gravel trails from the parking lot to the campsites. The sites are well-spaced and secluded. A modern facility with flush toilet and shower and drinking water is near the parking lot.

This is the only state park on the Great Lakes in which all campsites are "cart-in." The popular concept has been in place for more than ten years at Split Rock Lighthouse State Park.

During the summer and early fall, the campground is almost always full. There are plans for additional "cart-in" campsites at this park.

Four backpack camping sites in the park provide primitive and secluded camping.

Trails: Within the park are eight miles of trails for hikers, cross-country skiers and mountain bikers. There are some places, however, where skiing or biking is impossible. For example, on the Day Hill Trail is a stairway leading from a ridge line to the shoreline. Skis and bicycles would have to be carried on these stairs.

The Day Hill Trail is a circular 1.75-mile trail departing from the campground parking lot and passing through the campground. It circles around Day Hill and returns to the parking lot. Generally, the trail is comfortable to walk. A .1-mile spur takes you to the top of Day Hill. From here is an excellent view of the lake shoreline, the lighthouse, and surrounding woods and forests. In the fall the color from this vantage point is spectacular. If you plan to photograph the lighthouse from this lookout, bring a zoom lens. It is possible to see the Apostle Islands in Wisconsin in the distance.

The Corundum Mine Trail extends to Corundum Point where there is an excellent lookout onto Lake Superior. This trail goes on to Split Rock Point and then circles to the trailhead. This trail then brings the hiker to the mouth of the Split Rock River. It also connects with the Superior Hiking Trail after crossing the highway and proceeding on a separate trail for about a half-mile.

Little Two Harbors Trail extends along the lakeshore from the lighthouse station to the parking lot at the campground. This one-mile trail is easy to walk. Where it passes through the picnic area, it is asphalt. Along the shoreline are some of the best places to photograph the lighthouse.

The Superior Hiking Trail extends for about 5.5 miles through the park. The trail winds along the interior portion of the park, north of Minnesota 61.

Picnic Facilities: Along the lakeshore are two picnic areas, both on Little Two Harbors. The Pebble Beach Picnic Area is to the north and the Lakeview Picnic Area is to the south. Picnic tables and in-ground fire rings are spread throughout the birch woods on the edge of the lakeshore. The asphalt Little Two Harbors Trail passes through the picnic area. The Trail Center Picnic Shelter is in the Lakeview Picnic Area. On the rocks and boulders near this shelter is possibly the best place to get a good photograph of the lighthouse and Lake Superior shoreline. Also, a stone, gravel and rock beach is in this picnic area.

Winter Activities: Winter activities are becoming increasingly popular at Split Rock Lighthouse State Park. Camping is particularly popular with the "cart-in" concept.

Cross-country skiing is popular on all eight miles of the trail system. In addition, skiers can find many more miles of trails in the wilderness section of the park.

Split Rock Lighthouse State Park
2010A Hwy. 61 East
Two Harbors, MN 55616
(218) 226-3065

Historic Information:
Minnesota Historical Society
2010 HWY 61 East
Two Harbors, MN 55616
(218) 226-4372

Temperance River State Park

Temperance River State Park, established in 1957, is comprised of 539 acres. A new public information and office building was opened in November 1995, just inside the main park entrance.

The park is surrounded by the Superior National Forest. Also, the nearby 2,520-acre Cross River Wayside Area is administered by the Department of Natural Resources. In this wilderness area are numerous hiking, cross-country ski, and snowmobile trails along the Cross River.

The park is named after the Temperance River, so named in the 1860s because, unlike most other streams along the North Shore of Lake Superior, there is no bar at the mouth of the river. The Ojibwa Indian name for the river was "kawimbash," or "deep hollow river."

Location: Temperance River State Park is in Cook County, Minnesota, just north of Schroeder at the 80-mile marker on Minnesota

61.

Features of the Park: The park features the Temperance River, which winds its way through the park and empties into Lake Superior near the park campgrounds. The total length of the river is 98 miles, draining an area of 164 square miles. It originates at Brule Lake in northern Minnesota.

Within the park the river drops 140 feet, traversing a narrow gorge with many waterfalls along the way. The river cuts deep potholes in the soft riverbed. Over the years these potholes have dug deeper and wider, creating the gorge that is seen today.

The 320-acre Carlton Peak was donated recently to the state park by the 3M Corporation. This peak offers a fantastic view of Lake Superior. It is popular with hikers and rock climbers. Not adjacent to the park, this peak can be reached only by hiking the Superior Hiking Trail.

The Lower Campground is the only state park campground along the Lake Superior North Shore which is next to the water's edge.

Camping: There are 58 semi-modern campsites at Temperance River. The Upper Campground, on a hill overlooking the lake, has 39 campsites; the Lower Campground near the shoreline is comprised of 19 sites.

The Upper Campground is comprised of three loops: Loop A (campsites #1 - #8), Loop B (#9-#18) and Loop C (#19-#39). The campsites are in woods. Each has a picnic table, in-ground fire pit and grill. Loop A is along the river. Campsite #12 is on a bluff overlooking the water with an excellent view.

Electricity is available at the campsites in Loop C. Campsites #31, #32, and #33 are walk-in campsites. Carts are available for hauling gear to these campsites.

The Lower Campground entrance is just south of the highway bridge spanning the river. Campsites #L1 to #L5 face the water across the camp road from the picnic area. Campsites #10, #12, #14 and #20 back up to the highway. Water and pit toilets are available.

The flush toilet and shower facility is in the Upper Campground. Campers in the Lower Campground have access to this facility by walking a short distance over a bridge that crosses the river.

The Upper Campground was renovated in 1994. This project included paving roads and installing of electricity at 18 sites.

Seventy percent of the campsites are available by reservation; the remainder are on a first-come, first-served basis.

Trails: Eight miles of hiking trails are in the park. The most popular trail is the Cauldron Trail. The trailhead for this walk is the parking facility on Minnesota 61 at the bridge. The quarter-mile trail goes to Hidden Falls. Along this short distance are seven overlooks with informational plaques about the geology of the gorge and falls. They explain geological development of this gorge over millions of years. Though a short trail, it is not a particularly easy walk. There is some climbing and a lot of rocks to negotiate before arriving at the falls.

After the falls, the trail continues upstream along the Temperance River. This is part of the Superior Hiking Trail. As you walk along this trail, there are numerous cascades as well as gently flowing water. Less than a quarter-mile upstream from the gorge and waterfalls, the river becomes very placid and quiet. The trail proceeds along the edge of the river, providing excellent views and a very enjoyable hike.

The Superior Hiking Trail enters Temperance River State Park along the west side of the river and proceeds to the highway bridge. Here it heads back up river. Eventually it turns away from the Temperance River and goes toward the Carlton Peak addition to the park.

Picnic Facilities: A picnic facility is along the shoreline across from the Lower Campground. Here are several picnic tables, viewing overlooks, and a small stone and rock beach. The mouth of the river flows into Lake Superior here. The beach is a popular location to walk on the rocks, searching for agates and to fish.

Fishing: The Temperance River is a designated trout stream. As such, rainbow, brook and brown trout have been stocked in the river over the years. Also, chinook salmon and steelhead are found in the river.

Winter Activities: During the winter, park hours are greatly reduced. Yet the park is plowed and open for cross-country skiing, snowmobiling and snowshoeing. Twelve miles of cross-country ski trails are groomed in the park. These ski trails tie in with the Northshore Mountain Ski Trail system, which can take you from the park to Grand Marais. Snow camping is available during the winter. Usually there are several camping parties in the park each winter weekend. Most are snowmobilers planning to head into the surrounding forest lands. A trail connects to the North Shore Corridor Trail, which runs for miles throughout the surrounding woods.

Temperance River Sate Park
P.O. Box 33
Schroeder, MN 55613
(218) 663-7476

Tettegouche State Park

Tettegouche State Park is comprised of 9,346 acres, much of it undeveloped wilderness with no trail access. The park contains four lakes: Nipsiquit Lake, Mic Mac Lake, Tettegouche Lake and Nicado Lake. The park is surrounded by the Finland State Forest and Superior National Forest, which provide hiking trails, cross-country ski trails, snowmobile trails, and camping and fishing sites.

The land that today is the state park once was covered by virgin pine forests. In the late 1890s a lumber camp was established on the shores of Mic Mac Lake. For two decades these trees were harvested. After most of the Norway and white pines were cut, the land was sold in 1910 to a group of businessmen from Duluth who established a fishing camp and retreat. This group used the former lumber camp for recreational purposes until the 1920s. It eventually became privately owned. Over the years it became state land, with a state park established in 1979.

Today, aspen and birch second-growth forest dominate much of the park. Sugar maple and cedar trees also are common. Near the inland lakes sugar maple, yellow birch and white spruce trees are prevalent. In 1992 an addition of the Palisade Valley doubled the size of the park. This valley has two trout lakes with steep rock walls. You enter this area on the Superior Hiking Trail.

Location: Tettegouche State Park is in Lake County, four miles north of Silver Bay, Minnesota. The entrance to the park is at mile marker 58 on Minnesota 61.

Features of the Park: The park features the Lake Superior shoreline, Baptism River, the interior alpine lakes and the extensive hiking trail system.

About one mile of shoreline is in the park. The shoreline is beautiful but dangerous: solid rock with dropoffs of several hundred feet down to the water in places. The forest meets stones, rocks, and boulders along the shoreline. During the fall when the trees turn color, this shoreline is spectacular.

The Baptism River flows 1.8 miles through the park and empties into Lake Superior. The mouth of the river is a short walk from the park information center. Along the Baptism River as it flows through Tettegouche State Park are three falls: Baptism River Cascades, Two Steps Falls, and High Falls. High Falls is the most scenic, cascading 60 feet over the rocks.

Another feature within the park is the four lakes reached only by trails.

Nipisquit is a 50-acre lake with a small picnic facility. Near this lake, on the trail, is the Papasay Ridge overlook which gives a spectacular view of the lake and surrounding wilderness. Tettegouche Lake is 68 acres, Mic Mac Lake is the largest of the four lakes at 121 acres and Nicado Lake is the smallest lake with just 13 acres.

Visitor Center: At the park entrance is a visitor center with a small but interesting interpretive center. Here the visitor can become familiar with the features of the park and surrounding sites on the North Shore of Lake Superior. The center also serves as a campground sign-in office.

Camping: The campground is about 1.5 miles from the visitor center, where the only road in the park ends at the trailhead parking lot. The campground has a modern restroom and heated sanitation and shower building providing opportunity for year round camping. It is near campsite #34.

The heavily wooded campground has 34 sites. Generally, because of heavy underbrush and trees, it is not possible to see the campsite on either side of you or the one across the road. Each site has a picnic table and an in-ground fire pit and grill.

Five campsites (#6, #7, #8, #24 and #25) are walk-in sites. These are not located on the circular road, but campers must park their cars at a designated location and then walk a short distance to the campsite. Carts are available for carrying your gear.

Trails: In the park are 17 miles of hiking trails. The walk taken by most visitors include the three-fourths mile loop trail between the visitor center, the Lake Superior shoreline and the mouth of the Baptism River. The trailway along the Baptism River between the road and mouth of the river is easy and scenic.

Three overlooks should not be missed. At the mouth of the river is a sand and rock bar, and on either side stand tall rock and cliff formations. The walkway is on a bluff overlooking the lake. This part of the trail is asphalt, making it an easy trek and providing handicapped accessibility. Along this walkway are several picnic tables.

A half-mile self-guided trail, the Shovel Point Trail, extends from the edge of the shoreline, within sight of the visitor center, to Shovel Point. Shovel Point has 150-foot cliffs from which spectacular views of the Lake Superior shoreline can be seen. Also, rock climbers find these cliffs a challenge.

The trailhead for much of the interior trail system is at the end of the only road in the park, about 1.5 miles from the park entrance. Generally, the trails are well marked.

A short half-mile trail from the campground leads to High Falls, where there is an overlook. Another trail from the parking lot, about three-fourths of a mile, also leads to High Falls. While at High Falls, cross the suspension bridge that connects the two sides of the river.

This bridge was constructed as part of the Superior Hiking Trail. From the bridge it is possible to get a good view of the river as it flows toward the falls. After walking across the suspension bridge, your legs feel like rubber and will continue to "bounce" for a few minutes along the trail.

After viewing the falls from above, take a short walk to the water's edge for a different vantage point of the falls. Several excellent places to take photographs of the falls are found here.

The Superior Hiking Trail enters the park near Mic Mac Lake and proceeds to High Falls, then continues eastward. At one point on the trail, you must be cautious not to miss a turn. A sign indicating the "drain-pipe" can be easily missed and you will end up on a dead-end little

spur. Instead go downhill on the "drainpipe." The "drainpipe" is a series of rock steps, not particularly easy to maneuver.

Throughout the park trail system are about a dozen overviews that you should not miss. Most are on short spurs, five minutes or so, off of the trail. These overviews are well-marked on the trail map and are also indicated by signs along the trail. These overviews provide excellent places to see the surrounding lakes, valleys, mountains and Lake Superior.

The Lake Superior Water Trail has an access point at Tettegouche State Park.

Picnic Facilities: Two picnic areas are in the park. One is on Nipisiquit Lake, about 1.7 miles by trail from the parking lot. This picnic site includes two tables, a grill and a pit toilet deep in the woods on the eastern shore of this lake. From the parking lot, it takes 45 minutes to an hour of steady walking to this picnic facility.

The other picnic area is about 100 yards into the woods at the trailhead parking lot. Each picnic table is isolated from the others by underbrush and trees. Short spurs through the brush lead to several picnic sites, which have grills.

Also, across from the visitor center at the entrance to the park, are picnic tables. Each picnic site is separated by the brush and trees. Many are near the bluffs of Lake Superior and provide an excellent view of the lake.

Fishing: Fishing is excellent in all four interior lakes. Walleye and northern pike are common. Canoes can be used, but they must be portaged over the foot trails to the lakes. The distance to the lakes by trail is at least 1.5 miles and in some cases longer. Therefore, most fishing is done from the shoreline. Fishing in the Baptism River and in Lake Superior for rainbow trout and salmon is popular among anglers.

Wildlife: A variety of wildlife can be seen in this park. Deer, squirrel and beaver are common. Black bear, moose and red fox are in the vicinity; however, they usually are found in the more isolated sections of the park. Park literature identifies 140 species of birds that have been seen. Of particular interest are the thousands of hawks that migrate along the Lake Superior shoreline during the fall.

Palisade Head: Along Lake Superior is Palisade Head, which stands about 200 feet above the lake. You can drive to the top of this formation and walk a short distance to see spectacular views of the Lake Superior shoreline. This area provides rock climbing opportunities for experienced climbers.

Winter Activities: Tettegouche State Park is open year-round. Camping, snowshoeing, cross-country skiing and snowmobiling are the major winter activities. There are 11 miles of cross-country ski trails in the park. Snowmobiles can be unloaded at the parking lot near the park entrance and trails from there connect to snowmobile trails in the more isolated parts of the park and to the surrounding forests.

Historical Tettegouche Camp on Mic Mac Lake is a popular destination for cross-country skiers and snowshoers. Also, the cross-country ski trails take skiers to the four lakes in the park interior.

Tettegouche State Park
474 HWY 61E
Silver Bay, MN 55614
(218) 226-3539

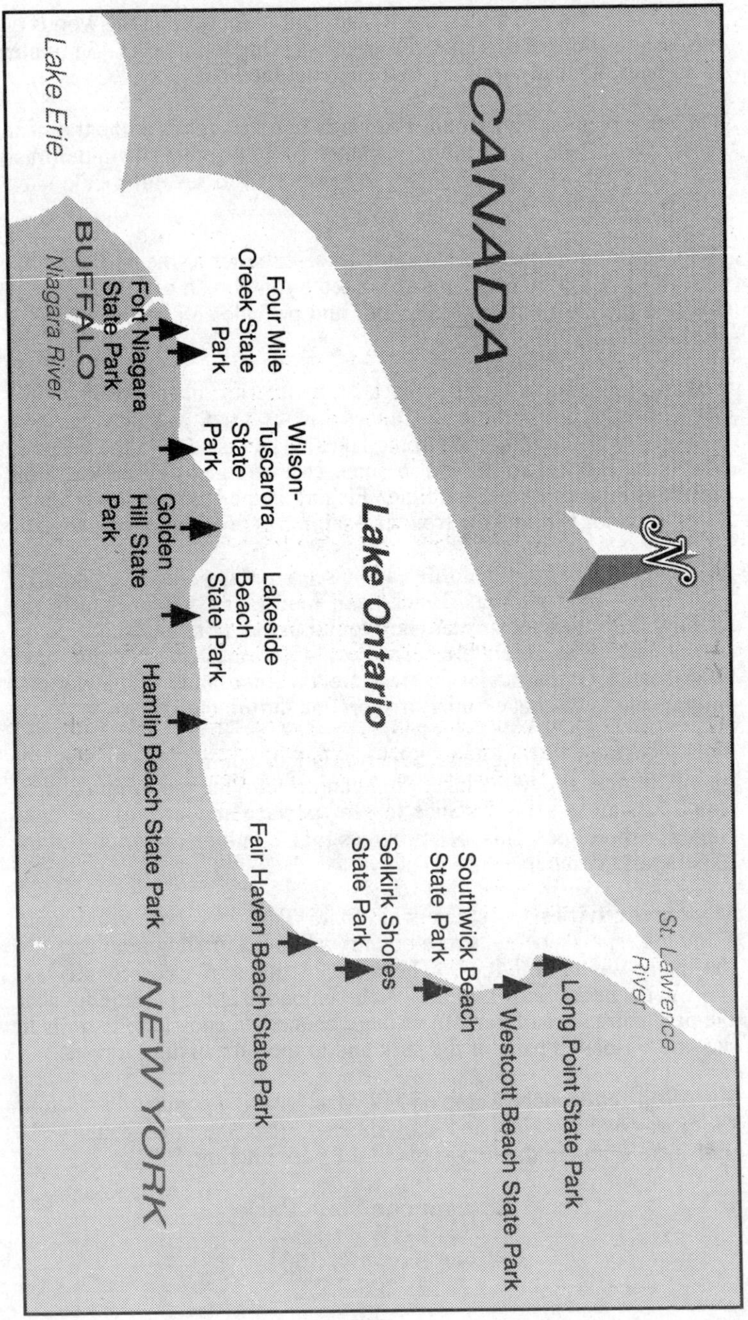
CANADA
Lake Erie
BUFFALO
Niagara River
Lake Ontario
Four Mile Creek State Park
Fort Niagara State Park
Wilson-Tuscarora State Park
Golden Hill State Park
Lakeside Beach State Park
Hamlin Beach State Park
Fair Haven Beach State Park
Selkirk Shores State Park
Southwick Beach State Park
Westcott Beach State Park
Long Point State Park
St. Lawrence River
N
NEW YORK

Lake Ontario

Lake Ontario is the easternmost of the Great Lakes. The entire southern and eastern boundary of this lake is on the border of New York.

There are 11 New York state parks on Lake Ontario. These parks are: Fort Niagara, Four Mile Creek, Wilson-Tuscarora, Golden Hill, Lakeside Beach, Hamlin Beach, Fair Haven Beach, Selkirk Shores, Southwick Beach, Westcott Beach and Long Point.

Most of them are not open year-round. Swimming is permitted only when there is a lifeguard on duty. This occurs from about the last weekend in June through Labor Day. Between Memorial Day and the last weekend of June, lifeguards are available only on weekends. Other services, such as concessions and pools, follow the same schedule.

Most of the parks along Lake Ontario are "carry-in, carry-out." Picnickers are expected to carry out all of their trash.

Reservations for campsites and cabins can be made up to three days, but not more than 90 days in advance at New York state parks. **Reservations: (800) 456-CAMP.**

Fair Haven Beach State Park

Fair Haven Beach State Park is at the junction of Little Sodus Bay and Lake Ontario, an area inhabited in the 1600s by the Cayuga and Seneca Indians. By the early 1900s the region had become a popular resort area. In 1927 work was begun to create a state park. During the 1930s the Civilian Conservation Corps (CCC) built a number of buildings, roads, walkways and campsites. During World War II, Fair Haven Beach was a prisoner of war camp for German prisoners.

Location: Fair Haven Beach is in Cayuga County, New York, with the park entrance in the town of Fair Haven on N.Y. 104A.

Features of the Park: Fair Haven Beach State Park is on three bodies of water: Lake Ontario, Little Sodus Bay and Sterling Pond. In addition to fishing, swimming, boating and sunbathing, there are a variety of other activities in this park of 865 acres, including cabins in the Pond Shore Cabin Area.

Beach: The beach, on Lake Ontario, stretches for about a half-mile between the lake and Sterling Pond. Swimming is permitted at the

beach when lifeguards are on duty. There are bathhouse changing and restroom facilities near the beach, as well as a recreation building. This facility is open during the summer for general use. In spring and fall it may be reserved through the park office, as can all shelters in the park.

Trails: There are two hiking trails, the Bluff Nature Trail and the Lakeshore Trail. The nature trail (.8-mile) passes through a hardwood forest forming a loop which begins near the bluff picnic area. The park nature trail brochure suggests walking the trail in a counter-clockwise pattern.

The Lakeshore Trail (1.2-miles) is a circular trail at the east end of the park, passing through a heavily wooded section. This trail is not well-marked. Bicycles are prohibited on the hiking trails.

Camping: There are 191 campsites in two areas: the Drumlin Camping Area and Bluff Camping Area. Forty-four sites are equipped with electricity. The campgrounds are open from mid-April to the end of October.

The Drumlin Camping Area is near Sterling Pond and the park entrance road, .4-mile from the beach and camp store. A sidewalk along Sterling Pond connects the beach with the campground. The campground itself

Fair Haven State Park

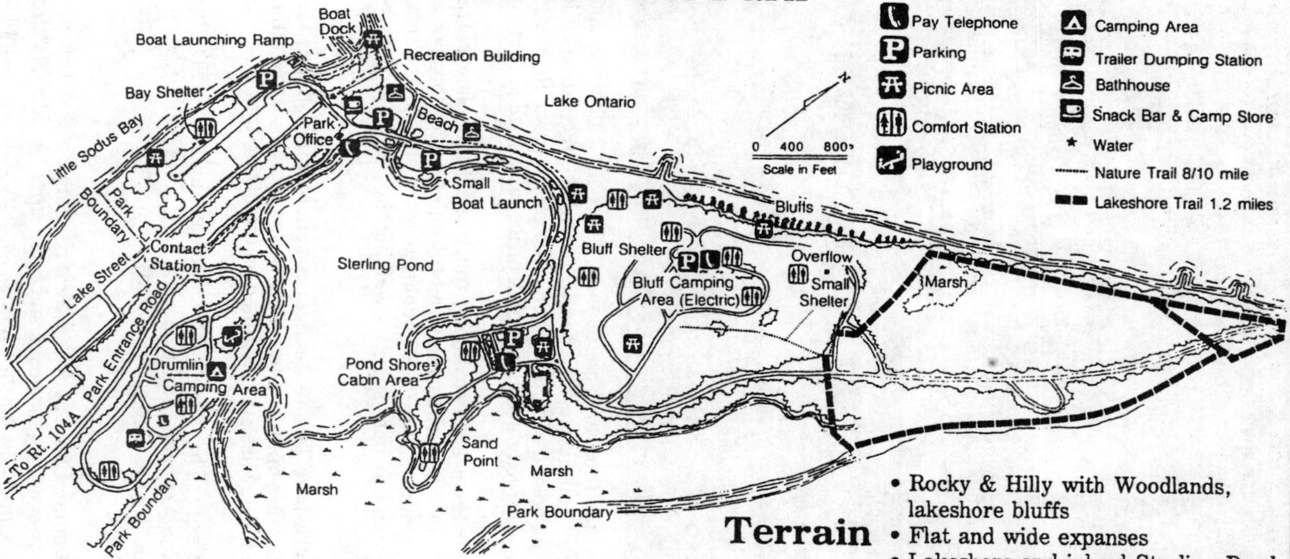

Terrain

- Rocky & Hilly with Woodlands, lakeshore bluffs
- Flat and wide expanses
- Lakeshore and inland Sterling Pond

is heavily wooded with much undergrowth and shrubbery between most sites. In many instances there is good distance between adjacent campsites. Each campsite has a picnic table, in-ground fire pit and grill. There are three modern toilet and shower buildings with hot shower and flush toilet facilities in this campground.

Campsites #165 to #175 are along Sterling Pond. The pond can be seen through the woods, since the sites are slightly above the pond on the small bluff.

The Bluff Camping Area has 44 campsites (#51-#94) on a bluff out of sight of the lake and pond. The campground is well shaded with small sites. Electricity is available at each site along with a picnic table, in-ground fire pit and grill. The modern toilet/shower building is in each circle.

From the end of June through Labor Day, the campgrounds are filled on most weekends and all holidays. During the week campsites are usually available. During July and August, several recreation programs are conducted by park personnel.

A camp store is near the beach and park office.

Cabins: Thirty-six cabins are on the point at Sterling Pond, called the Pond Shore Cabin Area. Some of the cabins (#5-#9 and #11-#14) overlook Sterling Pond, while others look out on the marsh at the south end of the pond. The cabins are well spaced and the area is well shaded.

All of the cabins have electric lighting, a refrigerator with small freezer, and an outside fireplace and table. The cabins vary in size. Several have accommodations for four individuals; others have three or four rooms. While most do not have heat or cooking facilities, there are some exceptions. Four of the cabins (#9, #12, #34 and #35) have a sink with hot and cold running water plus a four-burner gas stove with oven. One of these is a six-person cabin; the others are four person. Eight cabins (#1, #2, #4, #9, #12, #13, #17 and #33) are insulated and can be rented during the winter. Reservations may be made for a minimum of two nights during the spring and fall. During the prime summer season, the cabins can only be reserved on a weekly basis.

Picnic Facilities: Several picnic areas are scattered throughout the park. The Bluff Picnic Area is across from the entrance to the Bluff Campground. Included are picnic tables, children's swings and play sets, and a large play field with a softball backstop.

Another well shaded picnic area is on Little Sodus Bay, near the boat ramp. In this area most of the tables are placed on an asphalt slab. A grill is available at most picnic sites. A number of picnic tables are along Sterling Pond and in the beach area.

Boating/Fishing: Fishing is popular at Fair Haven Beach State Park, especially in Sterling Pond. The day of my visit I talked with several individuals fishing for northern pike. Also, you can fish in Little Sodus Bay and in the surrounding waters of Lake Ontario.

A boat launch with two ramps empties into Little Sodus Bay. Near the ramp is a large parking area for vehicles and boat trailers. A place to dock boats during the day can be found here, though overnight dockage is not permitted.

There also is a small boat launch on Sterling Pond, where rowboats are available for rent.

Winter Activities: The park is open year-round; however, there is no winter camping nor other services. Eight cabins are winterized and can be rented during the winter. These are popular among ice fishermen. Hiking, snowshoeing, cross-country skiing and ice fishing are popular during the winter as well.

Fair Haven Beach State Park
Route 104A
Fair Haven, NY 13064
(315) 947-5205

Fort Niagara State Park

Fort Niagara State Park is adjacent to the historic Old Fort Niagara, which is operated by a non-profit organization. Most visitors are unaware that the fort is not part of the state park, though they are next to each other. The park was dedicated in 1948 and is comprised of 240 acres.

Location: Fort Niagara State Park is at the mouth of the Niagara River, where it flows into Lake Ontario. It is on the Robert Moses Parkway about 15 miles north of Niagara Falls. There are two entrances to the park: the north entrance is reached from the parkway, while the south entrance is reached from Youngstown, New York.

Features of the Park: This park is basically a recreational area with facilities for picnicking, swimming, soccer and hiking.

Picnic Facilities: A large, grassy area for picnicking is along the Lake Ontario shoreline. There are numerous large trees throughout the picnic area. Extending to the water's edge is a sloping treeless grass area known as the Sun Lawn.

Another picnic area is across from the main soccer field. This wooded, grass-covered area has several grills and picnic tables.

There are shelters at both picnic areas.

Trails: A hiking trail departs from the picnic area and goes along the bluffs a short distance, turns south (right) and ends at the soccer fields. Less than .75-mile in length, there is no sign identifying the trail.

Swimming: Swimming is not permitted in Lake Ontario here. There is no beach or access to the water, but there is a large swimming pool complex adjacent to the picnic area. The pool is open from 11 a.m.-7 p.m. from late June until Labor Day. Next to the swimming pool is a snack and refreshment stand.

Boating/Fishing: There is a hard-surfaced boat launch into the Niagara River. A fee is charged to use this launch.

Recreational Fields: Two large areas in the park have about 17 soccer fields. The fields are used by the Niagara Pioneer Soccer Program, a non-profit, volunteer program for young people ages 5-19. Each summer tournaments attract up to 25,000 people. Everyone involved in the program are volunteers.

Camping: There are no camping facilities at Fort Niagara State Park. Camping is available two miles east on the Robert Moses Parkway at Four Mile Creek State Park.

Old Fort Niagara: On the point where the Niagara River flows into Lake Ontario is Old Fort Niagara, one of the oldest continuously occupied military sites in North America. This fort has been occupied as a military establishment since the latter part of the seventeenth century. The fort controlled access to the Great Lakes in those years.

In 1678 LaSalle erected temporary fortifications, Fort Conti, at the mouth of the Niagara River to protect French trading interests. In 1726 DeLery built for the fur trade on the Great Lakes a structure with stone walls, known as the "Castle." This structure, resembling a French chateau, is the oldest standing structure of the fort.

Possession of the fort changed hands several times during the latter part of the 1700s and the early 1800s. In 1759, after an 18 day siege during the French and Indian War, the English, under command of Sir William Johnson, captured the fort. The British improved the fort and used it for fur trading. During the American Revolution, Fort Niagara was a British base for raiding the American frontier. It wasn't until 1796 that American troops captured the fort.

Then during the War of 1812, following an American raid into Canada,

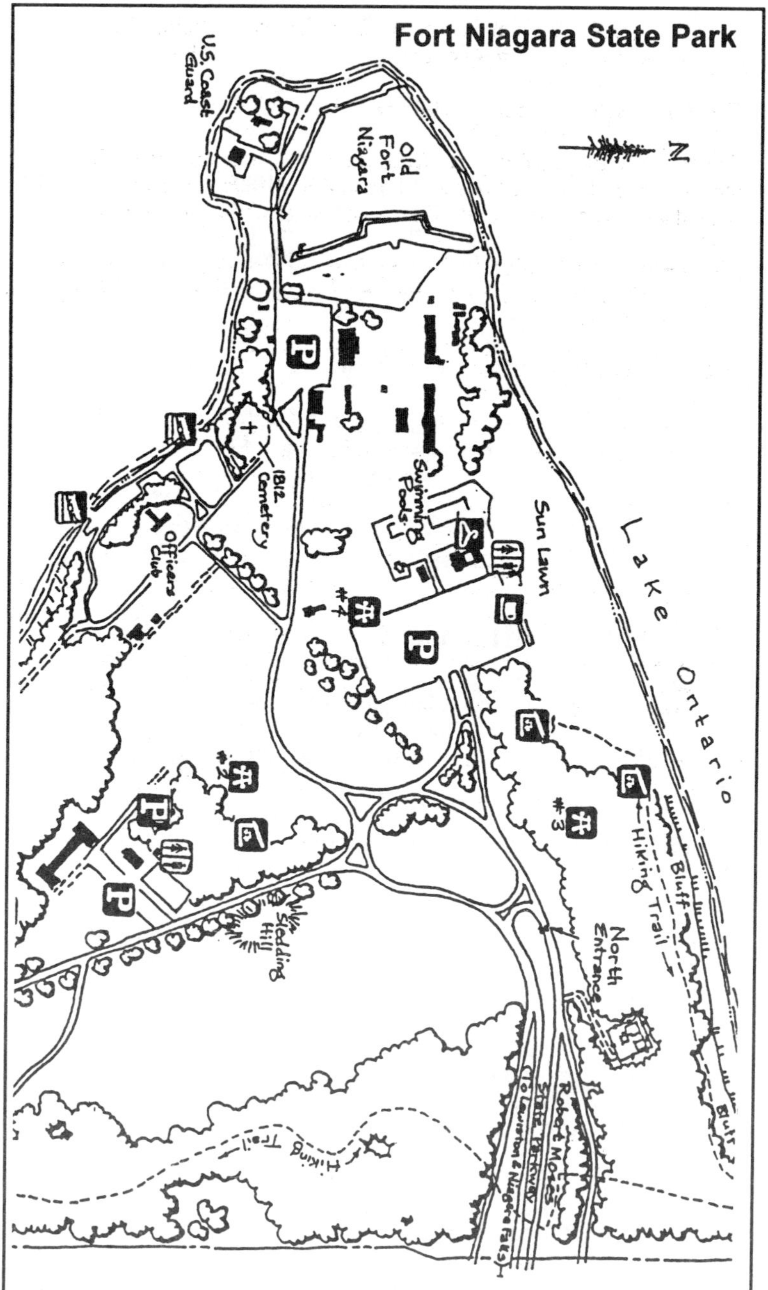
Fort Niagara State Park
U.S. Coast Guard
Old Fort Niagara
N
1812 Cemetery
Officers Club
Swimming Pools
Sun Lawn
Lake Ontario
#4
#2
#3
Sledding Hill
Hiking Trail
Bluff
North Entrance
Robert Moses State Parkway
(To Lewiston & Niagara Falls)

the British recaptured the fort in 1813. A peace treaty in 1814 returned the fort to the United States.

During the Second World War, Fort Niagara housed German prisoners of war.

Today, there is a self-guided tour of the fort grounds. The fort is open year round from 9 a.m. - 6:30 p.m. weekdays and 9 a.m. - 7:30 p.m. week-ends. Various demonstrations, re-enactments and special events are held from late June to Labor Day. These activities provide an opportunity for visitors to experience early history of this important part of America.

There is an admission fee to enter the fort.

Fort Niagara State Park
Youngstown, NY 14174
(716) 745-7611

Nearby

FOUR MILE CREEK STATE PARK

Four Mile Creek is a camping park about two miles east of Fort Niagara State Park on the Robert Moses Parkway in Niagara County, New York. The park rests where Four Mile Creek flows into Lake Ontario.

The park is comprised of 248 acres, most of which is the campground. Some of the acreage, not yet developed, is west of Four Mile Creek.

There are 266 campsites available from mid-April through the middle of October. Three modern shower and toilet buildings are in the interior of the three camping circles. Laundry facilities are available in these buildings. A picnic table, an in-ground fire ring and grill are available at each site. About 100 campsites have electricity.

This part of Four Mile Creek is marshy, making it possible to observe the typical marshland wildlife habitat. At the entrance to the park is a sign indicating that this park is open only to campers.

Four Mile Campsite
Youngstown, NY 14174
(716) 745-3802

Golden Hill State Park

Golden Hill State Park received its name from Golden Hill Creek, which flows into Lake Ontario at the old Cartwright farm near Thirty Mile Point. Daniel Cartwright was a pioneer who kept his cattle in a field bordering the lake near the mouth of Golden Hill Creek. The land, which became a state park in 1962, is comprised of 378 acres.

Tradition says that early French explorers were the first to call this location "Golden Hill." In the fall, the area appears like a hill of gold because of goldenrod blossoms that are prevalent.

Location: Golden Hill State Park is about three miles east of Somerset, New York, in the northeast corner of Niagara County. To arrive at the park, turn off of N.Y. 18 on Carmen Road and follow the signs about a mile and a half to the entrance.

Features of the Park: Golden Hill features a campground and the Thirty Mile Point Lighthouse.

Camping: The campground sits on a bluff, 10 to 15 feet above the shoreline overlooking Lake Ontario. The campground is grassy and open with no underbrush, much like camping in a field. A few small trees were planted recently. There is a picnic table at each of the 50 campsites, with electricity provided at 19 of them.

The campsites are around three short loops. Loop A is nearest the restroom and shower facility. Electricity is not provided to these sites. These campsites are on the outer side of the loop road. The sites are well spaced, with grills at each site. There are two shelters for picnic use in this loop, as well as a children's play area between Loop A and Loop B.

Loop B is near the lake, with electricity provided. Campsite #29 is next to the lighthouse. This site, along with #30 and #31 are on the bluff overlooking Lake Ontario. Directly on the bluff, across a road from Loop B, is a recreation hall which has ping-pong and several other games.

Loop C is the most shaded and scenic of the three campground loops. Electricity is not available. Campsites on the edge of the bluff overlooking the water are #36, #37, #39, #40, #46, #49 and #50.

There are several handicapped accessible campsites: #1 in Loop B, and #19 and #35 in Loop A.

Flush toilet facilities, a shower and hot water are at the entrance to Loop A. Basketball, volleyball and softball facilities are near the campground, which is open from mid-April through mid-October.

Trails: Six miles of trails exist in the park. A hiking and cross-country ski map is next to the parking area at the boat launch. The trails are marked by color code: The orange trail is 1.5 miles, the green trail is 1.16 miles, and the red trail is 1.52 miles. A series of blue trails provide access to trail systems outside the park. Another trail goes from the lighthouse to the mouth of Golden Hill Creek at the boat launch ramp..

Boat Launch/Fishing: The boat launch is on a road about a half-mile from the park entrance. The launch constructed in 1988, is where Golden Hill Creek flows into Lake Ontario. There is a fee for either launching or bringing in a boat. On the day of my visit several people fished along the shore of Lake Ontario and Thirty Mile Creek in this area.

Next to the boat launch is a small picnic area with several tables and grills. There also is a small open shelter with picnic tables.

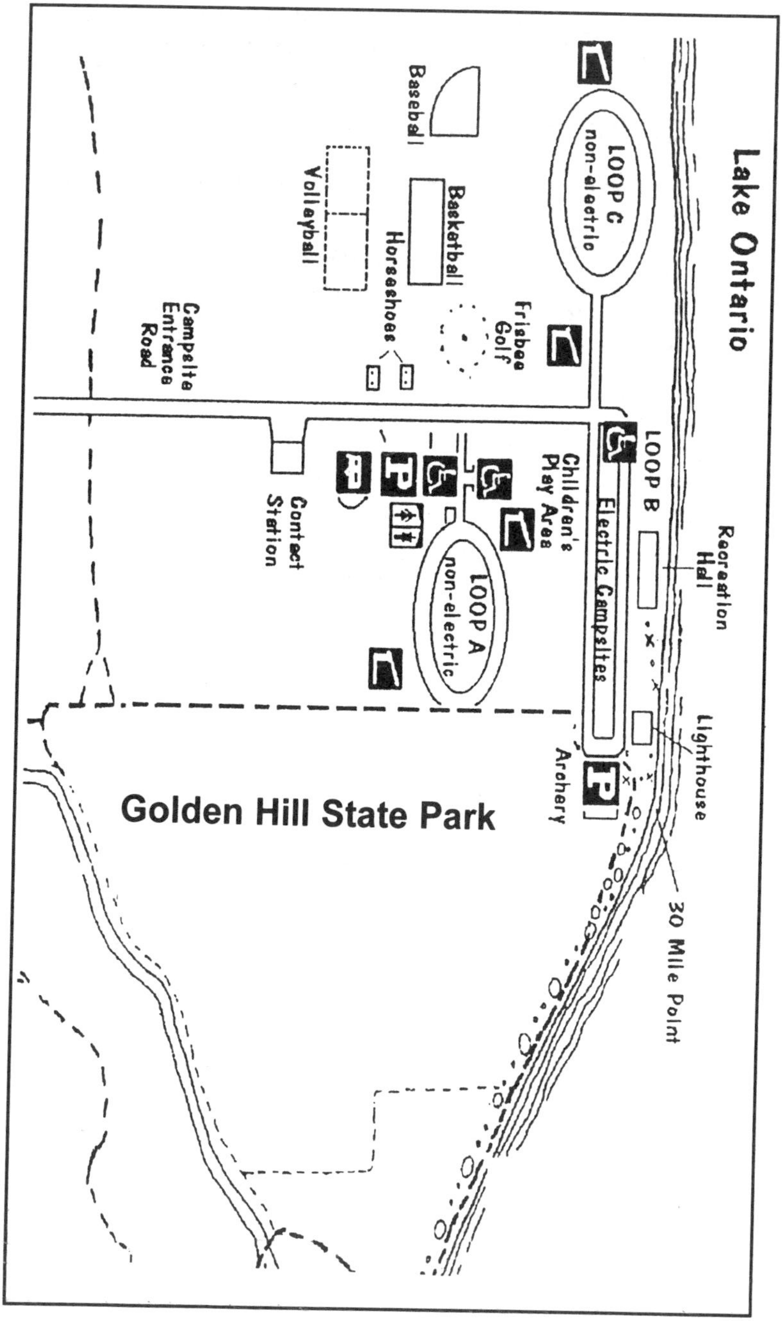
Lake Ontario
LOOP C
non-electric
Baseball
Basketball
Volleyball
Horseshoes
Frisbee
Golf
Campsite
Entrance
Road
LOOP B
Children's
Play Area
Electric Campsites
Recreation
Hall
Contact
Station
LOOP A
non-electric
Lighthouse
Archery
Golden Hill State Park
30 Mile Point

Pheasant and small game hunting is allowed in the park. Waterfowl hunting is allowed by permit. Small game season opens the first day of pheasant season and is open for rabbits until the end of February.

Thirty Mile Point Lighthouse: Thirty Mile Point Lighthouse was built at the mouth of Golden Hill Creek in 1875. It was built to warn approaching boats of a shifting sandbar and dangerous shoals stretching into the lake.

The lighthouse stands more than 60 feet high, has a slate roof, and is constructed of cut stone shipped from Chaumont Bay, near the source of St. Lawrence Bay. The lens, producing 600,000 candle power of light, was purchased from France. It was the most powerful lighthouse beacon on Lake Ontario. Its light could be seen as far as 16 to 18 miles. Inside is a circular steel staircase to the top from where there is an excellent view of the lake and surrounding area.

Two caretakers were on duty at the lighthouse. The families of the two lived in the lighthouse, with each caretaker working a 24-hour shift.

The lighthouse closed in 1958, replaced by an automated light now maintained by the U.S. Coast Guard. A brown horse stable and barn were constructed at the same time as the lighthouse in 1875. There is a garage and foghorn building that now serves as a recreation hall for campers. The foghorn building had compressed air tanks boxed in the ceiling which serviced a foghorn.

The lighthouse is open for visitors on Friday, Saturday and Sunday and on holidays from the first of July to Labor Day from 2-4 p.m. During the rest of the year, groups may request tours.

Beach/Shoreline: No swimming is permitted along the shoreline, which is mainly rock, stone, silt and gravel. Queenston shale, a sedimentary rock formed from sand, silt and clay, is found here. It has a rusty red appearance from small amounts of iron oxide. Geologists estimate that the shale was deposited here about 12,000 years ago when melting ice sheets retreated from this area.

Winter Activities: Snowshoeing and cross-country skiing are available in the park during the winter. However, there are no rental or winter camping services available.

Golden Hill State Park
9691 Lower Lake Road
Barker, NY 14012
(716) 795-3885

Hamlin Beach State Park

Hamlin Beach State Park, comprising 1,364 acres, became a state park in 1938.

Much of the early development in the state park was accomplished by the Civilian Conservation Corps during the late 1930s. From 1935 to 1941, members of the CCC constructed six buildings and reclaimed 90 acres of swamp in the east section of the park.

In November 1943, a prisoner of war camp was established on the site of the CCC camp. German prisoners of war lived here until the end of W.W.II in 1945.

Location: Hamlin Beach is near Hamlin in Monroe County, New York, about 25 miles west of Rochester on the Lake Ontario State Parkway.

Features of the Park: One feature of Hamlin Beach State Park is the shoreline, with two swimming beaches and five picnic areas stretching the length of the park. Another popular feature of the park is the heavily wooded campground. The Yanty Creek Nature Trail provides an opportunity to experience and learn about the marshy wetlands of the park.

Camping: Many people come to Hamlin Beach to camp. There are 264 campsites open from early May through Columbus Day in October. The road into the campground is near the Picnic Area 1 parking lot. The sites are on six circular loops (A through F), almost all of which are shady and well spaced. They are separated from each other by trees, underbrush and shrubs. In addition each has electricity, a picnic table, in-ground fire ring and grill. The numbered campsites are:

Loop A - #1 - #39
Loop B - #40 - #73
Loop C - #74 - #137
Loop D - #138 - #197
Loop E - #198 - #223
Loop F - #224 - #264

The camp store, laundry and a recreation building are at Loop C on the main campground road. Pets are permitted only in loops A and B. The campsites at the back of each loop are close to the highway; however, they are protected from the highway by heavy brush and woods. There is a group camping area at the western end of the park.

Trails: There are five trails in the park. All but one of the trails, which are color coded, start and finish in parking lot Area 1. Each trail has a wooden sign at the start and finish, and one at midpoint.

One hard-surface sidewalk runs the length of the park from Picnic Area 1 through Picnic Area 5, a distance of about two miles. It travels parallel to the shoreline, passing through woods and is scenic. Along the trail are hundreds of picnic tables and grills as well as several shelters. People were walking, jogging, roller blading and bicycling this walkway on the day of my visit.

Picnic Facilities: Five areas are designated for picnic activities, each with a large parking lot.

West Bluff Shelter II, at Area 4 adjacent to the parking lot, is enclosed, with several picnic tables inside. Outside are four barbecue pits.

West Bluff Shelter I is at Area 4, close to the beach. Near areas 3 and 4 is a concession building.

Swimming/Beaches: Swimming is permitted at beaches in Area 3 and Area 4 when lifeguards are on duty, usually from 11 a.m. to 6 p.m. from

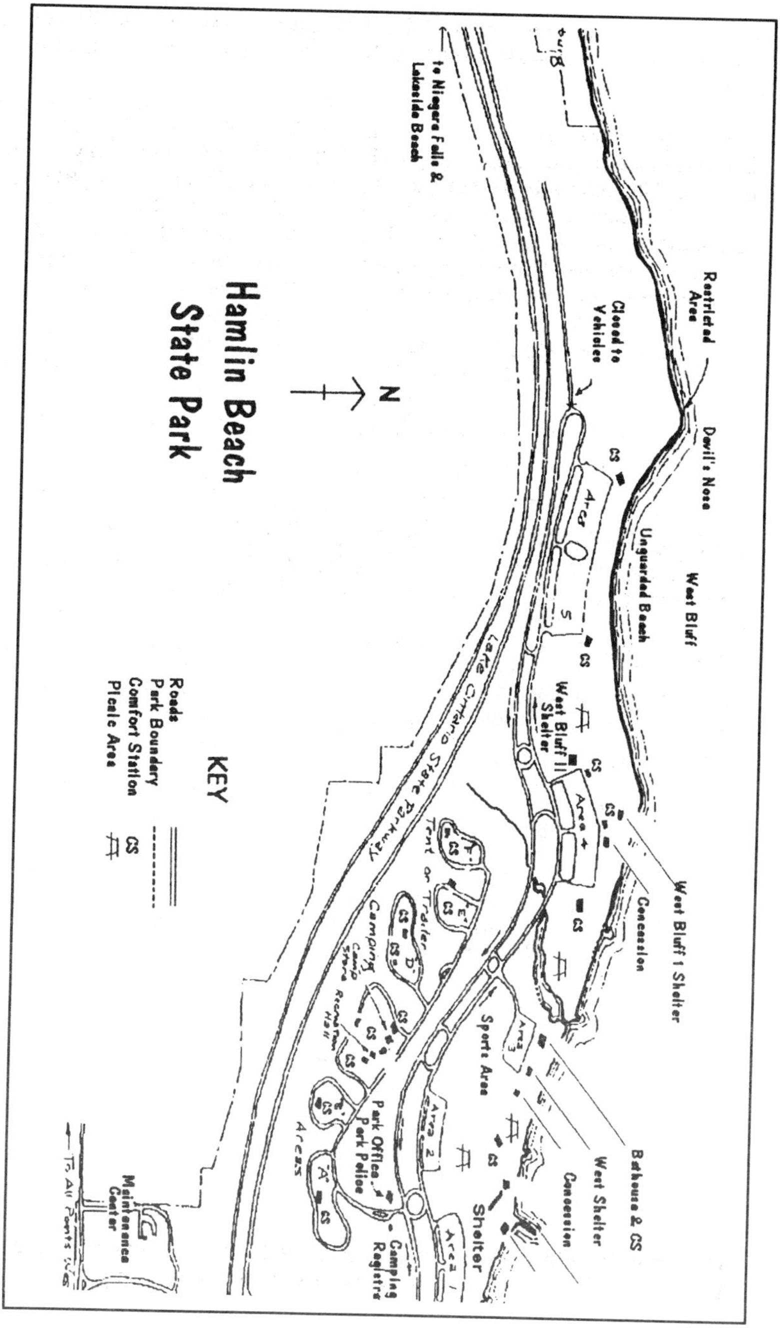
Hamlin Beach
State Park
N
KEY
Roads
Park Boundary
Comfort Station
Picnic Area
CS
to Niagara Falls &
Lakeside Beach
Restricted Area
Closed to Vehicles
Devil's Nose
West Bluff
Unguarded Beach
Area 5
CS
West Bluff II Shelter
Area 4
West Bluff 1 Shelter
Concession
Lake Ontario State Parkway
Tent or Trailer
Camping
Camp Store
Recreation Hall
F
E
D
C
B
A
Areas
Sports Area
Area 3
Bathouse & CS
West Shelter
Concession
Shelter
Area 2
Area 1
Park Office
Park Police
Camping
Registra
Maintenance
Center

late June through Labor Day. These combined beaches extend for more than a half-mile. The sand comes back a couple of hundred yards from the water's edge, plenty of sand for sunbathing and relaxing on a hot summer day.

Swimming is prohibited at picnic areas 1, 2 and 5. The shoreline here is sand, pebbles and small stones, with much driftwood.

Nature: At the eastern edge of the park is Yanty Creek. At the creek where it enters Lake Ontario is the 200-acre Yanty Marsh Environment Area. The .9-mile Yanty Creek Nature Trail provides environmental education about the area. Many school groups come to this area to learn of the surrounding environment. A guide for teachers is available. Along the trail you can observe marshlands fed by Yanty Creek. Also there is a coniferous woodlot, a deciduous woodlot, and a small pond.

Many species of birds can be seen at the park. A brochure provided to visitors identifies more than 250 species of birds that have been observed in this park. More than 65 species nest in the surrounding habitats. The best place to observe birds is in wetlands along the Yanty Creek Nature trail.

Boating/Fishing: A boat launch at the eastern end of the park can be used for launching small watercraft such as windsails, kayaks and canoes. Marine launch sites are available outside of the park at several nearby locations. Beaching of watercraft on park shores is prohibited.

Fishing is permitted along the shoreline in non-swimming areas. However, no fishing is permitted from the rock jetties extending into the lake.

Summer Activities: Once a week during July and August, concerts are conducted along the shore in picnic Area 3. During the Labor Day weekend, an arts festival attracts many people.

Hamlin Beach State Park
Hamlin, NY 14464
(716) 964-2462

Lakeside Beach State Park

Lakeside Beach State Park was established in 1962 and comprises 743 acres. The property had fruit orchards and lake front cottages.

Entering the park, the road to the left goes to the picnic area; the road to the right enters the campground. The roads are well manicured, with a wide swath of grass and shrubbery cut back a distance from the road. This is common in the state parks of western New York.

Location: Lakeside Beach is in Orleans County where N.Y. 18 changes from a two-lane road to four-lane Lake Ontario State Parkway. The park is between the shoreline of Lake Ontario and the parkway.

Features of the Park: Lakeside Beach is a camping and day-use park. There is no beach, with no swimming along the Lake Ontario shoreline, nor are there any hiking trails in the park. The park is not open in the winter.

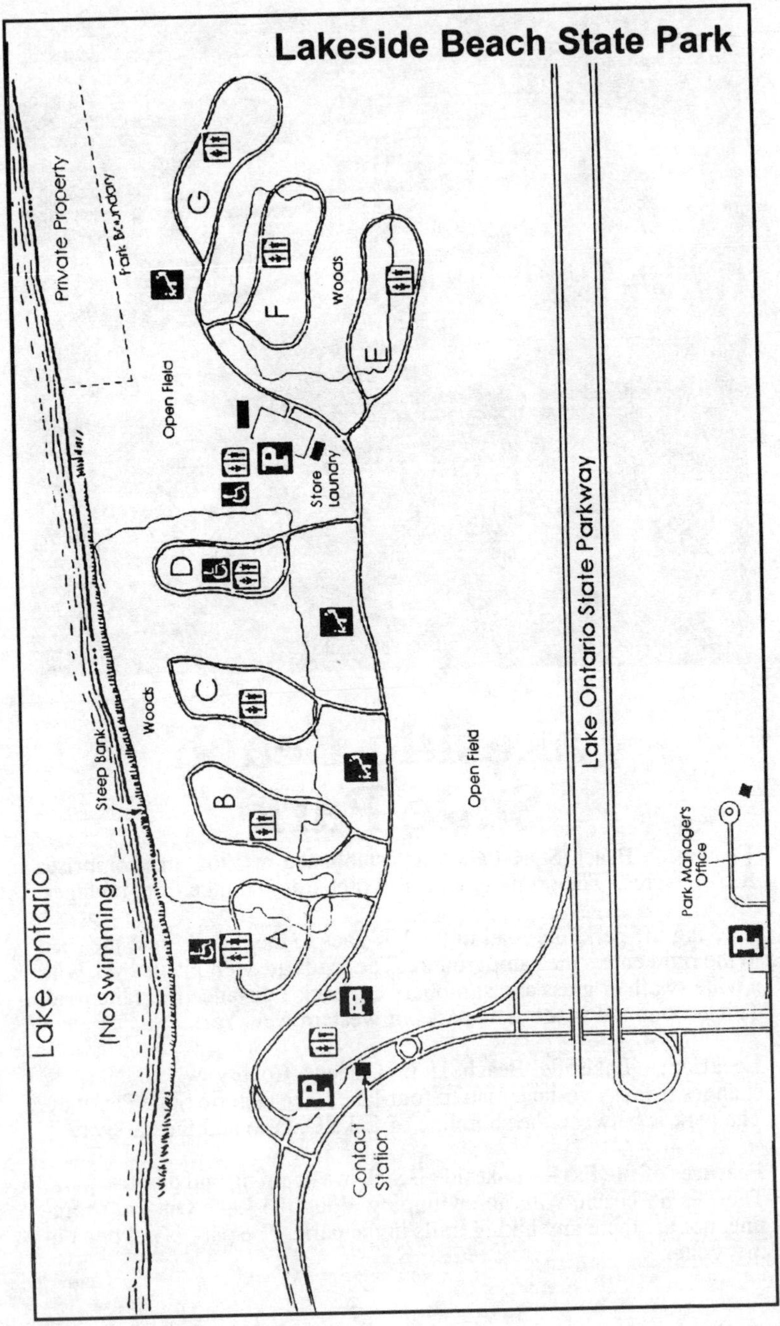

Lakeside Beach State Park
Lake Ontario
(No Swimming)
Private Property
Park Boundary
Steep Bank
Woods
Open Field
Woods
Store
Laundry
Open Field
Lake Ontario State Parkway
Park Manager's Office
Contact Station
A
B
C
D
E
F
G

Camping: There are 274 campsites along seven circular loops (A through G). Every campsite is equipped with electricity.

Loop A - There are 37 well-shaded, well-spaced sites in this loop. Campsites #A16, #A17, #A19, #A21 and #A22 are on the edge of the bluff overlooking the water.

Loops B, C and D - Loop B has 39 campsites, Loop C 40 and Loop D 36. Campsites in these loops are heavily wooded, with shrubs separating the sites, providing good privacy from neighboring campsites. Good distance separates each site.

Loop E - Campsites along this loop are in the open, with a few small trees. There are no shrubs between the 41 campsites here.

Loop F - The sites in this loop are in the woods and nicely separated from adjacent campsites. There are 40 sites in this loop.

Loop G - The 41 campsites in this loop are in the open, with little shade.

Each campsite has a picnic table, an in-ground fire pit and grill. Pets are prohibited in Loops A, B, C and D. Each loop has a modern toilet and shower building.

A camp store, with laundry facilities, is across from Loop E. An enclosed recreation building for campers also is here. Near campground loops A - D is a large open field for recreational purposes. The campground is open from late April until the latter part of October.

Picnic Facilities: Picnic tables are scattered from the large parking lot to the edge of the water, about a quarter of a mile. At the water's edge is a 5-to 10-foot bluff. In this grass covered picnic area there are no trees. The edge of the shoreline is rocky and stony. There is an open shelter with about a dozen picnic tables as well as a children's playground. A pavilion is available by reservation near the picnic area parking lot. This picnic area has a "carry-in, carry-out" designation, meaning you must take out all your trash.

Winter Activities: During the winter the park is available for cross-country skiing, hiking and snowmobiling. However, there are no services or winter camping.

Lakeside Beach State Park
Waterport, New York 14571
(716) 682-4888

Long Point State Park

Long Point State Park is a small park, principally a camping facility. It is the most remote state park on Lake Ontario to reach from the main highways.

There are several private cabins just across Long Bay and a private trailer court of about two dozen trailers, just a few hundred yards from the entrance to the park on Chaumont Bay. This is a "carry-in, carry-out" park; you must take your own trash out of the park.

The park is open from mid-May until shortly after Labor Day.

Location: Long Point State Park is on Point Peninsula in Jefferson County, New York, on a narrow peninsula between Chaumont Bay on Lake Ontario and Long Bay.

The park is about 15 miles from Cape Vincent, New York. To reach the park, travel north about two miles from the town of Three Mile Bay on state road 12E and turn onto Jefferson County road 57. Proceed on the county road for 8.1 miles. When road 57 turns right, continue straight ahead, 1.5 miles to the park entrance. This intersection is easily missed; there is a small painted sign, "Long Point," about 20 inches high, but was covered by tall grass on the day of my visit.

Features of the Park: This is an isolated camping park that is nearly surrounded by water. There are no recreational facilities, beach, or nearby commercial recreational interests; most people who camp come here to fish.

Camping: There are 94 campsites in this park. Eighteen around one circle road have electricity.

Generally, the campground is open with few trees providing shade. There are no shrubs or bushes between the campsites. A picnic table, large in-ground fire pit and grill are found at each campsite. The ground surface of the campground is freshly mowed grass.

The campsites in the middle of the circles have no shade. Some of the sites near the water have trees. Though water can be seen from anywhere in the campground, several sites are directly on the water's edge, along Chaumont Bay (#42, #44 to #49 and #50) and along Long Bay (#77 to #87 and #51 through #58). Several of these campsites are very small, however. There is one handicapped accessible campsite (#53), near the boat launch and fishing pier. This campsite has a hard-surface pad for placement of a trailer.

Two modern shower and toilet facilities are in the campground, which often is full on summer holidays and weekends. It is also packed on special fishing days, such as the first day of bass fishing.

In the campground is a pavilion which can accommodate about 40 people. Reservations are needed to use this facility; call Westcott Beach State Park (315) 938-5083. Swings and horseshoe pits are available in the campground.

Picnic Facilities: On the point of the park peninsula is a small, rustic picnic area with about a half dozen picnic tables and grills.

Boats/Fishing: A small fishing pier is near the picnic area. Adjacent is a small boat launch ramp and a marina with 32 floating docks.

Long Point State Park
7495 State Park Road
Three Mile Bay, NY 13693
(315) 649-5258

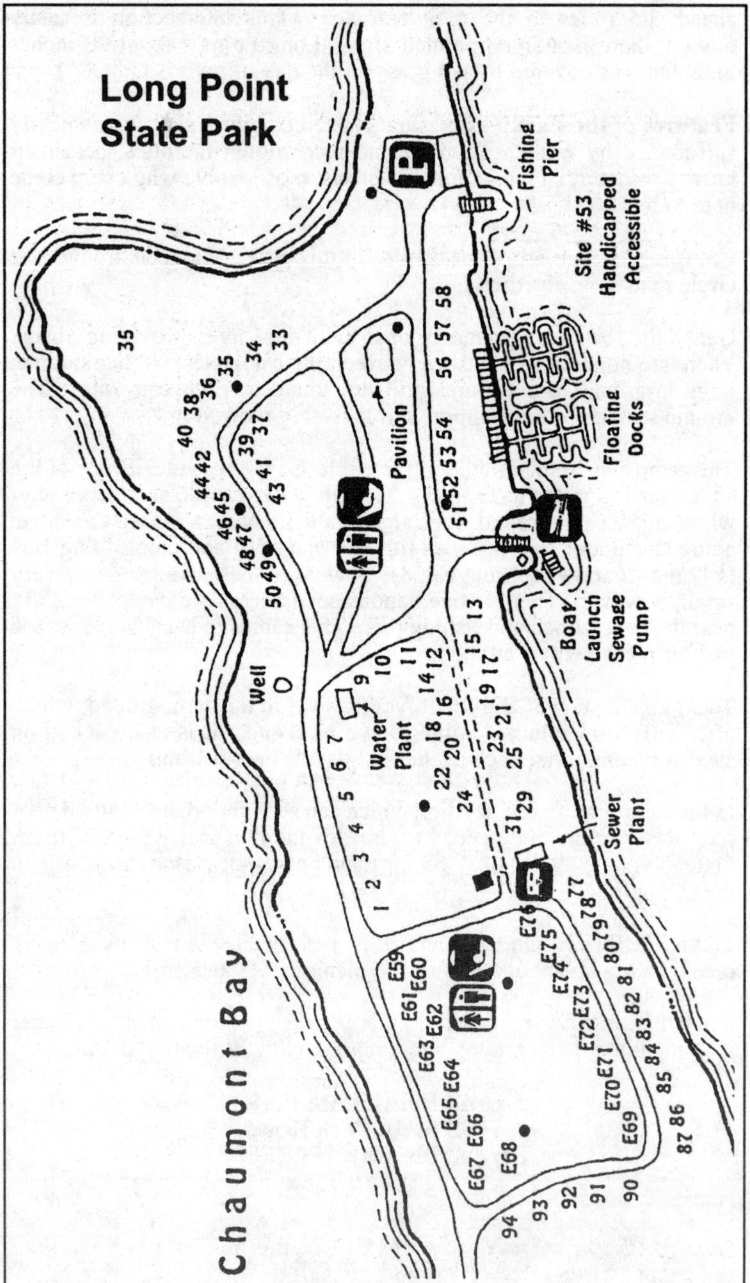

Long Point State Park
Fishing Pier
Site #53 Handicapped Accessible
Floating Docks
Pavilion
Boat Launch
Sewage Pump
Water Plant
Well
Sewer Plant
Chaumont Bay

Selkirk Shores State Park

The development of Selkirk Shores State Park began in 1925 with the construction of an administration building, a bathhouse and parking facilities. Between 1933 and 1937 the Civilian Conservation Corps (CCC) was busy at the park constructing cabins, the campground and several park facilities. A sign recognizing a CCC camp here from 1933 - 1940 is near the park entrance.

The park is comprised of 980 acres bounded on the south by Grindstone Creek and on the north by the Salmon River.

Entering the park, the entrance road divides. The road to the left goes to the beach and picnic area while the road to the right makes its way to the campground and cabins.

Location: Selkirk Shores is on the southeast shore of Lake Ontario in Oswego County, New York, on N.Y. 3, a short distance from Pulaski and about 20 miles from Oswego.

Features of the Park: Selkirk Shores is in a shady forest consisting of hemlock, sugar maple, birch, red oak and American beech trees.

The park features picnic grounds, shelter houses, fishing, cabins and camping facilities.

Camping: The campground, which is along the bluffs of Lake Ontario, has 148 sites, 88 of which provide electrical outlets, on four loops (A - D).

Most of the campsites are in the open with no trees, bushes or shrubs separating the sites. Behind the sites are woods, but the sites themselves sit in the open. There are picnic tables on cement slabs, large in-ground fire pit and a grill at each site.

In Circle A are 48 campsites. In circle B (#49 -#63) the sites are all on the outside of the road. Circle C includes sites #80 - #113. Circle D (#114 - #142) has a few sites that back up to the cabin area.

A camp store overlooking the lake is between Circle C and Circle D. Attached to the store is a recreation hall.

The campground is busy on weekends from the end of June until Labor Day. At other times the campground does not usually fill up.

A hard-surfaced trail of about a quarter-mile connects the campground with the picnic and beach areas. This path provides a nice walk through the woods.

Cabins: There are 24 cabins in an area known as the Cabin Colony. All of the cabins have a gas stove, a refrigerator with small freezer, cold running water, table with benches, a fireplace, beds and flush toilets. Each cabin also has a screened-in porch as well as an outside picnic table and fire ring. The cabins are scattered throughout the woods, more isolated and spread out than are the sites in the campground.

Two cabins (#29 - #30) have hot water and showers. Sixteen cabins have three rooms and are planned for four-person occupancy. Eight cabins have four rooms with six-person occupancy. Three cabins (#3, #10 and #24) are accessible to the disabled. Reservations can be made by calling the New York State Camping Reservation System.

People using the cabins must provide their own cooking and eating utensils, linens and firewood.

Cabins are rented for a two-night minimum and a two-week maximum. However, from the last weekend in June through Labor Day, cabins are rented for a minimum of one week.

Picnic Facilities: The picnic facilities, extending to the beach, are in a beautiful setting among hundreds of mature trees. The picnic area has tables and grills throughout the woods as well as a couple of open shelters.

On a bluff overlooking Lake Ontario in the picnic area is a large enclosed shelter with a stove, kitchen and about a dozen tables. Also, there are two large stone fireplaces in the building.

All of the buildings throughout the picnic grounds are made of similar log construction. They fit into the wooded forest setting well.

Beach: The beach swimming area is no more than a 100 yards long and wide. In the swimming area, the lake bottom is sandy. However, everywhere else the lake bottom is rocky and stony.

Swimming is permitted only when lifeguards are on duty. The beach is open from the last weekend in June through Labor Day from 11 a.m. to 7 p.m. daily.

At the entrance to the beach is a concession stand.

Trails: There are about 3.5 miles of hiking trails. A roughly drawn map is provided at the entrance booth.

Boating/Fishing: Fishing is popular along the Salmon River, in Grindstone Creek and also in the waters of Lake Ontario. Fish in Lake Ontario include chinook and coho salmon, steelhead, and brown and lake trout. Northern pike and brown trout are caught in the waters of Salmon River and Grindstone Creek. Also, bass fishing is popular.

Small boats can be put into Salmon River at the Pine Grove Boat Launch. Access to this launch is .9-mile from state road 104B, which is one mile from the park entrance. A fee is charged for use of the boat launch.

Larger boats and boats entering Lake Ontario can be launched at a facility operated by the state park at nearby Mexico Point.

A fish cleaning station is a short distance from the main park area along a dirt road near the maintenance building.

Nature: Selkirk Shores State Park is on a flyway for many birds during their spring and fall migrations. The habitat, particularly along Grindstone Creek, is conducive to many species of birds. A park brochure lists more than 200 species of birds that have been observed in the park.

A listing of these birds is provided for people interested in bird watch-

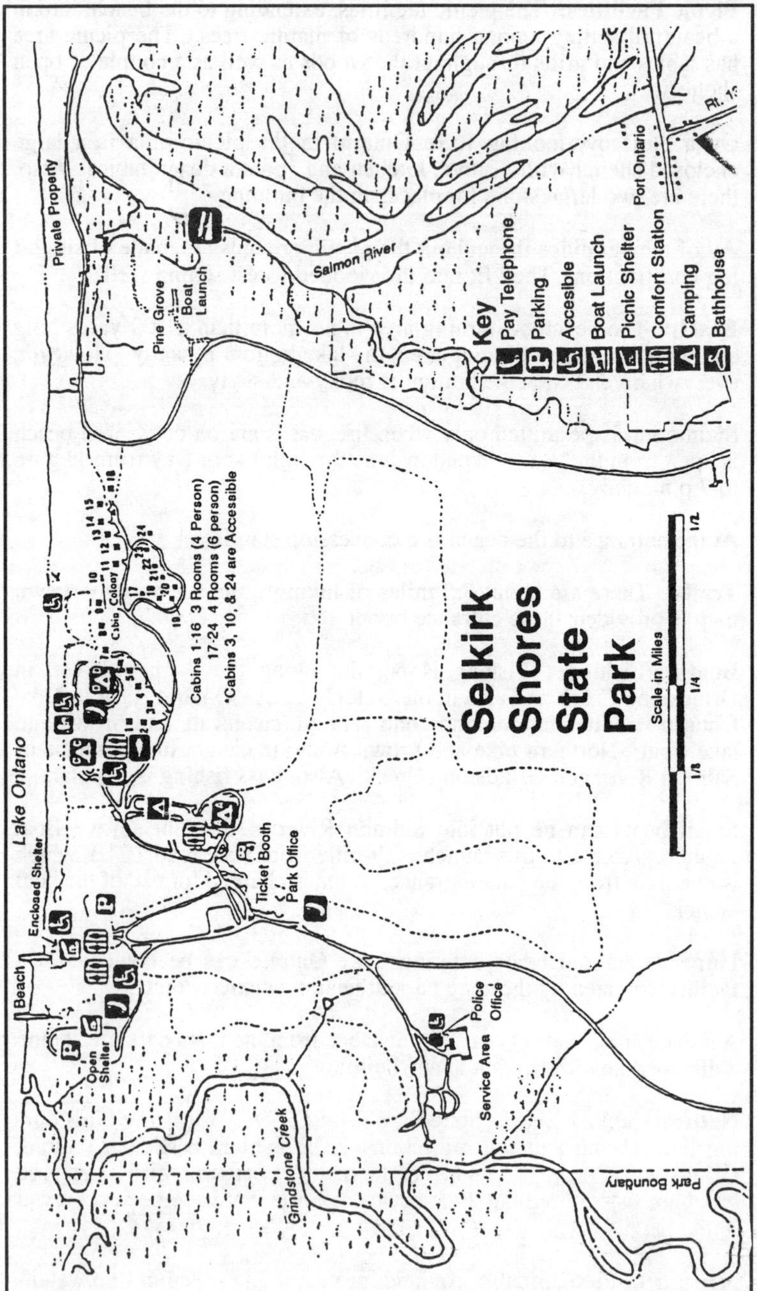
Lake Ontario
Private Property
Pine Grove
Boat Launch
Salmon River
Port Ontario
Rt. 13
Key
Pay Telephone
Parking
Accesible
Boat Launch
Picnic Shelter
Comfort Station
Camping
Bathhouse
Cabins 1-16 3 Rooms (4 Person)
17-24 4 Rooms (6 person)
Cabins 3, 10, & 24 are Accessible
Cabin Colony
Selkirk Shores State Park
Scale in Miles
1/8
1/4
1/2
Beach
Enclosed Shelter
Open Shelter
Ticket Booth
Park Office
Police Office
Service Area
Grindstone Creek
Park Boundary

ing. Migratory flights of hawks and eagles are often observed by visitors.

Winter Activities: The park closes in early November. There is no cross-country trail grooming; however, people do come to the park to cross-country ski and snowmobile. Skiing trails depart from the parking lot and follow the hiking trails. Snowmobiles can leave from the parking lot.

Selkirk Shores State Park
Route 3
Pulaski, NY 13142
(315) 298-5737

Southwick Beach State Park

Southwick Beach State Park received its name after the family who owned the property from 1870 to 1960. In the early 1920s week-end dances were conducted in a hall on the edge of the beach. This facility was destroyed by fire in 1925.

During the latter 1920s and early 1930s a popular recreational park, known as the "Coney Island" of northern New York, operated here. This park included a roller coaster, a dance pavilion, a midway, merry-go-round and picnic facilities. Large crowds made their way to this popular recreational site on Lake Ontario. By the end of the 1930s, economic hard times had brought to an end this popular amusement park.

In 1965 the area was purchased by the state and in 1966 the state park was opened. Today, the park is comprised of 500 acres and is open from mid-May through mid-October.

Location: Southwick Beach is at Port Ontario, New York, in Jefferson County off of N.Y. 3 at the intersection of N.Y. 193.

Features of the Park: The park features an excellent sand beach along Lake Ontario and the campground, particularly Loop B, which is next to the sandy lakeshore.

Beach: The beach extends the length of the park, about three-fourths of a mile. The lake bottom is clean and sandy, similar to the eastern shore of Lake Michigan. The beach looks west and is exposed to lake winds and weather patterns coming across Lake Ontario. There are no natural bays or manmade jetties to break up the action of the lake before it reaches the shoreline at the park. This beach is the best one at a state park on Lake Ontario.

All kinds of beach and swimming activities are possible here. However, swimming is permitted only when lifeguards are on duty.

At the north end of the beach and parking lot is a walkway for launching windsails for windsurfers.

Picnic Facilities: The picnic area is between the beach and a large parking lot. There are picnic tables and grills the length of the shoreline, which extends from a large recreation building near the south end of the parking lot to the north boundary of the park. The area has little shade; however, this openness provides picnickers with excellent views of the lake. This is a wonderful place to have a late afternoon picnic and watch the sun go down on the horizon over Lake Ontario. Some outstanding sunsets are visible from this location.

The large recreation building houses a store, several indoor picnic tables, and modern shower and restroom facilities. Groceries, camping supplies, refreshments, housewares, RV supplies, souvenirs and sporting goods are available at the store.

In the picnic area are two designated handicapped accessible picnic sites. These have tables on a hard-surface pad and a connecting path extending to the sidewalk, making them easily accessible to individuals in wheelchairs.

No dogs are allowed in the park.

This is a "carry-in, carry-out" park; you must clean up all your trash and take it with you.

Campground: The 112 campsites are around four loops. Forty-four sites have electricity.

There are few campsites on the Great Lakes where you can camp as

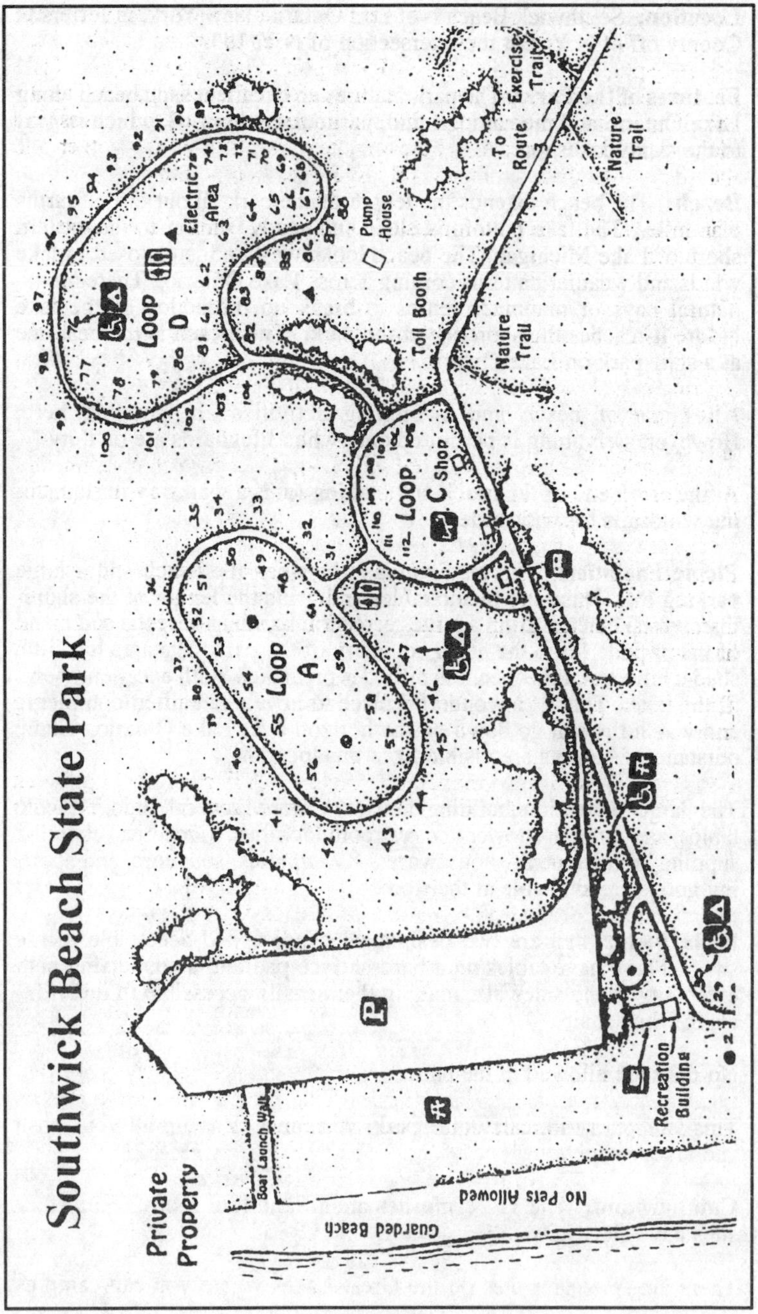
Southwick Beach State Park
Private Property
Boat Launch Wall
Guarded Beach
No Pets Allowed
Recreation Building
LOOP A
LOOP C
Shop
LOOP D
Electric Area
Pump House
Toll Booth
Nature Trail
To Route
Exercise Trail
Nature Trail

close to the shoreline and have a more spectacular view than you get at Loop B. There are 30 sites in this loop, which is on the beach. Each has an asphalt pad for a trailer or RV, a picnic table, an in-ground fire pit and grill. This loop runs about a quarter of a mile parallel to the shoreline. Campers can hear the continuing sound of the waves and view spectacular sunsets. The campsites are close to each other and there is a little shade from several large trees behind the beach.

Campsite #30 is reserved for disabled campers. This site is across the road from the shower and restroom facilities.

The campground has three other loops, Loop A (#31 - #60), Loop C (#105 - #112) and Loop D (#61 - #104). These loops are behind the parking lot near the entrance booth. The campsites on these three loops are small, generally in the open with little shade and have no brush separating the sites.

The electrical outlets are in Loop D. Loop C is on a short connector road between loops A and D. There are only eight campsites on this loop, all in an open field.

Behind the campsites is an area for recreational activities. Equipment for softball, volleyball, horseshoes and table tennis are available. Campsites #47 (in Loop A) and #76 (in Loop D) are reserved for the handicapped.

Trails: The park has a nature trail and an exercise trail, but no hiking trails.

Lakeview Wildlife Management Area: Adjacent to Southwick Beach State Park is the Lakeview Wildlife Management Area, with environmentally sensitive coastal sand dunes. You can observe wildlife and various types of plants common to the dunes, beach and shore environments. There are trails in this wildlife management area which can be accessed from Southwick Beach State Park.

Winter Activities: People can cross-country ski and snowshoe; however, there are no ski rental services available nor is there any winter camping.

Special Activities: During the summer, several special events are conducted on weekends and holidays. These include musical presentations, puppet shows and other types of entertainment.

Southwick Beach State Park
8119 Southwick Place
Woodville, NY 13650
(315) 846-5338

Westcott Beach State Park

The land on which Westcott Beach State Park stands was purchased in 1851 by Captain George Westcott. He and his descendants owned it until 1946, when Westcott's grandson sold the land to the state of New York. In 1950 the park was opened and today is comprised of 318 acres.

Location: Westcott Beach is on Henderson Bay two miles south of Sackets Harbor, New York, about 11.5 miles from Watertown.

The entrance to the park is off of N.Y. 3, which bisects the park. To the west of the highway is the larger of two campgrounds, the beach, marina and picnic area.

Features of the Park: The park features the day-use picnic area, beach and campgrounds. Also, there are 2,000 feet of shoreline in the park.

To the east of the highway are the Plateau Camping Area and hiking trails. No pets are permitted in this section of the park.

From the entrance booth, a 1.75-mile drive takes you to an overlook where you can see for miles in several directions. Nearby Stony Island and Gallo Island are visible from this spot, and in the distance Main Duck Island in Canada is visible. This location provides a spectacular view of the surrounding terrain and of Lake Ontario.

Camping: Camping is a major recreational activity of Westcott Beach State Park. A total of 168 campsites are divided between two locations. The largest is near the beach and shoreline. A great variety of campsites exist in this campground; some are open with no shade, others have shade. Some have hard-surface pads for picnic tables, while others do not. Each has a large in-ground fire pit and grill.

Electricity is available at 85 sites. Campsites #1 through #21 and even numbers from #40 to #58 have electricity. The campsites are close to each other. None is isolated by brush and shrubbery. The even numbered campsites from #110 through #128 and #129 are on the water's edge. Each has grass ground cover and there is a built-up wall providing protection from the waves.

Three campsites are accessible for the disabled (#1, #9 and #12). Each has an asphalt pad for your vehicle, and the picnic table. There are three restroom facilities in the campground, two of which have shower facilities.

To the east of N.Y. 3 is a smaller camping area, the Plateau Camping Area. The Plateau Camping Area (sites #130 - 169) is about two miles from the entrance booth. The 40 sites all have electricity.

There is a circular road with campsites on either side. The sites have no space between them. The inner side of the camp road is mostly a non-shaded, grassy surface. The campsites on the outside of the circle back up to the woods. They have a little more shade than do those on the inner ring. In the center of the circle is a modern toilet and shower building. Sites #130 and #148 are accessible to the disabled. These are both near the hard-surface walkway leading to the restroom and shower building.

Trails: There are about six miles of hiking trails in Westcott Beach. The general park map shows one trail beginning in the Plateau Camping Area, but there were no signs, trailhead indications or information about it. The trail system is located in the east section of the park.

Picnic Facilities: At the day-use picnic area is an open shelter, many picnic tables and grills. The picnic area is grass-covered and looks out onto Lake Ontario. It is an impressive and enjoyable day-use picnic

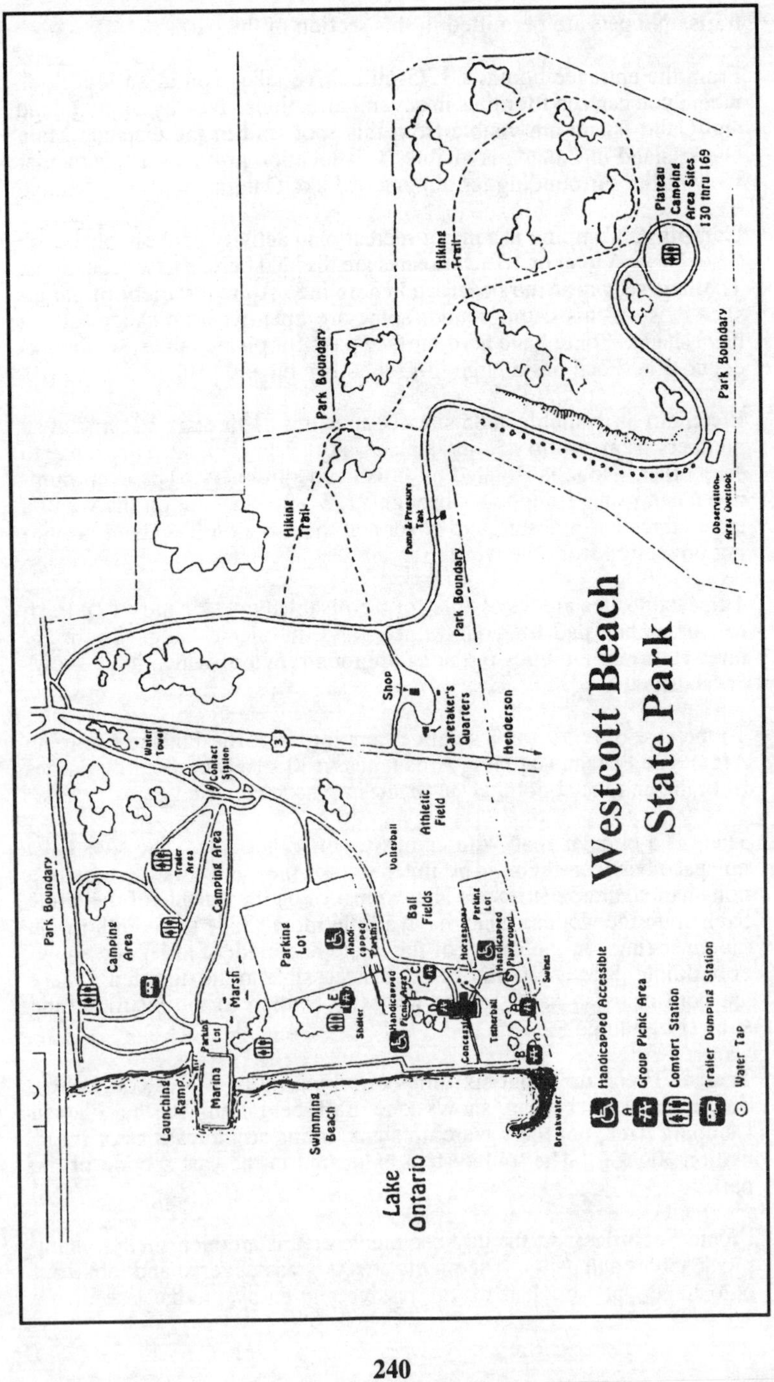
Westcott Beach State Park
Lake Ontario
Swimming Beach
Launching Ramp
Marina
Parking Lot
Marsh
Camping Area
Trailer Area
Contact Station
Water Tower
Park Boundary
Parking Lot
Handicapped Parking
Shelter
Handicapped Picnic Area
Concession
Tetherball
Swings
Playground
Horseshoes
Handicapped Parking Lot
Ball Fields
Volleyball
Athletic Field
Caretaker's Quarters
Shop
Henderson
Pump & Pressure Tank
Hiking Trail
Observation Area Overlook
Plateau Camping Area Sites 130 thru 169
Breakwater
Handicapped Accessible
Group Picnic Area
Comfort Station
Trailer Dumping Station
Water Tap

location.

Several handicapped accessible sites are available in the picnic area. Each has a picnic table on a cement pad. A hard-surface walkway connects the pad with the walkway, making it convenient for wheelchairs.

At the south end of the picnic area is a concession building, which includes a recreation room. Between the picnic area and the highway is a large athletic field. There are two backstops for softball and a volleyball court. Equipment is provided for those wishing to participate in these activities. At the south end of the picnic area is a children's playground.

Beach: The sandy beach extends from the marina to the south boundary of the park. It extends back from the edge of the water only about 15 yards. A cement walkway traverses the beach. The lake bottom is sandy, though in places it is covered with small stones. At the north end of the beach is a jetty extending a short distance into the water. A changing facility and restrooms are near the beach.

At the south end of the park is a smaller beach, no more than 50 yards wide. This beach is in a little cove which has a sandy lake bottom and is good for wading and child play. Between the two beaches is a walkway about five feet above the water. No jumping or diving is permitted from this walkway. The beach is open for swimming in late June, and remains open until Labor Day.

Boating/Fishing: There is a boat ramp and several docks where boats can be tied for short periods of time. It includes provision for mooring about two dozen boats.

Many people who come to the park to camp also bring their boats. Henderson Bay is excellent for boating because it is protected from the waves on Lake Ontario. Also, within a short distance from the park are several small towns and historical sites that can be reached by boat as well as by road. Best known is Sackets Harbor, a few miles north of the park, where a state historical park commemorates a battle between the British and Americans during the War of 1812.

Winter Activities: Westcott Beach State Park is open only from the middle of May through mid-October. As a result, there are no organized winter activities, camping or rental services at this park. However, people do come to the park to cross-country ski and snow shoe. Snowmobiling in the surrounding areas is popular.

Westcott Beach State Park
P.O. Box 339
Sackets Harbor, NY 13685
(315) 938-5083

Wilson-Tuscarora State Park

Wilson-Tuscarora State Park is a day-use only park. There are no camping or swimming facilities here. Neither are there any concessions or other services available. The 390-acre park became a state park in 1965.

Location: Wilson-Tuscarora State Park is a short distance west of Wilson, New York, on N.Y. 18, at the mouth of Twelve Mile Creek. The eastern park boundary roughly coincides with the East Branch of Twelve Mile Creek, which is a designated protected wetland area. This creek flows into Tuscarora Bay, which is separated from Lake Ontario by a strip of land known as "The Island." The west park boundary is the West Branch of Twelve Mile Creek.

Features of the Park: Wilson-Tuscarora is a picnicking and a boat launch/fishing park. The park contains woods, open meadows and marshlands.

Picnic Facilities: The park road parallels Lake Ontario, along which there are picnic tables and grills. The grass and brush on both sides of the road are well manicured and extend back a good distance. This area is on a bluff above the lake. Two picnic shelters near the entrance can be reserved by groups.

Boat Launch/Fishing: Fishing is a primary activity of park visitors. Several times throughout the year, organizations conduct fishing derbies at the park. Several hundred yards from the boat launch into Tuscarora Bay is a commercial marina. All the services needed by boaters and fishermen are available at the marina. Adjacent to the boat ramp is a small handicapped accessible fishing dock.

Near the park entrance is a short road to a fishing dock and a small boat dock on Twelve Mile Creek West Branch, about a quarter-mile from where the mouth of the river empties into Lake Ontario.

Beach/Shoreline: No swimming is permitted at the park. However, wind surfing in one section of the park is allowed by permit. Stretching back about 25 yards along the water's edge are stone, shale and driftwood. The lake bottom is gravel and stone. There is a little sand scattered among the stones and driftwood.

Nature: Birds, muskrats, opossum, turtles, frogs and raccoons are found in the marsh. Deer are commonly noted in the open meadow areas of the park.

The park provides a varied environment for trees. There are trees that live and grow beside creeks, rivers and lakes. Other trees live in a wetlands environment and in meadows. Trees identified on the park trail map include northern red oak, white oak, black locust, white ash, eastern cottonwood, eastern hemlock, birch, American beech, sugar maple, shagbark hickory, eastern white pine, weeping willow and black cherry. During the fall, small game hunting is permitted in the park. Duck hunting is also available.

Trails: The park brochure indicates that there are four miles of trails. The sign at the trailhead near the parking lot shows only about two miles of trails. The trailhead for the Tree Trail Trek (a 1.5-mile round trip) is at the parking lot near the boat launch. The trail traverses the eastern branch of Twelve Mile Creek.

Winter Activities: The park is open year round. Cross-country skiing and ice fishing are popular; however, no snowmobiling is permitted. Snowmobilers can connect to several snowmobile trails adjacent to the park.

Wilson-Tuscarora State Park
Wilson, NY 14172
(716) 751-6361

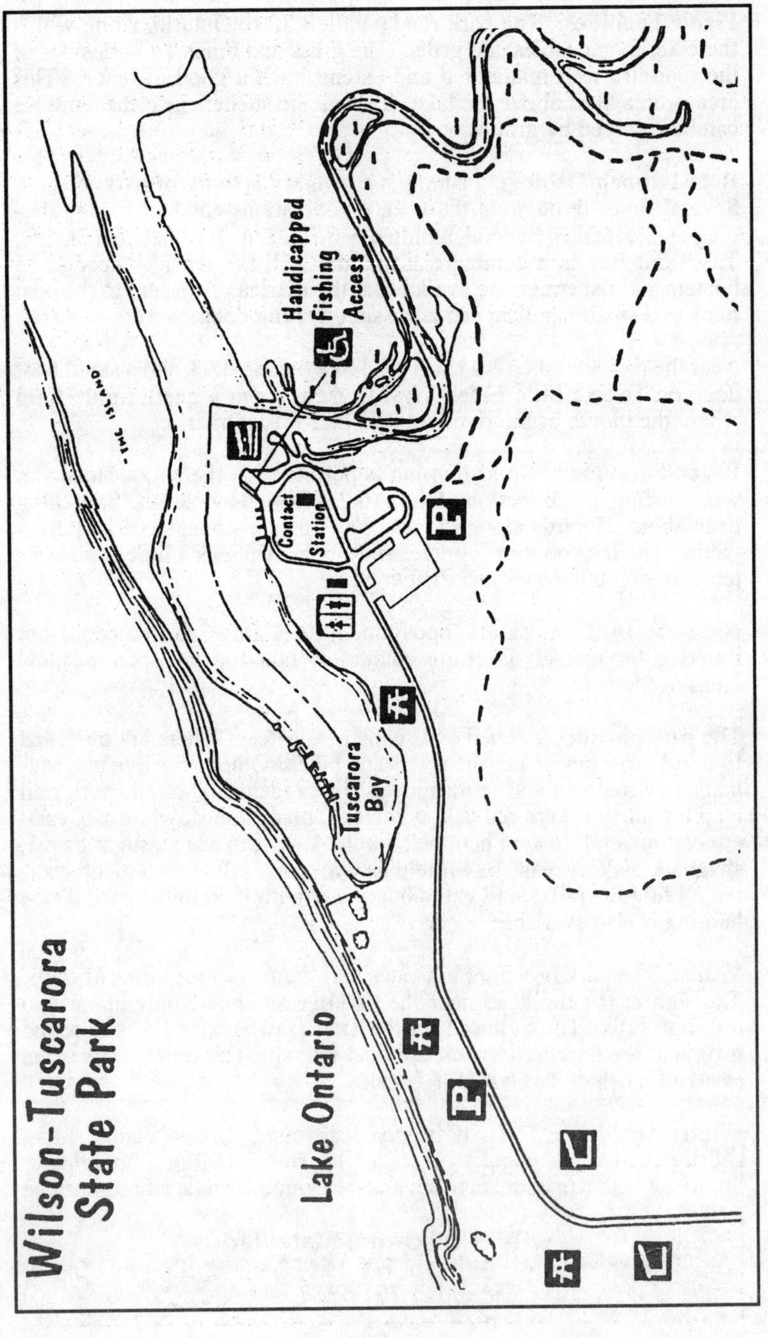
Wilson-Tuscarora
State Park
Lake Ontario
THE ISLAND
Tuscarora
Bay
Contact
Station
Handicapped
Fishing
Access

MICHIGAN'S UPPER PENINSULA
75
Lake Michigan
Straits State Park
Mackinac Island State Park
Colonial Michilimackinac State Park
Mill Creek State Park
Wilderness State Park
75
MICHIGAN'S LOWER PENINSULA
N

Straits of Mackinac

The waters of Lake Michigan and Lake Huron meet at the Straits of Mackinac, which separates the Upper Peninsula of Michigan from the Lower Peninsula. Since the late 1600s, a lot of history has passed through these waters of the upper Great Lakes.

Explorers passed through the Straits during the 18th and 19th centuries. During these years French fur traders, soldiers, missionaries and Indians used these waters. Native Americans used the waters for centuries before the explorers came.

Passing through the straits today are numerous sailing vessels: iron ore boats, ocean going vessels, recreational boats, plus sailboats of all sizes. You don't have to sit along the shore for long to see large ocean-going ships traveling from the ports throughout the Great Lakes to sites around the world. Also, the region is an extremely popular tourist site during the entire year.

On both shores and on beautiful Mackinac Island were forts which played significant roles in the early history of this region. Fort Michilimackinac was occupied from 1715 - 1781 and is today a state park where you can learn of its place in history. There was a fort at St. Ignace on the north shore of the Straits. Fort Mackinac on the island was built about 1715 by the French. In 1761, the British entered the fort and occupied it.

For years, the opposite shores of the Straits could only be reached by boats, canoes or in the winter by walking across the ice. People traveling by automobile or train through this area had to take ferries, which operated between Mackinaw City and St. Ignace. It was not until 1957, when the Mackinac Bridge opened, that the two shorelines were connected. Three years were needed to build this bridge, from 1954 to 1957, at a cost of $99.8 million.

The Mackinac Bridge is the longest single-span suspension bridge in the world—7,400 feet long. The bridge is supported by suspension cables which are 24.5 inches in diameter. There are 42,000 miles of cables in the structure. Concrete foundations for the bridge rest on bedrock up to 206 feet below the surface of the water. The roadway is 199 feet above the water.

There are five state parks along the Straits of Mackinac. Two are historical parks: Colonial Michilimackinac and Mill Creek. Michilimackinac State Park is at the southern terminus of the Mackinac Bridge in Mackinaw City. Mill Creek, which is one of the earliest industrial sites on the Great Lakes, is about four miles east of Mackinaw City. Wilderness State Park is about 12 miles west of Mackinac City along the southern shore of the Straits.

On the northern side terminus of the Mackinac Bridge is Straits State Park. Within sight of the shore on both sides of the Straits is Mackinac Island. More than 80 percent of this island is state park grounds. Mackinac Island State Park was the first state park in Michigan, established in 1894. The park includes historic Fort Mackinac. To get there, take a ferry from either St. Ignace or Mackinaw City, Michigan. Some people arrive by airplane at a small airstrip. Since no motor vehicles are allowed on Mackinac Island, you must travel by horse-drawn carriage, bicycle or on foot.

Colonial Michilimackinac Fort State Park

The reconstruction of Fort Michilimackinac, originally built in the early 1700s, is a 25-acre state park today at the southern terminus of the Mackinac Bridge. The park entrance and orientation center are underneath the bridge. The Michigan State Historic Park is co-administered with the Michigan Department of Natural Resources. A fee is charged for entrance to the historical park and fort.

The fort is open from early May to mid-October. From June 15 to Labor Day, it is open from 9 a.m. to 6 p.m.

History: Fort Michilimackinac began as a small trading post about 1715, where French explorers traded with the Indians. Furs and other traded items could be transported by water to settlements along Lake Huron and Lake Michigan and eventually on to the East Coast and to

France.

Over a period of time, the French built a more substantive fort. Traders and soldiers and their wives lived at the fort. This fort was needed by the French as a military base to protect the fur traders. There was increasing conflict with various Indian tribes in the area, and the fort provided military protection. French traders at Michilimackinac purchased corn and meat from Indians in exchange for cloth, blankets, beads and liquor which came from Montreal.

After the French and Indian War, the victorious British took control of the fort in 1761. In June 1763 the Chippewa Indians seized the fort, killing most of the small force and held it for a year. The British did not feel that this fort provided the protection they needed against the uprisings in the American colonies at this time. As a result, the British post was moved in 1781 to Mackinac Island, which was considered to be a better location for defense against American revolutionaries. They leveled and burned the Mackinaw City buildings that were left behind.

The Fort Today: Archaeological digging and study provided information needed to reconstruct the colonial fort.

Since 1959 archaeologists have studied the remains of the 18th century fort and buildings. Michilimackinac is the site of the longest ongoing archaeological program in the United States. Every summer since 1959, archaeologists have excavated and analyzed discoveries from the area.

From the museum and book store, a walkway leads to the fort. Outside the fort is a reconstruction of Native American houses and life.

Most people enter the fort through the Water Gate on the shoreline. In the fort are more than a dozen reconstructed buildings, including soldiers' barracks, the Church of Ste. Anne, the guard house, officers' houses, the King's storehouse, and storehouse facilities for the powder magazine. Around the fort is a walkway about 10 feet above the ground. From this walkway, you can get an excellent view of the interior of the fort as well as the sights outside the fort. A barnyard and corral are outside the back gate of the fort.

Throughout the fort and surrounding grounds, you can visit with guides dressed in period costumes. Live demonstrations depict making soap, cooking, growing gardens and other activities common to the people in the 1700s.

An excellent display of the archaeological work is presented in the basement of the British Traders House. More than 2 million artifacts have been uncovered from the sands around Michilimackinac. Hundreds of these are on display. Only half of the fort's buildings have

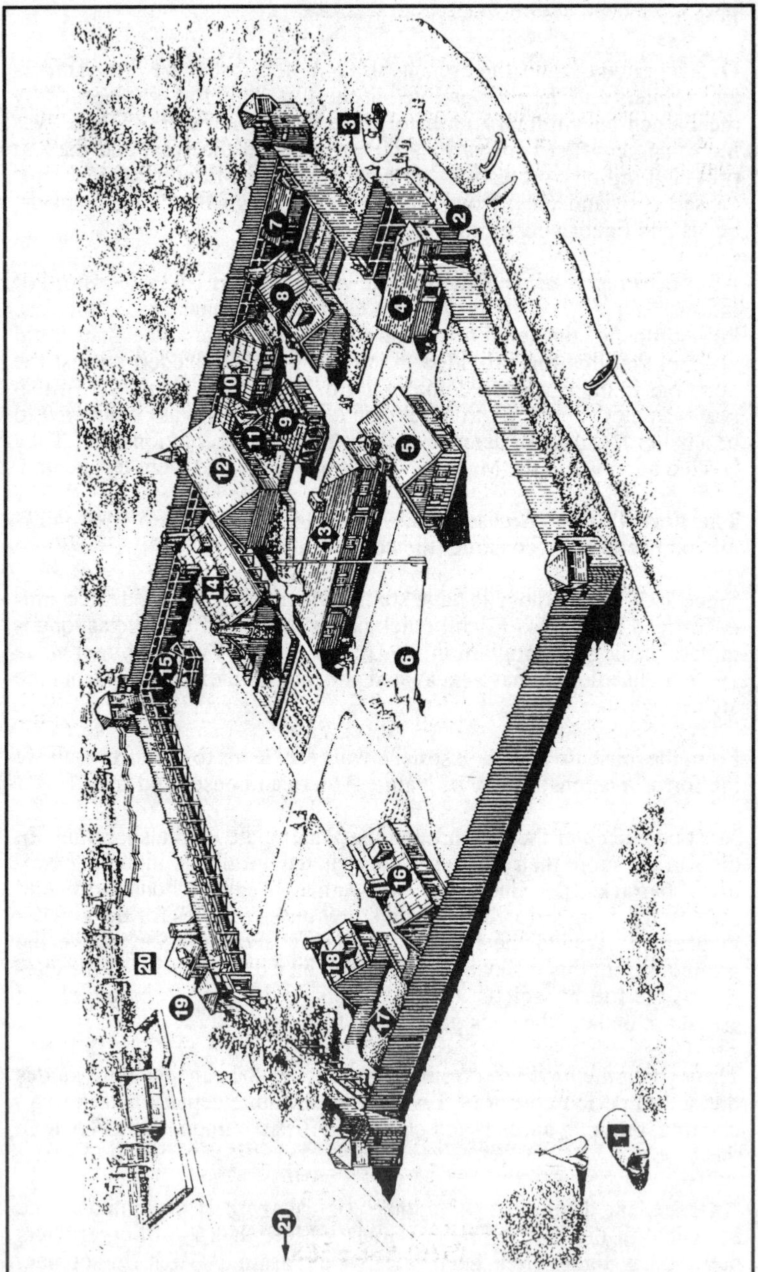

1
2
3
4
5
6
7
8
9
10
11
12
13
14
15
16
17
18
19
20
21

been excavated and reconstructed so far.

An interesting display entitled "Mysteries of Michilimackinac" presents 18 items in a case. Questions ask why visitors think these were found in this area. A book is next to the display where people may indicate why they think these items were in the fort area. Since this display is in the basement of a building that is not handicapped accessible, a 12-minute closed-caption video is available upon request for disabled individuals.

Throughout the summer, there are many demonstrations and activities for visitors. Each season the demonstrations change.

Always popular is the musket-loading and drill demonstration. Two "soldiers" explain how the muzzleloading rifle works and then the rifles are fired. This demonstration is given on the parade ground just inside the Water Gate entrance.

Cannon firing occurs four or five times a day outside the fort on the waterfront. There is a working blacksmith in the Blacksmith Shop. Also, cooking demonstrations are given in two locations in the fort.

Another interesting demonstration is the French colonial wedding and dance in the Church of Ste. Anne. Schedules for this event may be obtained from the park office.

For several years a birch-bark canoe builder has worked at the fort. The builder constructs a 15-foot canoe from authentic materials. While working, he answers questions and explains the process. Several completed canoes are on display in the fort.

Visitor Center/Museum/Store: A museum and store are inside the entrance booth beneath the Mackinac Bridge. As you browse the sound of passing traffic overhead is heard. The museum and store are well worth a visit. Audio-visual presentations are given on a regular basis in the small auditorium. Several items are displayed throughout the museum that have been found in the archaeological diggings of the fort.

The store contains an excellent supply of books on various aspects of the history of the Straits, Mackinac Island and Michilimackinac. Also, many books about Indians are available.

Colonial Michilimackinac State Park
Mackinac State Historic Parks
P.O. Box 370
Mackinaw City, MI 49757
(616) 436-5563

Mackinac Island State Park

At the northern end of Lake Huron is Mackinac Island. This popular tourist attraction is visited by nearly three million persons each year.

The island is about three miles long and two miles wide. High limestone cliffs circle the shoreline. Several ravines, natural bridges and geologic rock formations are spread throughout the island. Native Americans originally called the island Michilimackinac, which meant "great turtle." It has the shape and appearance of a turtle. Over time the name was shortened to Mackinac.

Most people come to the island by ferry from either St. Ignace or Mackinaw City. Three commercial companies provide boat rides that take just under an hour to reach the island from Mackinaw City and a half hour from St. Ignace. Each of these companies provides day and overnight parking in St. Ignace and Mackinaw City. Also, rides taking less than 20 minutes in hydroplanes and catamarans are available.

Your first impression of the island is of the many gift shops, candy stores selling fudge, restaurants, and the old Victorian houses near the boat landing. Most visitors are not aware that most of the island is a state park. About 80 percent, or 1,700 acres is state park land. The park is open year-round.

History: During the French and Indian War, the British defeated the French and took control of Fort Michilimackinac on the mainland. For several years the British occupied this fort but felt the need for a more strategic and secure setting. The high limestone bluffs of the island would provide protection against any attack, so the British moved to Mackinac Island in 1780-81 and established Fort Mackinac which they held for 15 years.

Following the Revolutionary War, the fort came under the control of the United States government. During the War of 1812 the British recaptured the island and held it for three years. Then a treaty returned the fort to United States control. A military presence continued there until 1895.

Before 1895, the federal government operated Fort Mackinac on the island. In 1875 the government established Mackinac as the nation's second national park, after Yellowstone. Then in 1894 it was returned to the state of Michigan.

Many military personnel at the fort were assigned duty to assist visitors coming to the island for recreation. Plans were put in place by the federal government to auction the park lands on the island. But as a result of the initiative of local residents, the fort and public land on the island were given to the state of Michigan as a state park.

Fort Mackinac: Fort Mackinac, on a bluff overlooking the city and harbor, today is a museum. Fourteen buildings have been preserved. Throughout the fort are costumed guides who conduct tours, provide colorful historical reenactments, and give cannon and rifle firing demonstrations as well as children's programs. The Fort Mackinac Tea Room with an outstanding view of the town, the Straits and the Mackinac Bridge serves lunch daily. Food service is provided by the Grand Hotel. The fort is open from mid-May until mid-October. There is an admission charge to visit the fort.

Outside the fort are several renovated buildings. The Early Missionary Bark Chapel is a reconstruction of chapels built on the island by Jesuit missionaries in the late 1600s. The Indian Dormitory was constructed in 1838. Today it has an Indian museum as well as a kitchen of the period of the mid-1800s. In 1996 an archaeological excavation of the old blacksmith's shop was begun.

Sights: It would take a book to describe all of the sights of interest on Mackinac Island. In fact, numerous published tour guides are available on various aspects of the island.

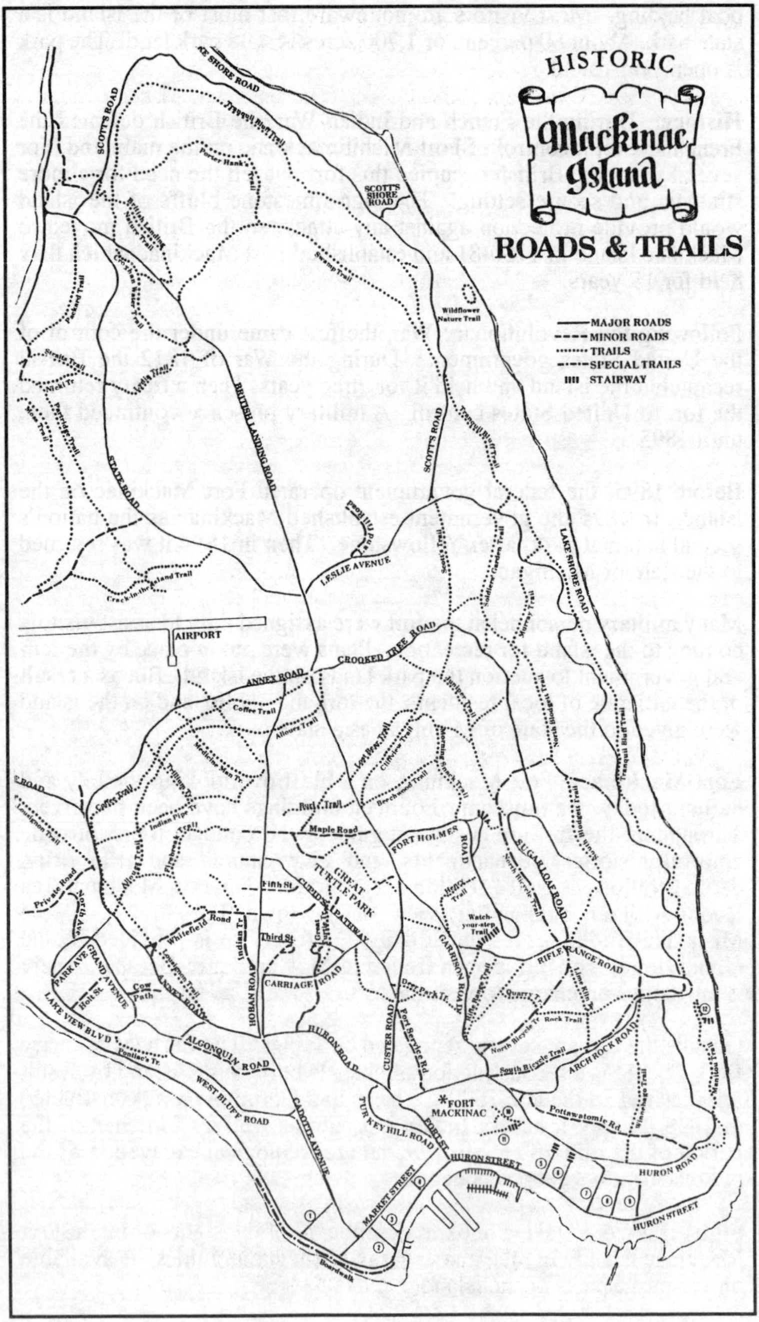

HISTORIC
Mackinac Island
ROADS & TRAILS
MAJOR ROADS
MINOR ROADS
TRAILS
SPECIAL TRAILS
STAIRWAY
SCOTT'S ROAD
SCOTT'S SHORE ROAD
LAKE SHORE ROAD
Tranquil Bluff Trail
Porter Hank's
Swamp Trail
Wildflower Nature Trail
BRITISH LANDING ROAD
STATE ROAD
Straits Trail
Leslie Avenue
LESLIE AVENUE
Crack-in-the-Island Trail
AIRPORT
CROOKED TREE ROAD
ANNEX ROAD
Coffee Trail
Allouez Trail
Medicine Man Tr.
Indian Pipe Tr.
Lost Bear Trail
Cliffview Trail
Beechwood Trail
Morning Star Trail
Soldiers Garden Trail
North Bicycle Trail
Rush Trail
Maple Road
FORT HOLMES ROAD
GREAT TURTLE PARK
CUPID'S PATHWAY
Fifth St.
Third St.
Whitefield Road
Indian Tr.
HOBAN ROAD
CARRIAGE ROAD
Private Road
PARK AVE
GRAND AVENUE
Holt St.
Cow Path
LAKE VIEW BLVD
Pontiac's Tr.
ALGONQUIN ROAD
WEST BLUFF ROAD
CADOTTE AVENUE
HURON ROAD
CUSTER ROAD
Fort Service Rd
Deer Park Tr.
GARRISON ROAD
Watch-your-step Trail
SUGAR LOAF ROAD
RIFLE RANGE ROAD
Quarry Tr.
Rock Trail
Lime Kiln Tr.
North Bicycle Tr.
South Bicycle Trail
ARCH ROCK ROAD
Pottawatomie Rd.
Winnebago Trail
Manitou Trail
FORT MACKINAC
TURKEY HILL ROAD
FORT ST.
HURON STREET
MARKET STREET
HURON ROAD
HURON STREET
Boardwalk

Several geological formations are of interest. Three popular ones are Arch Rock, Sugar Loaf and Scull Cave. Arch Rock is the most popular and prominent geologic feature on the island. Once, it was a solid mass of rock. Over time the softer material dissolved, leaving the arch. Sugar Loaf is the largest limestone stack, standing 75 feet. Scull Cave, formed by wave erosion, is one of the oldest formations on the island.

Lodging: No camping facilities are on the island. Most people planning to stay overnight make reservations at one of the several hotels, including the magnificent 320-room Grand Hotel. The Grand Hotel opened in 1887 and is noted for the 628-foot front porch

Transportation on the Island: No motor vehicles are permitted on the island. Transportation is by horse-drawn carriage, bicycle, horseback or on foot. A popular way to see island landmarks is by a horse carriage tour. Fringe-covered carriages seating a dozen people can be rented throughout the summer.

Many visitors to Mackinac Island enjoy bicycle riding. Bicycles are available for rental at several locations on the island, but many people bring their own. There are miles of trails and dirt roads which provide access to the interior of the island. The shoreline road encircling the island officially, is M-185. This is probably the only state highway in the nation which has never seen a motor vehicle accident. This road goes 8.2 miles along the water's edge. Many people walk along the roadway. You can take in spectacular scenery in all directions. The Mackinac Bridge can be seen to the west. Along the shoreline is a stone and pebble beach.

Activities: There are numerous festivals and water events during the summer on Mackinac Island. The Lilac Festival in June attracts many visitors. Lilacs were introduced in the 1600s on the island by French missionaries. Today many are large and during June when in full bloom, they are spectacular. The festival during June of each year runs for a week and includes a parade.

Also during the summer, Mackinac Island is the destination for two long-distance sailboat races: the Port Huron to Mackinac and the Chicago to Mackinac races. They attract some of the most beautiful sailboats on the Great Lakes. There are numerous size classifications of boats in these events. People on the island can observe the conclusion of the races and then visit the various boats and their crews following the races.

Mackinac Island State Park/Fort Mackinac
Mackinac State Historic Parks
P.O. Box 370
Mackinac Island, MI 49757
(906) 436-5563

Mill Creek State Park

Mill Creek State Park is four miles south of Mackinaw City on U.S. 23. This Michigan State Historic Park is co-administered with the Michigan Department of Natural Resources. A fee is charged for entrance.

The History: In the late 18th century, after the British had taken possession of Fort Michilimackinac from the French, the British moved to Mackinac Island to better defend the Straits of Mackinac. That meant there would be a tremendous demand for lumber to build the fort and other buildings on the island.

As a result, Robert Campbell purchased land on Mill Creek in the 1780s and built a sawmill there. Mill Creek, which flows into the Straits, was the only body of water large enough on which to establish a sawmill.

Campbell also built a gristmill. The mills were powered by the flowing water of Mill Creek. Lumber was cut much more rapidly by the sawmill than could be accomplished by hand. This became a source of

lumber to the British for buildings constructed at Mill Creek
.

In addition to the sawmill and grist mill, other buildings were constructed at Mill Creek: a blacksmith shop, several homes and a warehouse. An orchard was also established. This became the first industrial settlement in the upper lakes region of the new nation.

The mill was operated until 1819 when it was sold by relatives of Robert Campbell. In 1839, after several years of losing money, the sawmill and surrounding site were abandoned. By 1867 most of the buildings were gone and the area was in disrepair. A century later, there was no evidence of a once-thriving industrial complex. In 1984 the state began to reconstruct the sawmill and archaeologists began to dig and study among the ruins.

Today: As you enter Mill Creek State Park, there is a visitor center containing displays depicting the history of the area. An audio-visual presentation telling the story of the Mill Creek site is presented.

The reconstructed sawmill is the main feature. Here from June 15 to Labor Day demonstrations are given, showing how lumber was cut. Demonstrations occur each half-hour from 10 a.m. to 5:30 p.m. From May 10 to June 14 and Labor Day to Oct. 15, the demonstrations are every hour from 11 a.m. to 4 p.m.

It is interesting to observe the procedure and to see that there was no electrical or gas generated power, just the movement of water. Near the reconstructed sawmill a replica of a workshop has been built. This shop was built from lumber cut at the sawmill.

Under reconstruction is the millwright's house. It will take several years until this house is completed.

There is a scenic overlook on the Mill Pond Trail. Everyone should walk to this overlook to see a complete view of the mill site. Also, looking to the north, you can see Lake Huron and the Straits of Mackinac as well as Mackinac Island.

Trails: There are 625 acres that comprise the state park. Along Mill Creek through the surrounding woods, a hiking trail system has been developed. The trail can be walked in three loops. The shortest is the Mill Pond Trail, which takes less than 15 minutes and circles the exhibit area and Mill Pond. Going a little farther is the Evergreen Trail. This trail, walking time of about 25 minutes, provides information about the surrounding woods.

If you want to hike for about an hour, take the Beaver Pond Trail to several beaver ponds on Mill Creek. Near the ponds, two additional trails loop off. These trails, each a half-mile, are Aspen-Wildlife Forest Trail

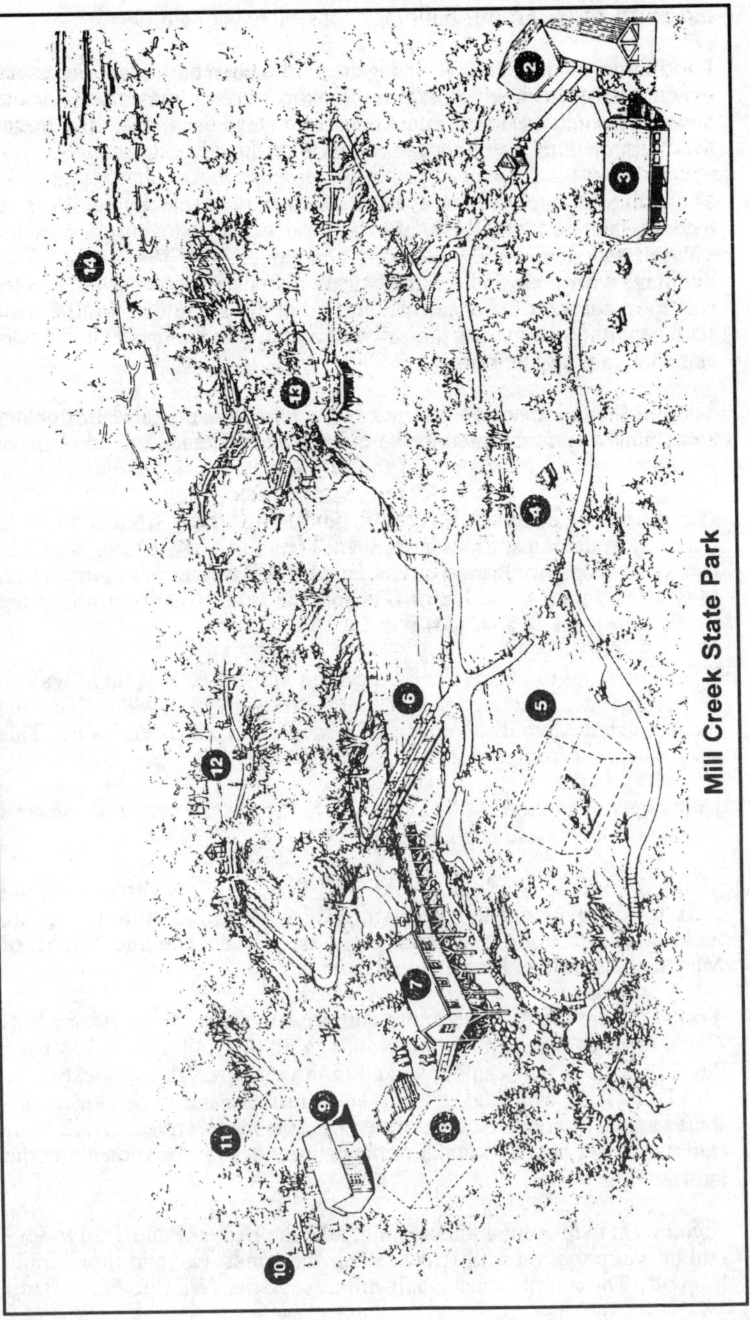

Mill Creek State Park

and Sugar Shack Forest Trail.

The Aspen-Wildlife Forest Trail takes you through a stand of aspen trees. Along the way are several signs providing information about these trees and measures being taken to manage the forest. The Sugar Shack Forest Trail goes through a hardwood forest, and passes a reconstructed maple sugar shack. Exhibits along the way explain the process of making maple sugar and features of managing this forest. Both of these loop trails are well marked.

The day of my visit, there were several school groups at the mill site. However, there were few people along the trails. On the Beaver Pond Trail, Aspen-Wildlife Forest Trail and Sugar Shack Forest Trail, I was alone.

Directly behind the visitor center are a refreshment stand and picnic area. Sandwiches, chips and soft drinks are available.

Mill Creek State Park
Mackinac State Historic Parks
P.O. Box 370
Mackinaw City, MI 49757
(616) 436-5563

Straits State Park

Straits State Park is at the northern terminus of the spectacular Mackinac Bridge in St. Ignace. The park contains 181 acres and was established as a state park in 1924.

Location: The main entrance to Straits State Park is reached by going east on U.S. 2 less than a half mile from the end of Mackinac Bridge to Church Street. The Father Marquette National Historic Site of the state park is west of the bridge. This site includes the Marquette Historical Memorial and Museum. To reach this section, turn west from the bridge and go several hundred feet along U.S. 2 to Marley Street. The entrance is a short distance south on this street.

Features of the Park: The major features that draw most visitors to the park are the camping facilities and the Father Marquette National Historic Site.

Most who camp at Straits State Park plan to take in various sites around the area, including Mackinac Island. The island, within view of Straits State Park, provides many activities for the tourist. Also in the area, at the southern end of the Mackinac Bridge, is Fort Michilimackinac in Mackinaw City. Here visitors can be entertained and learn about the history of the Straits area during the 1700s.

Boating and fishing are often activities that many participate in while camping at Straits State Park. There are no boat ramps in the park; however, launching facilities are available within a mile in the city of St. Ignace.

The shoreline provides scenic views from east to west looking south toward Mackinaw City. Both sunrise and sunset can be seen from the shores of the water.

There is no sand along the shoreline of this park, nor is there any swimming permitted.

The Father Marquette National Historic Site, a memorial to Father Jacques Marquette and a museum telling of his 17th century exploits, are in the western section of the state park.

Camping: There are four campgrounds with 275 modern sites at Straits State Park. A picnic table, in-ground fire pit and electricity are provided at each site. There is a modern building with hot showers and flush toilets in each of the four campgrounds.

Two campgrounds are near the water's edge. By far these are the most popular sites. These sites are small but offer a great view. Campsites #1 through #18 and #84 to #100 (the even numbers) are on the waterfront. The campground is well-shaded with most campsites having grass groundcover.

Campers near the water's edge have one of the most spectacular views of any state park camping ground on the Great Lakes. Here you see the Mackinac Bridge and a wide-angle view of the Straits of Mackinac. At all times of the day in all types of climate, the view is extraordinary. It is most spectacular to watch the sun set upon the water to the west with the magnificent bridge serving as a frame.

Throughout the day campers can simply sit at their campsites and watch the water. You won't have to wait long before seeing a large iron ore boat or an ocean going vessel pass under the bridge. On a calm, warm day with a light breeze blowing, there are any number of sailboats on the waterway. Mackinac Island can be seen to the east of the state park. Ferries ply the waters of the Straits of Mackinac taking visitors, supplies and residents between the island and the mainland.

Two additional campgrounds (campsites #131-#197 and #198-#226) are on a hill. The water of the Straits cannot be seen from these campgrounds. These campsites are not as shaded as those in the camp-

Straits State Park

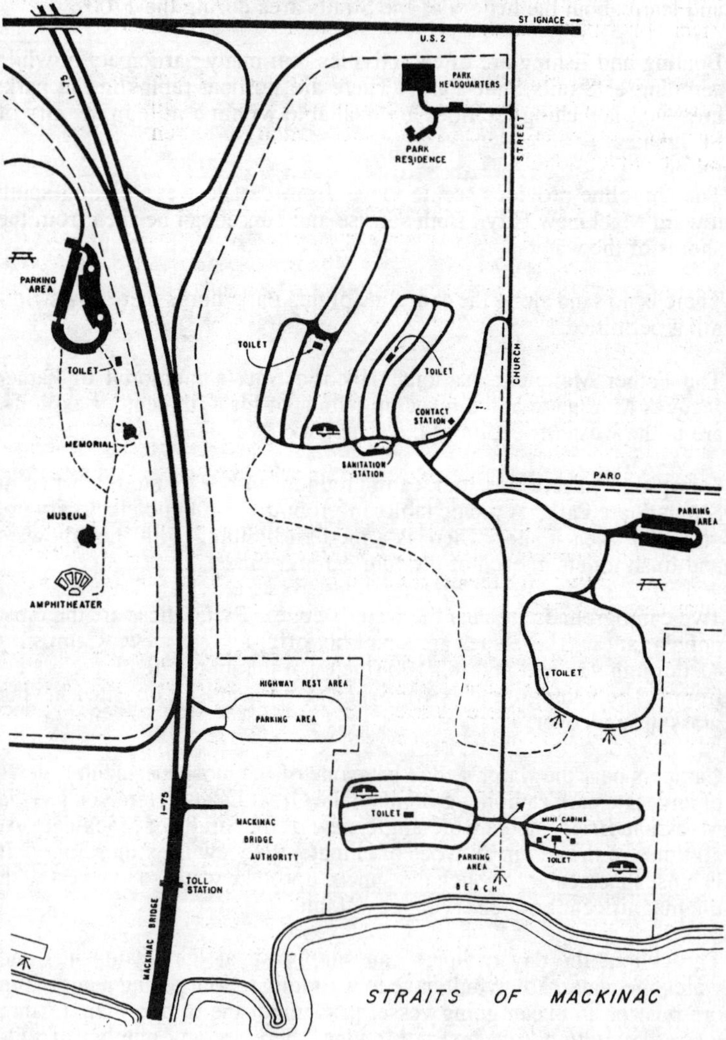

grounds nearer the water. The sites on the inner circle are small and open. Those on the outside of the road are more shaded and a little larger. A modern toilet and shower facility is in each campground. From this campground, there is a trail to a bridge overlook.

There are two mini-cabins in the campground. Four people can be accommodated in each of these cabins with bunks, mattresses and electric lights provided. These cabins are available on a rental basis, as are all the campsites.

Interpretive Center: An interpretive center is to the west of the "Big Mac" bridge. At this center are a museum and a national monument honoring Father Jacques Marquette. The museum is reached via a walk along a hard-surface path, about a quarter of a mile from a large parking lot. A memorial to Father Marquette is along a walkway several hundred feet from the parking lot.

Father Marquette arrived in North America in 1666. He was a Jesuit missionary who lived among the Indians until 1675. In addition to being a missionary, he was an explorer. Marquette learned several languages, which helped him communicate with the Native Americans.

In 1671, Father Marquette founded the mission of St. Ignace, two miles east of the monument. This mission was named in honor of St. Ignatius Loyola. Father Marquette died on May 18, 1675. His remains are buried in St. Ignace.

At the time of Marquette, this region of North America was claimed by France. Louis XIV ruled France and claimed territory throughout the Great Lakes. Marquette carried out exploration on behalf of France throughout the Great Lakes and Mississippi River.

Today, the history and events of that time are depicted at the museum. Displays provide information about the life of Native Americans in this region at the time of Marquette. Displays also describe trade routes, the development of religion among the Indians, and the relationships and interactions of Marquette among the Indians. A replica of an Indian house at the time of Marquette is featured. Also, a copy of Marquette's 1673 journal of his trip which led to the discovery of the Mississippi River is on display.

An auditorium where several films are shown on an hourly basis is located in the museum. There is a film about the life of Father Marquette, a film telling of the French occupation of this area in the 17th century, and other historical presentations. The museum is open daily from about Memorial Day to Labor Day from 9:30 a.m. to 5 p.m.

Near the museum, down the hill, is an amphitheater where programs are conducted during the summer. Also, along a walkway from the

museum is an overlook providing excellent views of the Mackinac Bridge.

Picnic Facilities: Along a one-way drive leading to an overlook are several picnic sites with tables, grills and other facilities. The views from these picnic areas permit you to see the Mackinac Bridge and much of the surrounding area on the water. The drive goes to an exceptional lookout of the bridge and Straits. Also, a playground for children is available.

Several picnic tables are also near the parking lot at the Marquette historical site.

Trails: Though there is a short hiking trail that leads from one campground to the scenic overview, few people come to this park to hike. It takes about 10 minutes to walk the trail.

Winter Facilities: The campground is not open in the winter, nor are park roads. Camping is allowed in the parking lot of the park headquarters. Cross-country skiing is permitted on the roads and picnic area; however, there are no groomed trails.

Straits State Park
720 Church St.
St. Ignace, MI 49781-1729
(906) 643-8620

Wilderness State Park

At the far northern end of the Lower Peninsula of Michigan, in Emmet County, is Wilderness State Park. This park is comprised of 7,514 acres, most of which is undeveloped wilderness.

Location: Wilderness State Park is about 12 miles west of Mackinaw City. From Mackinaw City, take C-81 west to the park. If traveling on I-75 exit at mile marker 338 and take C-81 to the park.

Features of the Park: The park features about 26 miles of shoreline. Several miles of sandy beach along the northern side of the park on Lake Michigan, plus the western side of the park along Sturgeon Bay provide opportunity to walk the beaches, swim, wade and fish. Sturgeon Bay is separated from Lake Michigan by two islands, Crane Island and Temperance Island, and Waugoshance Point.

The major development in the park is found on Big Stone Bay, a couple of miles inside the eastern boundary of the park. Here are the park office, campgrounds and several trailheads.

Camping: There are 250 campsites at Big Stone Bay in two locations. The Lakeshore Campground is near the shoreline of Big Stone Bay. The beach is next to the campsites.

Pines Campground is across the only road into the park. This camping area, in a pine woods, is about a quarter-mile from the water and the beach.

Both campsites have modern flush toilet and shower facilities.

A group camping area is on Big Stone Bay.

Rustic Cabins: Throughout the park are six rustic cabins and three bunkhouses. Four of these are on Lake Michigan, with entrance off of the county road. They are Big Stone Bay Cabin, Cap's Cabin, Station Point Cabin and Waugoshance Cabin. Each is isolated from the others, being a quarter-mile to a half-mile from the drive. Four to eight individuals can be accommodated in the cabins. They are located in the woods on the edge of the sandy beach.

The views from the beach are spectacular in all directions. From the cabins, you can see the Mackinac Bridge about 10 miles away. Also, large oceangoing vessels can be seen on the Straits of Mackinac.

You can walk for several miles along the beach. You easily get the impression that this area is little changed from what explorers experienced here a couple hundred years ago.

The morning we walked this area, we saw several deer coming down to the water and many ducks and other species of waterfowl and birds. Most people renting these cabins spend much of their time fishing near their cabins in addition to hiking, biking and enjoying the wooded surroundings near their cabins.

Another cabin, Sturgeon Cabin, is in the woods off of Sturgeon Bay Road, a short distance from Sturgeon Bay. Fishing in this area for bass is popular. The morning we were here, there were no other people along the bay; however, hundreds of ducks created a great amount of wilderness noise.

Nebo Cabin, in which four people can sleep, is about two miles from the main road along Nebo Trail. As with much of this park, Nebo Trail is a beautiful trail to bicycle. A short distance beyond Nebo Cabin, at the junction of South Boundary Trail and Nebo Trail, is a trailside shelter. Reservations are necessary to use it—and the cabins.

Trails: Most of the trails are two-lane tracks which are closed to vehicular traffic. They make for excellent bicycling as well as hiking. Also the single-road leading through the park from the east entrance to

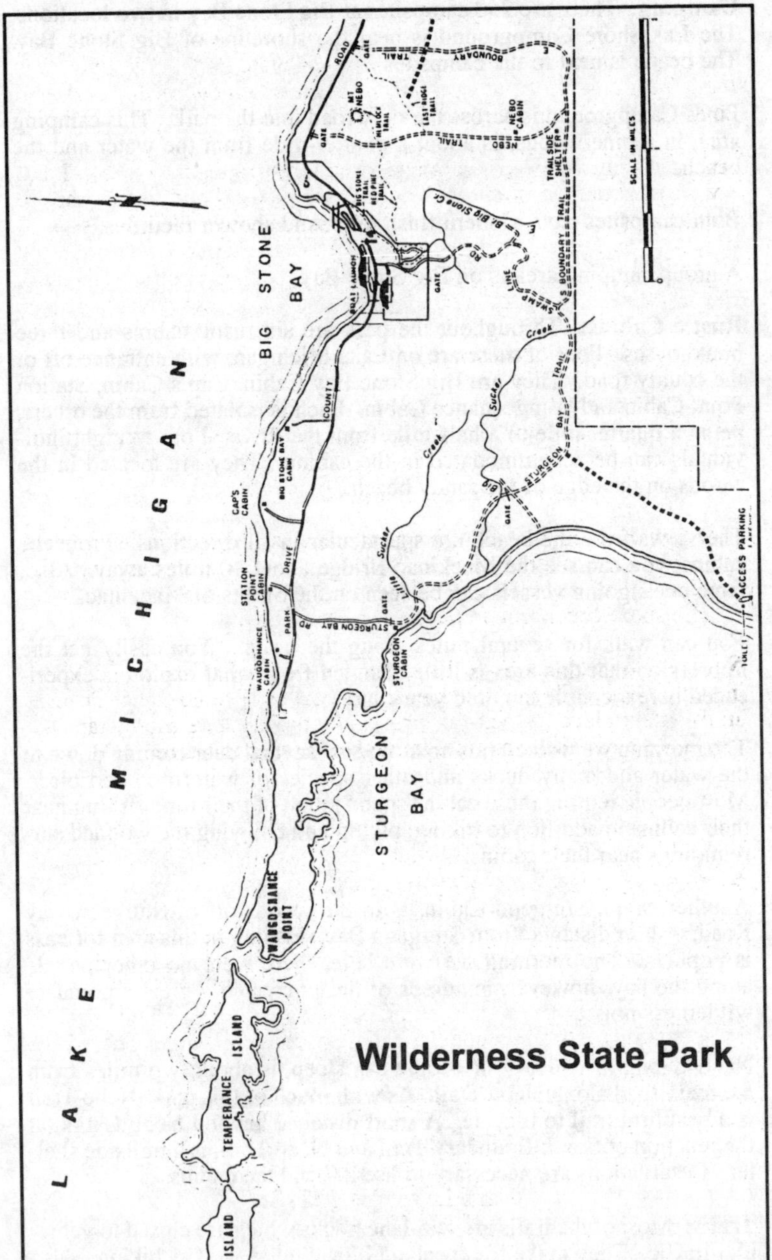

Wilderness State Park

Waugoshance Point is excellent for bicycling.

There are 16 miles of trails in Wilderness State Park. The longest is the 5.5-mile North Country Trail, from the south end of the park and connecting with the Sturgeon Bay Trail.

An interesting hike is the combined Red Pine Trail and Hemlock Trail, a walk of about 3.5 miles. It begins at the Goose Pond Dam, near the Pines Campground. There is a helpful brochure that identifies several points of interest along these trails. Using the character, Woody the Pileated Woodpecker, the brochure points out 30 points of interest. Various trees, leaves and animals are noted. Also, the remains of logging operations, in the area are identified. There are no provisions for horseback riding within the park.

Picnic Facilities: East of the campground is a picnic area. Tables are on the shoreline providing picnickers with a beautiful view of the Straits of Mackinac. There is a sandy beach alongside the picnic grounds.

Fishing: Fishing is one of the most popular activities at Wilderness State Park. A variety of lake fish are caught in the waters near the park. Smallmouth bass are particularly popular. There is a boat launch west of Lakeshore Campground on the Big Stone Bay.

Nature: Wilderness State Park has a variety of animals and birds, including whitetail deer, black bear and beaver. Waugoshance Point is an excellent place to look for birds. The park reports more than 100 species of birds either migrate through or nest in this area.

Winter Activities: Wilderness State Park is open throughout the year. This state park is an excellent location for cross-country skiing. There is usually an abundance of snow, the terrain is relatively flat, and there are about 12 miles of groomed ski trails.

It is possible to use the park cabins during the winter. Two of them, Nebo and Waugoshance can be reached only on skis since the drive is not plowed in the winter.

Snowmobiling is another popular activity during the winter. There are 12 miles of trails which are designated for snowmobiles, most of them in the southern section of the park.

Wilderness State Park
P.O. Box 380
Carp Lake, MI 49718
(616) 436-5381

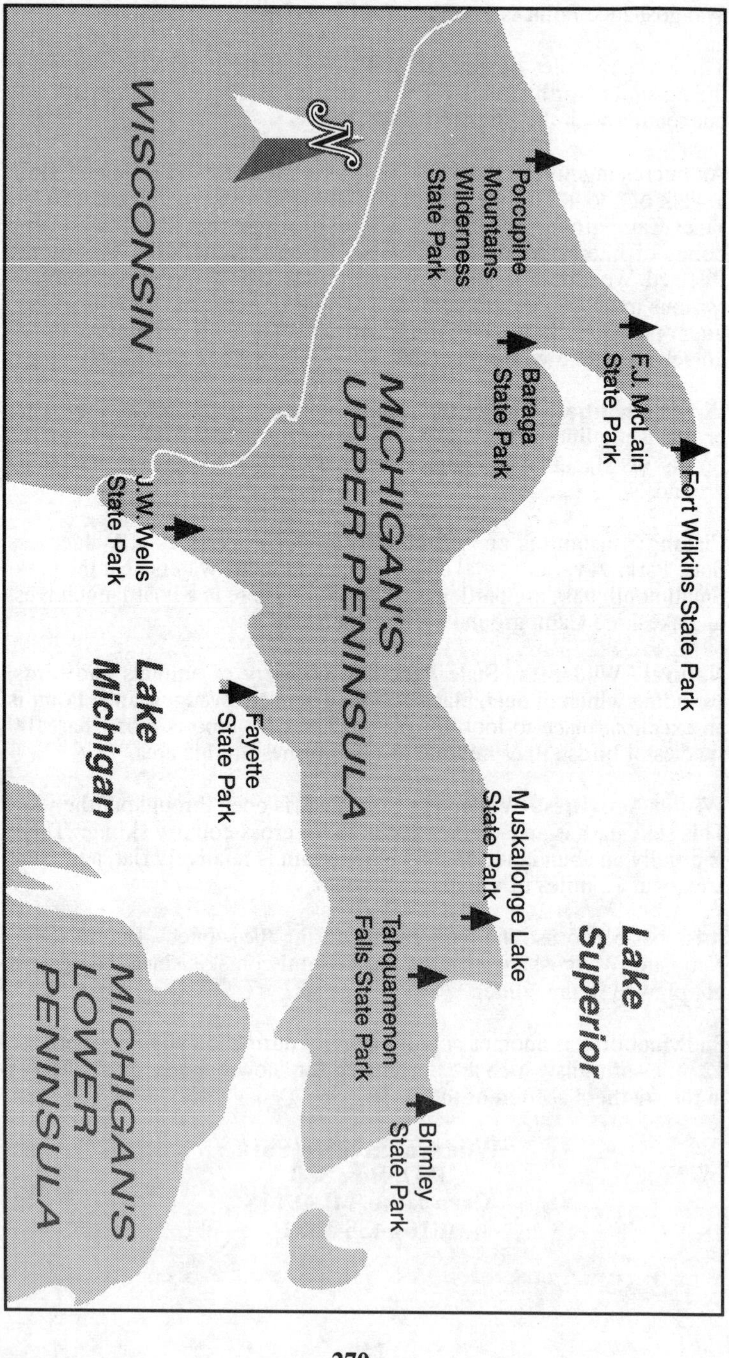
Lake
Superior
Fort Wilkins State Park
F.J. McLain
State Park
Baraga
State Park
Porcupine
Mountains
Wilderness
State Park
N
WISCONSIN
MICHIGAN'S
UPPER PENINSULA
J.W. Wells
State Park
Fayette
State Park
Lake
Michigan
Muskallonge Lake
State Park
Tahquamenon
Falls State Park
Brimley
State Park
MICHIGAN'S
LOWER
PENINSULA

The Upper Peninsula

The northern boundary of Michigan's Upper Peninsula extends along the shoreline of Lake Superior to Wisconsin. The northern shoreline of Lake Michigan forms part of the southern boundary of the Upper Peninsula. This region of Michigan is heavily wooded with numerous lakes, streams and rivers.

Though not heavily populated, it has become increasingly popular in recent years for its many tourist attractions. During the summer months, the lakes, waterways and forests provide unlimited opportunities for fishing, canoeing, hiking and camping. Fall finds the Upper Peninsula popular with tourists attracted by the beautiful fall foliage.

Also, in the fall and during the winter, visitors to the Upper Peninsula come for hunting, snowmobiling, downhill and cross-country skiing. Much of the Upper Peninsula is covered by heavy snow during the winter and early spring. Some winters, the snowfall exceeds 200 inches in places.

Nine Michigan state parks are on one of two Great Lakes. Seven are on Lake Superior: Baraga, Brimley, Fort Wilkins, F.J. McLain, Muskallonge Lake, Porcupine Mountains Wilderness and Tahquamenon Falls. Two are on Lake Michigan: Fayette and J.W. Wells.

Baraga State Park

Baraga State Park is the smallest state park in the Upper Peninsula, only 56 acres. This state park is primarily a camping facility.

Most campers travel throughout the Keweenaw Peninsula, visiting natural and historical sites.

Location: Baraga State Park is at the south end of Keweenaw Bay, which stretches south from Lake Superior. It is on U.S. 41 within a mile of Baraga in Baraga County.

Features of the Park: Most of the park is west of U.S. 41 which bisects the park.

Along the bayside of the park is a day-use picnic area with about a dozen picnic tables and children's play equipment. The campground is on the opposite side of the highway.

Camping: There are 119 campsites in the campground. The camping area is very attractive; there is excellent shading and the grounds are grassy and well maintained. The bay, across the highway, is visible from most of the sites.

Trail: A one-mile hiking trail begins at the campground and crosses a railroad track west of the campground. This trail, which is a loop, goes through birch, aspen and maple trees.

Picnic Facilities: From the picnic tables, you have an excellent view looking north of the Keweenaw Bay. Though there is no sand, there is a rocky beach where people can swim. Grass extends to the rocky shore.

Baraga State Park
Route 1, P.O. Box 566
Baraga, MI 49908
(906) 353-6558

Brimley State Park

Brimley State Park is one of the oldest state parks in Michigan. It was established in 1922, only a year after the Department of Conservation was formed. The initial 38 acres were given to the state for a park as a gift by the village of Brimley. Since then, additional acreage has been acquired through land exchange or purchase. Today the park comprises 151 acres.

Looking east from the beach, you can see Canada in the distance, as well as lake freighters passing through the channel from Lake Superior into the Straits of Mackinac.

Looking out on Whitefish Bay on a warm summer day, you may have trouble realizing that this section of Lake Superior can be extremely dangerous during a late-fall storm. Nearby here, the freighter Edmund Fitzgerald sank in 1973, taking many men to their deaths.

Location: Brimley State Park is on Six Mile Road one mile east of Brimley, Michigan, and 17 miles west of Sault Ste. Marie. From Sault Ste. Marie, go south on H-63 to Six Mile Road, turn west and go about eight miles to the park. From I-75, travel to exit 386 (M-28), then go west on Six Mile Road to the park.

Features of the Park: Brimley State Park, on Whitefish Bay, is primarily a campground and picnic facility.

Camping: There are 271 campsites which are open with no shrubbery or undergrowth separating them. The sites are about 50 feet wide.

At each campsite are a picnic table and an in-ground fire pit. The highest-numbered campsites are nearest the water. Twenty-five sites (even numbers from #222 to #244, then #245 - #247, and then odd numbers to campsite #269) are on the sandy shoreline of the Whitefish Bay.

A rent-a-tent (campsite #240) is along the shore.

There are three modern toilet and shower facilities. An underground electrical system provides electricity to all campsites. A mini cabin recently was built.

Campsites #245 and #271 have walkways leading to the beach.

A bulletin board in the campground provides information about ships on the Great Lakes that you might see offshore. It explains the meaning of different whistles the freighters use as well as the various flags that the vessels might fly.

Many campers visit other places of interest in the Upper Peninsula and in the Straits area. A display board in the campground provides information about them.

An area for organizational camping is near the western edge of the park, adjacent to the parking lot. Reservations are necessary.

Across the highway from the park entrance is a store offering food and camping supplies. The store is privately operated.

Picnic Facilities: The large, grass-covered picnic area has many tables, grills and a children's play area, including slides, swings and climbing equipment. A glass-enclosed shelter is also in the picnic area.

The picnic facilities are on the edge of the bay, where it is easy to watch passing ships. This is the largest picnic ground in an Upper Peninsula state park.

On the western edge of the park is a single-ramp boat launch. There are several ramps for larger boats in the surrounding area.

Beach: The beach extends the length of the park. It is sandy, stretching from the water's edge 25 to 50 feet. The sandy lake bottom has many small stones.

The water of Whitefish Bay is warmer than the rest of Lake Superior and provides an excellent beach for swimming and other water activities during the summer. There are no lifeguards.

Trails: There are no hiking or bicycling trails in Brimley State Park.

Winter Activities: Winter activities are minimal because the park is closed from the first of December until the end of March.

Brimley State Park
Route 2, P.O. Box 202
Brimley, MI 49715
(906) 248-3422

Fayette State Park

Fayette State Park includes the historic town of Fayette and encompasses more than 700 acres of forested land.

Location: Fayette State Park is in Delta County on Garden Peninsula, on M-183 about 17 miles south of U.S. 2, on Big Bay de Noc of Lake Michigan.

Features of the Park: The park highlights the restored town of Fayette, which fronts Snail Shell Harbor.

History of the Town: Fayette was an industrial community where pig iron was manufactured between 1867 and 1891. This ore was shipped to foundries south on the Great Lakes. Transportation was a costly venture, so Fayette Brown of the Jackson Iron Company established a company-owned furnace near the mine, where iron ore could be smelted into pig iron.

The furnace was built on Big Bay De Noc, where a natural harbor facilitated shipping of the processed pig iron. Also, there were limestone and hardwood forests in the area, both necessary for smelting the iron ore. In 1867 Fayette was established as a company town. Here, until 1891 when the facility was shut down by the company, an active, noisy, dirty industrial community thrived. Much of the population during this time was made up of immigrants.

Up to 500 people lived and worked in Fayette. Sites of the laborers' log cabins are noted as you walk along a path near the edge of Big Bay de Noc. There are other renovated and restored houses: the superintendent, the doctor, and the boarding house where workers lived. Three other interesting buildings are the Shelton House, which was a hotel, the town hall, and the company store and warehouse. In addition, an old opera house can be seen today.

About the grounds of the historic town are 22 buildings. Several have been renovated and are furnished with period artifacts. The largest building is the renovated furnace complex. Charcoal and lime kilns and the limestone quarry near the furnace help the visitor to understand the smelting process.

One reason that this town was chosen by Fayette Brown was that it sat on a small harbor, Snail Shell Harbor. Today, you can walk along the docks of this old facility and see much of the restored town.

Visitor Center: A scale model of the community accompanied with an explanation of the boom times of the late-1800s can be seen in the visitor center. Exhibits provide information for visitors. It is useful to spend some time listening to the story of the town and become informed about the history associated with the region before touring the various buildings. During the summer, tours through the town are given by park personnel. The visitor center is open daily from mid-May to mid-October.

Trails: Most tourists who come to Fayette State Park will spend a couple of hours walking about the town. They are not likely to spend much time hiking the park trails. However, there are about seven miles of hiking trails throughout the park. Not only do these trails take you through the historic town, but also among the beech and maple forests of the area. One trail, high on the bluff along the east side of Snail Shell Harbor, provides exceptional views of the town and Lake Michigan in the distance.

Camping: The campground has 80 sites. This semi-modern campground has pit toilets, water and electrical hook-ups at each campsite. Most sites have some shade. The campground is less than a half-mile walk from the town. It's about the same distance in the opposite direction to Sand Bay, which has a small beach. Here there is a changing building, along with playground equipment and facilities for picnicking.

Fayette State Park

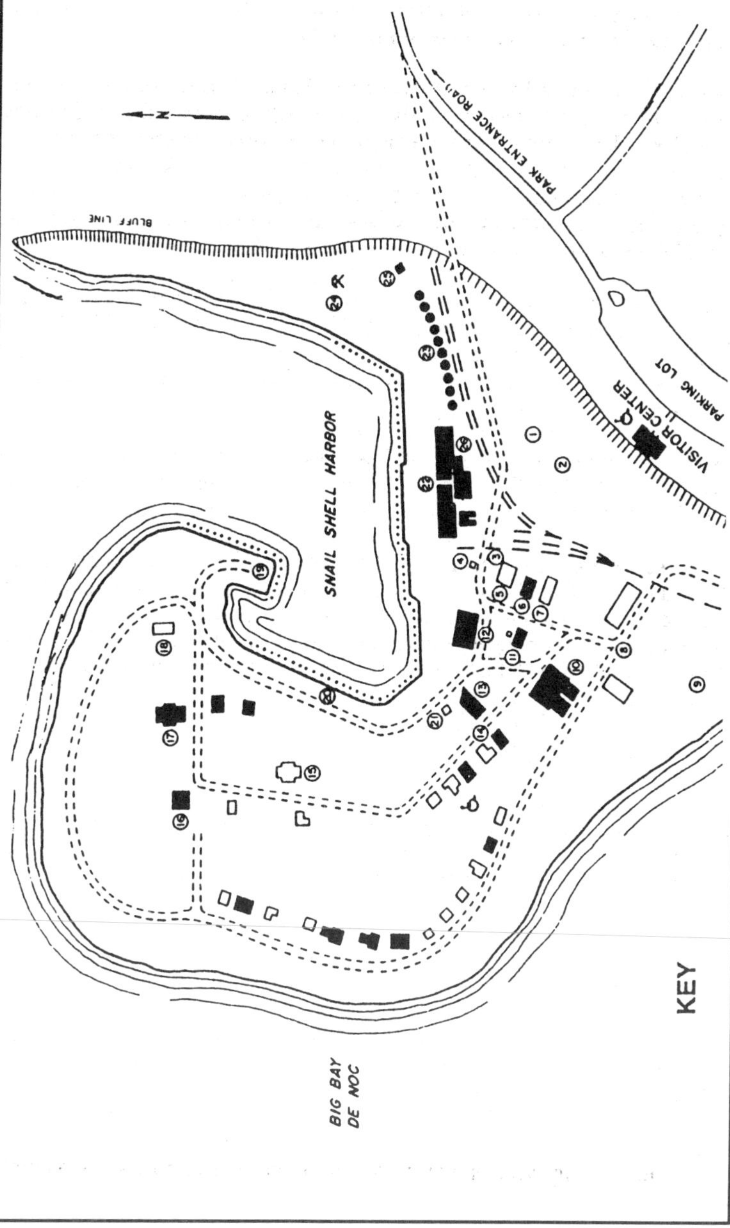

Fishing/Boating: Fishing for perch, smallmouth bass and northern pike are particularly popular in the waters of Lake Michigan near the park. Sometimes, there are walleye and salmon in these waters. Between the campground and beach is a boat launching site. It is possible to anchor your pleasure boat in Snail Shell Harbor. Spaces cannot be reserved; however, adequate space is generally available.

In Snail Shell Harbor, it is possible to scuba dive at certain times of the day. It is necessary to pay a fee and obtain a permit.

Winter Activities: As in most state parks in the Upper Peninsula, winter activities are available. Nordic skiing is particularly good in Fayette State Park because of the heavy amounts of snow around the area. Skiing along the trails through the town is particularly interesting, with the skier enjoying an empty snow-covered ghost town. Snowmobiling also is allowed in parts of the park.

Fayette State Park
13700 13.25 Lane
Garden, MI 49835
(906) 644-2603

Fort Wilkins State Park

In Fort Wilkins State Park is a restored fort built by the U.S. Army in 1844 on the southern shore of Lake Superior. Today 19 buildings remain. Twelve are original log and frame structures. This park is on 203 acres between Lake Superior and Lake Fanny Hooe.

Location: Fort Wilkins State Park is at the northern point of the Keweenaw Peninsula, just a mile north of Copper Harbor, Michigan. It is bisected by U.S. 41, which has its northern terminus one mile north of the park.

Features of the Park: The fort is on Lake Fanny Hooe, on the southern edge of the park. It is bounded on the west edge by Fanny Hooe Creek, which connects Lake Fanny Hooe with Lake Superior. The fort is open from 8 a.m. to dusk from mid-May to mid-October.

To the north, on the opposite side of U.S. 41, the park includes nearly two miles of Lake Superior shore. There also are a couple of islands and a peninsula across Copper Harbor that are incorporated in the park. On the peninsula is the Copper Harbor Lighthouse. This structure was built in 1866 and occupied until 1919. The federal government built a lighthouse at Copper Harbor in 1847. That structure was replaced by the present one in 1866. The state of Michigan purchased the lighthouse in the 1950s and today it has been restored and serves as a museum. It is necessary to take a tour boat from the Copper Harbor Marina to reach the lighthouse. At the lighthouse are a museum, narrative presentation about the history of the lighthouse, and trails.

There are no beaches or swimming facilities in the park. The waters of Lake Superior are too cold most of the summer for swimming. The day of my visit a few people were wading in the water, looking for colored stones along the bottom of the lake.

History of the Fort: Before the 1840s, most copper used in American industry was imported at highly inflated costs. Around 1840 geologists discovered copper in the Keweenaw Peninsula. In 1843 a boom in copper mining began in the region. Prospectors were causing problems, however, particularly with Indians. To maintain peace, the federal government sent troops to this area. A series of forts was established along the nation's western frontier all the way to the Gulf of Mexico. Fort Wilkins became the northernmost post in this national chain of defense.

The first soldiers arrived and established Fort Wilkins in 1844. However, the fort was occupied only for about two years, being abandoned in 1846. By this time prospecting for copper had subsided and the mining industry became the operation of large companies. The fort was again occupied from 1867 until 1870 because of insufficient barrack space elsewhere.

The fort today provides an example of army life on the northern frontier during the mid-19th century.

Costumed interpreters play the roles of individuals when Fort Wilkins was a military establishment in 1870. They may be working, walking the fort grounds, sitting in their "homes," or carrying out other activities of the past. You can enjoy a conversation with these individuals and will find that it helps you to feel a part of that time in history.

In the restored fort are an officers' quarters, enlisted men's barracks, and married personnel living facility. You can also see the kitchen, hospital, guardhouse, storehouses, bakery, carpenter shop and blacksmith shop. In each of these as well as other buildings are displays providing information.

The fort cemetery is several hundred yards along Lake Fanny Hooe, near today's parking lot.

If you take the time to read the various displays, listen to the video pre-

Fort Wilkins State Park

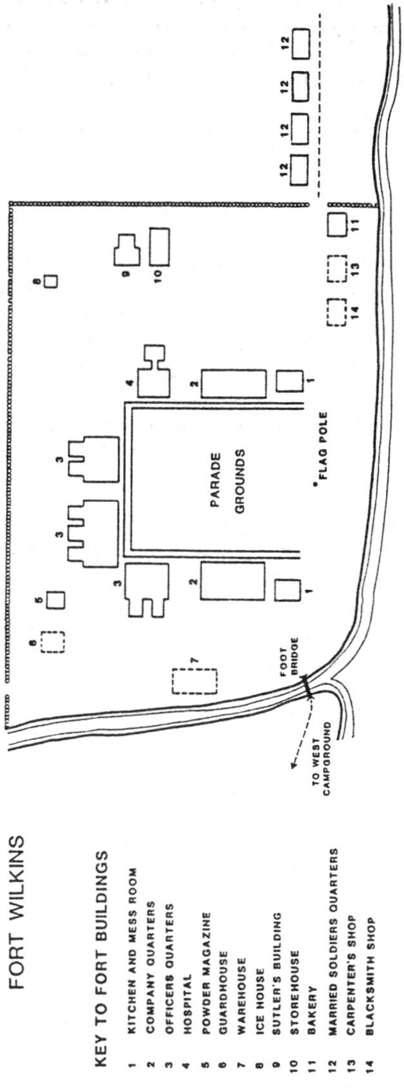
FORT WILKINS
KEY TO FORT BUILDINGS
1 KITCHEN AND MESS ROOM
2 COMPANY QUARTERS
3 OFFICERS QUARTERS
4 HOSPITAL
5 POWDER MAGAZINE
6 GUARDHOUSE
7 WAREHOUSE
8 ICE HOUSE
9 SUTLER'S BUILDING
10 STOREHOUSE
11 BAKERY
12 MARRIED SOLDIERS QUARTERS
13 CARPENTER'S SHOP
14 BLACKSMITH SHOP
PARADE GROUNDS
FLAG POLE
FOOT BRIDGE
TO WEST CAMPGROUND

sentations, talk with the interpreters and walk the grounds of the fort, you will come away with an increased appreciation for this period of American history.

Camping: There are two campgrounds, one to the east of the fort and one just west. Combined, there are 165 campsites. The west campground is connected to the fort by a short trail. Access to the Lake Superior shoreline is a short walk across U.S. 41. The east campground is near the day-use area and is a quarter-mile to Lake Superior.

There are also a group campground and one mini-cabin which can be reserved on a one-night rental basis.

Trails: About four miles of hiking trails exist in the park. One trail proceeds along Lake Fanny Hooe, starting at the campground and extending into Copper Harbor, a distance of about two miles. Another trail runs from the picnic area where Fanny Hooe Creek enters Lake Superior to the shoreline of Lake Superior. This trail is about one mile long. Lake Superior is within view along most of the trail. At any point along the way, you can stop along the shoreline and enjoy the scenery of the lake. The stone covered trail provides typical rugged Lake Superior scenery.

Picnic Facilities: To the east of the fort is a day-use area. There is a store where refreshments and curios can be purchased. Picnic tables and grills are in an expanse of grassy area where people can enjoy sporting activities and children can play on playground equipment.

Fishing: Fishing is popular in Lake Fanny Hooe. Rainbow trout, walleye and smallmouth bass are caught here. There is a boat ramp on Lake Fanny Hooe near the west campground, but none in the park into Lake Superior.

Winter Activities: Because of the isolation of this area and the usually heavy snow and cold winters, there are relatively few visitors during the winter. Several miles of cross-country ski trails are groomed; however, there is no ski rental in the park. Ice fishing on Lake Fanny Hooe is enjoyed by the most hardy individuals.

Fort Wilkins State Park
U.S. 41 East
Copper Harbor, MI 49918
(906) 289-4215

F. J. McLain State Park

F.J. McLain State Park encompasses 417 acres. Summer activities at McLain State Park include swimming, windsurfing, fishing, hiking and sunbathing. During the winter, cross-country skiing is a popular activity.

Location: F.J. McLain is in Houghton County on the Keweenaw Peninsula on M-203, 11 miles north of Hancock, Michigan. Most of the acreage and activity within the park are between the highway and lakeshore. On the opposite side of the highway the park extends about a quarter mile to Bear Lake.

Features of the Park: McLain State Park is along two miles of Lake Superior shoreline.

The sandy beach at the south end of the park is protected by a sea wall, which also serves as a fishing pier. At the end of the sea wall is a lighthouse. A public bathhouse, shelter and a concession store are near the beach.

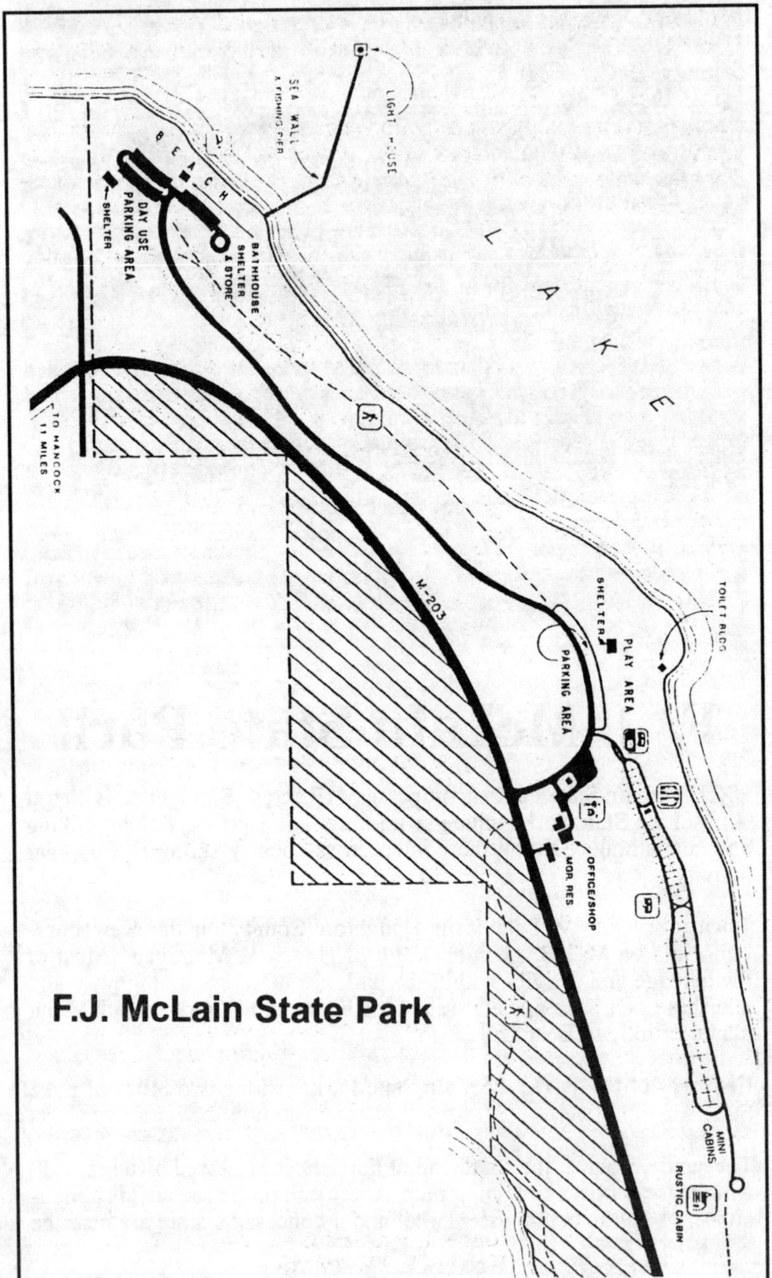

F.J. McLain State Park

In the midsection of the park, near the campground, is a play area with picnic facilities, a shelter and open grass where people can relax and enjoy the out of doors.

Camping: The campground has 103 sites, each with electrical service, in a forest of red pine and oak trees. It runs for more than a half-mile along the water on a bluff overlooking Lake Superior. Most sites have an excellent view of the lake.

Hot showers and flush toilet facilities are available in the campground. Facilities are also available for the Michigan rent-a-tent program at McLain State Park

Between the campground road and the shoreline bluffs are wooden chairs and swings where people can sit and relax while watching and listening to the water washing upon the shore. This provides a beautiful view and perfect place to read and talk with friends. It is spectacular in the evening as the sun sets over Lake Superior. The evening of our visit, the sky was clear and the setting sun provided numerous photographic opportunities.

At one end of the campground, four rustic cabins are on a bluff overlooking the lake. The cabins are available on a one night minimal rental basis.

Trails: In the park are two hiking trails. One, about a mile in length, connects the bathhouse and shelter at the beach with the day-use area. The other hiking trail, the Bear Lake Trail, is a circular path beginning in the campground. It crosses the highway and proceeds along Bear Lake, ending at the main entrance to the park.

There is a dock on Bear Lake, but there is little or no fishing here.

Fishing: Most fishing occurs from the seawall which provides protection for the sandy beach. Fishing during the summer is principally for Lake Superior whitefish. During the spring and fall, coho salmon fishing is popular.

Winter Activities: Winter in this part of the Upper Peninsula extends from early November until well into March. Most years, there is heavy snowcover in the park area during these months. Several miles of groomed cross-country trails exist in the park. Also, in the surrounding area outside the park are additional miles of cross-country trails. There are no facilities for ski rental at the park.

McLain State Park
Route 1, P.O. Box 82
Hancock, MI 49930
(906) 482-0278

Muskallonge Lake State Park

Muskallonge Lake State Park, comprised of 217 acres, is the most isolated state park on the Great Lakes.

The park is on the site of the old town of Deer Park, Michigan, a lumbering town in the late 1800s. In 1876, a sawmill was built there by the Cook and Wilson Lumber Company. A hotel, store and family homes were built. Lumber was shipped from a dock which extended into Lake Superior. White pine logs were brought by way of narrow-gauge railroad lines to Muskallonge Lake, which served as a mill pond.

By the turn of the century the forests became depleted, lumbering ceased to be profitable, and the mill closed. By 1906, the surrounding land was badly scarred from the removal of the trees. The lumbering company left the area, taking all of its equipment. Most of its buildings were loaded on barges and taken to Canada where another "boom" town was established.

Still seen in the water at the Lake Superior shoreline are remains of the old dock. The dock and other remnants of the town are scenic and worth photographing.

Location: Muskallonge Lake State Park is in Luce County on Lake Superior 28 miles north of Newberry, Michigan, on road H-37 (county road 407), which is a hard-surface road. This highway bisects the park. From the west the park is 18 miles from Grand Marais. This road is a narrow, gravel road which becomes blacktop at the western boundary of the park.

Features of the Park: The park is about a quarter of a mile wide between the shoreline of Lake Superior on the north and Muskallonge Lake on the south.

The water level of Muskallonge Lake is 32 feet higher than Lake Superior. This is because the sand of Muskallonge Lake resists water penetration. An elevated lake such as this is called a "perched" lake.

Across the road from the campground entrance is a wooden walkway which goes to the Lake Superior shoreline. The shoreline extends about a mile and a half, the length of the park, east and west. The

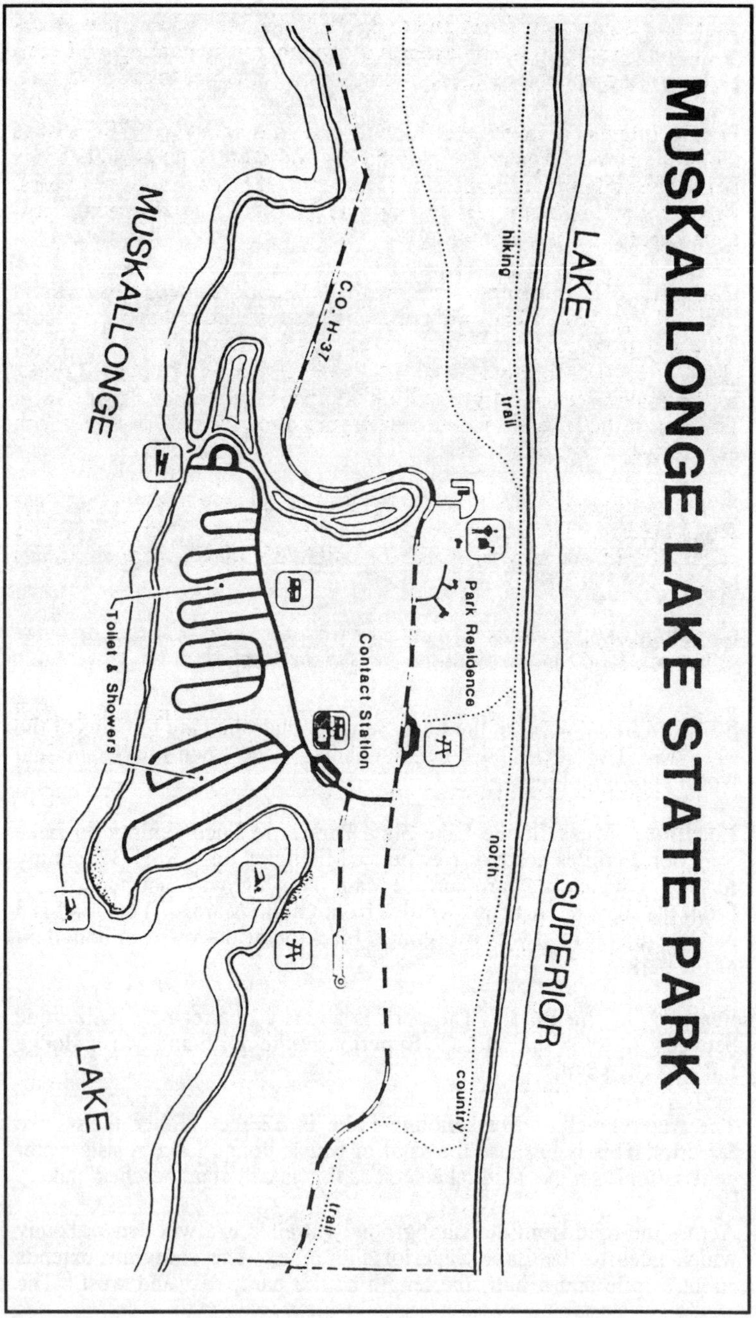
MUSKALLONGE LAKE STATE PARK
LAKE
SUPERIOR
hiking
trail
north
country
trail
C.O. H-37
Park Residence
Contact Station
Toilet & Showers
MUSKALLONGE
LAKE

shoreline is generally stony and rocky. Although there are a few places with some sand, it is not extensive enough for swimming and sunbathing. At places along the shoreline, dune bluffs rise to about 75 feet.

People interested in rock collecting can find many colorful stones along the shore. Agates are particularly common. The agate belongs to the quartz family of minerals. Development takes millions of years. Agate collecting is not new; as early as 3500 B.C., the Egyptians collected agates from the desert.

Camping: The campground, with 179 well-shaded sites, is on Muskallonge Lake. They are grass-covered sites, each having a picnic table and ground fire pit. The lake can be seen from most of the campsites. Sites #149 through the #170s are nicely isolated from each other, well wooded, and have ground underbrush to provide some privacy. The rest of the sites are wooded with grass groundcover, but not much underbrush separating them.

At the campground is a beach about 200 yards long with an excellent sandy bottom. The sand extends back up to 20 feet from the water's edge. There are several pieces of children's play apparatus at this beach.

Camping supplies and food can be purchased at two private stores one mile in either direction from the campground entrance.

Picnic Facilities: Just to the left of the campground entrance is a small picnic area. About a dozen picnic tables, several grills and children's play sets are in this area. A very small sandy beach is also here. This picnic/swimming area is on an arm of Muskallonge Lake. The campground is just across the water from the picnic site.

Trails: There is a 1.5-mile hiking trail in the park. This trail connects with the North Country Hiking Trail, an east-west trek from New York to North Dakota, which will be 3,240 miles long when completed. However, the park trail is poorly identified.

Fishing: Fishing on Muskallonge Lake is excellent for northern pike, perch, smallmouth bass, walleye, muskies and rock bass. There is a boat launch ramp into Muskallonge Lake, as well as a parking lot for about a half-dozen cars and trailers, on the west edge of the campground.

Muskallonge Lake State Park
Rt. 1, P.O. Box 245
Newberry, MI 49868
(906) 658-3338

Porcupine Mountains Wilderness State Park

Porcupine Mountains Wilderness State Park is the largest state park on the Great Lakes. It was established in 1945.

This park comprises more than 58,000 acres stretching for nearly 20 miles along the beautiful and rugged shoreline of Lake Superior. The hills in the park reach 1,958 feet high. Summit Peak is the tallest point in the park. Porcupine Mountains Wilderness State Park comprises some of the most spectacularly beautiful wilderness east of the Rocky Mountains.

Location: Porcupine Mountains Wilderness State Park is along Lake Superior, 17 miles west of Ontonagon, Michigan. Most people coming to Porcupine Mountains Wilderness State Park enter along M-107.

Features of the Park: The Lake Superior shoreline is rugged, yet extremely beautiful. There are places where you can walk along the stony shore, picking up various colored stones. There are many examples of beautifully shaped driftwood along the shores of the lake.

From the east entrance to the park, the main road follows along the shoreline for about 10 miles. This scenic road ends at a parking area where there are facilities for picnicking. However, most individuals who come to this spot will take a short walk on a hard surface footpath, about a quarter of a mile, to an overlook. Here is one of the most spectacular views in the park, a view of Lake of the Clouds, one of four lakes in the park. The lake sits in the Big Carp River Valley. At this observation point you are almost 1,300 feet above the lake and surrounding valley. The lake is accessible by trail from this point, as are several other trails.

Many activities draw visitors to this park: hiking, fishing, walking along the lakeshore, downhill and cross-country skiing, mountain climbing and sightseeing. Probably the most popular is hiking.

Several waterfalls are found in Porcupine Mountains Wilderness State Park. At the western side, along the Presque Isle River within easy walking distance of the camping area, are three falls: Manabezho, Manido and Nawadaha Falls. Others are on the Little Carp River. The highest falls in the park is Shining Cloud Falls on the Big Carp River. This falls can be reached by hiking on the Big Carp River Trail.

History: This region of the Upper Peninsula was an area of copper and silver mining during the 1800s and early part of the 20th century. The first mining in the Porcupine Mountains was the Union Copper Mine, which started in 1845 and was part of the first mining in this part of the country. Today, the one-mile Union Mine Trail takes you to several points of interest in that early mining time. Several numbered locations along the trail provide information about the Union Mine. This mine, along with most other mining operations of that time, eventually failed. In the early 1900s logging became an important business in this region of the Upper Peninsula.

Visitor Center: Near the entrance to the park, about a half-mile south of the main road is a visitor center. It offers information about the geology and history of this area. A large three-dimensional relief map of the park depicting the trails, roads, lakes and streams will help you decide what to do. There is a small theater where film presentations are given, providing visitors with highlights of the park.

Individuals planning to backpack overnight must make reservations with park personnel at the visitor center.

Trails: There are nearly 90 miles of trails for the day-hiker, the backpacker and the extended hiker. The longest trail in the park is the Lake Superior Trail, which follows the shore of Lake Superior for about 16 miles. Along the trail are many excellent views of the lake. This trail stretches from Presque Isle River on the west end of the park to M-107 at the eastern entrance.

There are 20 trails ranging in length from the one-mile Union Mile Trail to the Lake Superior Trail. Most of the trails intersect with at least one and often several other trails, allowing you to plan trips of any length.

An interesting walk is the one-mile round trip to the observation tower at Summit Peak, at 1,958 feet the highest point in the park. From this 40-foot tower, you can see a broad panorama of surrounding territory, as far as 40 miles away. The Apostle Islands to the west are in view from this tower.

Two hiking trails, the North Mirror Lake Trail (4 miles) and the South Mirror Lake Trail (2.5 miles), lead to Mirror Lake, situated at 1,532 feet, the highest lake in the park.

Possibly the most scenic trail is the four-mile Escarpment Trail. This trail traverses the escarpment over Cloud Peak and Cuyahoga Peak, high above the Lake of the Clouds. The views of the lake and the Carp River Inlet, several hundred feet below the trail provide spectacular scenery for hikers. This trail is particularly beautiful in September when the valley is covered with the autumn colors.

The Little Carp River Trail is the second longest trail, at 11 miles. A number of rapids and waterfalls of the Little Carp River provide many scenic spots along the trail. Brook trout fishing is common along the river.

The Big Carp River Trail is nine miles long. Along this trail you will see the highest falls in the park, the Shining Cloud Falls, in addition to a variety of other rapids. Brook trout fishing is also popular along this trail.

Throughout the park, accessible by the various trails, are miles of streams and rivers. These scenic rivers and streams tumble along through the forest and rocks flowing eventually into Lake Superior.

There are numerous waterfalls in the park. The easiest falls to walk to are along the Presque Isle River, where within about a half-mile you can see the Manido Falls, Manabezho Falls and Nawadaha Falls. These falls can be reached by walking along a comfortable boardwalk. Along the boardwalk are several viewing platforms where you can stop to photograph the falls or simply observe the river, rapids and flowing cascades. Fishing in many of the streams that empty into Lake Superior will often reward you with catches of salmon and trout.

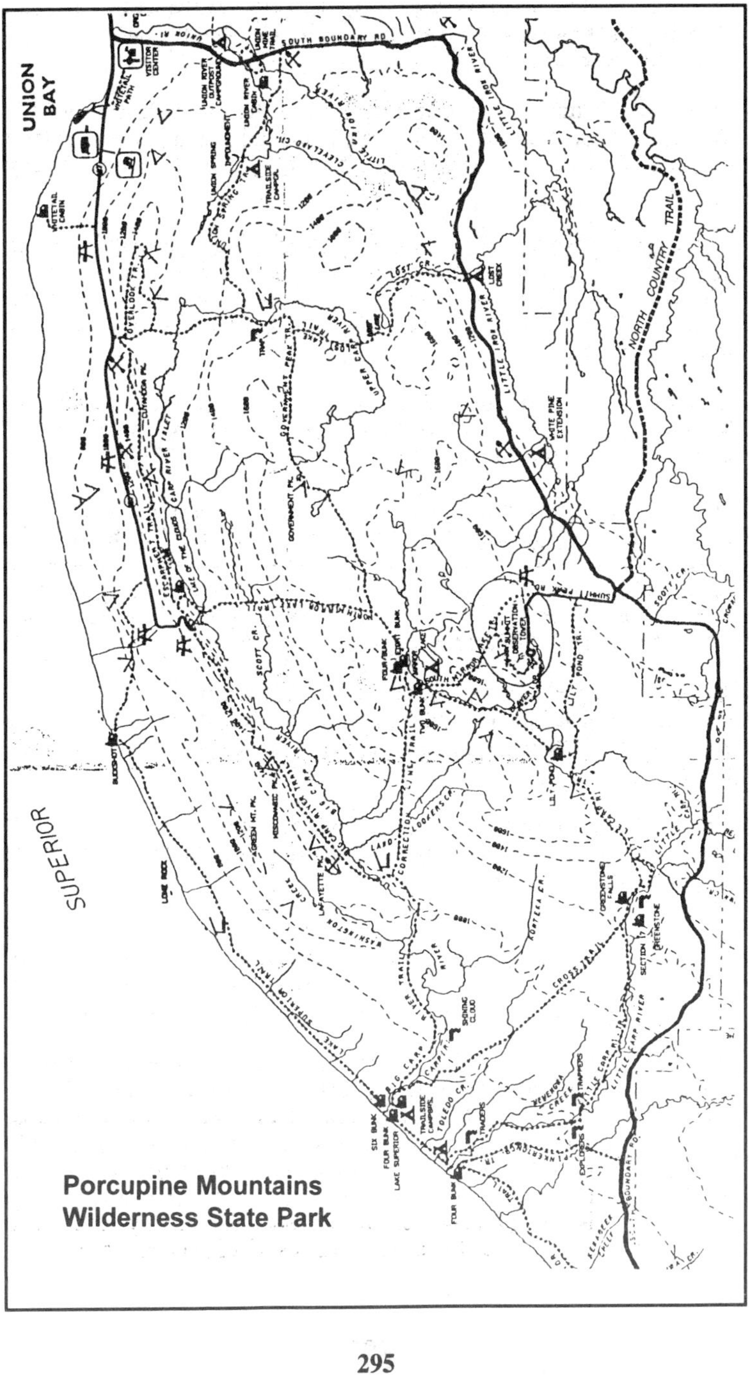
UNION BAY
SUPERIOR
NORTH COUNTRY TRAIL
SOUTH BOUNDARY RD.
Porcupine Mountains
Wilderness State Park

Camping: There are two campgrounds in the state park. One, with 95 sites, is near the eastern entry point to the park. This campground, the Union Bay Campground, is near the shore of Lake Superior. Flush toilets, hot showers, a sanitation station and electricity are available.

On the western side of the park is the Presque Isle Campground, near the mouth of the Presque Isle River, with 88 campsites. At this campground are restrooms and showers; however, there is no electricity for trailer hook-ups. Several of the campsites are on a bluff overlooking Lake Superior. We camped at one of these sites and found the view to be spectacular.

Because of the popularity of the campgrounds, it is necessary to make reservations about six months in advance for summer camping.

There are four areas in the park where rustic camping is allowed. Near the visitor center is a group camping site. Throughout the park on the various trails are a number of other camping facilities. These facilities include small walk-in campsites. These sites do not have the facilities you would find at more developed campgrounds. They are excellent for serious hikers, however.

Along the many trails are small wilderness rustic trailside cabins and shelters. Some of these overlook Lake Superior; others are on the shore of Lake of the Clouds or along the streams of the interior wilderness. The cabins are available for rental from April through November and should be reserved in advance. The cabins have bunks that will accommodate eight to 12 individuals. Provided at each cabin in addition to the bunks with mattresses are a sink, wood stove, table, benches, cooking utensils, dishes, and an ax and saw. Those using the cabins must provide their own food, bedding, lighting and other personal needs. A rowboat is provided at the cabins on Lily Pond, Mirror Lake and Lake of the Clouds. Those with reservations for the cabins must get the key at the park office before venturing into the wilderness.

Only bunks are provided at the trailside, or Adirondack shelters, which are available on a non-reservation, first-come, first-served basis.

Trailside camping is permitted in the interior of the park. Backpackers must not camp within a quarter-mile of any cabin, Adirondack shelter or road. At several locations there is a dry tent pad, a campfire ring and rustic toilet. Backpackers must take out all non-combustible trash.

Nature/Wildlife: You are likely to see a variety of northwoods wildlife in the park. Deer are abundant. Black bear are to be found. Visitors are warned to keep all food away from their campsites because of potential bear visits.

Winter Activities: Wintertime brings as much as 200 inches of snow each year to this part of the country. This makes for excellent skiing, both downhill and cross-country. Porcupine Mountains Wilderness State Park is one of two state parks on a Great Lake with alpine ski facilities.

There are 14 downhill ski runs in the park—four expert, seven intermediate and three novice trails. The longest run is one of the novice runs, 5,800 feet long. There are a triple chair and T-bar lift as well as a double chair and handle tow serving the "Bunny" slope. The lift capacity is 3,600 skiers per hour. There is an A-frame chalet that provides a cafeteria, ski rentals and fireplaces.

More than 25 miles of groomed cross-country ski trails are tracked through the wooded hill country. Nordic skiing enthusiasts can experience some of the most beautiful trails in the Midwest. Back-country nordic skiing is permitted. However, the cold winter conditions and amount of snow demand that back-country skiers register at the ski chalet and carry extra provisions as well as snowshoes.

Equipment is available for rental. Several park cabins are available for use during the winter on a ski-in basis. It is necessary to carry snowshoes and cross-country skis to reach these cabins. Reservations must be made in advance at the park office.

The South Boundary Road is not open after the end of November. M-107 is kept open only as far as the ski area during the winter.

Porcupine Mountains Wilderness State Park
412 S. Boundary Road
Ontonagon, MI 49953
(906) 885-5275

Tahquamenon Falls State Park

Tahquamenon Falls State Park is the second largest park on the Great Lakes, comprising nearly 40,000 acres. Nearly half of the 40,000 acres are undeveloped. There are few roads, no buildings and minimal development in this section of the park.

The park extends along the Tahquamenon River, which flows east entering Whitefish Bay of Lake Superior at the Rivermouth section of the park.

Location: The Upper and Lower Falls in the park are 23 miles north of Newberry, Michigan, and 10 miles west of Paradise on M-123. The Rivermouth area is about five miles south of Paradise on M-123.

Features of the Park: The Tahquamenon River with the waterfalls is the principal feature of the park.

Tahquamenon River: The 94-mile Tahquamenon River originates in a small group of lakes in western Luce County, north of McMillan. In its entire course, the river drains an area of about 9,000 square miles.

The water over the Upper Falls flows over an escarpment of Cambrian Age sandstone. This sandstone is sediment deposited as marine beaches during the Cambrian Age, more than 500 million years ago.

The water over the Upper Falls has a unique root beer color, the result of tannic acid in the cedar hemlock swamps along the river. At the bottom of the Upper Falls is a lot of white foam, which is the result of the water being churned by the drop over the falls. This foam has been the trademark of the Tahquamenon River since the early days of exploration. At the Upper Falls is a maximum flow of more than 50,000 gallons a second and a minimum flow of about 2,000 gallons a second. On either side of the falls is rock and Cambrian Age sandstone.

Sections of the Park: There are four sections to this park: the Rivermouth area, Upper Falls, Lower Falls and the isolated wilderness in the northwestern part of the park.

Rivermouth - The Tahquamenon River flows into the Whitefish Bay section of Lake Superior at Rivermouth.

Upper Falls - The Upper Falls is one of the largest waterfalls east of the Mississippi River. The water drops nearly 50 feet and is nearly 200 feet across.

Lower Falls - The Lower Falls are four miles downstream from the Upper Falls. These are a series of five smaller falls and cascades which circle an island.

Wilderness area - No motorized vehicles or boats can enter this area. This is known as the Tahquamenon Natural Area and covers roughly 20,000 acres. In this section are three isolated lakes: Betsy Lake, Clark Lake and Sheephead Lake.

History: The Rivermouth area is near a historical town, Emerson, once a thriving hub of pine lumbering. This town was immortalized in Longfellow's poem "Hiawatha." The village was founded by Curt Emerson, a lumberman from the Saginaw Bay area in the early 1880s. Emerson erected a sawmill, which was sold in 1884. In the early 1900s the town had 30 homes, a post office and a general store. In 1913 lumbering and milling operations ceased. Commercial fishing became the major economic contributor to this area. Today, little remains of the town except for several building foundations among the rubble.

Camping: The park contains four campgrounds. Two modern campgrounds are at the Lower Falls and a modern and rustic campground are at the Rivermouth area. Each of the modern campgrounds has about 90 campsites, each equipped with electrical outlets, a picnic table and an in-ground fire ring. Modern toilet and shower facilities are found at each modern campground.

Lower Falls Campgrounds - None of these sites is directly on the water, yet they are within easy hiking distance to the water. The Rivers Bend Campground has 88 sites, all of reasonable size. There is little underbrush, so visibility across the campground is easy. Sites #1 through #13 are on the bank of the Tahquamenon River.

The other campground, with 100 campsites, is the Overlook Campground. The road leading to it turns right at the park entrance booth. This campground is heavily wooded. Each campsite has a table and an in-ground fire ring as well as electricity hook-ups. The campsites in the inner circles are close together. There is no underbrush separating the campsites. Ground cover is dirt, grass and leaves. The campsites on the outside section of the campground tend to be bigger, deeper and wider.

Rivermouth Campground - There are 76 campsites at the modern Rivermouth Campground, which is along the Tahquamenon River. It is heavily wooded with campsites well-separated from one another. Each site has a picnic table and an in-ground fire ring. Most sites have grass and leaves covering the ground.

A gravel road leads to the rustic campground with 57 campsites. These sites begin about a quarter of a mile from the campground booth. They extend a little over a quarter-mile along the river on either side of the gravel road. The setting is beautiful with excellent views of the river and island in the river. The campsites on the north (right) side of the road are directly on the river. The campground is in a heavily wooded pine forest, with a table and an in-ground fire ring at each campsite. There are no modern facilities in this campground, only pit toilets. Campers can tie their boats up within a few feet of their campsite.

Generally, the campsites at the Rivermouth section are less crowded than are those at Lower Falls. These campgrounds are most popular among people wishing to fish. A boat ramp there provides the only access to the river below the Lower Falls and Whitefish Bay.

Upper Falls - There are no campground facilities at the Upper Falls.

Trails: There are about 45 miles of trails in Tahquamenon Falls State Park.

At the Upper Falls is a hard-surface, wide trail leading four-tenths of a mile from the parking lot to the falls. About a quarter of a mile from

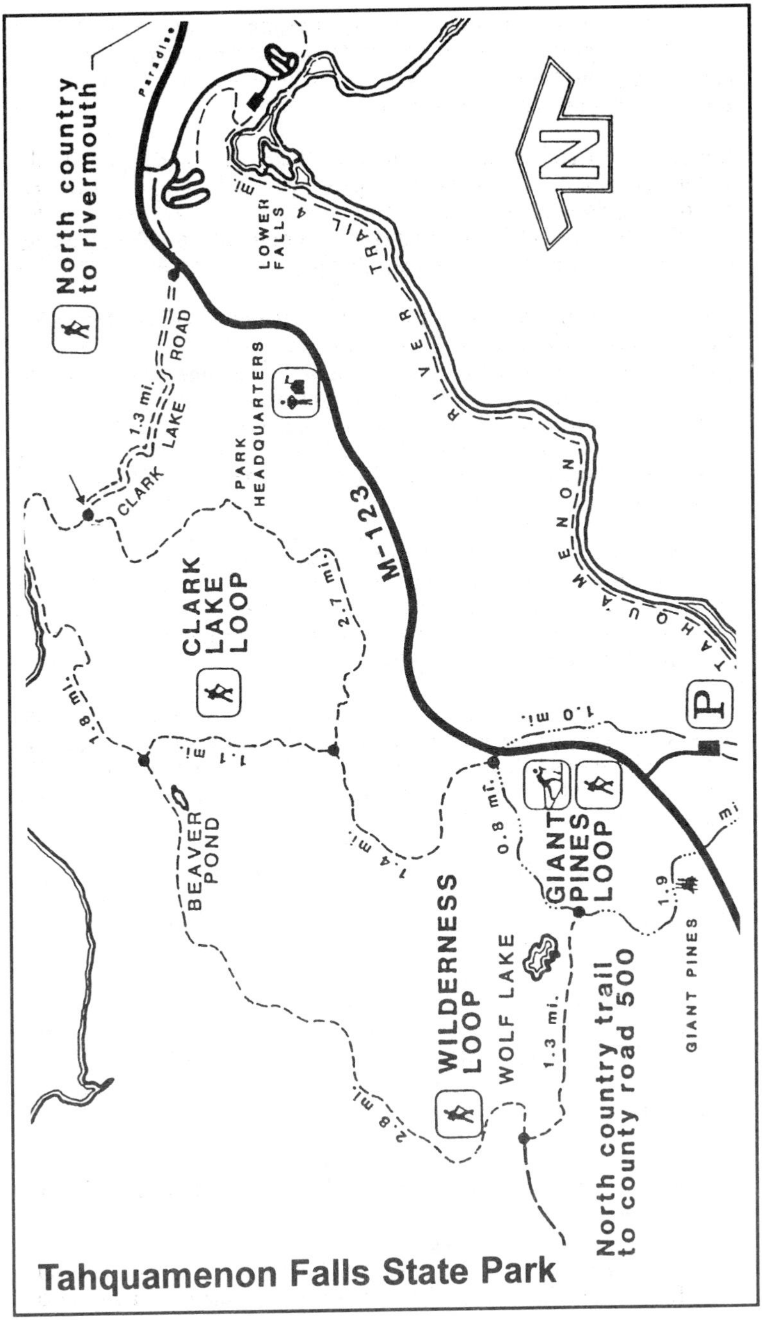
Tahquamenon Falls State Park
North country trail to rivermouth
North country trail to county road 500
Paradise
CLARK LAKE ROAD
1.3 mi.
PARK HEADQUARTERS
M-123
LOWER FALLS
RIVER TRAIL 4 mi.
TAHQUAMENON
CLARK LAKE LOOP
2.7 mi.
1.8 mi.
1.1 mi.
1.4 mi.
BEAVER POND
1.0 mi.
0.8 mi.
GIANT PINES LOOP
1.9
GIANT PINES
WILDERNESS LOOP
WOLF LAKE
1.3 mi.
2.8 mi.
N
P

the parking lot the trail divides; the right branch goes to the top of the falls and the left branch to the stairway that takes you to the bottom of the falls. The left branch also takes you to the trailhead of the four-mile River Trail to the Lower Falls.

The trail to the Upper Falls is easy to walk and is handicapped accessible. As you approach the end of the trail, several overlooks provide views of the falls. Each is scenic and provides a different view of the falls. The best overview to give a complete view of the falls is the first one to the left of the "Y" in the trail.

From above the falls to the brink is a stairway with 74 steps. The stairs from the trail to the bottom of the falls include 116 steps. The walk down is not difficult. At the brink of the falls is a large, wooden viewing area. There are benches for rest and plenty of space to walk about and see the falls from different vantage points.

Year round, this is a very scenic trail. During the fall with the forest colors, it is beautiful. In the winter it serves as a cross-country ski trail providing a spectacular scene of white snow and ice formations created by the falls. The best time to photograph the Upper Falls is in the morning, up to noon. In the late afternoon the sun is behind the falls and not as conducive to good photography.

There is a .3-mile nature trail, Old-Growth Nature Trail, that returns to the parking lot from the falls trail. Much of the forest along this trail is old growth. American beech, sugar maple and hemlock are the predominant trees in this area. These are large trees that are long-lived and able to reproduce in their own shade. Today, less than one percent of old growth forests are left and a good number of them are found in Michigan state parks.

A popular hiking trail is the four-mile River Trail which connects the Lower Falls with the Upper Falls. The trail proceeds along the river. It is difficult in places, going over tree roots and wet spots. Nevertheless, it is scenic with the falls, the river and the woods.

The trail extending from the parking lot at the Lower Falls to the viewing area is a .3-mile hard-surface trail, becoming a wooden trail. It is handicapped accessible and follows the river with the falls and island in view most of the way. An interpretive guide exists for this trail. At the falls, your destination, is a viewing platform.

A hiking trail circles the island at the Lower Falls.

A short distance on M-123 from the entrance to the Lower Falls campground is a single-lane dirt road, Clark Lake Road, leading 1.5 miles to a trail that takes you to Clark Lake. It is narrow and best traveled on foot or bicycle. I rode my bicycle along this road and found it solid for

biking. In places it was sandy and necessitated walking the bike a short distance. At the end of the road is a turnaround parking space for motor vehicles. It was necessary to park the bicycle and proceed to Clark Lake by hiking trail for two-tenths of a mile.

Clark Lake is in a wilderness setting, surrounded by trees. A number of ducks, geese and other birds were around the lake, which is boggy around the perimeter. There are two wooden walkways over the bog to the edge of the lake. The lake bottom drops immediately at the edge of the water and bog; it is impossible to see the bottom.

Beyond Clark Lake is a much bigger and more isolated lake, Betsy Lake. Sheephead Lake is still further north and east of Betsy Lake.

Hiking is popular on the Giant Pines Loop Trail, 3.7 miles, whose trail-head is at the Upper Falls parking lot; the Wilderness Loop Trail, slightly more than seven miles; and the Clark Lake Loop, nearly seven miles, access being off of the Clark Lake Road.

The North Country National Scenic Trail extends nearly 20 miles through the park. This trail, when completed, will be a 3,240-mile-long trail crossing seven states from the state of New York to the Lewis and Clark Historical Trail in North Dakota. In the Upper Peninsula of

Michigan, the trail comes north from St. Ignace through the Hiawatha National Forest to Tahquamenon Falls State Park. The trailhead at Tahquamenon Falls State Park is at the Rivermouth campground. The trail follows along the river, past Camp 10 Lakes to the Lower Falls. From here it goes into the Natural Area, leaves the park and continues north through Lake Superior State Forest, eventually coming to Muskallonge Lake State Park and then on to Pictured Rocks National Lakeshore.

Nature: Moose have been seen, particularly in the Natural Area and along the marshy river waters near the mouth of the river. According to park information, the Tahquamenon area is home to 25 moose. In recent years moose sightings have been increasingly reported. Black bear and deer are seen throughout the entire park.

The park is an excellent place for viewing any number of birds, particularly at the mouth of the river the Rivermouth Region. Osprey and bald eagles are often seen in the park.

Picnic/Concession Facilities: A picnic ground at the Upper Falls parking lot has several tables and grills.

At the Upper Falls parking lot are spaces for several hundred motor vehicles. There is a new concession building known as Camp 33. Pasties, a dish unique to the Upper Peninsula of Michigan, hand-dipped ice cream, sandwiches, beverages and a Tahquamenon Falls root beer float in a souvenir cup are available. Also, there is a large souvenir shop. A number of picnic tables are on a wooden deck overlooking the forest at the concession building.

At the Lower Falls are picnic facilities next to the large parking lot adjacent to the river. The picnic area is well-shaded, having a couple of dozen picnic tables and several grills as well as an open shelter house. Children's swing sets are available at this site.

Also at the Lower Falls is a concession facility with a gift shop and a cafe (Big Boy Park Cafe) which is open from Memorial Day through mid-October. There is a wooden deck with tables where you can enjoy refreshments and the surrounding woods. At the Rivermouth area are picnic facilities within view of the river mouth. M-123 is adjacent to the picnic area.

Activities at the Park: The Tahquamenon River provides a wide range of sport fishing opportunities. At the mouth of the river walleye, muskies, northern pike and perch are caught. Upriver, northern pike, yellow perch, walleye, smallmouth bass and muskie are caught by anglers.

Yellow perch and northern pike are caught in the wilderness lakes of the Natural Area. These lakes are only accessible by walk-in. No motor vehicles or motorized boats can be taken to the three lakes.

A boat ramp is at the point where the river flows into Lake Superior. There are parking spaces for about a half-dozen vehicles with trailers.

At the Lower Falls, it is possible to rent a canoe or rowboat at the concession facility. This is the only way onto the island.

During July and August until Labor Day, nature programs are presented on the deck of the Camp 33 Reception Center at the Upper Falls. Also, various interpretive programs are conducted by park naturalists on a daily basis at various locations throughout the park. There are a five-hour canoe trip, a bog walk, a junior ranger program for children, and other activities.

Winter Facilities: Winter camping is available at the Overlook campground, located at the Lower Falls. There are electricity, vault toilets and water taps in the campground. During the winter the entrance road and parking lot at the Lower Falls are plowed. Likewise, the Upper Falls entrance road and parking lot are plowed. Also, during the winter backpack camping is available in the park.

The Upper Falls are spectacular during the winter with beautiful ice formations created by the falls and spray.

There are several groomed cross-country trails in the park. The 3.7-mile, Giant Pines Loop, cross-country ski trail leaves from the top of the Upper Falls. The Wilderness Loop trail covers about seven miles, taking you past Wolf Lake and Beaver Pond.

The Clark Lake Loop, around six miles, goes to Clark Lake. In addition to these marked and groomed trails, there are miles of other trails which are good for cross-country skiing.

Snowmobile access to hundreds of miles of trails throughout the surrounding national forests and wilderness areas in the region is possible.

Tahquamenon Falls State Park
Star Rt. 48, P.O. Box 225
Paradise, MI 49768
(906) 492-3415

J. W. Wells State Park

J.W. Wells State Park encompasses about 678 acres and extends for about three miles along the shoreline of Green Bay. Offshore from the park, Green Bay becomes part of Lake Michigan.

J.W. Wells State Park was established in 1925. The land was donated to the state of Michigan by the family of John Walter Wells, for whom the park is named. Mr. Wells was a prominent lumberman in the area and mayor of Menominee in the 1890s.

Much of the construction in the park was carried out by the Civilian Conservation Corps (CCC) in the 1930s and 1940s. Roads in the area, fire lanes and some buildings were built by CCC workers. The park campground is the original site of the former CCC Camp Wells. Other activities carried out by the CCC in this area included planting trees and clearing trails, along with a variety of other construction projects.

Location: J.W. Wells is on Green Bay about halfway between Escanaba and Menominee, Michigan, on M-35 in Menominee County. The entrance to the park is about two miles from the town of Cedar

River.

Features of the Park: This state park offers swimming, fishing, camping, picnicking and hiking. In the winter it is an excellent place to cross-country ski and ice fish. To the north, west and south surrounding the park are thousands of acres of state forest lands. During hunting season hunters camp at the state park and hunt on the forest lands.

Along the nearly three-mile shoreline of the park are a beach, picnic area and campground with modern facilities. Extending north from the campground is Timber Trail, which goes through the woods about one mile along the edge of the shore. The trail leads to an area where six rustic cabins are available for rental.

Camping: In the campground are 178 campsites. About 40 of them are along Green Bay, providing an excellent view. Electrical hook-ups, flush toilets and shower facilities are available in the campground for use by campers. The campground is well-shaded, with most of the campsites having grass ground covering. Each site has a picnic table and an in-ground fire pit.

Similar to many other state parks during the summer, a volunteer campground manager checks in the campers and serves as the host/hostess. The summer I visited, the volunteer manager provided coffee at 10 a.m. to anyone coming to his campsite. This provided an opportunity for campers to get to know one another, and it also helped the volunteer program of the state parks to be better understood by those staying at the campground. There are no facilities for purchasing camping equipment and supplies in the park. You must go to nearby towns to obtain camping supplies. It is about two miles from the park to the nearest town of Cedar River.

During the summer, the campground receives wide use. Often on weekends the campground fills up. Campsites can be reserved in advance either by mail or phone. Though the park is open year round, the campground is open only from mid-April to mid-October.

Cabins: Six rustic cabins are along Green Bay in the north section of the park. Three of these cabins can accommodate up to eight persons. They are named Detroit, Poverty and Summer, after the Grand Traverse islands which can be seen about 20 miles offshore on a clear day. These islands, running in a chain from Door Peninsula in Wisconsin to Garden Peninsula in Delta County, Michigan, designate the boundary where Green Bay becomes Lake Michigan.

Three other cabins can accommodate up to 12 persons. These also are named for the offshore islands: Washington, Plum and St. Martin. Each of the cabins has bunk beds with mattresses, a wood stove for heat, firewood, table and chairs, and an outdoor charcoal grill. No stove, dishes or cooking utensils are provided by the park service.

No electricity or modern toilet facilities are available in the cabins. For this reason bring lanterns and flashlights. Pit toilets and drinking water are available in the vicinity. There are two outside water pumps available for use by those staying in the cabins. Cabin visitors may use the showers in the campground for an additional cost of two dollars per person per day. The cabins are in the woods along the shoreline. The view is spectacular and the setting is quiet and peaceful.

The cost to rent the rustic cabins is on a nightly basis regardless of the number of persons in the group. Parking is available in the area; however, renters must walk a short distance from the parking area to their cabins. No pets are allowed in the cabins or the cabin area. Reservations can be made in advance by mail or phone for the campsites as well as the cabins.

Picnic Facilities: There is a large day-use area south of the campground, along the edge of the water, designated for picnicking and swimming. Two picnic shelters can be reserved for a small fee. Each of these buildings has modern restrooms. In this area are picnic tables, charcoal grills, a playground and facilities for playing horseshoes and volleyball. Also in this day-use area is a bathhouse for use by individuals coming to the beach.

Trails: There are seven miles of hiking trails in the park. Going south from the picnic area in a loop trail is the Ridgewood Trail. This trail goes almost to the southern end of the park.

Extending from the campground and traversing for about a mile is Timber Trail. This is a very interesting trail to hike. It is within a few feet of the edge of Green Bay and provides excellent views and scenery. This trail brings hikers to the rustic cabins.

Two other trails, Cedar River Trail and Evergreen Trail, add about 2.5 miles to the hike. These two trails are inland from the water's edge and extend to the Big Cedar River, which marks the north boundary of the park. Along the trails are several stone shelters where you can stop for a rest. These shelters were built in the 1930s by the CCC.

Fishing: Many people who visit J.W. Wells State Park come to fish. Fishing is very good for walleye, pike, smallmouth bass, trout and salmon. Park rangers will tell you that the best time to fish is in early April, when the ice is breaking up on the lake. At this time brown trout fishing is usually excellent along the shore of the park. There are no facilities for boat launching in the park; however, boat ramps and charter boat services are available in the nearby town of Cedar River.

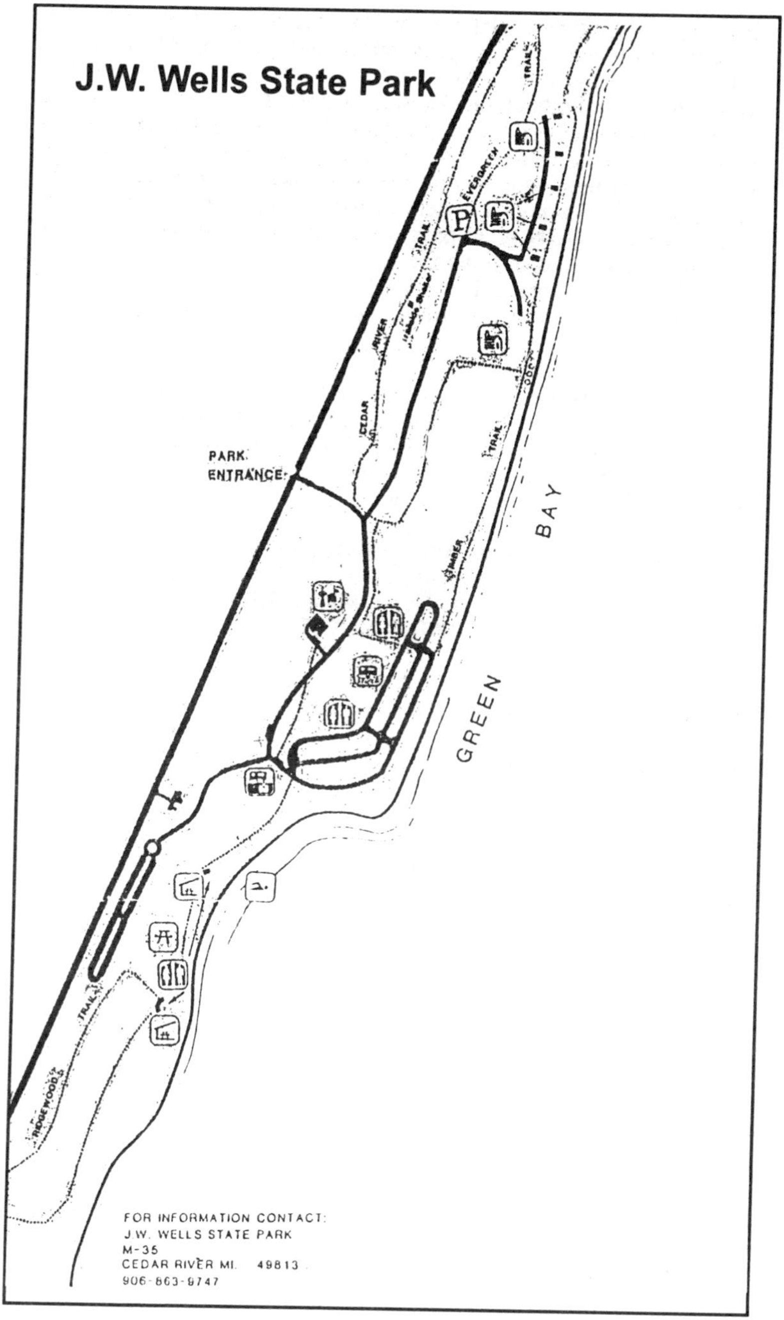
J.W. Wells State Park
PARK ENTRANCE
GREEN
BAY
CEDAR
RIVER
TRAIL
EVERGREEN
TRAIL
TIMBER
FOR INFORMATION CONTACT:
J.W. WELLS STATE PARK
M-35
CEDAR RIVER MI. 49813
906-863-9747

Hunting: Hunting is not permitted in the park. However, the surrounding area is one of the best deer hunting regions of the Upper Peninsula. Many hunters hunt squirrel, rabbit, duck, pheasant and waterfowl. Throughout the hunting season, many hunters use the camping facilities.

Winter Activities: As in most of the state parks of Michigan's Upper Peninsula, winter brings a variety of recreational opportunities. J.W. Wells is a particularly good park for cross-country skiing. The park grooms several miles of trails for skiing during the winter. The park is relatively flat, making it enjoyable for novice skiers. Along the trails, shelters are used as warming huts with wood available to keep the fire going.

The rustic cabins are used during the winter by many cross-country skiers. There is no ski rental in the park. While snowmobiling is permitted in the park, it is prohibited on the ski trails. With the thousands of surrounding acres of state forest land, the snowmobiler has miles of trails available for winter enjoyment.

J.W. Wells State Park
Michigan Route 35
Cedar River, MI 49813
(906) 863-9747

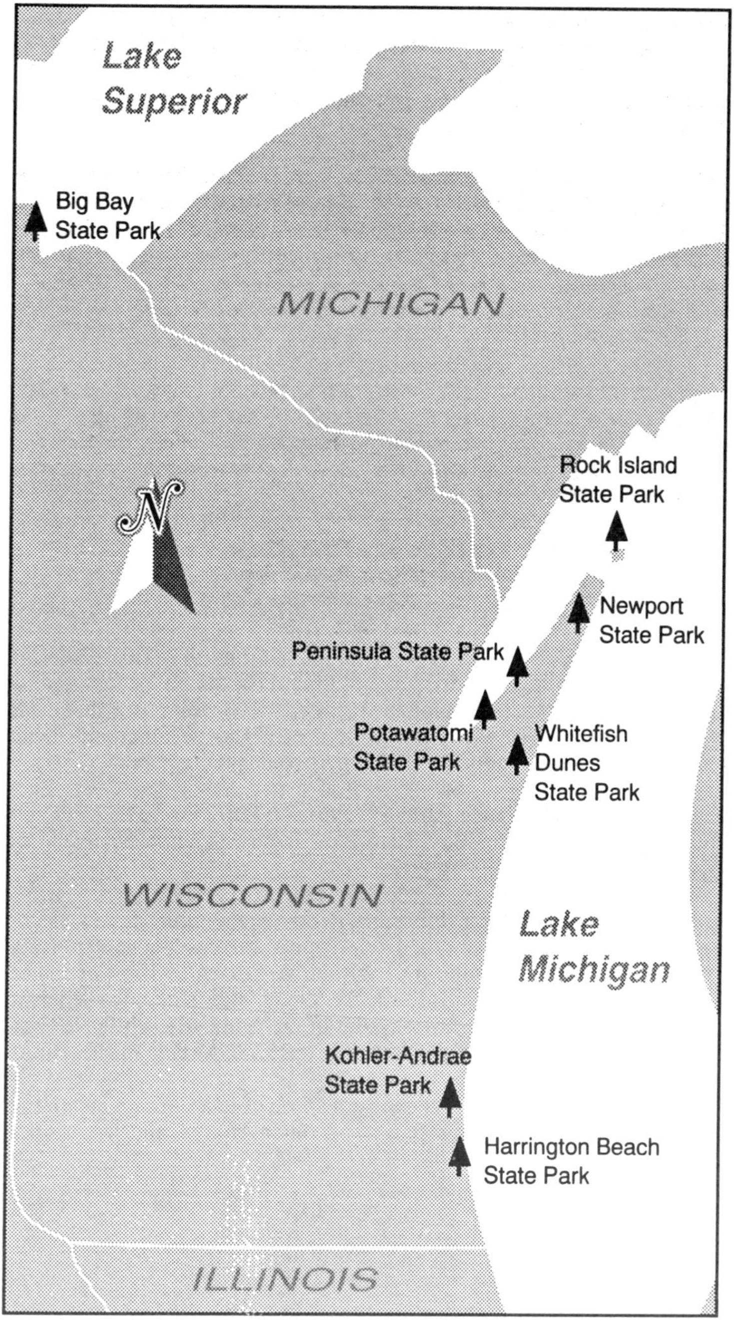
Lake Superior
Big Bay State Park
MICHIGAN
N
Rock Island State Park
Newport State Park
Peninsula State Park
Potawatomi State Park
Whitefish Dunes State Park
WISCONSIN
Lake Michigan
Kohler-Andrae State Park
Harrington Beach State Park
ILLINOIS

Wisconsin

Two Great Lakes border Wisconsin: to the far north is Lake Superior, and Lake Michigan forms a major part of the state's eastern boundary. Jutting into Lake Michigan for nearly 100 miles is a peninsula which separates Lake Michigan from Green Bay. A large part of this peninsula is Door County, a scenic and popular tourist area.

Eight of Wisconsin's state parks are on Lake Superior, Lake Michigan and/or Green Bay. Big Bay State Park is on Madeline Island in the Apostle Islands on Lake Superior.

The remainder of Wisconsin's state parks on the Great Lakes are on Lake Michigan. Five are in the Door County area: Newport, Peninsula, Potawatomi, Rock Island and Whitefish Dunes. Two of these, Peninsula and Potawatomi are on the Green Bay side. Rock Island State park is at the northernmost point of the peninsula, while Newport and Whitefish Dunes state parks are on the Lake Michigan shoreline.

North of Milwaukee along the western shore of Lake Michigan are two additional Wisconsin state parks: Kohler-Andrae and Harrington Beach.

Big Bay State Park

Located on Madeline Island, the largest of the 22 Apostle Islands in Lake Superior, is Big Bay State Park. This park is the northernmost Wisconsin state park. It was established in 1963 and today comprises about 2,383 acres.

Location: The principal means of transportation to Big Bay State Park is by ferry from the town of Bayfield, on the Wisconsin mainland. It is about three miles across the North Channel of Lake Superior from Bayfield to Madeline Island. The ferry runs regularly from the spring breakup of ice, usually in March or April, until the winter freeze. During the summer the ferry runs every half-hour to accommodate the many tourists. The 3-mile ferry ride to the island takes about 20 minutes. Once on the island the park entrance is six miles away.

Features of the Park: The park features a 1.5-mile sandy beach that curves around Big Bay.

Visitors enjoy walking along the water's edge, sitting in the sun, relaxing and playing in the water. The day of our visit there were five groups of people wading in the surf and walking the beach. The water of Lake Superior is cold and not conducive to swimming except on the warmest days during July and August.

An interesting feature of the park is an acid bog lake lagoon which covers about 120 acres.

Trails: The hiking system includes more than seven miles of trails. An interesting boardwalk nature trail extends parallel to the shoreline for about a half-mile behind the beach. Along this trail are signs describing the trees and vegetation within sight of the walkway. At all times, you can see the beach and lake, making for a very enjoyable walk. This is an easy walk that can be experienced by anyone, regardless of age or physical condition.

A 1.3-mile trail, the Bay View Trail, meanders along the lake between the campground and picnic area. It goes mainly through woods, with the shore 25 to 50 yards from the trail. Along this trail the shoreline is rocky, with several places where you can leave the trail and find a place to sit and enjoy the sandstone rock formations of Lake Superior. The wave action on Lake Superior has worn small caves in the bluffs along the edge of the water. These caves are interesting to observe and photograph. The path is comfortable to walk and is well maintained. The day we walked it, there were a few places where we had to walk through mud. The park department was moving the trail about 10 yards back because of erosion that was damaging the trail. A sign at the trailhead warned us of possible wet spots.

Another trail, the Point Trail, is a 1.5-mile loop that begins and ends in the picnic parking lot. It extends about halfway along the shoreline, then circles back through the woods.

This park is not a good spot for bicycling. Though bicycles are available for rental in nearby Lapointe, once at Big Bay State Park the only place that the bicycles can be ridden are on the few roads in the park and campground. Bikes are prohibited on the trail system and there is no bicycle trail in the park.

Camping: Sixty campsites are available at Big Bay State Park. The campground has drinking water along with toilet and shower facilities, but no electrical outlets. The campground is near the beach and the hiking trails. Seven sites can be reached only by walking a shcrt distance to the site.

An indoor group camping facility is alongside the lagoon on the Lagoon Ridge Trail. Groups of up to 20 can make reservations to use the facility.

Picnic Facilities: There are two picnic areas in the park that include

Big Bay State Park

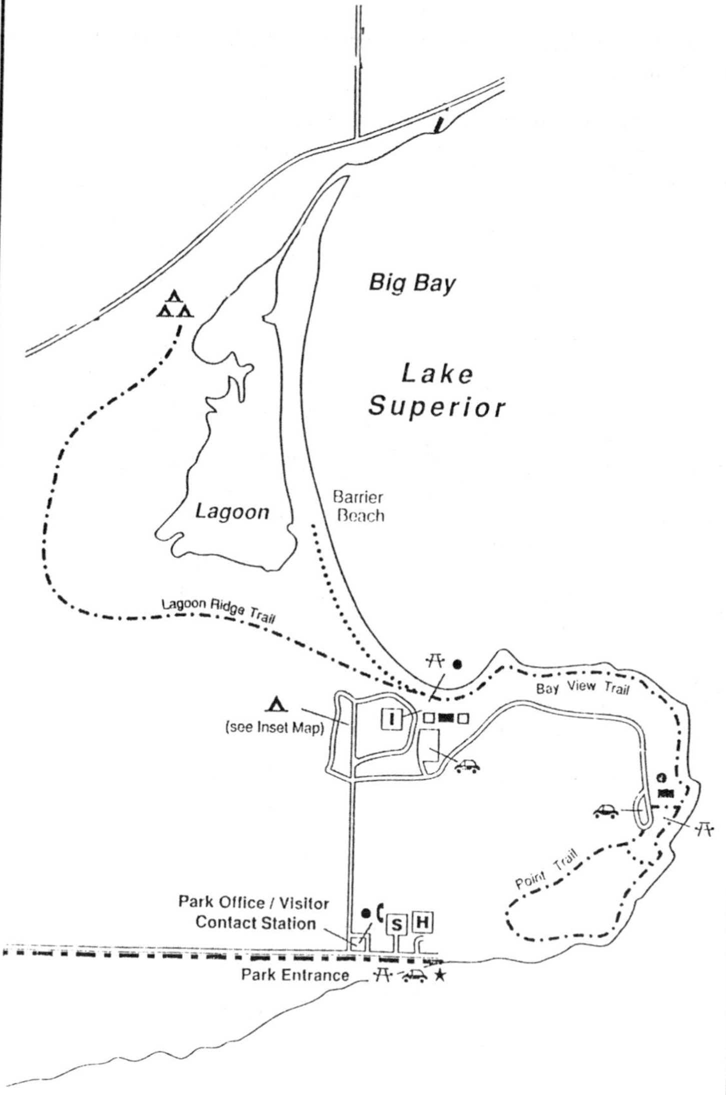

tables, grills, water and toilet facilities. Some tables are among trees with pine needles and pine cones covering the ground. Both trails, Bay View Trail and Point Trail, begin at this picnic area.

Fishing: Fishing, primarily for northern pike, is a popular activity in the Big Bay Lagoon. Fishing for trout and whitefish are popular among anglers in Lake Superior. However, there are no boat docks or launching ramps in the park.

Nature: A popular activity at Big Bay State Park is nature study. There are many kinds of wildflowers that appear in mid-April and grow through the summer until the end of September. Wildflowers in the park tend to bloom one to two weeks later than those on the mainland. Also, in the fall the trees turn color a week to two later. This is due to the cold temperatures of Lake Superior cooling the climate on the island.

Throughout the park many kinds of ferns and mosses grow on the floor of the forest.

Throughout the entire Apostle Islands, area more than 240 species of migratory and nesting birds have been spotted. Many of these can be seen while visiting the state park. A brochure indicating the season when each species is likely to be seen is provided to park visitors.

Periodic evening naturalist and environmental presentations and guided nature hikes are conducted by Wisconsin Department of Natural Resources naturalists during the summer. Also, a ranger program of the Apostle Island National Lakeshore Park is conducted weekly at Big Bay State Park during the summer.

Winter Activity: Cross-country skiing and hiking are permitted; however, there are no groomed skiing or snowmobile trails in Big Bay State Park. You must bring your own equipment. The only way onto the island during winter is by snowmobile or by driving across the ice roadway between Bayfield and Lapointe. Deer hunting is permitted during the state hunting season in November.

Big Bay State Park
P.O. Box 589
Bayfield, WI 54814
(715) 779-3346 (winter)
(715) 747-6425 (summer)

Harrington Beach State Park

Harrington Beach State Park is a day-use facility with no camping or boat launching facility. The park, on the western shore of Lake Michigan, includes about 636 acres.

Location: Harrington Beach is in Ozaukee County, half-way between Sheboygan and Milwaukee. To get there, drive about 10 miles north of Port Washington on I-43, then take County Highway D east to the park.

Features of the Park: Located at Puckett's Pond is a large parking facility. During summer weekends and holidays, motor vehicles are not permitted beyond this point. A shuttle system provides transportation for people to other picnic areas along the Lake Michigan shore, to the beach, and to scenic locations around Quarry Lake. The shuttle bus traverses a three-mile road. We bicycled this road, which was enjoyable without car traffic.

A major feature of the park is Quarry Lake, which covers about 26 acres and is about 50 feet deep. A hiking trail goes around the lake, providing many opportunities to see the beauty of this lake. Care must be taken as there are steep dropoffs into the water from the limestone rocks. Care must be taken when hiking in wet weather since the trail becomes slippery. White cedar trees are found along the trail.

Fishing for smallmouth bass, bluegill and panfish is popular in Quarry Lake. Fishing licenses are required for individuals ages 16 to 65. Boating and swimming are forbidden.

The waters of Lake Michigan are beautiful at Harrington Beach. However, even on the warmest summer days the water is not warm. Swimming is permitted, but you must be careful to adjust gradually to the temperature of the lake.

Several hundred yards offshore in about 80 feet of water are the remains of the freighter Niagara, destroyed by fire in 1856. Up to 169 people perished in that fire. Today, scuba divers can explore the ruins of this submerged ship. The anchor of the freighter is on display in the Point Picnic Area.

History of the Park: The historical development of Quarry Lake is interesting. Quarrying of limestone began in this area in the 1890s. Much of the limestone taken from this area was used for roadbeds after being crushed. During the first two decades of the 20th century, the place which is now Quarry Lake was a rather profitable limestone quarry. Here the Lake Shore Stone Company conducted a prosperous mining business until about 1920, when washed gravel replaced limestone as the stone substance in roadbeds. A number of houses where the miners' families lived were located in the quarry. Barracks that provided living accommodations for workers without families also were located in the area.

After the mining operations were shut down by the end of the 1920s, the surrounding lands were sold or left to stand idle. The 50-foot-deep quarry gradually began to fill with water. Today, as you stand on the edge of Quarry Lake, it is hard to believe that fewer than 80 years ago at the bottom of this lake was an active limestone quarry.

Throughout the park, along the hiking trails and the roadway, are signs providing information about mining operations. These signs include pictures of various mining activities that were taken nearly 100 years ago. The individual who stops to read each of these signs will not only better understand the activities that took place years ago, but will have a greater appreciation for the history of this area.

Picnic Facilities: This is a day-use facility with six picnic areas. One, is near the park entrance. This is Puckett's Pond Picnic Area. Puckett's

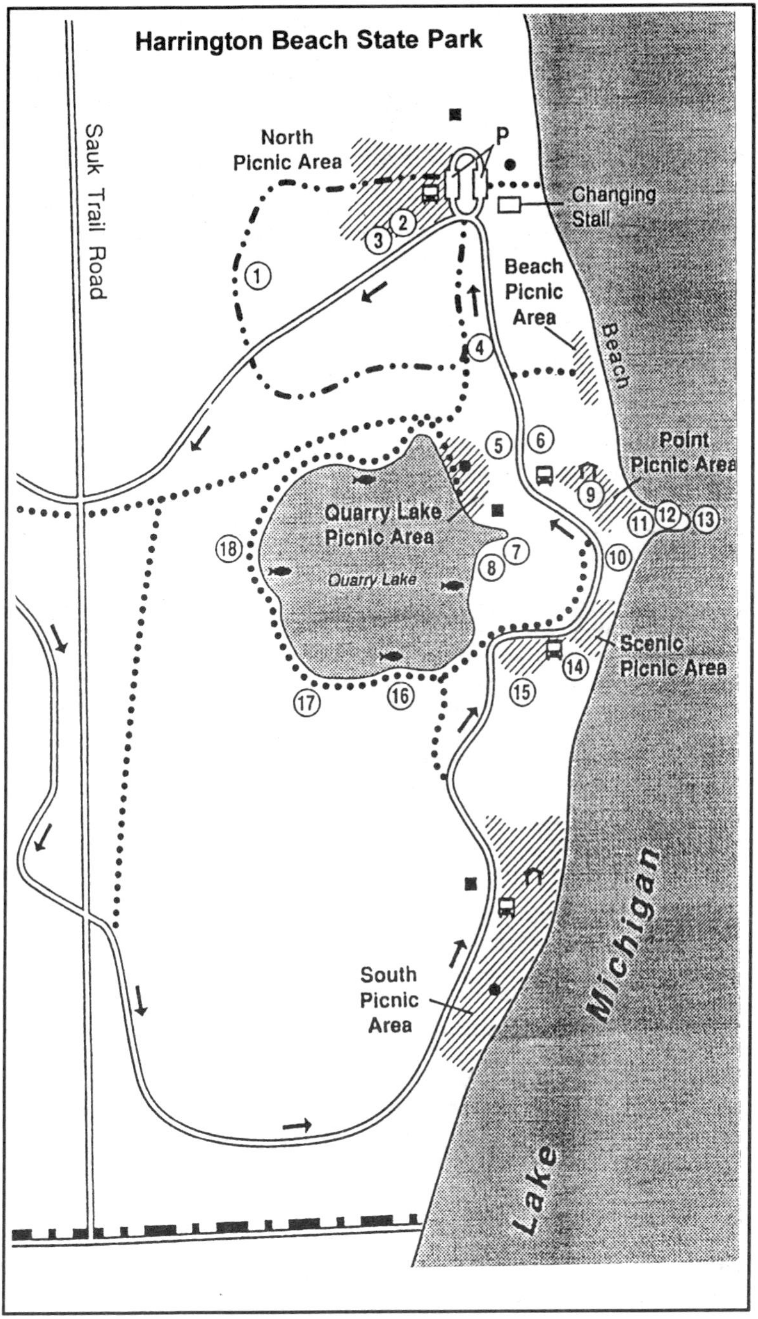

Harrington Beach State Park
Sauk Trail Road
North Picnic Area
P
Changing Stall
Beach Picnic Area
Beach
Point Picnic Area
Quarry Lake Picnic Area
Quarry Lake
Scenic Picnic Area
South Picnic Area
Lake Michigan
1
2
3
4
5
6
7
8
9
10
11
12
13
14
15
16
17
18

Pond is a small scenic body of water where fishing is popular.

Harrington Beach State Park is an excellent place to observe a broad range of birds. The park is on one of the main routes, the Mississippi "Flyway," that migratory birds take spring and fall. Many species of ducks and geese can be seen here. The open fields near Puckett's Pond provide habitat for many of the song birds.

The Point Picnic Area, Scenic Picnic Area and South Picnic Area are on the shore of Lake Michigan. Each provides a magnificent view of the lake.

North Picnic Area is near the north parking lot, and the Quarry Lake Picnic Area is on Quarry Lake.

Grills and picnic tables are provided at all of the picnic areas.

Fishing: Fishing in the surf of Lake Michigan for trout and salmon is a popular activity. Wisconsin fishing licenses are required.

Park Programs: A unique program at Harrington Beach is the annual photography contest. Every person who comes to the park is encouraged to take pictures and submit entries in four categories: plants, wildlife, people and landscapes. Pictures must be taken in or of Harrington Beach State Park. The awards are not lucrative (a $20 gift certificate); however, it certainly encourages people to be aware of the beauty and features about them as they experience the park.

During the summer, the park service provides interpretive programs on wildlife, waterfowl and the many trees and wildflowers in the park. In addition, these programs tell of the quarrying activities that took place around the turn of the century.

Winter Activity: A 2.5-mile cross-country ski trail goes from the lower parking lot along the shuttle bus road to the upper parking area. There also is a snowmobile trail at the western edge of the park.

In winter the shoreline of Lake Michigan becomes covered with ice, which creates a scene of beauty.

Harrington Beach State Park
531 Highway D
Belgium, WI 53004
(414) 285-3015

Kohler-Andrae State Park

Kohler-Andrae State Park, which is open year-round, is a combination of two properties owned and operated by the state Department of Natural Resources. The Andrae portion of the park, constituting about 122 acres, was given to the state by the wife of Frank Theodore Andrae, owner of an electrical supply company in Milwaukee. The Kohler parcel of land, comprising about 280 acres, was given to the state as a memorial to the founder of the Kohler Company, John Michael Kohler, the leading industrial corporation in Sheboygan County and the second largest plumbing manufacturer in the United States. This combination of land, with an additional 358 acres purchased by the state, comprise about 760 acres that is managed as one unit today.

Location: Kohler-Andrae State Park is about five miles south of Sheboygan, Wisconsin, in Sheboygan County. It is reached by exiting I-43 five miles south of Sheboygan and going east to the park entrance.

Features of the Park: Your first impression is of the beautiful sand beach and dunes, with the waters of Lake Michigan washing upon the shore. The beach extends about two miles along the shore of the lake. During the summer the usual beach activities of swimming, sunbathing and beachcombing are popular. There are no lifeguards along the beach. Winds from the lake make windsurfing another popular summer recreational pursuit.

Nature Center: In the northern section of the park is the Sanderling Nature Center. Open during the summer, the center is built into the dunes overlooking the lake. In the nature center are numerous displays telling of the history of the park. Also, information about the natural features, animals, wildflowers and formation of the sand dunes is available. An auditorium is the setting for audio-visual presentations during the summer.

On the top of the building is a viewing deck, which is accessible from a stairway on the inside. From this deck is an excellent view of the lakeshore and a fine spot for taking pictures. During the summer, a naturalist is available at the center to talk with visitors, to conduct programs and to explain the various exhibits.

In addition, the nature center is staffed by local volunteer workers. These people present various informational programs in the center auditorium and are also responsible for the development of displays.

Throughout history there have been many shipwrecks in the waters of Lake Michigan. It is believed that more than 50 ships have gone down near this park. In 1852 an 87-foot schooner sunk offshore near Kohler-Andrae State Park. This ship, the Challenge, was the first centerboard, clipper-type schooner. In 1982 a section of the keel from this ship washed ashore at the park. The keel is now a part of the display at Sanderling Nature Center.

Camping: There is a 105-unit campsite at Kohler-Andrae. The campground, though not directly on Lake Michigan, is within easy hearing distance of the crashing waves on the shore. Most of the campsites are surrounded by trees, making for an enjoyable wooded location. It is a short walk to the beach. There are hook-ups for electricity at 49 sites, and a shower and toilet building. An enclosed shelter with stone fireplace is across from the shower building. There is one "Teepee" campsite, an authentic Native American Teepee tent.

Reservations are offered for only half of the campsites; the others are available on a first-come, first-served basis. Except for July and August, you can usually get a comfortable campsite without a reservation. On one of my visits in early October, there were about a half-dozen camping units occupied.

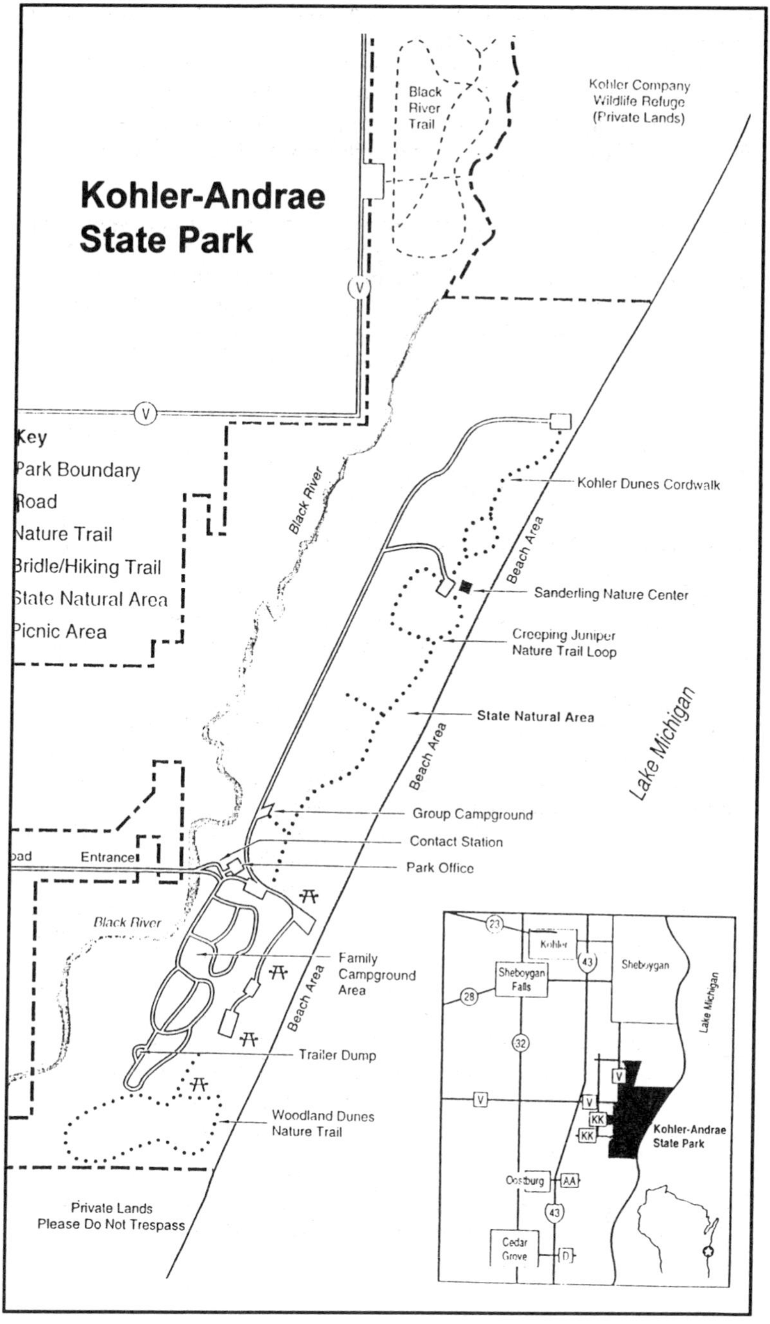
Kohler-Andrae
State Park
Black River Trail
Kohler Company Wildlife Refuge (Private Lands)
V
Key
Park Boundary
Road
Nature Trail
Bridle/Hiking Trail
State Natural Area
Picnic Area
Black River
Kohler Dunes Cordwalk
Beach Area
Sanderling Nature Center
Creeping Juniper Nature Trail Loop
State Natural Area
Lake Michigan
Group Campground
Contact Station
Park Office
Entrance
Black River
Family Campground Area
Trailer Dump
Woodland Dunes Nature Trail
Private Lands
Please Do Not Trespass
23
Kohler
43
Sheboygan
Sheboygan Falls
28
32
V
KK
Kohler-Andrae State Park
Oostburg
AA
Cedar Grove
D

There are two sites where groups of up to 50 people can camp. Only tent camping is permitted in these sites.

Picnic Facilities: Many picnic tables and grills are along the lake at the south end of the park. The picnic area extends for about a half-mile. Snacks can be obtained from vending machines during the summer.

Trails: Four hiking trails are in the park. Two are short self-guided nature trails. The Creeping Juniper Trail is just south of the Sanderling Nature Center. This trail traverses the sand dunes. A "cordwalk" on the trail is made of boards and rope that make walking easy over the dunes. It keeps hikers on the trail, thus providing protection to the dunes. There is more of this "cordwalk" in the Kohler-Andrae State Park than any other park on the Great Lakes.

In this area you will see Sand Reed grass and Marram grass. The Sand Reed Grass is deep-rooted and drought tolerant; it is the initial grass that grows on the sand dunes. The Marram grass stabilizes the sand long enough for other plants to take root. The other self-guided nature trail, Indian Pipe Nature Trail, traverses through a wooded section of the park south of the campground.

There are two longer hiking trails. The Black River Trail is a 2.5-mile trail in the northwest section of the park. To reach the trailhead, you must leave the park at the main entrance and travel a couple of miles north over county roads. On this trail, mountain biking and horseback riding are permitted in addition to hiking.

The other hiking trail is the Kohler Dunes cordwalk. This trail extends for about 2.5 miles through the dunes north and south of the nature center. The entire trail is on the cordwalk. Along the way are two lookout points and several benches where hikers can stop to rest and observe the surrounding terrain.

At various sites the views of Lake Michigan are spectacular. A photographer can find numerous spots from which to take beautiful pictures.

Fishing: Fishing in Lake Michigan is popular in the park. Surf fishing for trout and salmon are favorites as there are no boat ramps or docks. People wishing to fish either must charter a fishing boat in a nearby community or put their boat in at public launch facilities in the area.

Nature: Wildlife in the park include deer, squirrel, chipmunks, rabbits, oppossums and an occasional fox, coyote or beaver. Many species of birds have been sighted throughout the park; a brochure identifies more than 150 species of birds that live in or migrate through the park.

Particularly interesting are ducks that are seen in huge numbers during the spring and fall migratory seasons.

Up to 5,000 ducks may be seen in the waters of Lake Michigan at a time. Falcons, hawks and eagles are also found during the migrations. Hunting and trapping are prohibited in Andrae-Kohler State Park.

Winter Activities: As is true in much of the Midwest, outdoor winter activities are popular in this park. During the winter cross-country skiing, tobogganing and snowshoeing are common activities.

There is a two-mile marked ski trail in the south section of the park.

Winter camping is permitted in 28 of the campsites with electrical hook-ups, with water available for campers at the park office.

Kohler-Andrae State Park
1520 Old Park Road
Sheboygan, WI 53081
(414) 452-3457

Newport State Park

Newport State Park is near the tip of Door Peninsula on Lake Michigan. This 2,440-acre park is a designated wilderness area of the Wisconsin Department of Natural Resources. As such, motor vehicles are restricted to the roads and campers must carry all supplies into the isolated campsites. There are less than 1.5 miles of roadway in the entire state park. The road runs from the park entrance to two parking lots.

Location: Newport State Park is reached by traveling three miles north of Ellison Bay, Wisconsin, on W-42, then turning right on South County Road NP and going four miles to the park entrance.

Features of the Park: Newport State Park extends for 11 miles along Lake Michigan. The shoreline is undeveloped and provides plenty of places to walk along the water's edge. Both clear sandy beaches and rocky cliffs make up the shore's boundary. There are innumerable opportunities for fishing along the shoreline.

History: Modern history of this area began in the 1880s when Hans

Johnson established a settlement on Rowleys Bay. He named the village Newport. The early settlers were mainly Germans, Bohemians and Scandinavians, who cut and hauled wood. Ships came to the settlement to pick up lumber. By the early 1890s about 300 people lived in Newport.

By 1919, lumbering activities in the village came to an end. At that time Ferdinand Holty, a diamond merchant from Chicago, purchased the village and used it as a private retreat. During this time much of the land reverted to wilderness. In 1966 the state of Wisconsin purchased the land and established Europe Bay State Park. A few years later, at the urging of local people, the park's name was changed to Newport in memory of the original village.

Camping: There are 16 campsites throughout the park. To reach these sites, campers must hike one to three miles. All supplies, food and water must be carried in as there are no water sources at the campsites and no stores in the park. Eleven campsites are on the south end of the park along Varney Point and Duck Bay. Two campsites are on Lynd Point overlooking Lake Michigan. Three others are three miles from the trailhead in the Europe Bay region, two on Europe Lake.

Half of the sites, the even numbered ones, can be reserved in advance. The odd numbered sites are available on a first-come, first-served basis. Backpackers must register and pay a camping fee before going to their site. No more than five persons may occupy any one campsite. Pit toilets are near each site. Drinking water is available only at the park office, in the picnic area near the trailheads, and at the Europe Lake area. All trash and garbage must be carried out.

Trails: Thirty miles of hiking trails are found throughout Newport State Park. The longest is the Europe Bay Trail extending from the trailhead at parking lot #3 to Europe Lake. This seven-mile round trip passes through a heavily wooded region. The trail is about a quarter-mile from Lake Michigan. At several points there are offshoot paths leading to the water's edge.

This trail, combined with the Hotz Trail, brings hikers to the northern boundary of the park and Europe Lake. This lake is bounded on the eastern shore by the park. The north and west shores are private lands. It's interesting to hike the three-plus miles through deep woods and wilderness to Europe Lake, look across the south bay a short distance and see more than a dozen houses. The day of my visit there were builders just a short distance across the water building a large lake home. There is about a mile and a half of park boundary along the Europe Lake shoreline. The lake's bottom in this area is sandy, making for excellent swimming, wading, fishing, and birdwatching. Two campsites are in beautiful settings along the shore of Europe Lake.

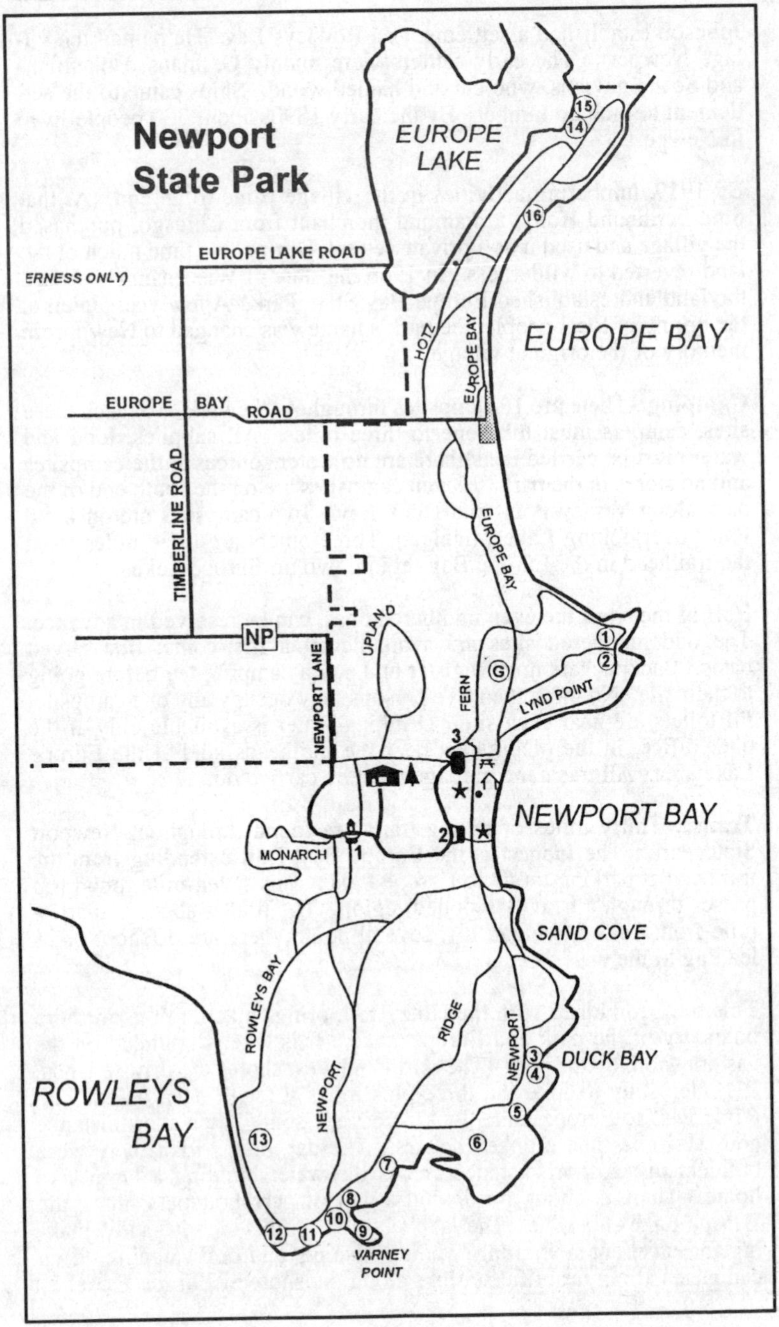
Newport
State Park
EUROPE
LAKE
EUROPE LAKE ROAD
ERNESS ONLY)
EUROPE BAY
HOTZ
EUROPE BAY
EUROPE
BAY
ROAD
TIMBERLINE ROAD
EUROPE BAY
NP
NEWPORT LANE
UPLAND
FERN
LYND POINT
MONARCH
NEWPORT BAY
SAND COVE
ROWLEYS BAY
RIDGE
NEWPORT
NEWPORT
DUCK BAY
ROWLEYS
BAY
VARNEY
POINT

Three trails, Rowleys Bay Loop Trail (4 miles), Newport Loop Trail (5 miles) and Ridge Trail (2 miles), are in the south part of the park. There is a two-mile nature trail.

All of the trails begin at parking lot number 3.

Newport State Park is well suited for bicyclists. More than half of the trails, 15 miles, are open for off-road bicycling. These trails are clearly marked. The trails are not hard-surfaced, but dirt, sand and rocks. The trails are flat, with only slight upgrades. Campers can bicycle to most of the campsites.

We biked most of the trails where cycling was permitted. This provided us with an excellent opportunity to see much of the park, the woods, Europe Lake and the Lake Michigan shoreline. It is refreshing to be in a semi-wilderness park where riding mountain bikes is not only permitted but encouraged. One of the statements of a park brochure captures this by stating: "Skillfully ridden mountain bikes leave no more impact than a hiker's boot."

Picnic Facilities: On Newport Bay is a picnic area with a shelter and a half-mile sandy beach. There is a shelter where sunbathers and swimmers can change into swimming attire. There is no lifeguard. Facilities for picnics include tables, grills and a shelter.

Also at this area is a board with pictures and information depicting the history of the village of Newport and the development of the area into the state park. A small nature center is located at the office. The center provides some pictures of the area and information about the geological development, wildlife in the area, and other information of interest.

Nature: As with other state parks in Door Peninsula, whitetail deer are abundant in this park. Porcupines, squirrels, foxes, coyotes and raccoons are often seen by visitors. More than 175 species of birds have been seen in the park.

Winter Activities: Newport State Park is open in the winter. Cross-country skiing is popular with 23 miles of trails available for the Nordic skier. Winter camping is permitted at the various campsites. However, campers must register before walking in or skiing to the campsite. Winter campers can hike, ski or snowshoe to their sites; however, snowmobiles are not permitted in the park. Ice fishing on Europe Lake is popular among many winter outdoor enthusiasts.

Newport State Park
415 S. County Road NP
Ellison Bay, WI 54210
(414) 854-2500

Peninsula State Park

At 3,763 acres, Peninsula State Park is the third largest state park in Wisconsin and the largest of Wisconsin's state parks on the Great Lakes. The park was established in 1909, making it the second oldest park in Wisconsin.

Peninsula is one of the most popular and widely used state parks in Wisconsin. Opportunities exist for many activities throughout the year.

Location: Peninsula State Park is on a peninsula jutting into Green Bay at Fish Creek, Wisconsin, on W-42. The park extends for more than seven miles along Green Bay in Door County.

Activities at the Park: Along the north shore of the park is Eagle Tower. This 75-foot tower was built in 1914 and was reconstructed in the 1930s. The tower stands 250 feet above the waters of Green Bay. From the top of the tower, you get a spectacular view of the surrounding waters. The shoreline of Michigan 40 miles away is visible on a clear day.

There is a par 71, 6,200-yard golf course in the park. The course is open daily from May through the middle of October. The clubhouse provides food service and a full range of golfing equipment and supplies. The course, on the bluffs overlooking Green Bay, is well designed, with several holes providing beautiful views of the bay.

During the summer there is an American Folklore Theater production at Peninsula State Park. The production usually begins in late June and runs until late August, with three or four shows performed each summer.

Along Shore Road near the northern tip of the park is the Eagle Lighthouse, constructed in 1868. The lighthouse is listed on the National Register of Historic Places. Guided tours are provided during the summer by the Door County Historical Society. A fee is charged for this tour.

Just off the shore is Horseshoe Island, a part of the park. Because no boat service runs to the island, you must bring your own boat or rent one. Hiking and picnicking are the only activities permitted on the island. No camping, fires or facilities are provided on the island.

Camping: Peninsula State Park has 470 campsites, the most of any state park in Wisconsin. This is one of the largest camping facilities of any state park on the Great Lakes. The campsites are at four locations. The largest is the Tennison Bay campground with 189 campsites, some heavily wooded where the camper gets a feeling of being secluded from neighbors. Other campsites provide little shade. One section of the campground is in a spruce forest. It is possible to see through this forest and see many campsites at one time. Near the Tennison Bay Campground is a ramp where small boats can be launched. Also, the Sunset Bike Trail skirts the edge of the campground.

The Nicolet Bay campground, with 188 sites, is divided into northern and southern sections by the beach. There is a boat ramp in the northside campground. A number of the campsites at Nicolet Bay are directly on the water. These are the even-numbered sites. It is not easy to get one of these sites without a reservation during the summer and on fall weekends.

The other two campgrounds, Weborg Point and Welcker's Point, are smaller. Weborg Point has only 12 sites, all with electrical hook-ups. These sites have little shade and no shower facility. Therefore, most campers bring RVs and/or trailers with their own bathing and washing facilities.

The Welcker's Point campground, with 81 sites, is heavily wooded. It is on the far north point of the park between Nicolet Bay and Green Bay.

Reservations can be made for the even-numbered campsites in the Nicolet Bay and Welcker's Point campgrounds. Reservations can be made for all campsites in Weborg Point and Tennison Bay campgrounds. Reservations are available in January; camping starts in May and ends the last weekend of October.

Beach: There is only one beach in the park where swimming is permitted. This is a natural sand beach at Nicolet Bay. The beach is open daily from May into October, with a bathhouse having showers available. No lifeguards are provided at the beach.

Located at the beach area is a concessions facility. Here, groceries, food service, some camping supplies, as well as boat and bicycle rental are available. Rentals include rowboats, canoes, sailboats, kayaks and windsurf boards.

Trails: Throughout the park are 11 hiking trails, comprising more than 20 miles. These range from the half-mile White Cedar Nature Trail, which begins near the Nature Center and tells of the ecology of the whitetail deer, to the Skyline Trail, which is three miles long. Some of the trails are easy walking, others rather difficult. Many intersect.

The Eagle Trail, a distance of two miles, is one of the more popular. This trail goes along the water's edge and climbs the bluffs to Eagle Terrace. It is a steep, rocky trail which connects Eagle Terrace with Eagle Harbor.

A one-mile exercise circuit, the Vita Course, is near Nicolet Beach and includes exercise stations. The trail winds through the forest. Participants can run, walk or jog from one station to the next.

Bicycling: Peninsula State Park is a bicyclist's paradise. It's common to see several bicycles at nearly every campsite. People of all ages, ride the trails and roads of the park.

There is a 5.1-mile hardpacked fine limestone bicycle trail, the Sunset Bike Trail, which runs from the park entrance to the beach at Nicolet Bay. One section of the trail runs along the shoreline. This section is scenic; you can stop almost anywhere to observe the waters of Green

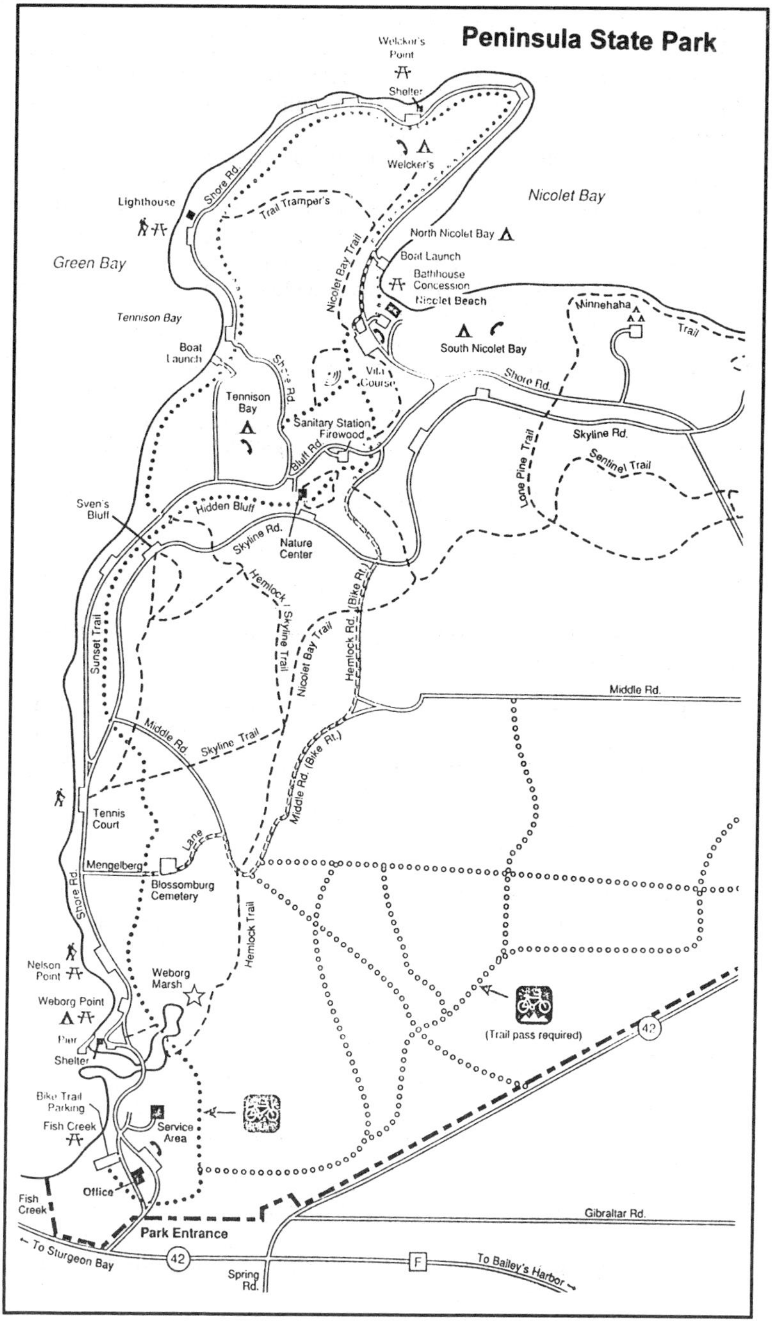
Peninsula State Park
Welcker's Point
Shelter
Welcker's
Nicolet Bay
Lighthouse
Shore Rd.
Trail Tramper's
Nicolet Bay Trail
North Nicolet Bay
Boat Launch
Bathhouse
Concession
Nicolet Beach
Green Bay
Tennison Bay
Boat Launch
Minnehaha
Trail
South Nicolet Bay
Vita Course
Shore Rd.
Tennison Bay
Sanitary Station
Firewood
Bluff Rd.
Skyline Rd.
Sentinel Trail
Lone Pine Trail
Sven's Bluff
Hidden Bluff
Skyline Rd.
Nature Center
Hemlock / Skyline Trail
Hemlock Rd. (Bike Rt.)
Nicolet Bay Trail
Sunset Trail
Middle Rd.
Middle Rd.
Skyline Trail
Middle Rd. (Bike Rt.)
Tennis Court
Lane
Mengelberg
Blossomburg Cemetery
Shore Rd.
Hemlock Trail
Nelson Point
Weborg Marsh
Weborg Point
Pier
Shelter
(Trail pass required)
42
Bike Trail Parking
Fish Creek
Service Area
Office
Fish Creek
Park Entrance
Gibraltar Rd.
To Sturgeon Bay
42
F
To Bailey's Harbor
Spring Rd.

Bay.

Four miles of roadways have been identified as a designated bicycle route. In addition, there are about 20 miles of asphalt roadways throughout the park that are excellent for bicycling. In places these roads can get crowded, particularly in the busy summer.

About eight miles of backwoods trails have been designated as off-road bicycle trails. These trails are in the southern section of the park between Middle Road and the southern park boundary. These trails are not smooth and require skill to ride. To bicycle on these off-road trails, a fee is required.

Picnic Facilities: Six picnic sites are scattered throughout the park. Picnic tables and grills are found at each site. A shelter house is at the Welcher's Point picnic site on the north tip of the peninsula. There are no garbage cans at any of the picnic sites; picnickers are expected to carry out their trash. It all makes for an environmentally clean area with no ugly, overflowing garbage cans.

Nature Center: The White Cedar Nature Center has several displays telling of animal life, park history and photographs depicting sights that can be seen in the park. A narrated diorama provides an overview of the park, places of interest in the park, and information of the natural history of the area.

Nature: Whitetailed deer are abundant in the park. Smaller animals such as fox, raccoons and porcupines are sometimes observed. A list provided for bird watchers includes more than 125 species that have been identified in the park. An informational sheet provided at the entrance noted that wild turkeys are common in the park, though in the more remote areas.

Fishing: Fishing is good in Green Bay. Common fish include northern pike, perch, smallmouth bass, coho and chinook salmon, and several varieties of trout (brown, rainbow and lake). A Wisconsin fishing license is required before fishing in the waters surrounding the park. At the Weborg Campsite there is a fishing pier.

Winter Activities: Peninsula State Park, like the other parks in Door County, is open year round. There are many visitors during the winter. Both snowmobiling and cross-country skiing are important activities during the season.

Twenty miles of cross-country trails are groomed and include nine ski trails ranging in distance from the relatively easy one-mile Yellow Trail to the more difficult and hilly Blue Trail, which is a seven-mile loop. The most challenging cross-country ski trail is the six-mile Purple Trail.

Eighteen miles of trails are set aside for snowmobiles. Snowmobiles must be registered and can only be operated on trails and roads designated for snowmobile use. They are not permitted on plowed roads or ski trails.

Winter camping occurs in part of Tennison Bay Campground. There are electrical hook-ups available as well as a winter water supply and pit toilets.

In addition to cross-country skiing and snowmobiling, sledding and tubing are permitted on a steep hill on the 17th fairway of the golf course. People come to the park to hike and snowshoe on the various trails in winter.

Two miles of marked snowshoe trails are designated, with trailheads at Eagle Tower and Nicolet Bay. Hikers are prohibited from walking on the cross-country trails.

Ice fishing is a popular activity at Peninsula State Park. Trout, perch and walleye are the most commonly caught fish. It is possible to drive on the ice in winter to ice fish. However, as anywhere, care must be taken when going out on the ice of any body of water.

Peninsula State Park
P.O. Box 218
Fish Creek, WI 54212
(414) 868-3258

Potawatomi State Park

Potawatomi State Park was establised in 1928 and named after the Potawatomi tribe of Native Americans. These people resided throughout this part of Wisconsin. They called themselves Bo-de-wad-me, which means "Keeper of the Fire." Over time the name became Potawatomi.

Technically, this 1,231-acre park is not on a Great Lake or on a bay of the lake. This park is at the entrance to Sturgeon Bay, from where you can go either into Green Bay or Lake Michigan.

Location: Travel three miles south of Sturgeon Bay, Wisconsin, on W-42 and W-57, then turn north and follow the signs to Potawatomi State Park.

Features of the Park: Along the shore of Sturgeon Bay, the park has rugged limestone cliffs, providing many scenic views. Throughout, the park is heavily forested.

Fall is a particularly popular time for tourists who come to enjoy the spectacular tree colors. Beech and maple trees along the shoreline of

Sturgeon Bay offer colorful scenery during the autumn.

An interesting sight at the north end of the park on a 150-foot bluff overlooking Sturgeon Bay is a 75-foot observation tower. This tower was built in 1932 and provides an excellent view of Sturgeon Bay, Green Bay and the surrounding territory. Combining the height of the tower and the bluff on which the tower stands, the deck of the tower is 225 feet above the water level.

A boat launch is in Sawyer Harbor at the north section of the park. There are two boat ramps and a large asphalt parking lot at the launch area. Most people bringing boats to the park head to one of the bays (Sturgeon Bay or Green Bay) and Lake Michigan to fish. Bass, walleye, northern pike, salmon and perch fishing is particularly popular.

No beach exists in Potawatomi State Park. The shoreline is rocky and has steep dropoffs, making swimming impossible.

Trails: There are 6.5 miles of hiking trails in the park. The favorite trail for hiking is the Tower Trail, along the edge of the cliffs from the campground to the observation tower. There are steep drop-offs to the water. The trail winds back to the campground, passing through woods in the interior part of the park. It passes the downhill ski area.

The Hemlock Trail (2.5 miles) circles through the south section of the park. This trail passes through the picnic area along the water's edge. In the picnic area, the trail is blacktop for easy walking. In the interior of the park the Hemlock Trail becomes more rugged.

A four-mile off-road trail and about 8.5 miles of roadway provide bicycling throughout the park. The road leading from Shore Road to the boat launch is scenic to cycle along the water's edge.

A half-mile nature trail, the Ancient Shores Nature Trail follows the edge of two post-glacial shorelines which are now as high as 60 feet above the present Green Bay waters.

Camping: A 125-site modern campground, which is open year around, is in the middle of the park. Twenty-five sites have electrical hook-ups. Odd-numbered campsites may be reserved starting in January for the period May 1 through the last weekend in October. The other campsites are available on a first-come, first-served basis. During the summer, most of the reservable sites are taken, particularly on weekends.

The campground, which is separated into two sections by a road, is nicely wooded with adequate distance separating most of the sites. There are a picnic table and ground metal grill at each site. None of the campsites is on the water; however the water can be seen through

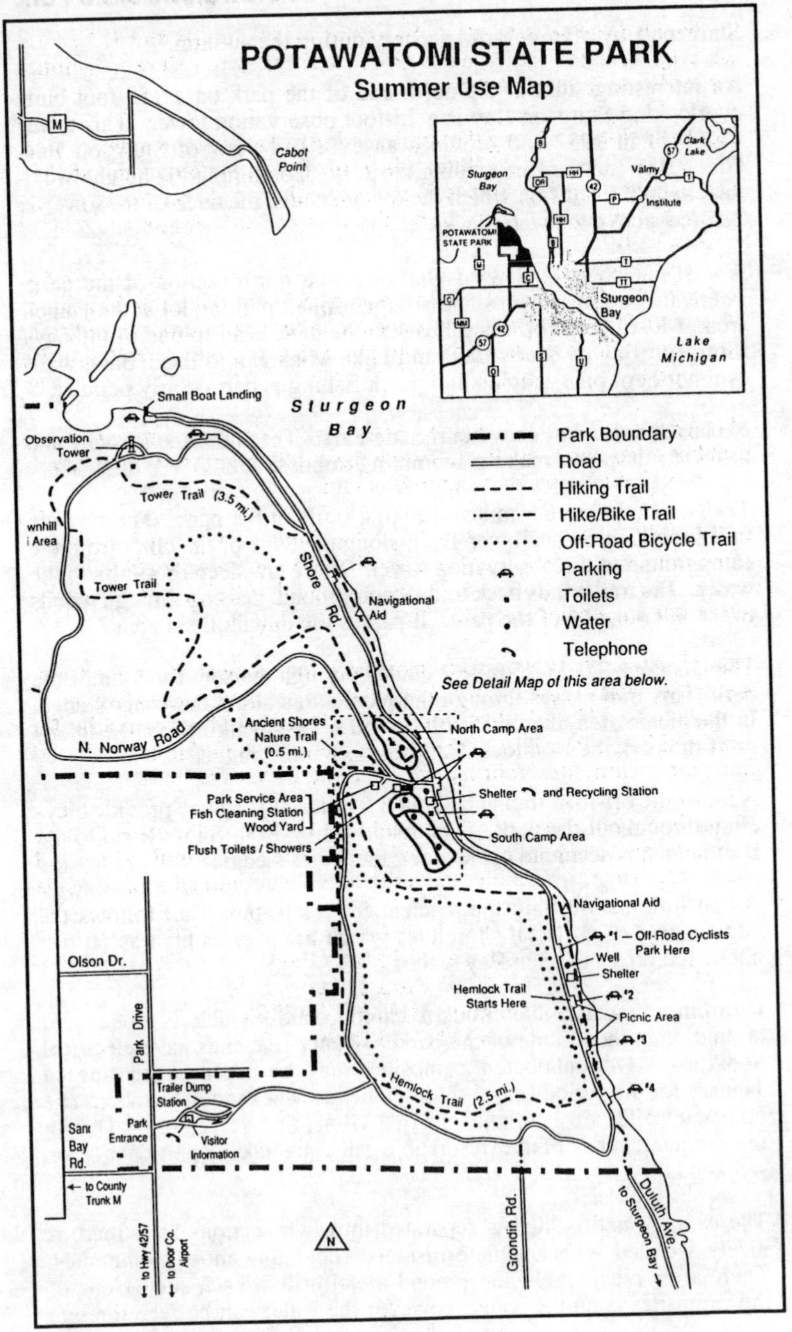
POTAWATOMI STATE PARK
Summer Use Map
M
Cabot Point
Sturgeon Bay
POTAWATOMI STATE PARK
Clark Lake
Valmy
Institute
57
42
HH
DR
B
P
T
TT
C
M
MM
S
U
Q
Sturgeon Bay
Lake Michigan
Small Boat Landing
Sturgeon Bay
Observation Tower
Tower Trail (3.5 mi.)
wnhill
i Area
Tower Trail
Shore Rd.
Navigational Aid
Park Boundary
Road
Hiking Trail
Hike/Bike Trail
Off-Road Bicycle Trail
Parking
Toilets
Water
Telephone
See Detail Map of this area below.
Ancient Shores Nature Trail (0.5 mi.)
North Camp Area
N. Norway Road
Park Service Area
Fish Cleaning Station
Wood Yard
Flush Toilets / Showers
Shelter and Recycling Station
South Camp Area
Navigational Aid
1 – Off-Road Cyclists Park Here
Well
Shelter
Hemlock Trail Starts Here
2
Picnic Area
3
4
Olson Dr.
Park Drive
Hemlock Trail (2.5 mi.)
Trailer Dump Station
Park Entrance
Visitor Information
Sand Bay Rd.
← to County Trunk M
to Hwy 42/57
to Door Co. Airport
N
Grondin Rd.
Duluth Ave.
to Sturgeon Bay

the woods from several sites. Two campsites (sites 1E and 4E) are set aside for disabled individuals. Both flush toilet and shower facilities are available in the campground.

Picnic Facilities: Along the south section of the park are a picnic area, which provides an excellent view of Sturgeon Bay, and shelter. Throughout the picnic area is an asphalt walking trail, providing opportunity for everyone, particularly the disabled and senior citizens to enjoy a walk.

Nature: Bird watchers find Potawatomi State Park an ideal location. More than 200 bird species have been reported in the park. In addition, there are whitetailed deer, raccoon, porcupine and other small animals in the park.

Winter Activities: Potawatomi State Park is open year-round with a number of activities available during the winter months. Winter camping is available in south campground unit.

A downhill ski slope is operated by a local nonprofit group. There are three runs, two rope tows, a double chairlift and snow-making equipment. The ski run looks out on the surrounding fields and woods. A snack bar and chalet are at the bottom of the hill.

Other winter activities include snowmobiling, snowshoeing, sledding, ice fishing and cross-country skiing. There are more than 16 miles of cross-country ski trails that provide a variety of skill opportunities for Nordic skiing enthusiasts. Walking on the trails is prohibited. The ski trails are identified as four loops of varying distances.

More than eight miles of snowmobile trails exist in the park. These trails intersect with park roads and cross-country ski trails at several locations. The snowmobiler can connect with additional trails outside the park.

Potawatomi State Park
3740 Park Drive
Sturgeon Bay, WI 54235
(414) 746-2890

Rock Island State Park

Rock Island State Park is at the northern tip of Door County, beyond Washington Island, where Green Bay and Lake Michigan meet. It's about a 15-minute boat ride from the Jackson Harbor boat landing on Washington Island. This park encompasses the entire 912-acre island. No motorized vehicles, bicycles or horses are permitted on the island. The only means of movement about the state park island is on foot.

Location: To get to Rock Island from the Wisconsin mainland, you have to take a half-hour ferry ride from Lakeport, Wisconsin, to Detroit Harbor on Washington Island. It is eight miles from that boat landing to Jackson Harbor Where a park service boat takes you to Rick Island. Round-trip fees from the mainland come to about $30. There is no other way onto Rock Island except by private boat. However, there is no marina and it is not advisable to bring small boats to the island.

Features of the Park: As you approach the island by boat, you will see the Thordarson estate. This building, with its Viking Hall, is listed in the National Register of Historic Places. On the north side of the island are high limestone bluffs along the shoreline, while at the south end of the park is a sand beach. A forest of pines, maple, beech and yellow birch trees covers most of the island.

There are several points of interest on the island. On the northernmost point is the Potawatomi Lighthouse, which is reached by walking a little over a mile from the boat dock along the Thordarson Loop Trail.

The lighthouse was built in 1836 and is the oldest lighthouse in Wisconsin. It is not open to the public; however tours can be arranged. You can take a stairway down to the water's edge, passing over Dolomite cliffs.

On the southeastern section of the island is the Stone Water Tower, which also is listed in the National Register of Historic Places. Near the water tower is a former fishing village. There is little evidence of the village today.

History of the Park: The island has an interesting history. Indians may have inhabited the island as early as 500 B.C. In more recent times the Hurons, Ottawas, Chippewas and Potawatomi Indians lived on the island. Early explorers, particularly LaSalle, visited the island. It is believed that LaSalle was the first North American explorer to discover Rock Island in 1679. By the mid-1800s about 200 people, mostly fishermen, lived on the island.

In 1910, the island came under the private ownership of a wealthy inventor of electrical devices, Chester Thordarson, originally from Iceland. He came with his family in 1873 to Milwaukee. By the early 1900s Thordarson had designed and built transmitters for sending high-voltage electricity over long distances.

Thordarson paid $5,725 for the island. He owned the property for the next 55 years, when it was sold to the state of Wisconsin.

Thordarson was interested in Rock Island because it reminded him of his homeland. It was his intention to build a house which would have features of a Viking house and the Parliament building in Iceland, his home country. He built a combination boathouse-great hall with a large fireplace. However, Thordarson never built his planned mansion.

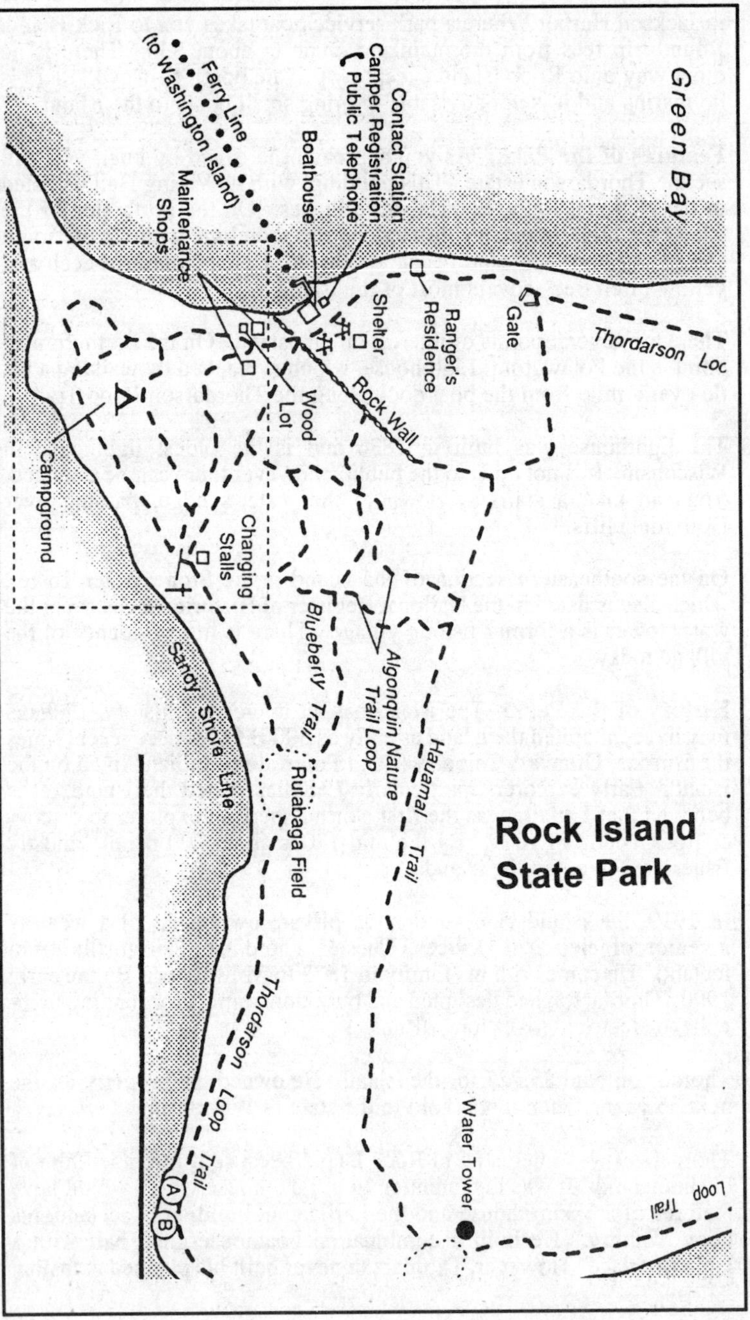
Rock Island State Park
Green Bay
Thordarson Loc
Gate
Ranger's Residence
Shelter
Contact Station
Camper Registration
Public Telephone
Boathouse
Ferry Line (to Washington Island)
Maintenance Shops
Rock Wall
Wood Lot
Campground
Changing Stalls
Blueberry Trail
Algonquin Nature Trail Loop
Hauamal Trail
Rutabaga Field
Sandy Shore Line
Thordarson Loop Trail
Water Tower
Loop Trail
A
B

He built the boathouse from Rock Island limestone. The Viking Hall was constructed atop the boathouse. Today, this hall serves as an information center for visitors. Displays explain the history of the island, show Indian artifacts found on the island and provides information about animals, birds and the flora of the island. Also in this hall is a large display of Thordarson's original Icelandic carved oak furniture.

Thordarson died in 1965 and in 1966 the island came under the ownership of the state of Wisconsin for use as a state park.

Camping: Since no motor vehicles are permitted on the island, only walk-in camping is allowed. There are 40 campsites available from early May through November.

Thirty-five sites are within a half-mile of the boat dock on the southwest section of the island. Most of these campsites are on a sand bluff on the edge of the lakeshore, providing beautiful views of the lake.

Five campsites along the Thordarson Loop Trail in the southeast section of the park can only be reached by backpacking. These sites are along the shore of the lake.

In addition, there are two group campsites.

Pit toilets, picnic tables, and fire rings are provided in the campground. Campers must bring all food and other supplies, as there is no store on the island. Also, all trash must be carried out. During the summer, you should have a reservation. Fishing is a popular activity for many who come to the island to camp for a few days.

Trails: Hiking is the major activity for most of those visiting Rock Island State Park. More than 10 miles of hiking trails are well-marked and not difficult to walk. For the most part, the hiking trails pass through forests.

The Thordarson Loop Trail circumnavigates the entire island. This 6.5-mile trail connects most of the important features of interest on the island. Along the eastern side of the island, this trail goes near the shoreline.

The 1.5-mile Fernwood Trail, crossing the middle of the island, connects with the Thordarson Trail on the east and west sides. Another east-west trail is the Hauamal Trail, about 1.5 miles. In addition, there is a one-mile nature trail, the Algonquin Nature Trail Loop.

The Beach: On the south shore of the island is a beach, which is reached by walking southeast about a half-mile along the Thordarson Loop Trail from the boathouse. The beach extends about a half-mile along the shoreline. The water bottom is sandy, making for an excellent place to wade and swim. The beach is near the campground, convenient for those camping on the island. A changing stall is at the beach for those needing to change into swimming attire.

Picnic Facilities: Several picnic tables are near the boathouse. All trash must be carried out as there are no waste containers.

Nature: The most common wildlife on the island are whitetail deer and squirrels. On occasion bear, coyote and fox have been sighted. On a board in the nature center is a listing of 121 birds that have been spotted on the island.

Rock Island State Park
Washington Island, WI 54246
(414) 847-2235

Whitefish Dunes State Park

Whitefish Dunes is an 863-acre park on a strip of land between Lake Michigan and an inland lake, Clark Lake. At one time Clark Lake was a bay of Lake Michigan. Through the years the land filled in from the movement of the sand.

This park features the highest dunes on the western shore of Lake Michigan. Unlike the eastern side of Lake Michigan where dunes reach several hundred feet in height, large sand dunes are not common on the west. The tallest dune in Whitefish Dunes State Park is "Old Baldy," which rises 93 feet above the level of Lake Michigan. A wooden walkway permits hikers to go to the top of this dune. Visitors are prohibited from climbing any of the other dunes.

The park was established as a state park by the state of Wisconsin in 1967 for the purpose of preserving and protecting the dunes.

Location: The park is reached by traveling about eight miles north of Sturgeon Bay, Wisconsin, on W-57, then east for four miles on county

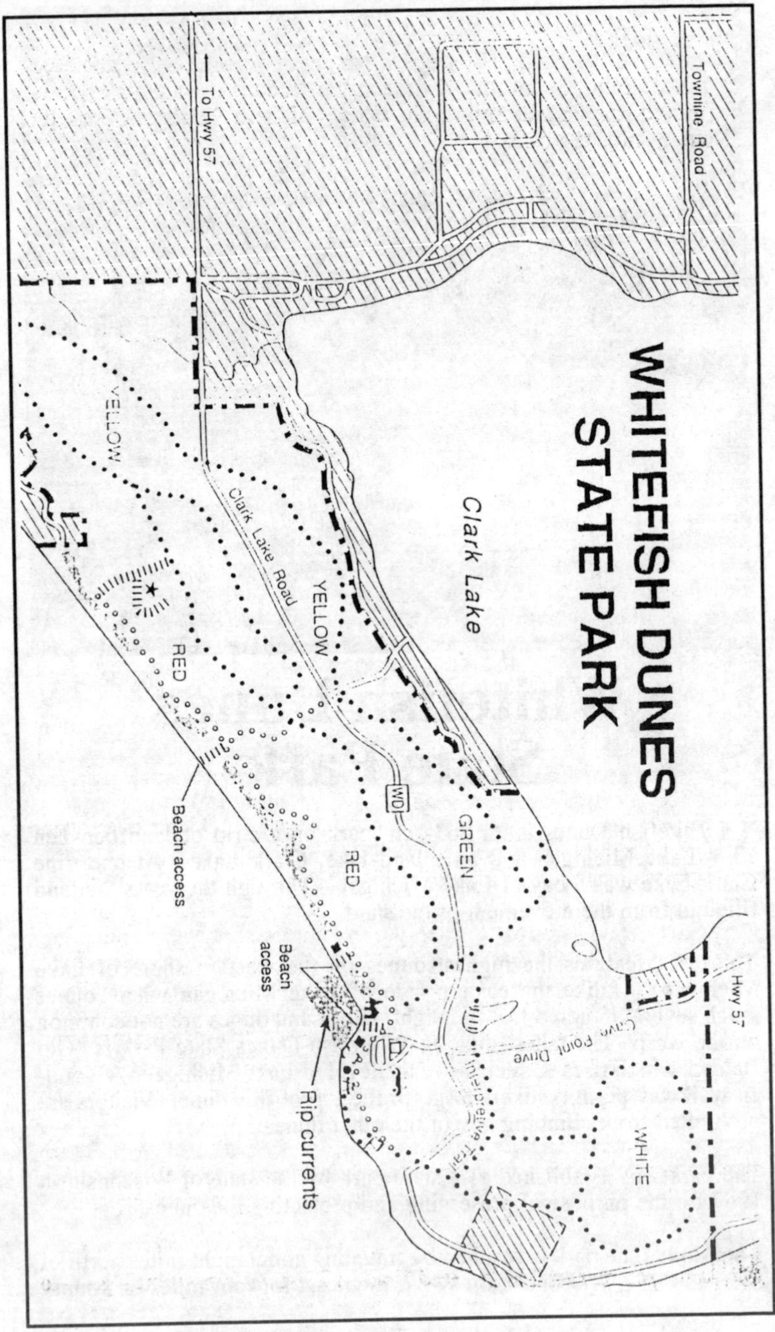
WHITEFISH DUNES STATE PARK
Clark Lake
Townline Road
To Hwy 57
Hwy 57
Clark Lake Road
Cave Point Drive
Interpretive Trail
WD
YELLOW
YELLOW
GREEN
RED
RED
WHITE
Beach access
Beach access
Rip currents

road WD.

Features of the Park: Whitefish Dunes is a day-use only park, having no camping facilities. Most people who come to the park picnic, swim and play in and around the waters of Lake Michigan, walk the beach, or hike the trails.

The beach, which is the focal point of the lakeshore, extends more than a half-mile along Lake Michigan. Access to the beach is permitted only at three locations where there is a walkway or a wooden plank board walkway over the sand. No lifeguards are provided. However, people come by the thousands in the summer to enjoy the water, to sunbathe and to walk along the water's edge. Swimming is prohibited along a 200-to 250-yard section of the beach where there is the greatest danger of severe rip tide currents. Signs, ropes and buoys in the water designate this area. Throughout the park are warning signs instructing people what to do if they become caught in a rip tide current. Rip tide currents are particularly a danger when there are large waves on the lake.

Nature Center: There is a modern, nicely designed and informative nature and interpretive center on the north edge of the beach. This center opened in 1990. The facility has a 60-seat auditorium where visitors can view audio-visual presentations about the history of the park, development of the sand dunes, information about natural features and what to look for along the trails and beach. Also, the center hosts several naturalist presentations for visitors of all ages throughout the summer. During the remainder of the year school groups, as well as other interested organizations, come to the park to learn about the dunes and surrounding environment. Displays depict the development of sand dunes, history of the area, and recent archeological digs in the park.

History in the Park: Much has been learned about the history of this area as the result of archeological diggings in the park in 1986 and 1992. Eight separate occupations have occurred in this area beginning about 100 B.C. The earliest people residing in this region were the North Bay people from about 100 B.C. to 300 A.D. Various artifacts excavated in 1992 identified other people groups: the Heins Creek people (from about 500-750 A.D.), the Late Woodland people (800-900 A.D.), and the Oneota (900 - about 1390 A.D.). Jars, pottery, stone tools, animal remains and other artifacts have provided much information about the previous history and occupation of the land.

Trails: There are 13 miles of hiking trails in the park. All of the trails begin near the nature and interpretative center. The longest is the 4.2-mile Yellow Trail which passes through a dry, sandy, desert-like section of the park.

The most popular trail is the Red Trail, a 2.8-mile loop which goes to

The most popular trail is the Red Trail, a 2.8-mile loop which goes to Old Baldy, a dune. Here it is possible to walk along a wooden walkway to an observation point on top of the sand dune. From the observation point you can get a good view of Lake Michigan and a glimpse of Clark Lake. At two locations along the trail is boardwalk access to the beach.

Another trail, the Green Trail (1.8 miles), passes along the base of an old stabilized dune. Along this trail you can see how a sandy area can become heavily forested over many years. Along the trail are growths of white pine, hemlock trees, beech and maple trees. A short spur off of this trail (0.7 mile) brings hikers to Clark Lake. Most of Clark Lake is surrounded by private land, cottages and homes. You can relax, fish and swim in the waters of the lake.

Also in the park is an interesting 1.5-mile Interpretive Trail with 16 marked points of interest. This trail begins at the picnic area and returns to the nature and interpretative center.

Because the sand dunes are fragile walking or climbing the dunes is prohibited. This preserves the plants, grass and flora growing in the sandy soil.

On about two miles of the hiking trails, bicycles may be ridden. However, due to the sandy nature of the trails, it is necessary to use bicycles with wide, mountain-bike tires.

Picnic Facilities: There is a shaded picnic area near the parking lot overlooking the rugged shoreline of Lake Michigan. This area is near the beach and nature center. Picnic tables, grills and a shelter are provided for the picnicker.

As is the case in other Wisconsin state parks, there are no garbage cans in the picnic area. People who come for a picnic are expected to take their waste with them or place them in large bins in the parking lot.

Nature: A large variety of flowers, trees and shrubs have found a toehold in the sand dunes. Two plant species found in the park, the dwarf lake iris and dune thistle, are listed on the federally threatened species list. In addition, there are five plants in the park which are listed on Wisconsin's endangered and threatened species list.

Visitors are provided with a brochure with a list of birds seen in the park. This list includes more than 120 species of birds.

Winter Activities: During the winter, about 10.5 miles of hiking trails are open for cross-country skiing. The trails are relatively flat and excellent for the novice skier. Groomed trails range from .7 to 4.2

The White and Interpretative trails are open for hiking, snowshoeing and Nordic skiing. Trailheads for all of the trails begin and end near the nature center. A warming shelter in the picnic area provides a fireplace.

Snowmobiles are prohibited in the park.

Nearby Feature: A visitor to Whitefish Dunes State Park should visit Cave Point County Park. The state park surrounds this tiny county park, where you can see the results of rugged battering waves along rocks on the shoreline.

This water action has formed numerous caves in the limestone bedrock along the shore which is part of the Niagara Escarpment which underlies all of this area of Door County.

Whitefish Dunes State Park
3701 Clark Lake Road
Sturgeon Bay, WI 54235
(414) 823-2400

About the author

Dean Miller has taught for 27 years at the University of Toledo and nine years at colleges, junior high and elementary levels.

He is also the author of 16 other books about personal health, safety, community health, school law and elementary school health.

Dean has visited several hundred state and national parks where he enjoys cycling, hiking and outdoor photography. He is often in demand as a lecturer where he uses his photographs to share his expertise about outdoor recreation and parks.